Switching to Windows Vista for Sł

Studio Visual Steps

Switching to Windows Vista for SENIORS

Become familiar with the new features in Windows Vista

This book has been written by Yvette Huijsman, Henk Mol, Alex Wit and Ria Beentjes, using the Visual Steps™ method.
Translated by Yvette Huijsman and Chris Holingsworth.
Edited by Jolanda Ligthart, Marleen Vermeij and Ria Beentjes.

Cover design by Studio Willemien Haagsma bNO

First printing: November 2007
ISBN 978 90 5905 045 7

Would you like more information?
www.visualsteps.com

Do you have questions or suggestions?
E-mail: info@visualsteps.com

Website for this book:
www.visualsteps.com/switchtovista
Here you can register your book.

Register your book
We will keep you aware of any important changes that are necessary to you as a user of the book. You can also take advantage of our periodic newsletter informing you of our product releases, company news, tips & tricks, special offers, etcetera.
www.visualsteps.com/switchtovista

Table of Contents

Appendices

Foreword

Even if you are already familiar with *Windows XP*, switching to the totally new appearance of *Windows Vista* will probably take some getting used to. Some features and windows can be found in a different place. New features have been added. *Vista* also comes packaged with some new programs, in addition to the familiar programs you already know from *Windows XP*.

This book is a practical guide to help you switch from your *XP* computer to a *Vista* computer. The content is targeted for users who are already familiar with *Windows XP* and is not intended to be a guide for beginners. The clear instructions, explanations and screenshots in this book will quickly help you find your way in *Vista*.

We hope you have a lot of fun exploring *Windows Vista*!

The Studio Visual Steps Authors

PS Your comments and suggestions are most welcome.
Our e-mail address is: mail@visualsteps.com

Visual Steps Newsletter

All Visual Steps books follow the same methodology: step by step instructions with screenshots.

An overview of all books can be found on **www.visualsteps.com**
On this website you can also subscribe to the **free Visual Steps Newsletter** that is sent by e-mail.

The Visual Steps Newsletter provides periodic information about:
- the latest titles and previously released books;
- special offers, free guides and discounts.

Our Newsletter subscribers have access to free information booklets, handy tips and guides which are listed on the web pages **www.visualsteps.com/info_downloads** and **www.visualsteps.com/tips**. You can visit the free online Visual Steps quiz website at **www.ccforseniors.com**. Please be assured that we will never use your e-mail address for any purpose other than sending you the information you have requested and we will not share this address with any third-party. Each newsletter contains a one-click link to unsubscribe from our newsletter.

Introduction to Visual Steps™

The Visual Steps' manuals and handbooks offer the best instruction available for anyone new to computers. Nowhere else in the world will you find better support while getting to know the computer, the Internet, *Windows* and other computer programs.

Visual Steps manuals are special because of their:

- **Content**
  The adult learners needs, desires, know-how and skills have been taken into account.
- **Structure**
  Get started right away. No lengthy explanations. The chapters are organized in such a way that you can skip a chapter or redo a chapter without worry. Easy step by step instructions and practice exercises to reinforce what you have learned.
- **Illustrations**
  Every single step is accompanied by a screenshot. These illustrations will guide you in finding the right buttons or menus, and will quickly show you if you are still on the right track.
- **Format**
  A sizable format and pleasantly large letters enhance readability.

In short, I believe these manuals will be excellent guides.

Dr. H. van der Meij

Faculty of Applied Education, Department of Instruction Technology, University of Twente, the Netherlands

What You Will Need

In order to work through this book, you will need a number of things on your computer:

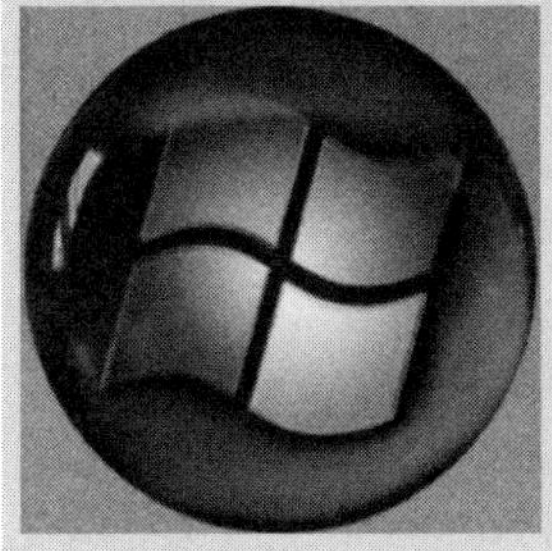

The primary requirement for working with this book is having the US version of ***Windows Vista*** on your computer.
Windows Vista is available in various versions. This book can be used with the editions:

- *Windows Vista Home Basic*
- *Windows Vista Home Premium*
- *Windows Vista Ultimate*

Are you still thinking about purchasing *Windows Vista*? Then you can start by reading the information on this subject in chapter 1.

Network and Internet
View network status and tasks
Set up file sharing

You need a functioning **Internet connection** to work with *Windows Mail* and *Internet Explorer.*

The editions *Windows Vista Home Premium* and *Windows Vista Ultimate* include:

Windows Media Center

Windows DVD Maker

- *Windows Media Center*
- *Windows DVD Maker*

If you do not have *Windows Media Center* and *Windows DVD Maker* you can just read through the sections about this programs.

Register Your Book

You can register your book. We will keep you aware of any important changes that are necessary to you as a user of the book. You can also take advantage of:
Our periodic newsletter informing you of our product releases, company news, tips & tricks, special offers, etcetera.

How to Use This Book

This book has been written using the Visual Steps™ method. The method is simple: have the book near you as you work on your computer, read the relevant section and perform the tasks as described. By using clear instructions with screenshots to visualize each step, you will quickly be able to do what you want with your computer.

In this Visual Steps™-book, you will see various icons. This is what they mean:

Techniques
These icons indicate an action to be carried out:

The mouse icon means you should do something with the mouse.

The keyboard icon means you should type something on the keyboard.

The hand icon means you should do something else, for example insert a CD-ROM in the computer. The hand icon is also used for a technique you have learned before or a specific order you have to carry out.

Extra help is given when we want to alert you about a particular topic.

Help
These icons indicate that extra help is available:

The arrow icon warns you about something.

The bandage icon will help you if something has gone wrong.

1 Have you forgotten how to do something? The number next to the footsteps tells you where to look it up in the appendix *How Do I Do That Again?*

In separate boxes you find general information and tips about computers and *Windows*.

Extra Information
Information boxes are denoted by these icons:

The book icon gives you extra background information that you can read at your convenience. This extra information is not necessary for working through the book.

The light bulb icon indicates an extra tip for using *Windows*.

The Reading Order

The book is set up in such a way that you do not necessarily need to work through the book from beginning to end. You can read the table of contents to see which subjects interest you first. Work through the chapters at your own pace and in the order you want.
Chapter 1 is specifically meant for users that need more information for purchasing *Windows Vista*: which edition to buy, whether to use a new computer or 'upgrade' an *XP* computer to *Vista.* Even though it may seem like a lot of information, it is presented in the easy to follow, step by step *Visual Steps* manner.

The Screenshots

The screenshots in this book may not be exactly the same as what you see on your computer. This will depend on which *Vista* edition is installed on your computer. This makes no difference however in performing the requested actions. In the text it will be noted when a difference could occur and in which *Vista* edition a certain feature or specific program may not be available.

Test Your Knowledge

When you have worked through this book, you can test your knowledge by doing one of the free tests available online on the website **www.ccforseniors.com**
These multiple choice tests will show you how thorough your knowledge of *Windows Vista* is.
If you pass the test, you will receive your free computer certificate by e-mail.

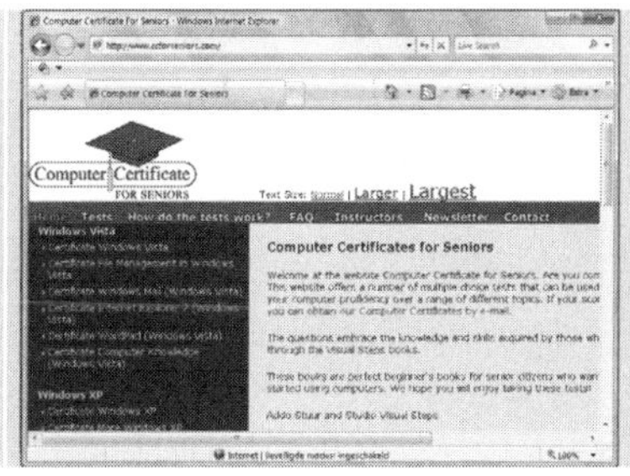

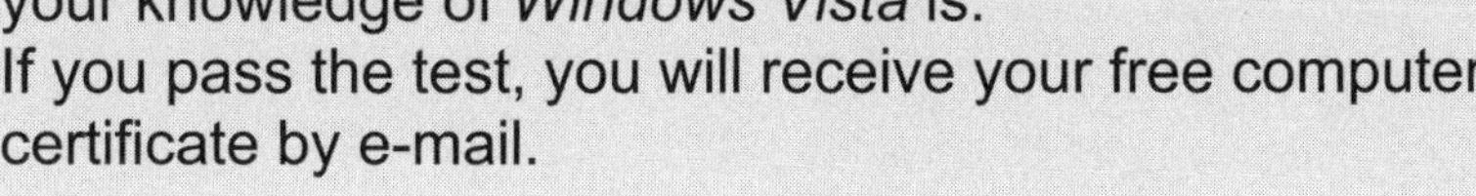

How to Continue After This Book

When you have worked through the book *Switching to Windows Vista for SENIORS*, there may be subjects that you want to know more about. You can gain more *Vista* skills by using the other books in the *Windows Vista for SENIORS*-series. On the website **www.visualsteps.com** you will find extensive information about other available titles, along with the complete table of contents and chapter excerpts (PDF files) for each book. This is a good way to check if a book meets your expectations. All Visual Steps books have been written using the same step by step method. If you like this method, there is no need to hesitate to buy another Visual Steps book. Would you like more information? Send an e-mail to **info@visualsteps.com**

1. From XP to Vista

Microsoft, the creator of *Windows*, has published various versions of the *Windows* operating system over the past two decades. *Windows Vista* is the latest version, the successor to *Windows XP*. Many *Windows XP* users are wondering if they should switch to *Windows Vista* right away or wait for a while. This is a decision you must make on your own. To help you decide, the advantages and disadvantages of switching to *Windows Vista* are listed in this chapter.

In case you do decide to trade in your trusted *Windows XP* for *Windows Vista*, you will have to make a lot of choices. For example, which edition of *Vista* are you going to use? Are you going to use your old computer, or will you buy a new one? Is your old computer capable of running *Windows Vista*? If that is the case, are you going to upgrade your *Windows XP* system to *Vista*, or will you start with a clean installation? These are all choices you have to make for yourself, but the information provided in the first part of this chapter will make that a lot easier.

In the second part of this chapter you will read how you can perform an upgrade and a clean installation. Furthermore, you will see how you can use *Windows Easy Transfer* to secure your files and settings. With the special *Easy Transfer* cable you can transfer data between an *XP* and a *Vista* computer.

In this chapter you will find information on the following subjects:

- the advantages of *Windows Vista* compared to *Windows XP*;
- the disadvantages of switching to *Windows Vista*;
- the different editions of *Windows Vista*;
- the system requirements;
- using *Windows Vista Upgrade Advisor*;
- upgrading *Windows XP*, a complete installation or a new computer;
- performing an upgrade from *Windows XP* to *Windows Vista*;
- downloading, installing and using *Windows Easy Transfer*;
- performing a complete installation on an empty or an *XP* computer;
- completing the installation;
- importing data into *Vista* using *Windows Easy Transfer*;
- using an *Easy Transfer* cable to transfer data;
- setting up a dial-up account.

1.1 The Advantages of Windows Vista

Every new version of the *Windows*-operating system contains improvements. For example, improvements in security. There are also improvements made in response to feedback received from users, like improved user-friendliness and help-functions, as well as a better looking interface. The most important advantages of *Windows Vista* compared to *Windows XP* are:

More security and stability

Compared to *Windows XP*, the level of security has improved in *Windows Vista.* As an *XP* user you might have wondered about the number of updates you had to install to keep *Windows XP* safe. A more stable and secure base structure is incorporated in *Windows Vista.*

Increased safety in Internet use

The growing use of Internet applications is also a risk for computer users. *Windows Vista* contains two programs that help battle dangers lurking on the Internet: *Windows Firewall* and *Windows Defender*.

Windows Firewall checks the source of the flow of data coming from the Internet or a network, and then either blocks it or allows it to pass through to your computer, depending on the settings you have chosen. This is a useful tool to protect your computer against hackers or malicious software.

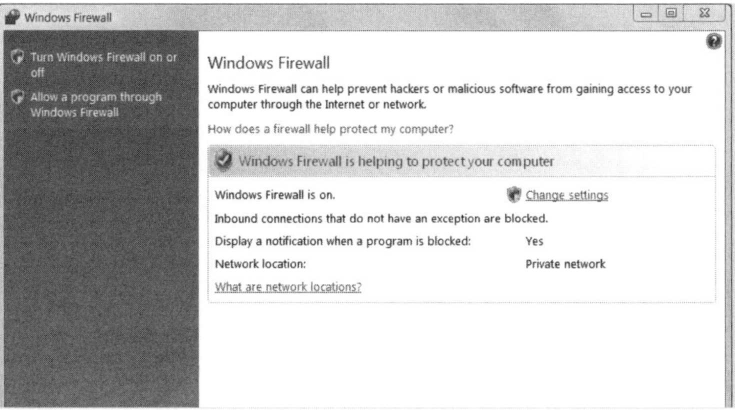

Windows Defender protects your computer against the installation of spyware or other unwanted software.

Please note: *Windows Defender* by itself is not enough to protect your computer against viruses. You should purchase and install an antivirus program to further protect your computer.

User Account Control

As an added security measure, the *User Account Control* has been improved in *Windows Vista. User Account Control* can help prevent unauthorized changes to your computer.

In *Windows Vista* you will frequently see your screen go dark. A window appears in which *Windows* asks your permission to continue before a task is completed:

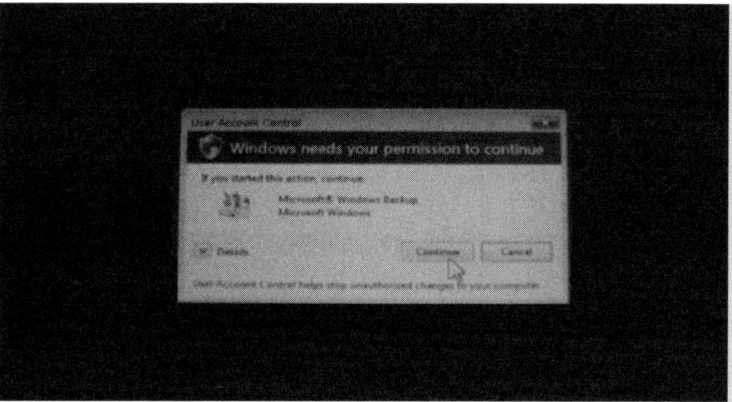

In case you have a standard user account instead of an administrator user account, you will have to enter the administrator password when you see this window. This will prevent programs being installed or changes being applied by users that do not have permission to do so.

Improved search feature

The search feature in *Windows XP* left a lot to be desired. The improved search feature in *Windows Vista* makes it a lot easier to find documents and other files on your computer's hard drive.

At the bottom of the *Start menu* and in the top right corner of each folder window you find a handy *Search Box*:

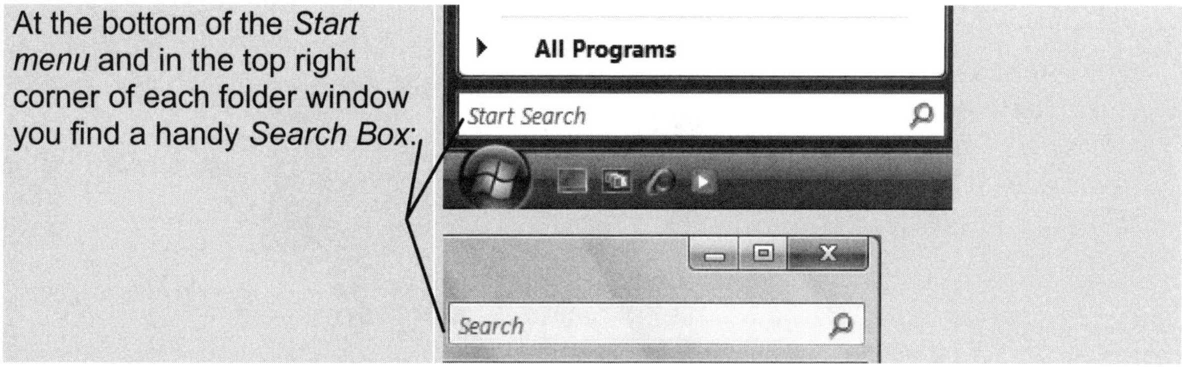

Improved interface with *Windows Aero* and *Windows Flip 3D*

Windows Vista looks a lot different than *Windows XP*. In developing *Vista*, a lot of attention has been given to the overall 'look and feel'.

The new *Windows Aero* interface is an eye-catcher:

When you use *Windows Aero*, you see transparent window frames in the color of your choice:

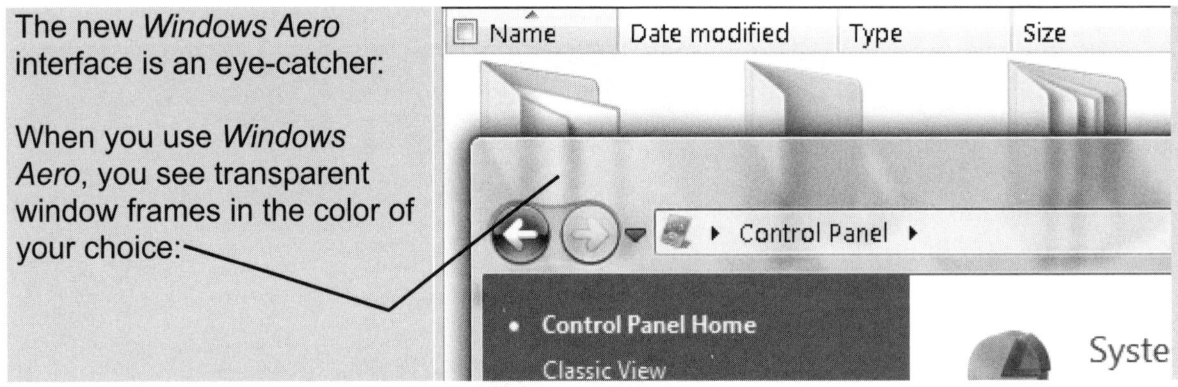

To be able to run *Windows Aero* smoothly, you need a fast graphics card. If your graphics card does not meet the minimum requirements, *Vista* will automatically choose another appearance which can be run properly.

A fun part of the *Windows Aero* interface is *Windows Flip 3D*: this is a way to preview your open windows in a 3D stack without clicking the individual buttons on the taskbar.

Flip 3D shows all opened windows in a stack on your desktop. You can flip through the stack, and open the desired window by clicking it:

Please note: several key *Vista* features such as *Windows Flip 3D* are not available in *Vista Home Basic*.

Parental Controls

You can use this feature to help manage how your (grand)children use the computer.

You can set limits on:

- the number of hours they can log on to the computer
- which games they can play and what programs they can run
- which websites they can visit

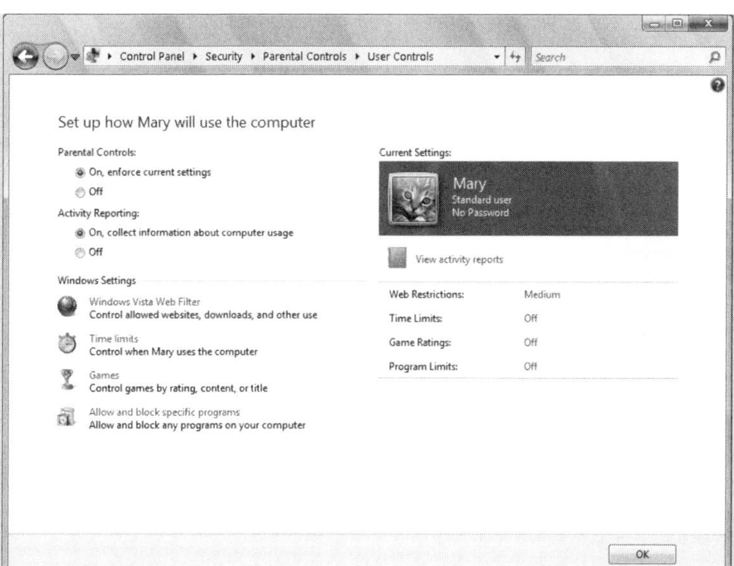

1.2 The Disadvantages of Switching to Vista

Of course there are disadvantages to be considered in switching to *Windows Vista*. In the end you will have to decide for yourself if the advantages of *Vista* outweigh the disadvantages you can encounter in switching to *Vista*.

Cost

It will be obvious that you will have to spend money to switch to *Vista*. The *Windows Vista* software alone is a considerable expense. But that is not all. There is a good chance that your current computer is not capable of running *Windows Vista*. Even for *Windows Vista Home Basic*, the most simple edition, the system requirements are demanding. It is possible that you will also have to add the cost of a new computer, or the cost to upgrade your current computer. In the following sections you can read more about the different editions of *Vista* and their system requirements.

Older software does not run anymore

A lot of programs that run on an *XP* computer, are not automatically compatible with *Windows Vista*. In many cases this issue can be resolved by downloading an update for or a new version of the program from the manufacturer's website. You need to take into account that there will be some programs that are no longer supported for *Windows* versions newer than *XP*. This means you will have to find similar software that is suitable for *Windows Vista*.

Devices do not function anymore

When you switch to *Windows Vista*, it is possible that devices like printers, webcams and scanners no longer function. In many cases this can be resolved by downloading a new *driver* for the device from the manufacturer's website. Be aware that there may be no *Windows Vista* drivers available for older devices.

Getting used to *Vista*

When you start to use a new operating system, you will need time to get used to it and to get to know the different parts. It will take a while before you are as familiar with it as you are with *Windows XP*.

Improved security

Oddly enough, the improved security in *Windows Vista* can be experienced as annoying by some users. When you change the settings of your computer, you will frequently be interrupted and asked for your permission to continue.

1.3 The Different Editions of Windows Vista

Windows Vista is released in five different editions. Two editions for the business market (*Vista Business* and *Vista Enterprise*) and three editions for the consumer market. As a home user you can choose from:

- ***Windows Vista Home Basic*:** this is the most simplest edition, with the most important general features of *Windows Vista*. This edition also contains the new security features. *Windows Vista Home Basic* is ideal for homes with basic computing needs like e-mail, surfing the Internet, and viewing photos.
- ***Windows Vista Home Premium*:** this more extensive edition is suitable for the more demanding user. In this edition extra attention has been given to digital media and entertainment (*Windows Media Center*), and to features for laptops (*Windows Mobility Center*). This edition also offers support for users that use a tablet with an electronic pen instead of a mouse.
- ***Windows Vista Ultimate*:** this is the most complete edition of *Windows Vista* with all features for power management, security, mobility and entertainment. This edition is very suitable for people that use the same computer for business use as well as for private use.

You may have read about some of the new features in *Vista.* However, they are not available in all editions. The most important differences are listed in this table:

	Home Basic	***Home Premium***	***Ultimate***
Windows Firewall	yes	yes	yes
Windows Defender	yes	yes	yes
Parental Controls	yes	yes	yes
Making backups	yes	yes	yes
Making automatic backups	no	yes	yes
Windows Aero interface	no	yes	yes
Windows Flip 3D	no	yes	yes
Windows Media Center	no	yes	yes
Windows Mobility Center	no	yes	yes
Tablet-pc support	no	yes	yes
Remote desktop	no	no	yes
Windows Meeting Space	no	no	yes

Tip

Will you choose the 32-bit or the 64-bit version?
It is possible that you already have a computer with a new 64-bit processor, instead of the usual 32-bit processor. Each of the different editions of *Windows Vista* is available in both a 32-bit and a 64-bit version.

Even if you have a 64-bit processor, it is probably a better idea to choose the 32-bit version. This version is perfectly suitable for normal home use. Using the 64-bit version requires that you use 64-bit versions of all hardware drivers. In addition, all software has to be 64-bit as well. You can **no longer** use 32-bit software and drivers.

Tip

What is Windows Vista Starter?
Windows Vista Starter is a stripped edition of *Home Basic*, developed especially for 'emerging markets' like developing countries. This edition will not be available in the USA and Canada.

1.4 System Requirements

To be able to install and run *Windows Vista Home Basic* your computer has to meet the following minimum system requirements:

- 800 MHz 32-bit (x86) or 64-bit (x64) processor, like an Intel Pentium 4, AMD Athlon or Celeron processor;
- 512 MB of system memory;
- 20 GB hard drive with at least 15 GB of available space;
- Support for Super VGA graphics;
- CD-ROM drive.

A computer that is five years old or more will probably not meet these requirements. Computers that were sold right before the introduction of *Vista*, carry this sticker if they meet the minimum requirements:

Home Basic can be installed on a computer that meets the minimum requirements. However, there is no guarantee that the performance of *Vista* will be optimized. Some product features may not be available.

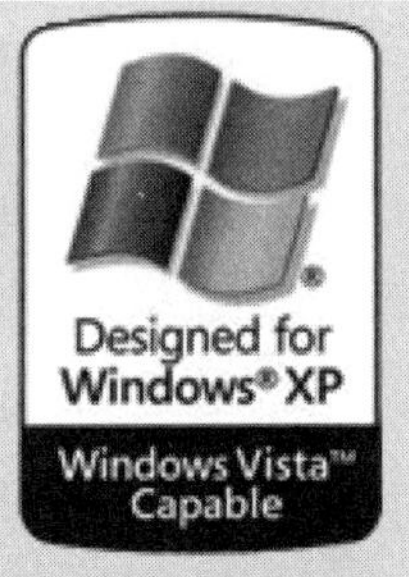

These are the recommended system requirements for an optimized performance of *Windows Vista Home Basic*:

- 1 GHz 32-bit (x86) or 64-bit (x64) processor;
- 512 MB of system memory;
- 20 GB hard drive with at least 15 GB of available space;
- graphic support for DirectX 9 and 32 MB of graphics memory;
- a DVD-ROM drive;
- audio output;
- Internet access.

These are the recommended system requirements for an optimized performance of *Windows Vista Home Premium* and *Ultimate*:

- 1 GHz 32-bit (x86) or 64-bit (x64) processor;
- 1 GB of system memory;
- 40 GB hard drive with at least 15 GB of available space;
- graphic support for DirectX 9 with WDDM driver, a minimum of 128 MB graphics memory, Pixel Shader 2.0 in hardware and support for 32 bits per pixel;
- a DVD-ROM drive;
- audio output;
- Internet access.

To be able to use all of the features of *Windows Media Center* in *Windows Vista Home Premium* and *Ultimate* you will also need a TV tuner card. *Windows Tablet and Touch Technology* requires a Tablet PC or a touch screen.

1.5 Windows Vista Upgrade Advisor

It is possible that the system requirements mentioned in the previous section do not mean a whole lot to you. Or you may have no idea what the current specifications of your computer are. *Microsoft* has thought of this as well.

On the *Microsoft* website you can download the program *Windows Vista Upgrade Advisor* for free. This program can determine if your computer can run *Vista* and if yes, which edition. You will also receive tips on parts that possibly need replacement, devices that might not function anymore and programs that are not compatible with *Vista*.

You can download the *Windows Vista Upgrade Advisor* from this website:

http://www.microsoft.com/windows/products/windowsvista/buyorupgrade/upgradeadvisor.mspx

HELP! This web address no longer exists

Content on the Internet, including the *Microsoft* website, is frequently updated. If the web address listed above no longer exists, you can surf to **www.microsoft.com** and use the *Search Box* on the website to search for 'upgrade advisor'.

You can download and install the *Upgrade Advisor* as follows:

- **Use the link Download Windows Vista Upgrade Advisor to go to the download page. There you can enter which type of Internet connection you use, and (if necessary) change the language of the download**

- **Click Download to start the download**

- **Click Run in the window *File Download - Security Warning***

The download starts right away and you see the progress.

- **Click Run in the window *Internet Explorer - Security Warning***

The installation begins. In the wizard that appears:

Agree to the terms of use

When the installation is completed, *Windows Vista Upgrade Advisor* is opened. If that does not happen automatically on your computer, you can use the shortcut that has been placed on your desktop: .

You see the first window of the *Upgrade Advisor.*

Before you start the scan, plug in any devices that you use regularly with your computer, such as printers, scanners or external hard drives.

Click 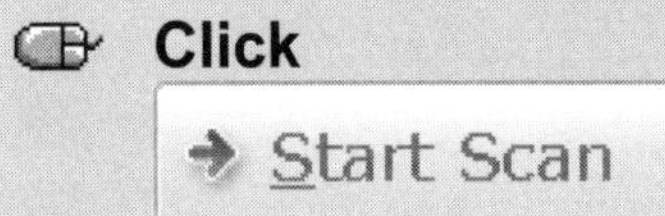

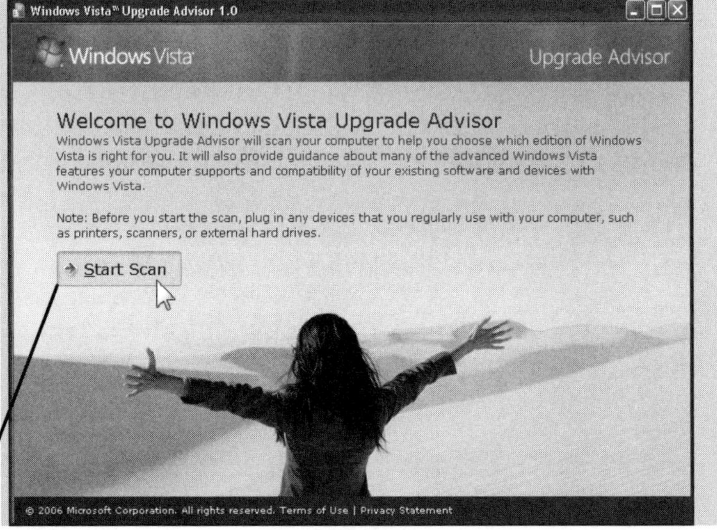

Your computer is being scanned. This might take a few minutes.

In the meantime, you can use the buttons at the bottom of the window to read more about the different editions of *Windows Vista*:

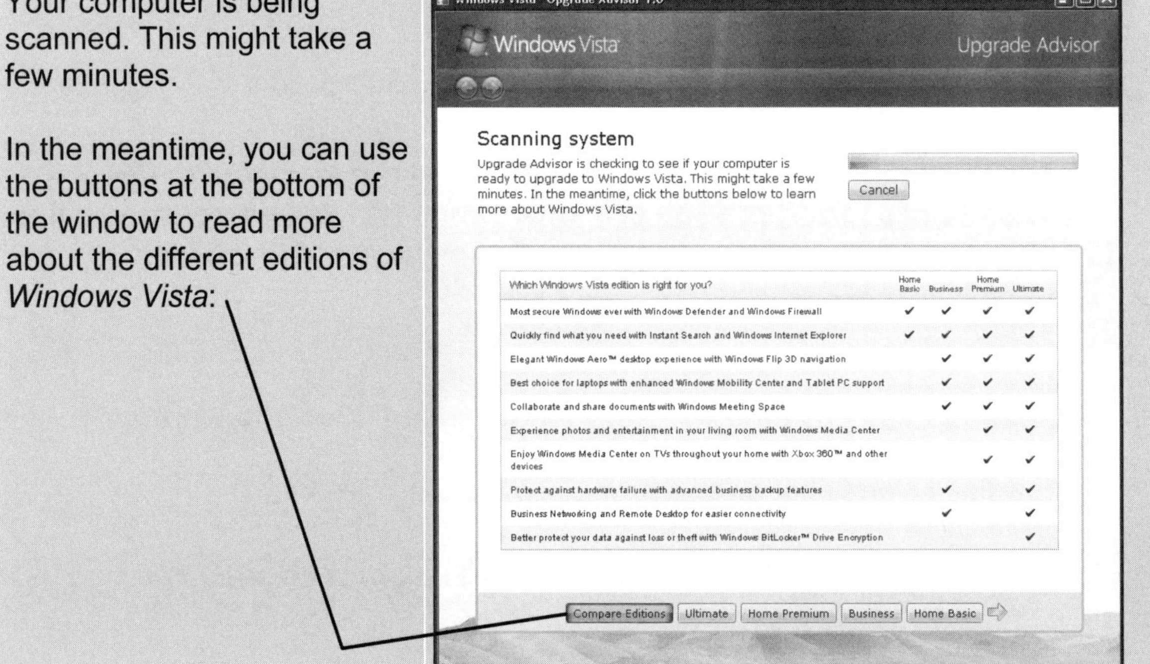

When the scan is complete you can view the results.

Click See Details

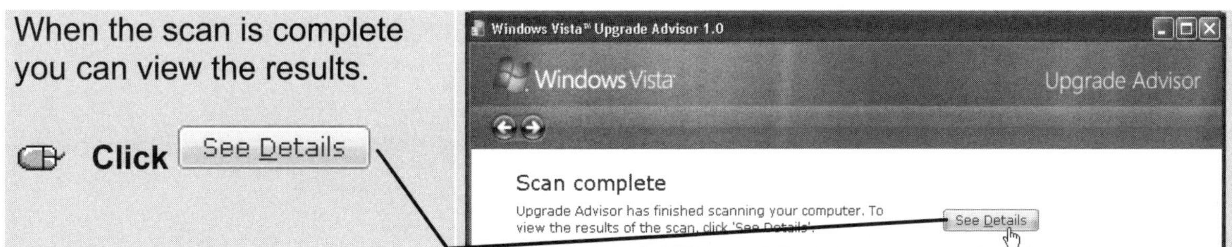

In this example the *Upgrade Advisor* gives a positive report, and indicates that *Home Basic* is probably the most suitable edition:

By clicking the names of the other editions, you can check the report to see if your computer might be able to run these editions:

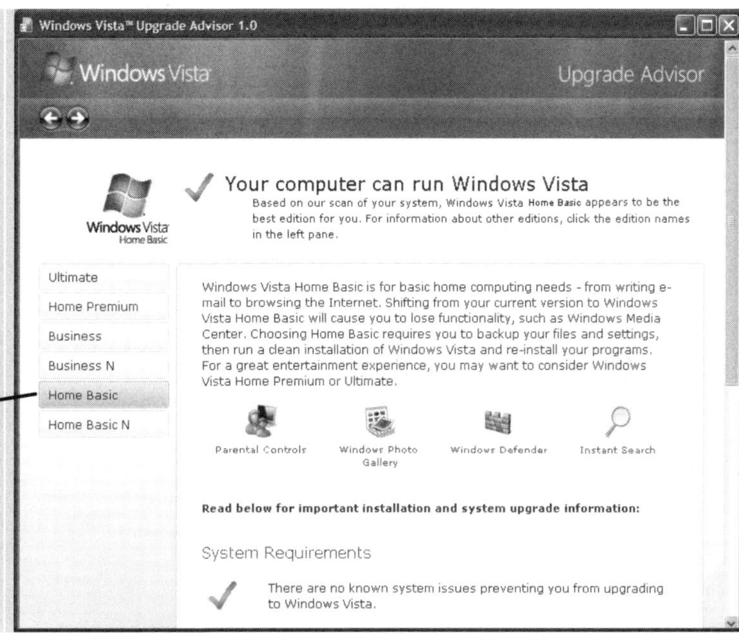

When you scroll down, you see the summaries of the reports for the other items: system requirements, devices and programs.

Only the items with ✓ have no problems.

With the buttons See Details you can open the reports:

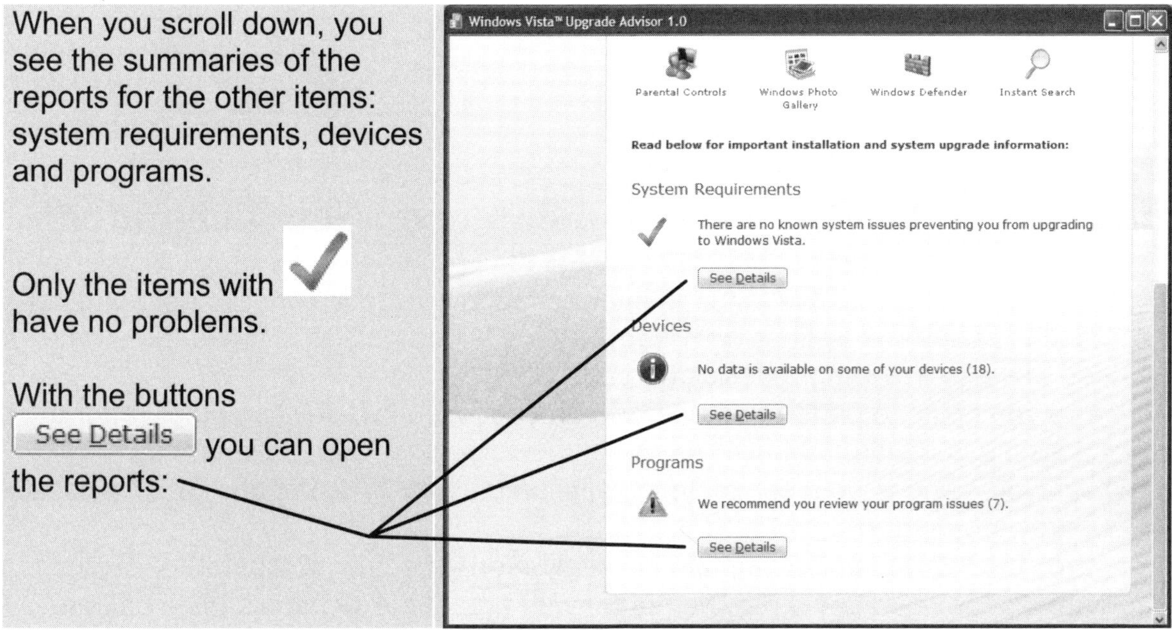

In the report on programs there may be certain items that need your attention:

- means that a program should be removed before a possible upgrade to *Windows Vista* can take place.
- indicates *Vista* compatibility problems causing a program not to run well or not to run at all. Using the links given in the report you may wish to download updates, or visit the manufacturer's website for more information.
- these items have no known compatibility problems.

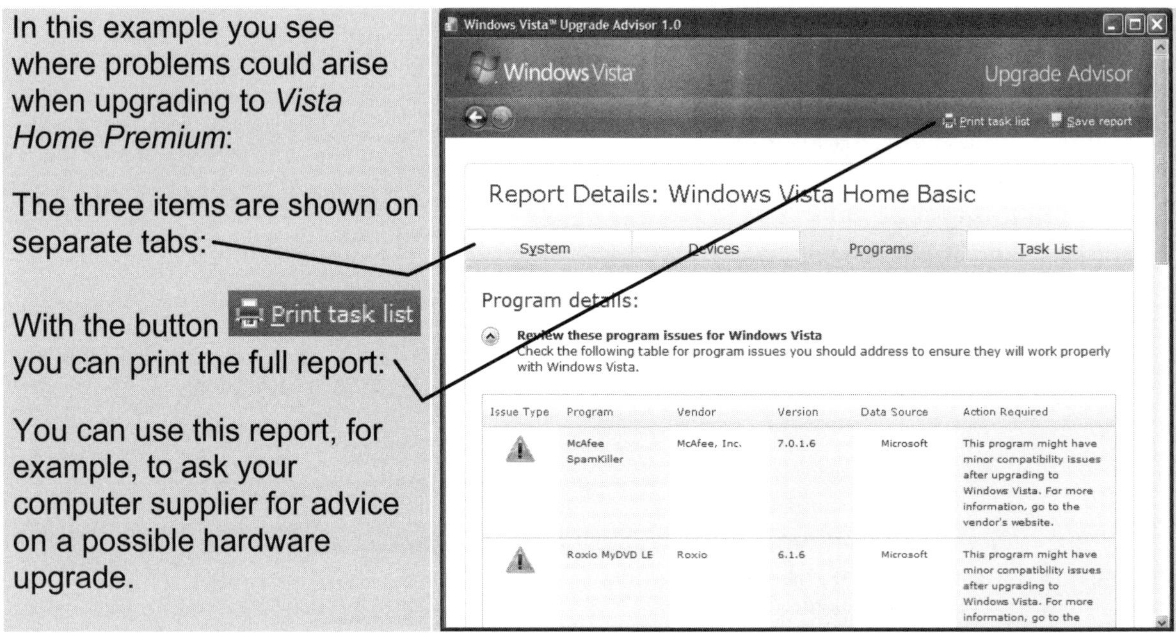

In this example you see where problems could arise when upgrading to *Vista Home Premium*:

The three items are shown on separate tabs:

With the button Print task list you can print the full report:

You can use this report, for example, to ask your computer supplier for advice on a possible hardware upgrade.

1.6 Upgrade, Complete Installation or New Computer?

By now you have received enough information to decide whether or not you want to switch to one of the editions of *Windows Vista*. If you decide to make the switch, you need to make a few more decisions:

- are you going to perform an upgrade on your *Windows XP* computer (after a possible hardware upgrade) to one of the *Windows Vista* editions?
- are you going to do a complete installation on your *XP* computer (after a possible hardware-upgrade)?
- are you going to do a complete installation on an empty computer?
- are you going to buy a new computer with one of the *Windows Vista* editions already installed?

If you are considering an upgrade from *Windows XP* to an edition of *Windows Vista*, be aware of the following points:

Choose the right edition

The edition of *Windows XP* on your computer will be the deciding factor as to which edition of *Vista* is best suited for your upgrade. From *Windows XP Professional* it is only possible to upgrade to *Vista Ultimate* or *Vista Business*. From *Windows XP Home Edition* you can upgrade to all editions: *Home Basic*, *Home Premium*, *Ultimate* and even the *Business* edition.

Choose the right language

The language of your current edition of *Windows XP* should be the same as the language of the *Vista* software you want to use. For example, it is not possible to upgrade a Spanish *XP* computer to an English language edition of *Vista*. If the language does not match, you will only be able to do a complete install.

Upgrade copy or full copy?

To perform an upgrade from *Windows XP Home Edition* to *Windows Vista Home Premium* you can purchase a special upgrade copy of *Windows Vista*. The price of an upgrade copy is lower than the price of a full copy of the *Vista Home Premium* software. A disadvantage is that if you ever need to reinstall *Vista*, you have to do a complete reinstall of *Windows XP* including *Service Pack 2*. After that, you can perform the upgrade to *Vista*.

It is definitely worth considering buying the full version of the *Windows Vista* software. With the full version, you can upgrade *Windows XP* and if necessary, you can do a complete install, without needing your *XP* software.

Advantage of an upgrade

The biggest advantage of upgrading *Windows XP* to *Windows Vista* is that you can keep your programs, files and settings, (like contacts and favorites) as they were in your previous version of *Windows*. The version of *Windows* on your computer is not overwritten, but only updated. As mentioned before, after an upgrade to *Vista*, there is a possibility that some of your programs or devices will not run well or may not even run at all.

 Tip

Safety first!
Before you start an upgrade, be sure to make a backup of files that are important to you, such as documents, photos or music. A good way to do so is to write a copy of these files to one or more CDs or DVDs. You can also copy your personal files to a USB stick. If you have an extensive library of larger sized files (such as videos) you may want to copy these files to an external hard drive.

In chapter 6 of the book **More Windows XP for SENIORS** you can read more about writing Data CDs in *Windows XP*. To write a Data DVD you can refer to the manual of the program you use for writing DVDs. Information on working with a USB stick can be found on **www.visualsteps.com/info_downloads.php** in the free guide **Working with USB sticks in Windows XP**.

 Tip

What will happen to the music you have bought?
Music you have bought in online stores such as *Rhapsody* and the *iTunes Store* is protected with *Digital Rights Management*. It is possible that you will no longer be able to play these music files on your *Vista* computer. Once you switched to *Vista* and have transferred your music and video files, you will need to retrieve new media usage rights for any protected files transferred.

In many cases, *Windows Media Player 11* handles media usage rights acquisition for you. When you attempt to play a song that requires new media usage rights, the *Player* will typically try to download them automatically. If it cannot do so, usually an error message appears that instructs you what to do next (for example, verify that you are connected to the Internet, sign in to your online store, and so on.) If you are unable to download new media usage rights contact your online music store for assistance.

Tracks that have been bought in the *iTunes Store*, can be played on a maximum of five computers. These computers (for example your *Vista* computer) have to be authorized in the *iTunes*-program. When you upgrade from *Windows XP* to *Windows Vista* it is advised to deauthorize all computers first. After installing *Vista* and *iTunes* you can authorize your computer again through the *Store*-menu in *iTunes*. For more information, please refer to the online Help-section of *iTunes*.

Please note:

Do you use the *Windows*-program *Back-up* to create backups in *Windows XP*?
By default, it is **not** possible to import the.BKF-files you make with *Windows Back-up* in *Windows Vista*. To be able to do that, you need a special program that can be downloaded from the *Microsoft Download Center*:
www.microsoft.com/downloads/Search.aspx?displaylang=en

On this page you use the search terms 'Backup restore utility':

Search | All Downloads | Backup restore utility | Go

Open the page for the program with this link Windows NT Backup - Restore Utility.
Follow the instructions on this page for downloading, installing and using this program.

When you perform a complete installation, none of your settings will be retained and all programs will need to be reinstalled. A complete new version of *Windows* is placed on your computer. All files on the hard disk of your computer, will be overwritten when *Vista* is installed. Therefore, before you do a complete installation, be sure to back up your important files. You can do this with *Windows Easy Transfer*.

In section 1.8 you can read how to download and install *Windows Easy Transfer*.

Are you going to upgrade your *Windows XP* computer to *Windows Vista*?
Just continue reading.

Are you going to perform a complete installation on your *Windows XP* computer?
Skip the next section and continue reading at section 1.8 *Downloading and Installing Windows Easy Transfer*.

Are you going to perform a complete installation on a computer where *Windows* has not yet been installed?
Skip the next sections and continue reading at section 1.10 *Performing a Complete Installation*.

Have you purchased a new computer with *Windows Vista* already installed?
Skip the next sections and continue reading at section 1.11 *Completing the Installation*.

1.7 Performing an Upgrade

An upgrade from *Windows XP* to *Windows Vista* can be performed like this:

Place the *Windows Vista* DVD in the DVD-ROM drive

Wait until the DVD starts automatically

An installation window appears.

Click the option

Now you see the window *Get important updates for installation*. It is recommended to choose the option *Go online to get the latest updates for installation*. This means that an online check will be performed to see if there are new installation files available. This way you can make sure that the latest *Vista* files are installed.

Click

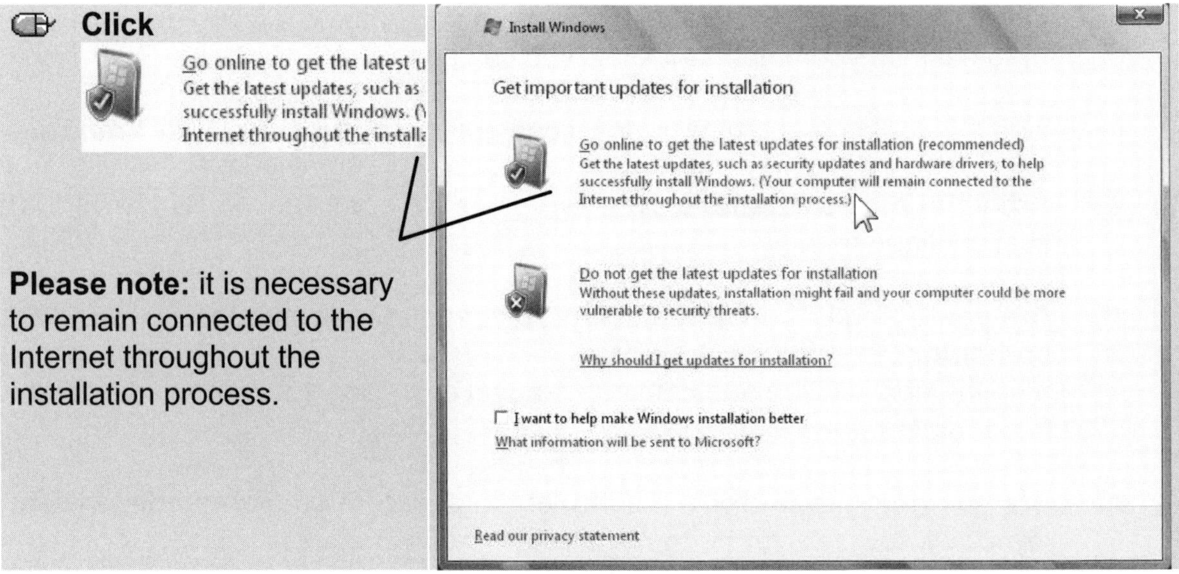

Please note: it is necessary to remain connected to the Internet throughout the installation process.

Now enter the product key, which consists of five groups of five letters and digits. You can find the product key on the *Windows Vista* box or the DVD sleeve. You do not need to type the dashes in the product key, they will be added automatically.

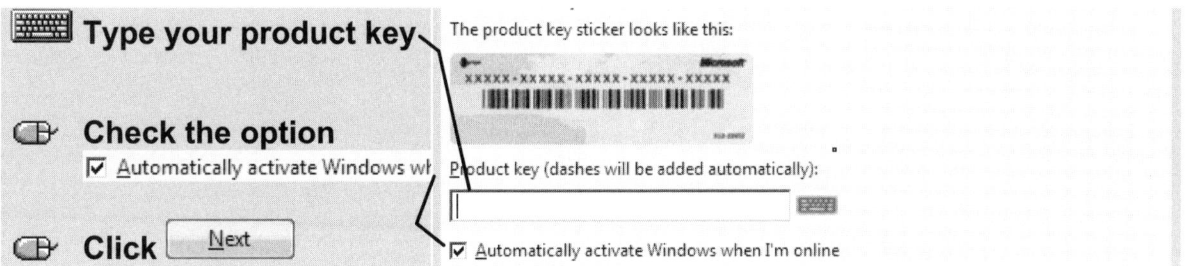

Activation of *Windows Vista* is necessary, because otherwise you can only use the program for fourteen days. If necessary, you can activate *Vista* later through the *Welcome Center*.

Please note:

Did you not enter the product key? Then you must select the exact edition you have purchased in the window *Select the edition of Windows that you purchased*.
If you did enter the product key the edition will be determined automatically and you will not see this window.

In the next window you have to accept the software license terms. Then you are asked which type of installation you want to perform. It is very important to make the right choice here. To perform an upgrade from *Windows XP* to *Windows Vista* and keep your files, settings and programs:

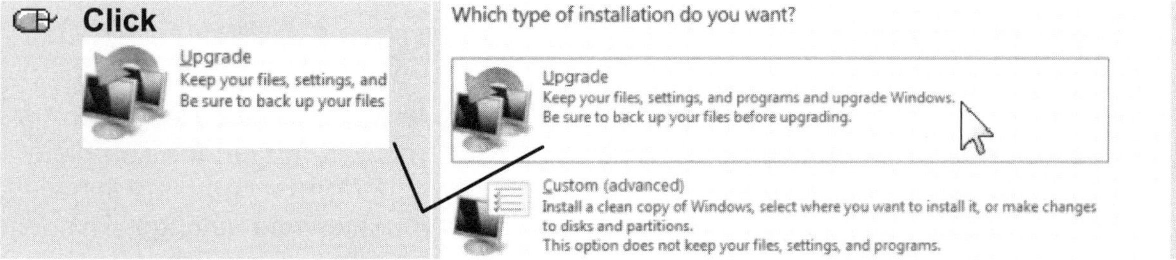

Before the upgrade procedure begins, a check is made for possible compatibility problems with the hardware and software on your computer. This is the same check that is performed by the *Windows Upgrade Advisor*.

When a compatibility problem is found, you will see a window with a report of that specific problem and a suggestion on how to solve the problem.
It may for instance be necessary to remove a program before you can perform the upgrade.

☞ **Follow the instructions in this window**

Click the button *Close*

When the problems have been resolved, you can start the upgrade again. The same check will be performed to see if the upgrade is now possible.

The upgrade is done automatically, you do not need to click or enter anything. The complete upgrade can take up to a few hours, depending on the configuration of your computer and programs already installed.

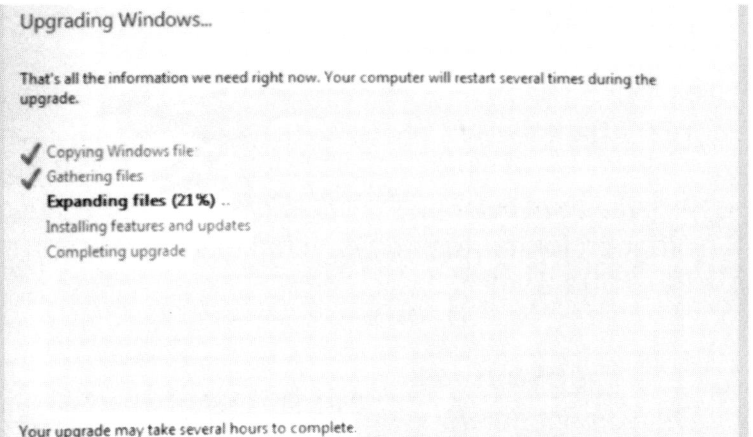

During the upgrade the computer will restart automatically a couple of times.

☞ **Do not turn off the computer during the upgrade procedure, even when it looks like the computer has not responded for a while!**

☞ **Skip to section 1.11 *Completing the Installation***

1.8 Downloading and Installing Windows Easy Transfer

All data on the hard disk of your computer will be overwritten when you perform a complete install. When you install *Vista* on a new 'empty' computer the complete installation is the only available option. But when you perform a complete installation on your *Windows XP* computer, you will lose all of your files and settings. This can be prevented by securing your files and settings using *Windows Easy Transfer*.

Windows Easy Transfer is a wizard that helps you transfer your personal files, photos, music, e-mails and important settings for *Windows* (program settings, *Favorites*, Internet settings, e-mail settings and contacts) to a safe place. The data can be wrote on a CD or DVD or copied to a USB stick or an external hard disk. After installing *Vista* the data can be imported again.

Let op!

Windows Easy Transfer does **not** copy the programs you have installed on your *Windows XP* computer. You will need to reinstall these programs yourself in *Vista*. *Windows Easy Transfer* can copy program settings. For example things like high scores in games, or the settings you use for the toolbars in *Microsoft Office*.

The first step is to download and install *Windows Easy Transfer* on your *XP* computer.

Open the website
www.microsoft.com/downloads/search.aspx?displaylang=en

The *Microsoft Download Center* is opened. Here you can search for the program you need:

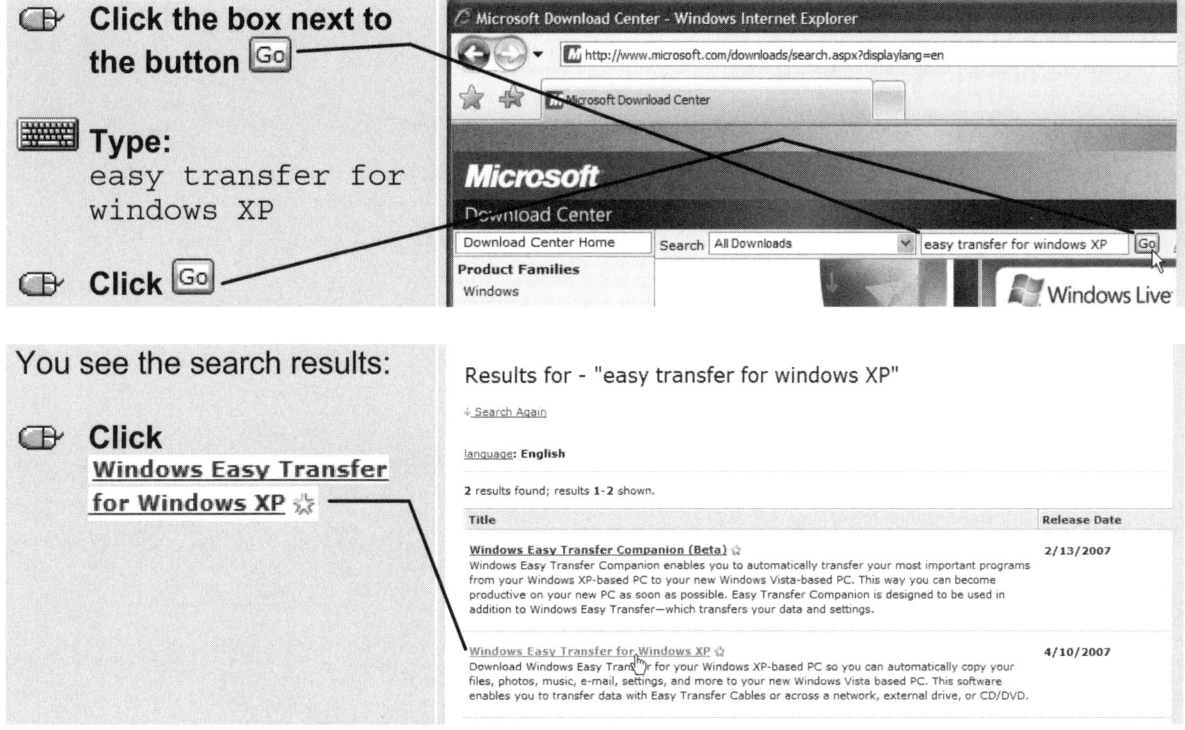

You see a webpage with a description of the program *Windows Easy Transfer for Windows XP*. To be able to download the program validation is required: this means that a check needs to be performed to ensure that you have a genuine version of *Windows XP*. You can start the validation process by clicking the button Continue.

Please note:

If you have never validated your version of *Windows XP* before, it may be necessary to install an ActiveX-control. Follow the instructions that appear in the information bar and install this control.

After validating your version of *Windows XP* you can download and install the program *Windows Easy Transfer for Windows XP*. This procedure will go as follows:

- If necessary, you can change the language of the download on the download page.
- Use the link ⇩ Download files below to show the part of the webpage where you can choose your download.

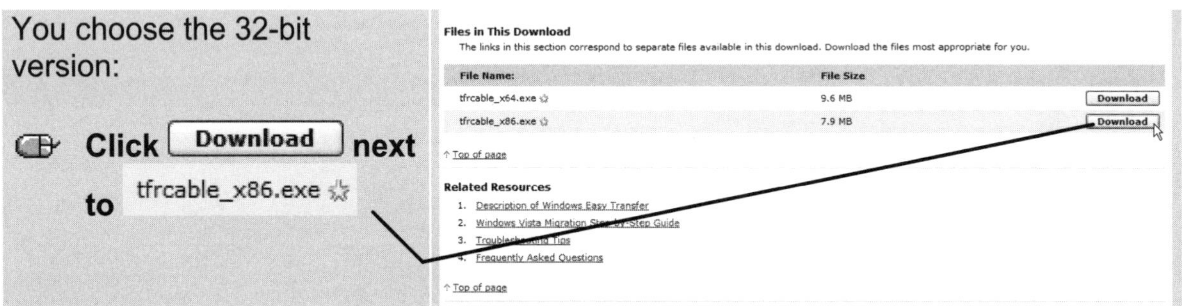

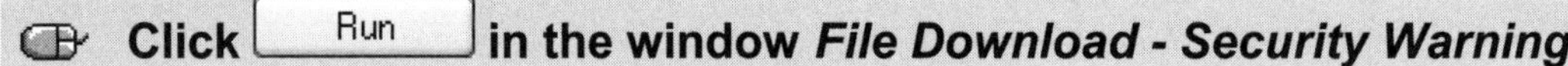

The download starts and you see the progress.

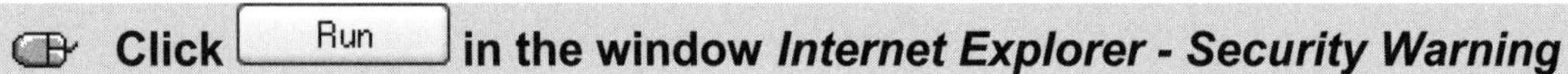

The files are unpacked. You see the start window of the *Wizard Install Software-updates*.

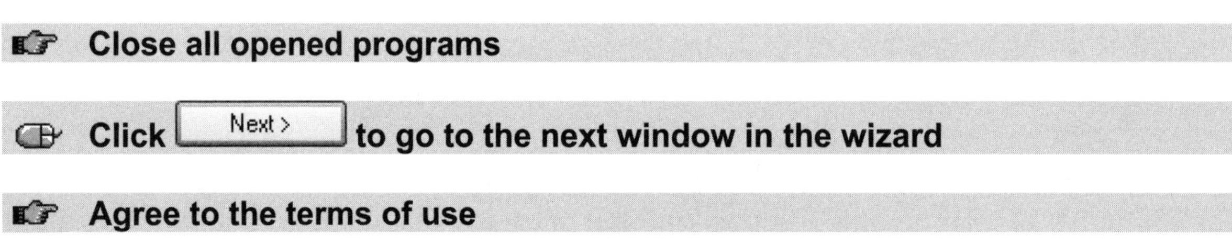

Now the installation starts.

1.9 Using Windows Easy Transfer

In *Windows XP* you can start *Windows Easy Transfer* as follows:

Close all programs and windows that are still open

Click start, All Programs, Windows Easy Transfer

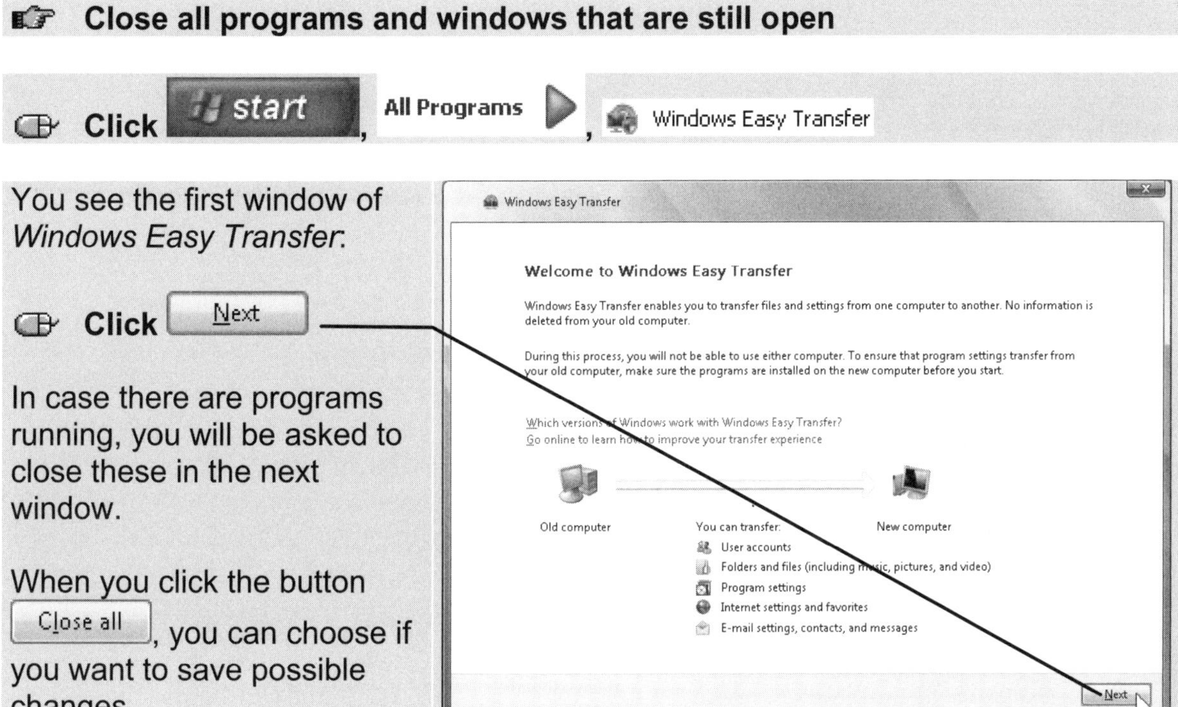

You see the first window of *Windows Easy Transfer*.

Click Next

In case there are programs running, you will be asked to close these in the next window.

When you click the button Close all, you can choose if you want to save possible changes.

Now you have to choose how you would like to transfer the files and settings to *Windows Vista*.

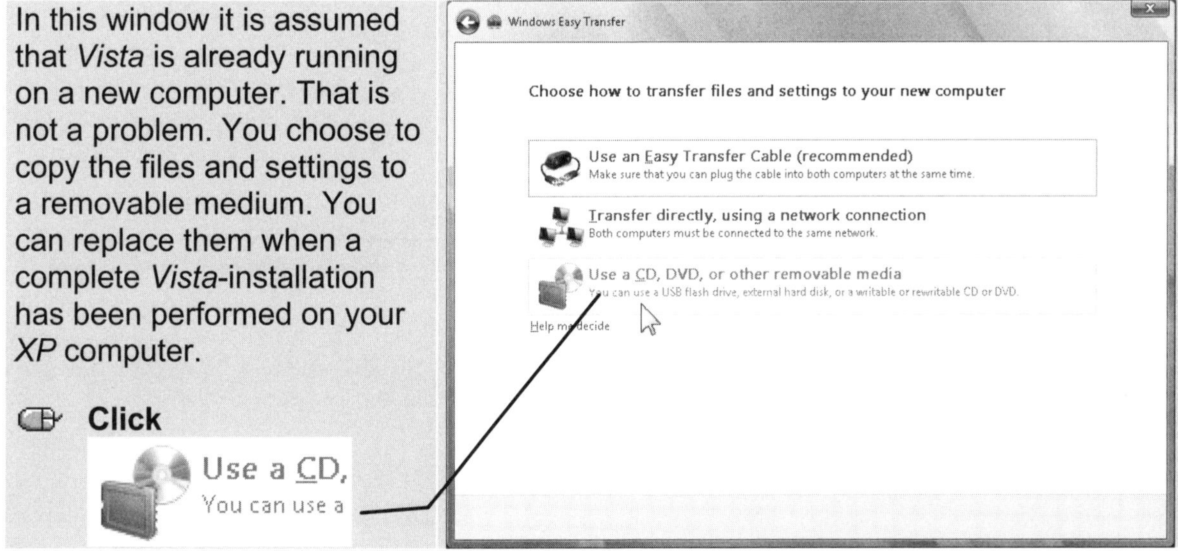

In this window it is assumed that *Vista* is already running on a new computer. That is not a problem. You choose to copy the files and settings to a removable medium. You can replace them when a complete *Vista*-installation has been performed on your *XP* computer.

Click Use a CD, You can use a

In the next window you choose which type of removable media you want to use to store the data.

If you want to use a CD or DVD writer:

Click **CD**

You can also choose a USB stick or an external hard disk.

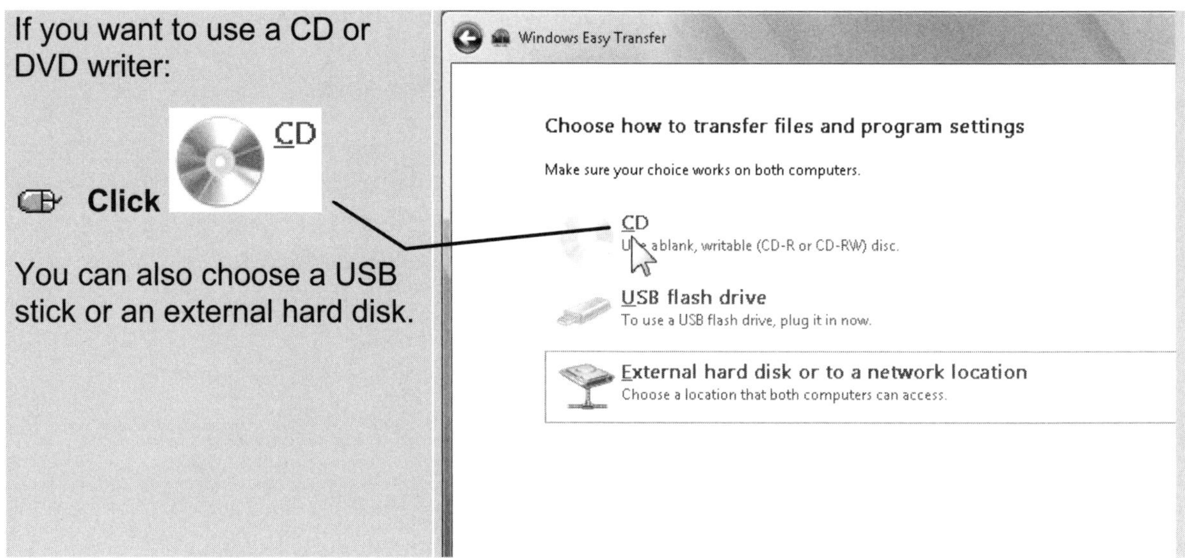

In this example the data will be written to a blank DVD.

Check if the correct drive has been selected

Place a blank DVD in the DVD writer

Here you can enter a password to protect the DVD(s) if necessary:

Click **Next**

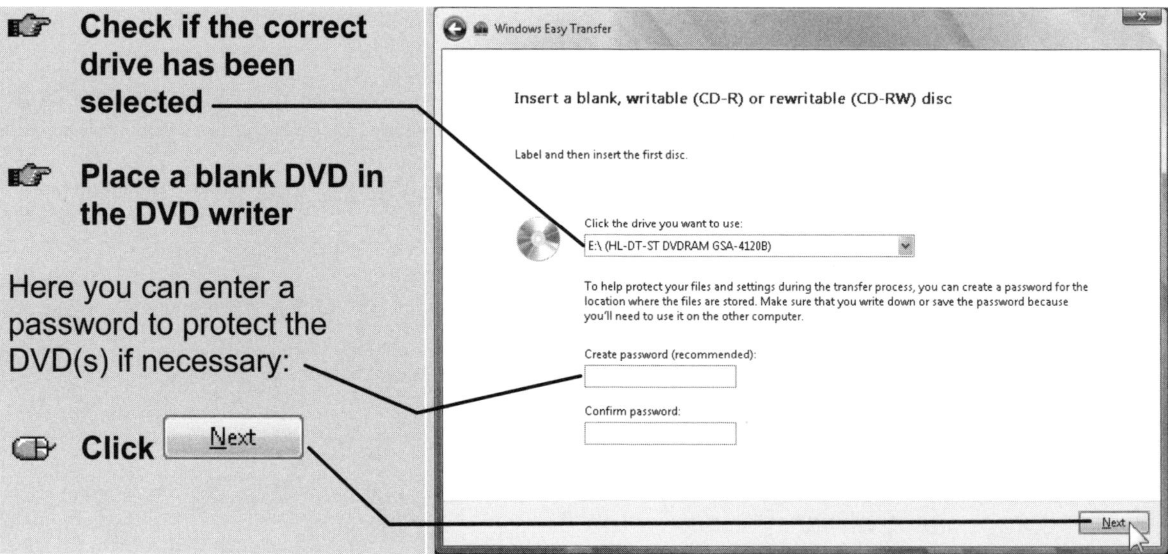

Tip

More information

If your computer is connected to a network, you can also secure your files and settings on an network location. For more information you can refer to the extensive Help-function of *Windows Vista*.

- **Click** , Help and Support

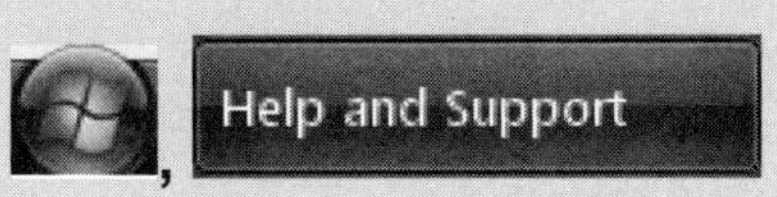

Type:
windows easy transfer

- **Click**

When you click the first search result, you will reach a goldmine of information on *Windows Easy Transfer*.

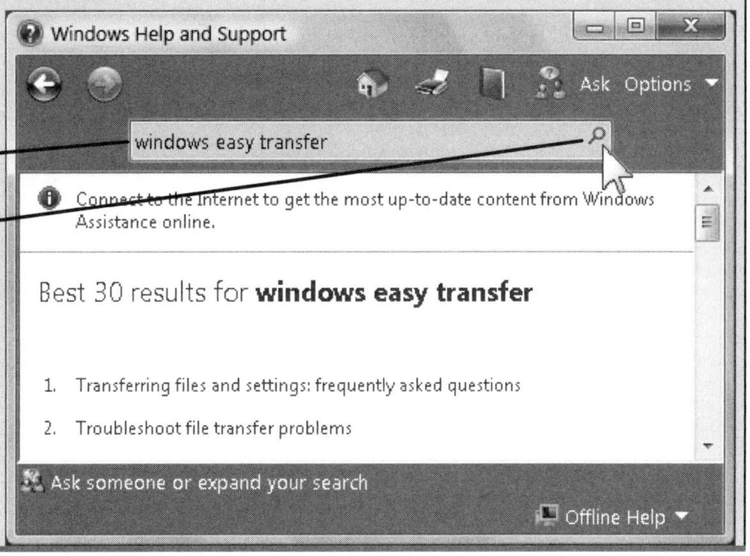

In the next window you choose which files and settings you want to transfer to *Windows Vista*. The recommended option, *All user accounts, files, and settings*, will result in a very large amount of data. That is no problem if you transfer your data using a cable, network or external hard disk. But if you are going to write the data to a CD or DVD, you probably want to reduce the size of the file. This is how you can do that:

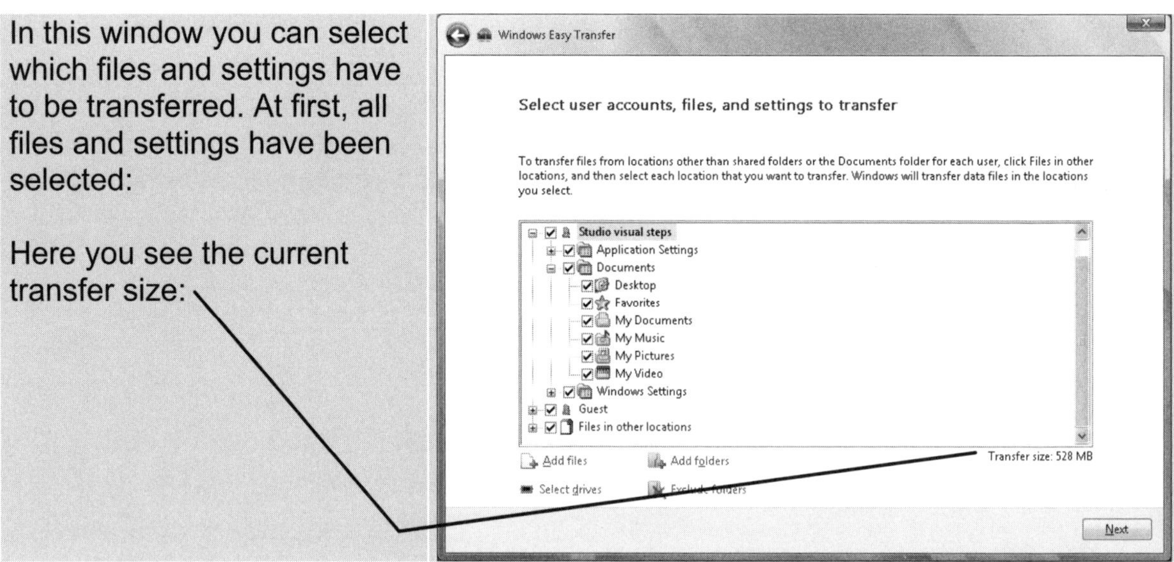

In this window you can select which files and settings have to be transferred. At first, all files and settings have been selected:

Here you see the current transfer size:

For example, you can choose to open Files in other locations and remove the check mark ☑ in front of large folders with photos and other files. This will reduce the transfer size. You should only do this if you are sure that you have made a backup of these files. It is advised to select all folders with the names of the users like ☑ Studio visual steps.

When you have finished selecting files:

Click Next

In the next window you will see that the data to be transferred is being collected and verified.

Now the data is written to the DVD:

It is advised to have a few discs on hand, in case you need more than one DVD for the transfer. When transferring the data to *Vista* the discs have to be entered in the correct order.

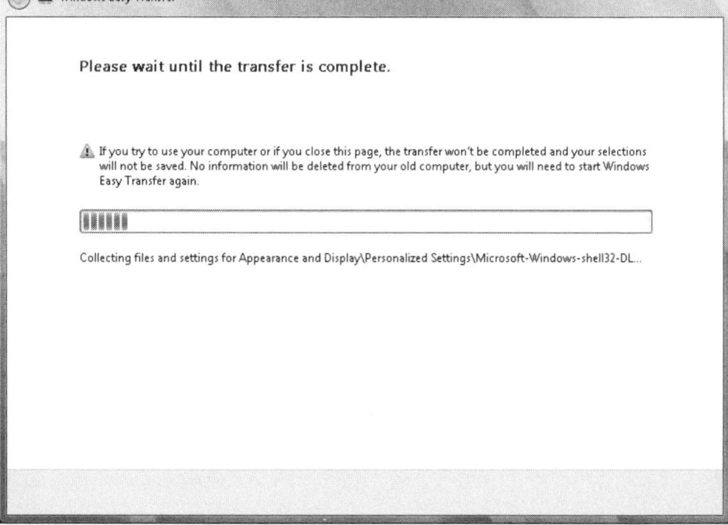

If another disc is needed, you will be asked to place it in the drive. In the end you will see the window *You're ready to transfer files and settings to your new computer.* You can close this window. You have secured your files and settings. When you have installed *Vista* on your *XP* computer, you can transfer the data (see section 1.12).

 **Please note:**

Windows Easy Transfer can also be used to transfer files and settings directly between two computers. For example from your old *XP* computer to your new *Vista* computer. This can be done with the special *Easy Transfer* cable. But if you do not have this cable, you can also copy the data on the *XP* computer as described in this section.
The use of the *Easy Transfer* cable will be described in section 1.13.

1.10 Performing a Complete Installation

When you perform a complete installation of *Windows Vista* all data on the hard drive of your computer will be overwritten. When you install *Vista* on a new 'empty' computer this is the only available option.

 **Please note:**

When you are going to install *Windows Vista* on your *Windows XP* computer, first check if you have a good backup of your important files (like documents and photos). In case you have not yet secured your files, folders and settings using *Windows Easy Transfer* you can do so now.

The start of the complete installation on an *XP* computer is slightly different than on an empty computer.

When you install *Windows Vista* on an *XP* computer:

 **Place the *Windows Vista* DVD in the DVD-ROM drive**

Wait until the DVD starts automatically

When you install *Windows Vista* on an empty computer, you will need to boot your computer from the CD/DVD drive. This will not automatically be the case on all computers.

 **Check the documentation for your computer to see if it will boot from the DVD drive or ask your hardware supplier for information.**

If necessary, let your hardware supplier adjust the settings of your computer

When your computer can boot from the DVD drive:

Place the *Windows Vista* DVD in the DVD drive

Restart the computer

In the window that appears you can enter the proper country and language settings:

Select the proper setting for language and country

For the keyboard setting, select *United States of America (international)*

Click the button *Next*

After this window the installation on the *XP* computer will continue in the same manner as on an empty computer. The installation window appears:

Now you enter the product key, which consists of five groups of five letters and digits. You can find the product key on the *Windows Vista* box or the DVD sleeve. You do not need to type the dashes in the product key, they will be added automatically.

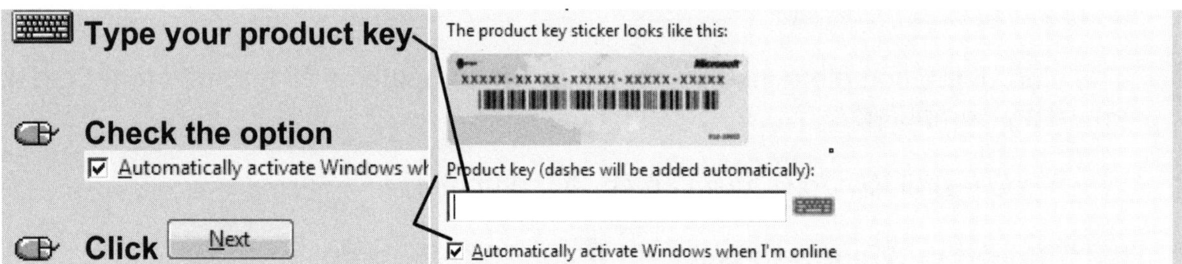

Activation of *Windows Vista* is necessary, because otherwise you can only use the program for fourteen days. If necessary, you can activate *Vista* later through the *Welcome Center*.

 **Let op!**

Entering the product key during the installation is not mandatory. You can also do this after the installation. When you install *Windows Vista* on a new computer, the sticker with the product key might be attached to the bottom or the back of the computer. In that case it will be more convenient to enter the product key later.

In this case you must select the **exact** edition you have purchased in the window *Select the edition of Windows that you purchased*. On the *Windows* DVD the software is the same for all editions of *Vista*. The product key you enter decides which edition of *Vista* is installed. *Windows Vista* does not accept a product key that does not match the edition you have selected. In that case you have to reinstall *Vista*, or purchase a new product key for the edition you have installed.

Now you have to accept the software license terms. Then the installation starts.

In the next window you will be asked which type of installation you want to perform. The option Upgrade will not be available on an empty computer.

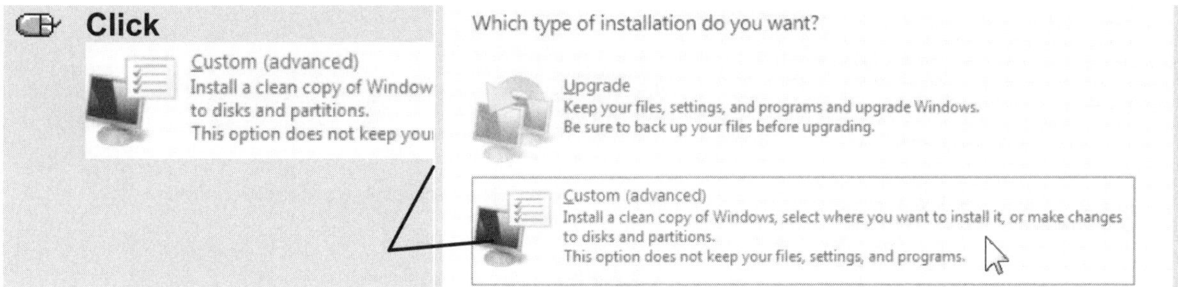

In the window *Where do you want to install Windows?* you choose the hard disk where *Windows Vista* will be installed. You can use the link Drive options (advanced) to open another window where you can choose to partition or format your hard disk during the installation.

If the hard disk you chose for the installation already contains a version of *Windows*, it will be saved in a separate folder with the name *Windows old*. After the installation you can copy files from this folder to *Windows Vista* if necessary. The folder only contains *Windows*-specific files, folders and settings. This means that a folder with your photos will not be saved!

The rest of the installation is done automatically, you do not need to click or enter anything. The complete installation will take about thirty to forty minutes, depending on the specifications of your computer. During the upgrade the computer will restart automatically a couple of times.

Do not turn off the computer during the upgrade procedure, even when it looks like the computer has not responded for a while!

1.11 Completing the Installation

Once the upgrade or the complete installation has finished, your computer will need to restart. You are now ready to adjust the settings in *Windows Vista*. If you bought a computer with *Windows Vista* already installed, these are the first windows you see when you start your computer for the first time,

Use the button  Next each time you want to go to the next window:

Enter a name for the administrator account:

It is a good idea to secure this account with a password right away:

Just like in *Windows XP* you can assign a picture to go with this user account:

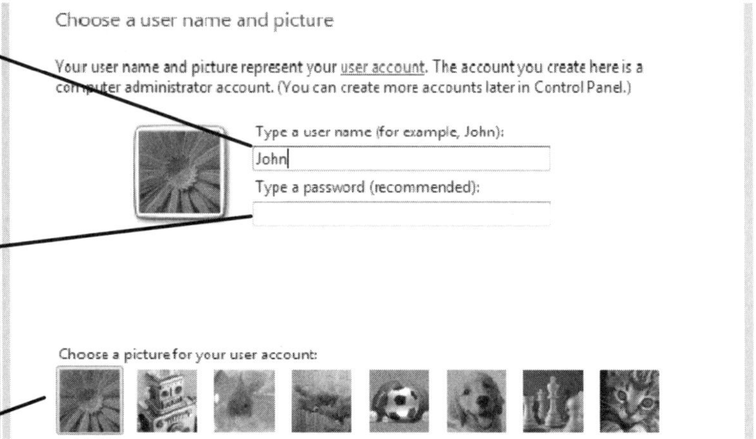

Choose a user name and picture

Your user name and picture represent your user account. The account you create here is a computer administrator account. (You can create more accounts later in Control Panel.)

Type a user name (for example, John):

John

Type a password (recommended):

Choose a picture for your user account:

Then enter a name for your computer:

This name can be used to identify your computer in a network.

Here you can choose a desktop background:

Type a computer name and choose a desktop background

Type a computer name (for example, Office-PC):

John-PC

Choose a desktop background (you can make changes later in Control Panel):

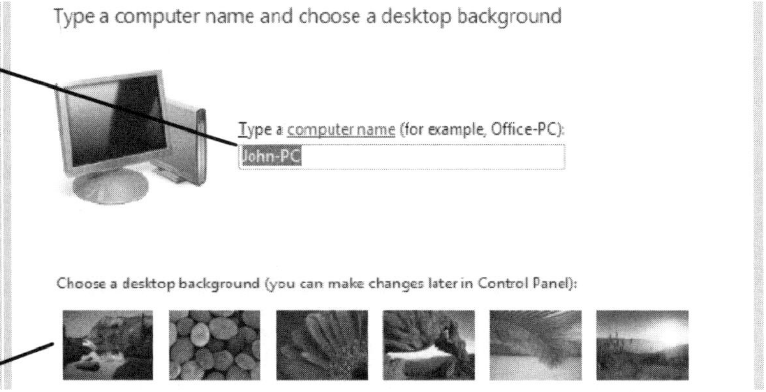

In the next window you can determine how you want to use the security features in *Windows Vista*.

It is highly recommended to choose the first option:

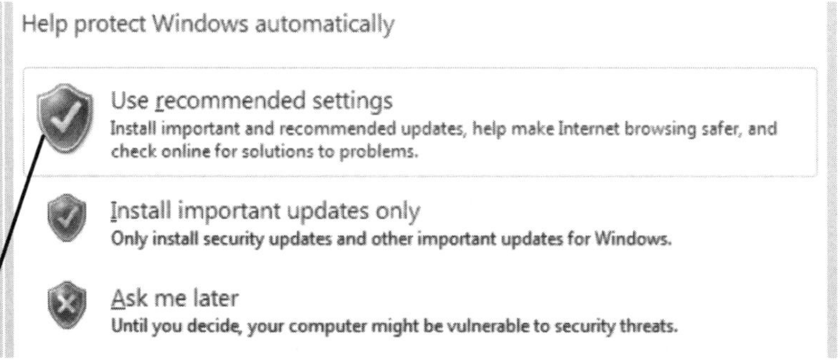

Help protect Windows automatically

Use recommended settings
Install important and recommended updates, help make Internet browsing safer, and check online for solutions to problems.

Install important updates only
Only install security updates and other important updates for Windows.

Ask me later
Until you decide, your computer might be vulnerable to security threats.

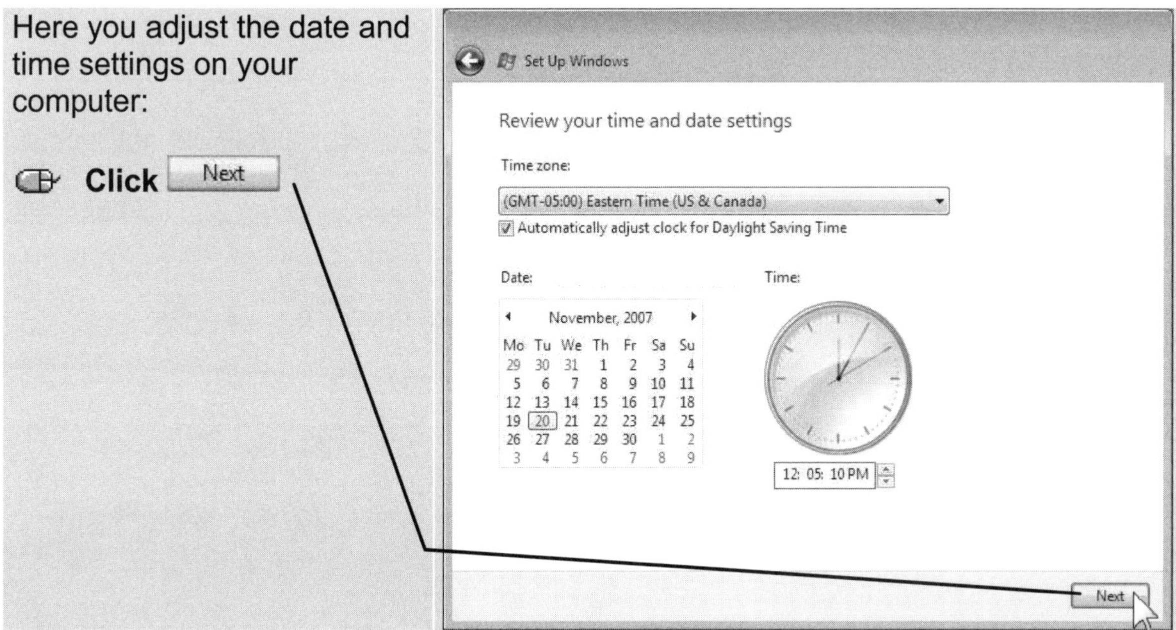

Windows Vista is now ready to use. You will see the final set up window:

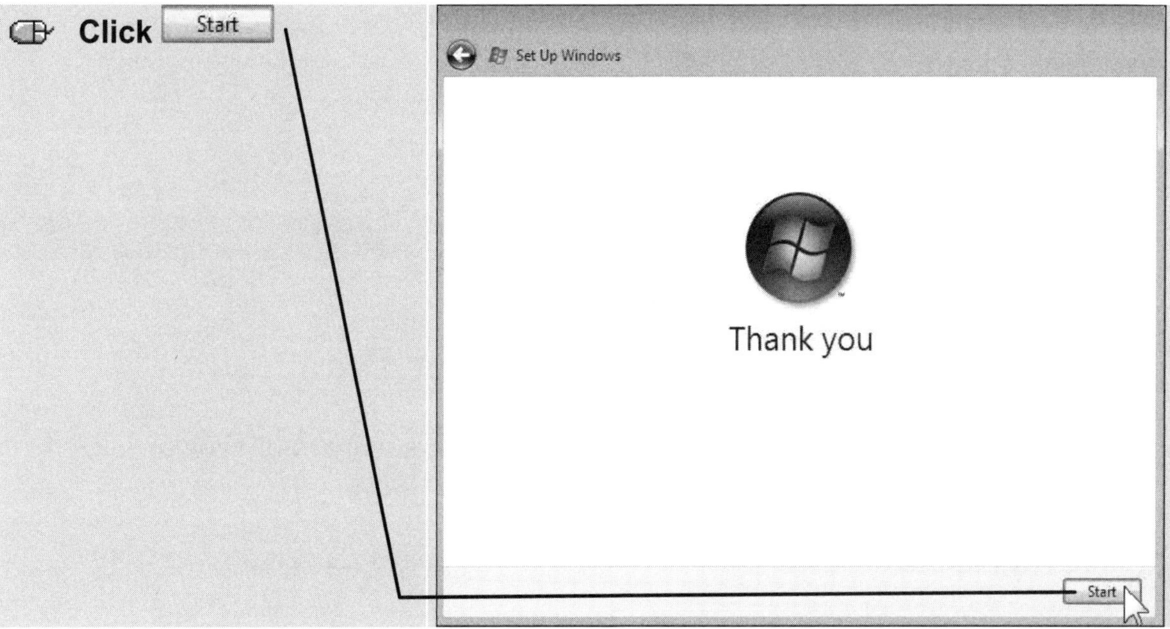

The computer is restarted one last time. Now *Windows Vista* rates the performance of your computer, you see a system check message. Your desktop is configured based on the results of this system check.

If you entered a password for the administrator account you will first see the *Welcome Screen*. After entering the password, your desktop appears.

Tip

Make a recovery DVD
If you bought a computer with *Vista* already installed, you probably did not receive a *Vista* installation DVD. As soon as you start using your computer, *Windows Vista* will urge you to make a recovery DVD. In case of computer problems you can use this DVD to repair the installation.

Creating this recovery DVD is highly recommended. Follow the instructions on your screen to do so.

When you see *Vista* for the first time, the *Welcome Center* is displayed:

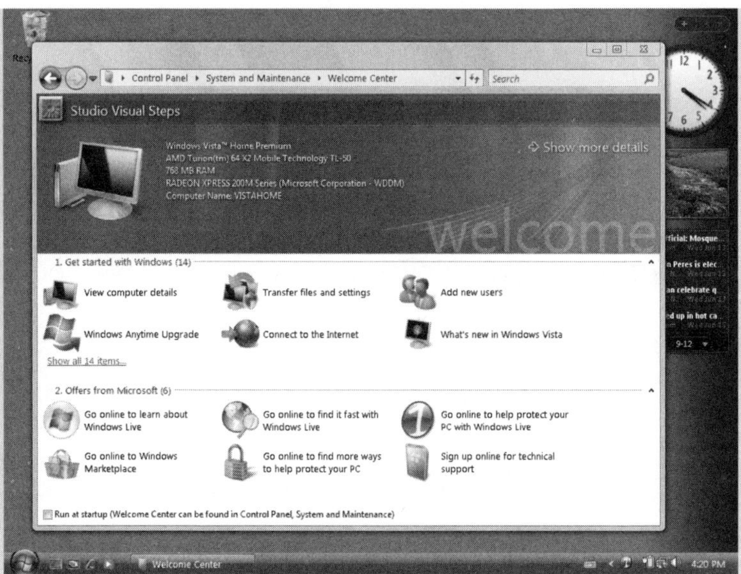

1.12 Transferring the Easy Transfer Data

If you used the program *Windows Easy Transfer* to secure your *Windows XP* files and settings, you can transfer the data to *Windows Vista*.

☞ **Insert the (first) CD-ROM or DVD-ROM in the DVD drive**

or:

☞ **Connect the external hard disk or USB stick**

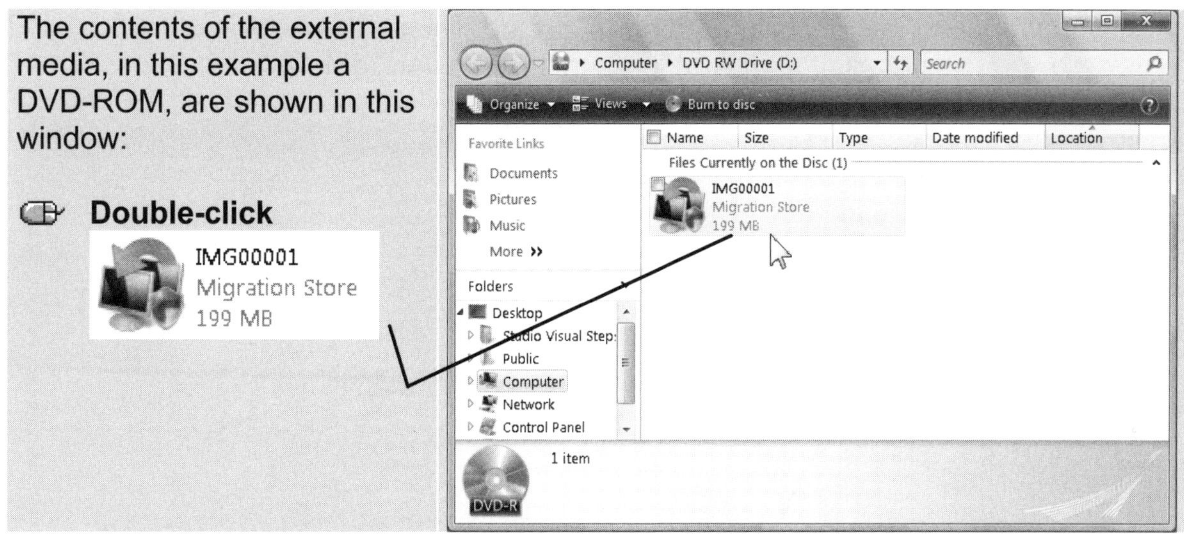

You will be introduced to the improved security in *Windows Vista* right away: your screen goes dark and a window appears. In this window you need to give permission to continue with the transfer. You do this by clicking the button Continue.
Now the transfer starts automatically. First the data is read from the removable media. If your data is divided over multiple discs, you will need to insert the next disc in the drive as soon as *Easy Transfer* asks for it.

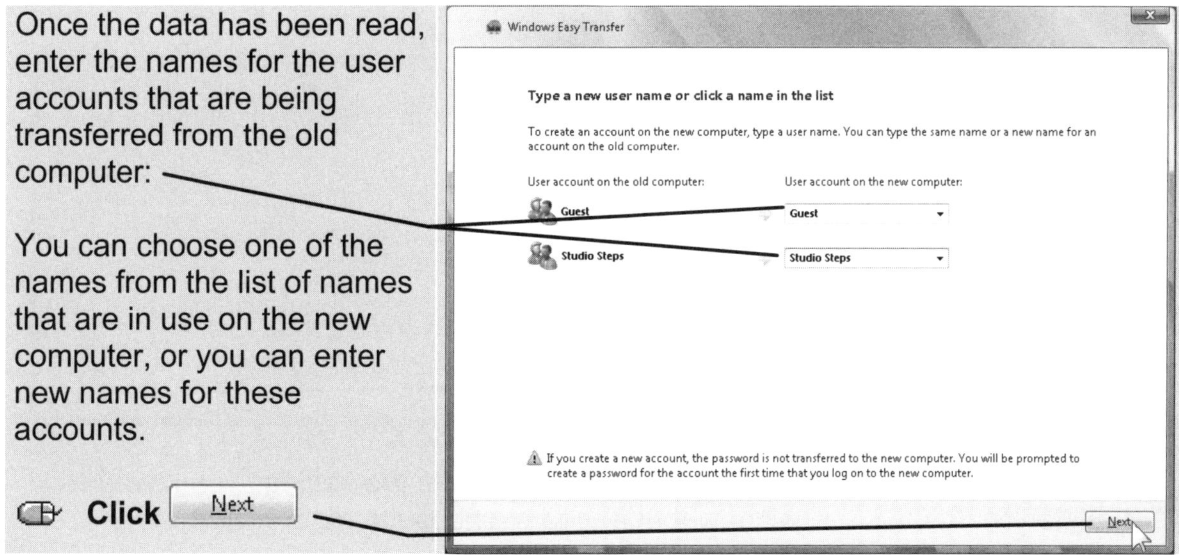

If your computer has multiple hard disks or hard disk partitions, you will see a window where you can choose the disk(s) to store the transferred data.

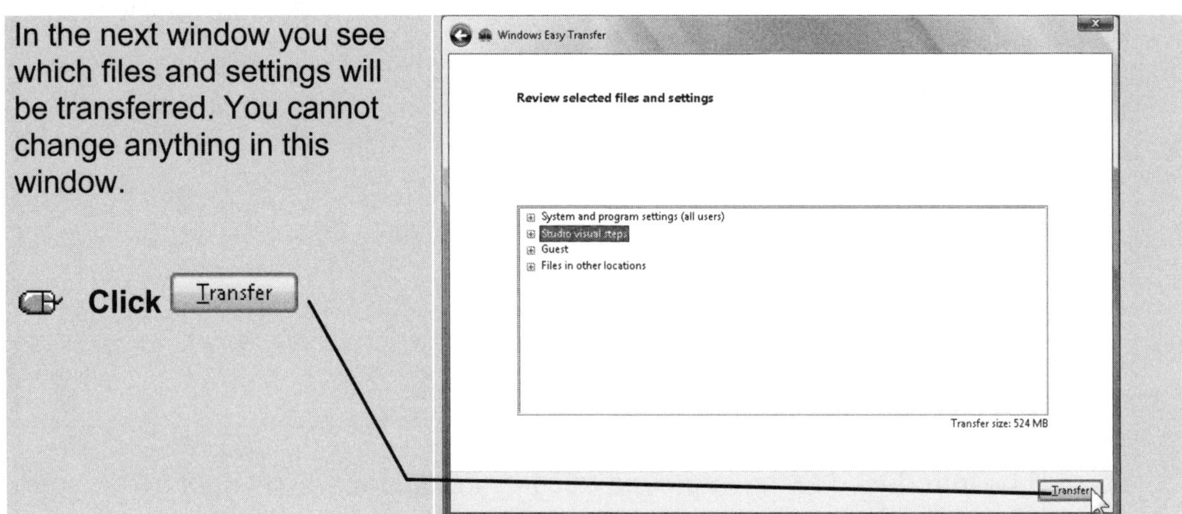

The transfer starts. The moving green bar keeps you apprised of the transfer progress.

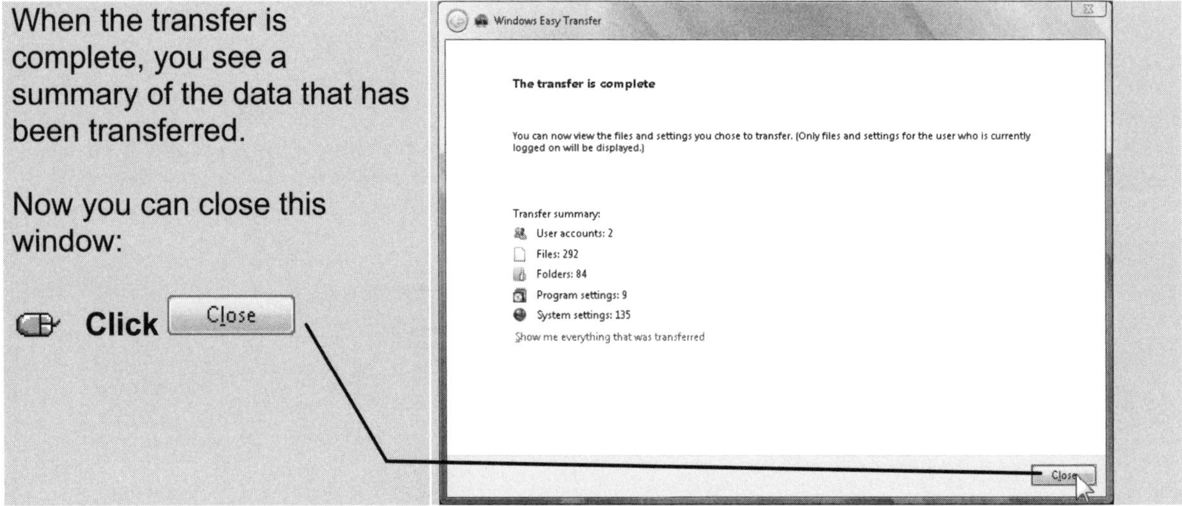

You need to restart the computer in order to activate the settings you have just transferred. In the small window that appears, choose to restart now.

When the computer has restarted, you will find the new user accounts you made during the transfer process on the *Welcome Screen*. If an account was password protected on the *XP* computer, the password has not been transferred. You will have to enter a new user name and password for this account. For accounts that were not password protected on the old computer you do not need to enter anything. Clicking the button with the arrow is enough.

1.13 Using an Easy Transfer Cable

If you kept your old *XP* computer, you can use a special *Easy Transfer* cable to transfer your files and settings directly to your new *Vista* computer.

Tip

Easy Transfer cable
The *Easy Transfer* cable is a special type of USB cable with a connecting piece in the middle. It is not possible to use a regular USB cable for this type of transfer. The cable is offered by different suppliers such as Belkin.

When you buy a cable, check the box for this *Vista* logo:

Each *Easy Transfer* cable comes with a CD-ROM containing special software that needs to be installed on the *Windows XP* computer.

Close all programs on your *XP* computer

Insert the CD-ROM in the CD-ROM drive of your *XP* computer

After inserting the CD-ROM, the installation starts automatically. You will see the first window of the *Software Update Installation Wizard.*

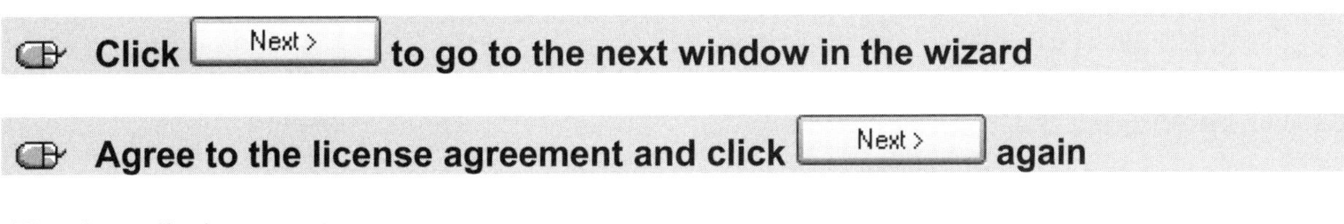

The installation starts.

Please note:

If you want to transfer data from multiple user accounts at the same time from the *XP* computer to the *Vista* computer, you need to be logged in as administrator on both computers.

Connect one end of the *Easy Transfer* cable to a USB port in the *XP* computer. Connect the other end to a USB port in the *Vista* computer

The cable driver is installed automatically on the *Vista* computer.

You see this window on the *Vista* computer:

Click Transfer files and settings using Windows Easy Transfer

Your screen goes dark and you need to give your permission to continue.

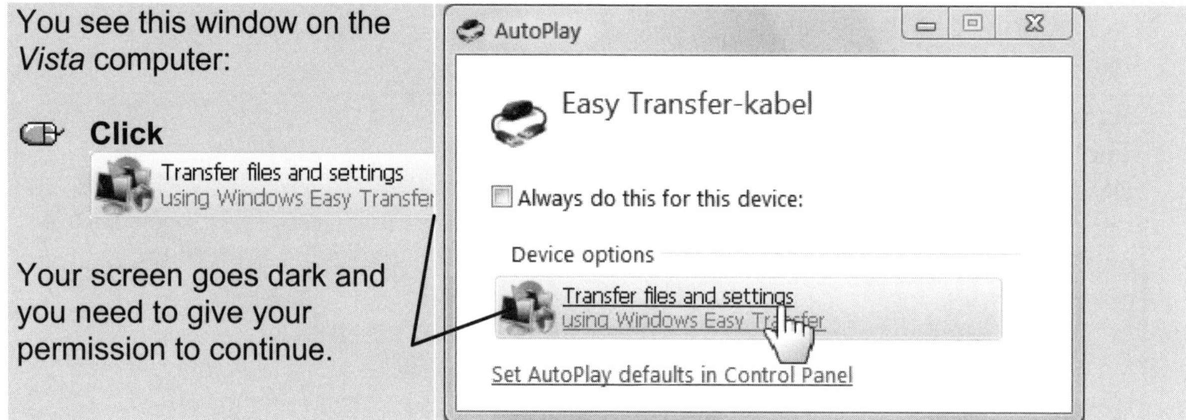

You see the same window on your *XP* computer, in the familiar blue *XP* style. Here you also choose the option Transfer files and settings using Windows Easy Transfer.

Both computers show the first window of *Windows Easy Transfer*:

Click Next

If there are programs still running, you are asked to close these in the next window.

When you use the button Close all, *Windows* will ask if you want to save the changes.

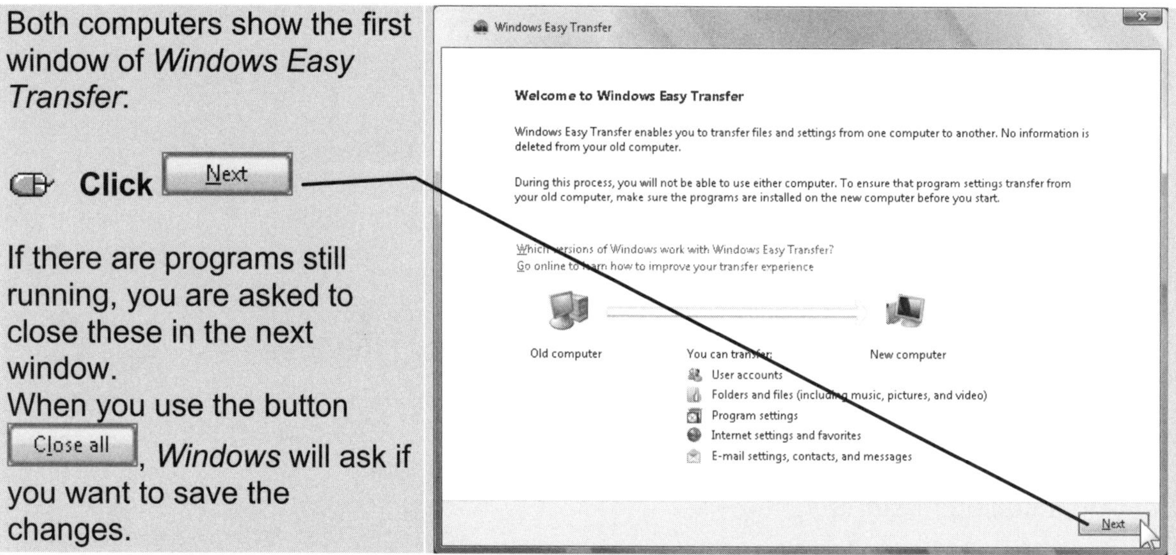

Depending on the speed of your computer, you might see the window *Choose how to transfer files and settings* on your *XP* computer:

Click the option

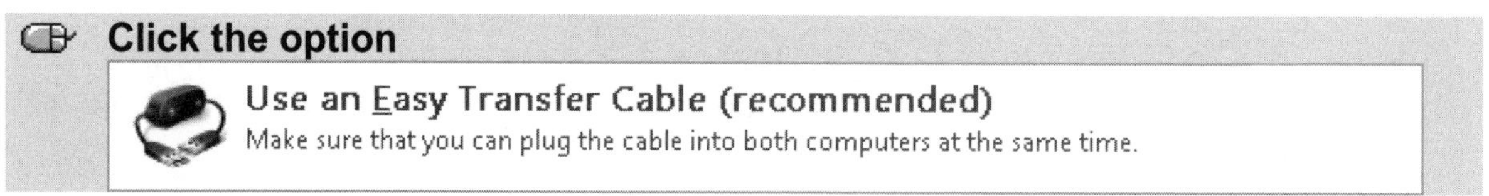

You see a window with instructions for connecting the cable and installing the software.

This window will change as soon as the *XP* computer connects to the *Vista* computer, and vice versa.

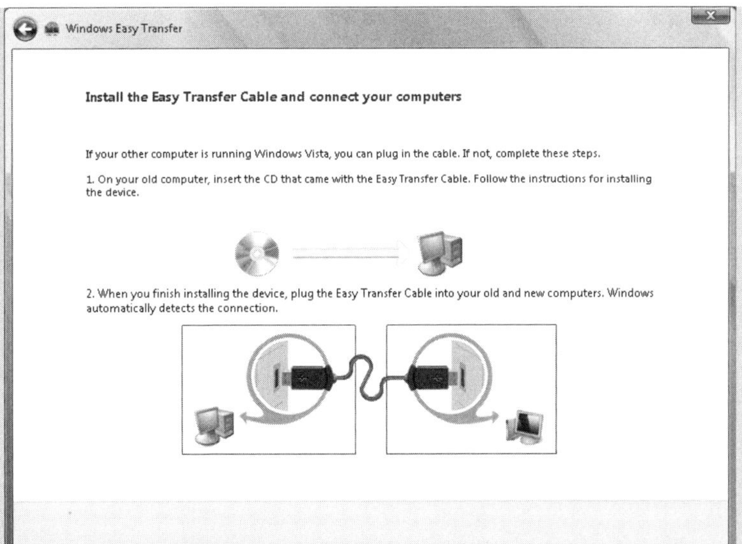

A connection is made between the two computers.

On your *Vista* computer you see this message:

Your computers are now connected

Windows Easy Transfer is running on both computers. Do not unplug the cable, or use or turn off your new computer.

On your old computer, start selecting the files and settings that you want to transfer.

On your *XP* computer you can select the user accounts, files and settings you want to transfer. The recommended option, *All user accounts, files and settings,* will result in a large amount of data. This is not an issue when you use the *Easy Transfer* cable. If you prefer to see exactly what is transferred:

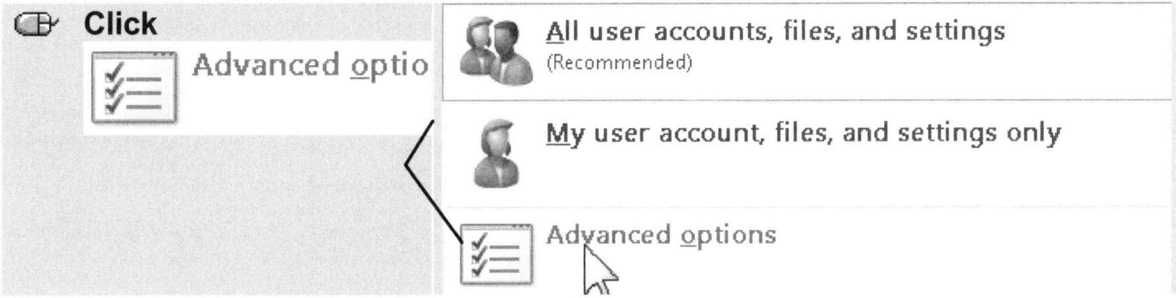

In this window you can choose which files and settings to be transferred. By default, all files and settings have been selected:

Here you see the current transfer size:

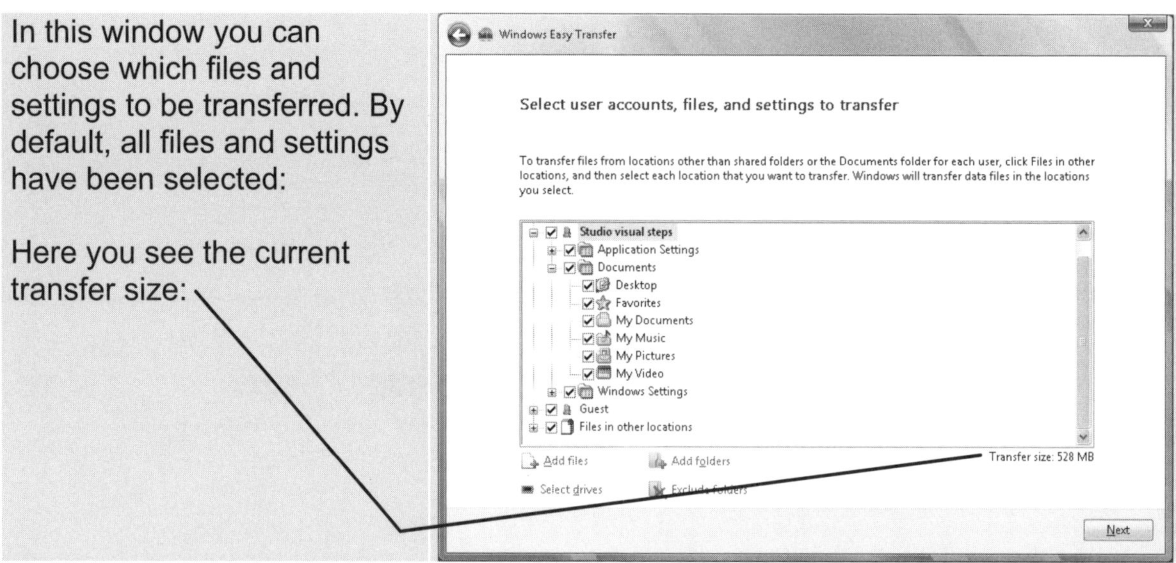

If there are files that you do not want to transfer, you can remove the check marks ☑ next to them. By opening Files in other locations you can see the other folders that have been selected in addition to the user accounts and personal settings. There might be some files that you prefer to keep on your *XP* computer instead of transferring them to your *Vista* computer as well. It is advised to select all folders with the names of the users like ☑ Studio visual steps.

When you have finished selecting files:

Click Next

Now you need to enter names for the user accounts that are transferred from the old computer:

You can choose one of the names from the list of names that are in use on the new computer, or you can enter new names for these accounts.

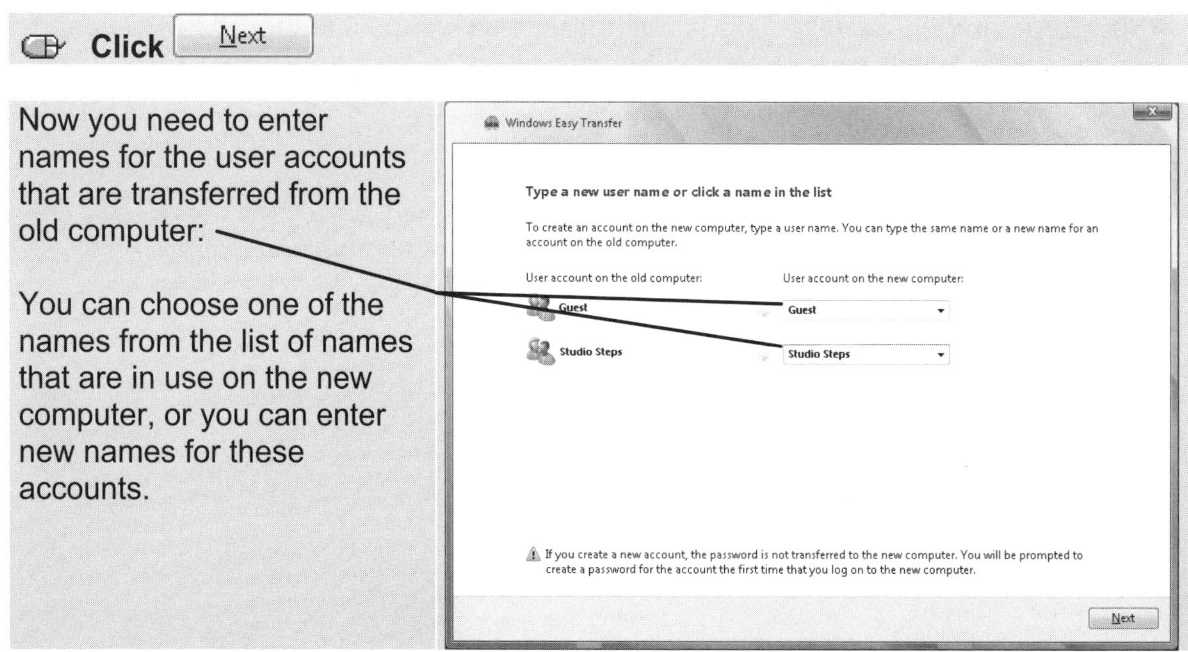

In the next window all the data that you have selected for the transfer is gathered together. After it is collected, the transfer will begin:

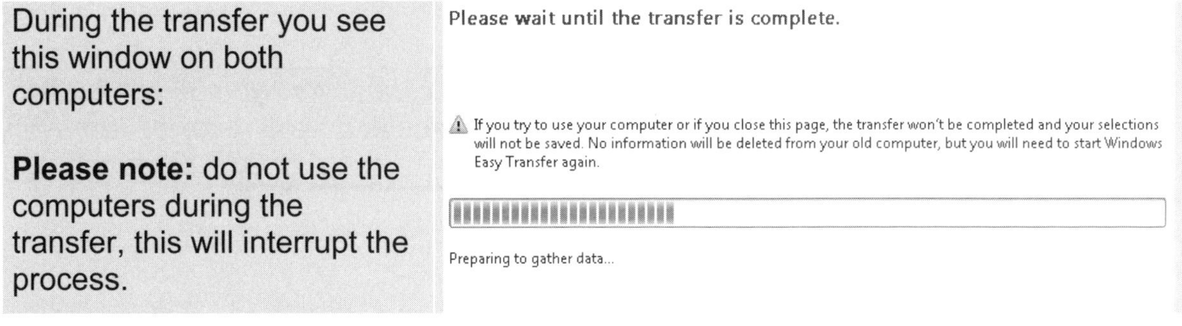

During the transfer you see this window on both computers:

Please note: do not use the computers during the transfer, this will interrupt the process.

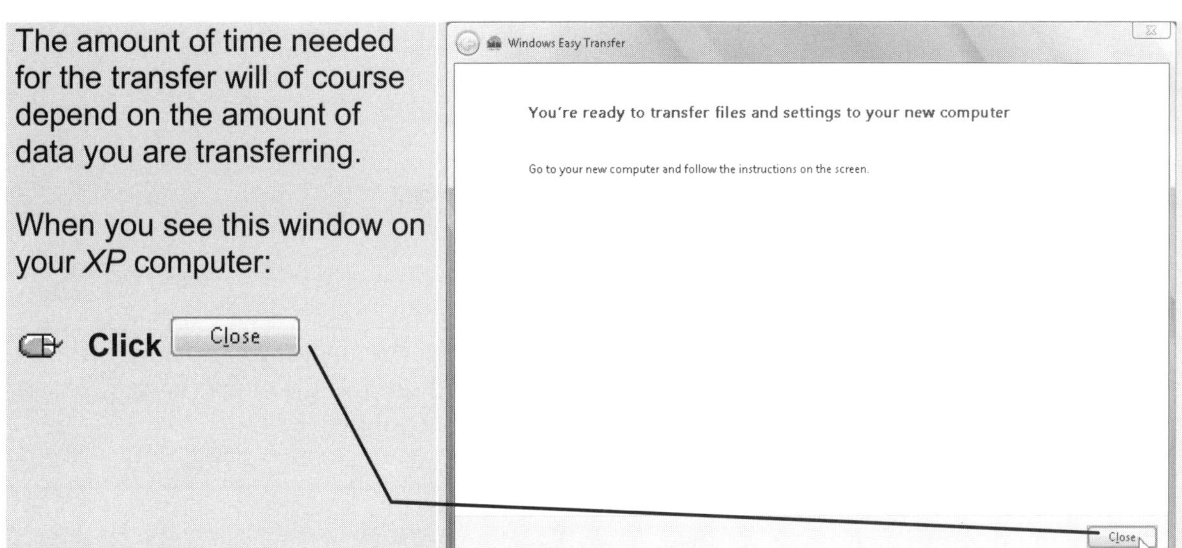

The amount of time needed for the transfer will of course depend on the amount of data you are transferring.

When you see this window on your *XP* computer:

Click Close

When the transfer is complete, a window on your *Vista* computer appears with a summary of all the data that has been transferred.

You can close this window:

Your files and settings have been transferred to your *Vista* computer.

1.14 Setting Up a Dial-Up Connection

In *Windows Vista* it is very easy to set up a dial-up connection to connect to the Internet.

 **Please note:**

If you connect to the Internet using a cable or DSL connection, you do not need to set up a dial-up account. Please refer to the documentation you received from your Internet provider for information on how to set up your cable or DSL connection.

First, check if your modem is ready:

Make sure your modem is connected to the telephone line

Do you have an external modem?

Turn the modem on

Do you have an internal modem?

You do not have to do anything

 **Please note:**

If you have an Internet access subscription, your *Internet Service Provider* (ISP) has given you a **user name** and a **password**. Also, you should have received a **phone number** that is to be used to contact your ISP's computer.
Make sure to have these details ready.

The folder window Network is opened. Now go to the window where you can add a new network.

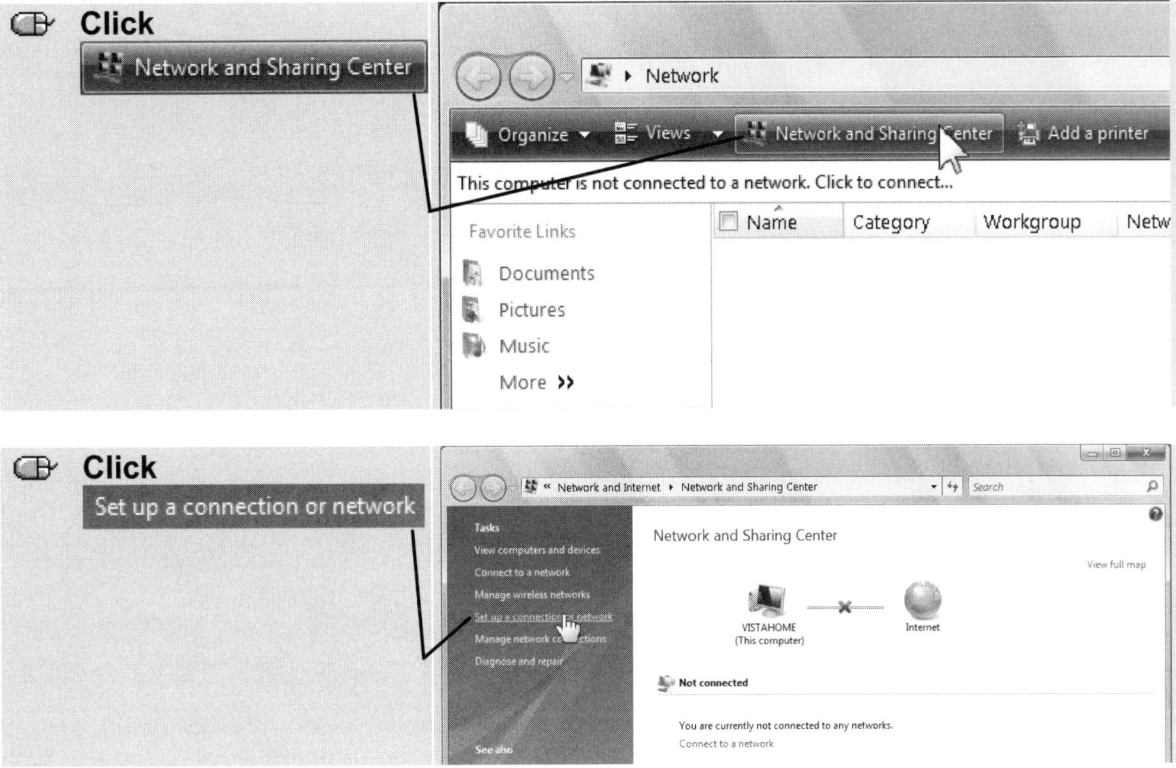

Select *Set up a dial-up connection*:

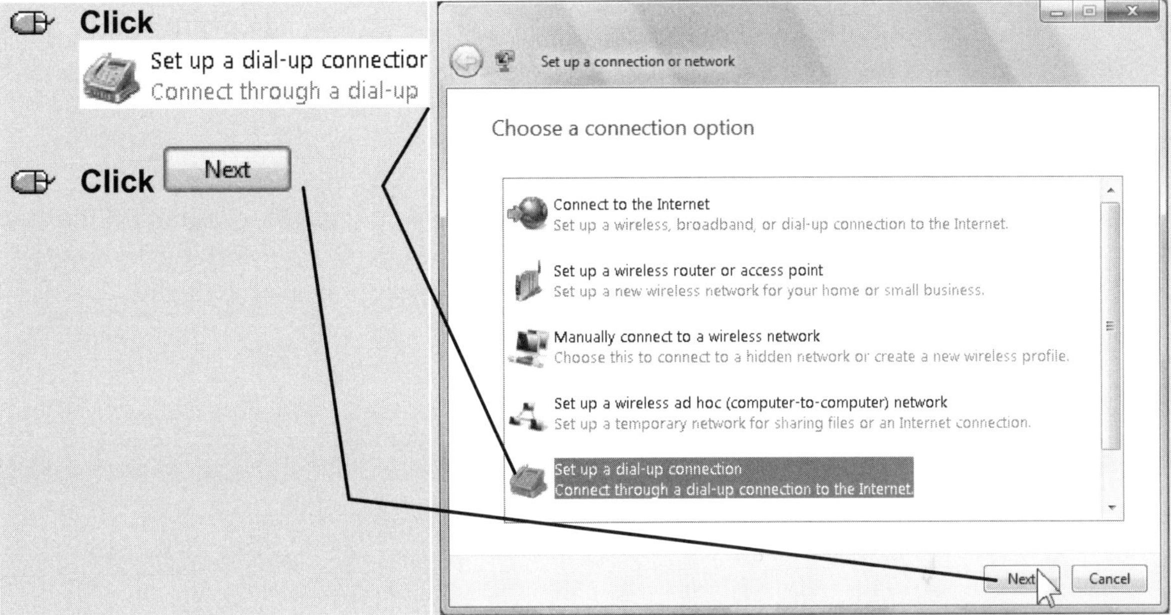

Now you can enter the details for your dial-up connection:

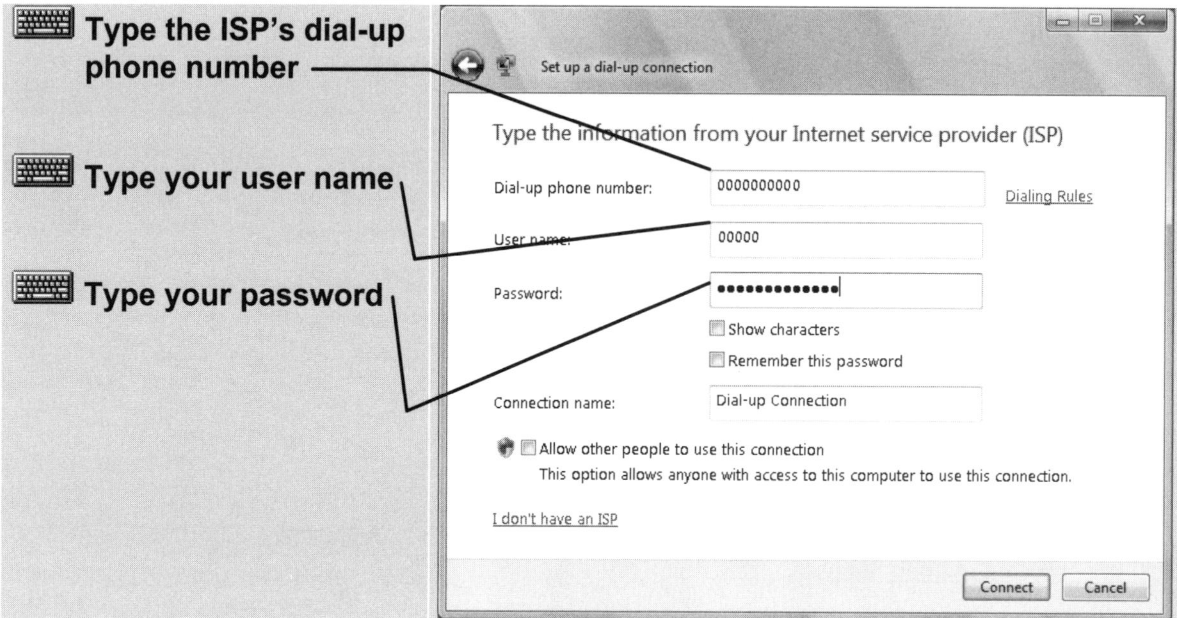

Please note:

Whether you want *Windows* to remember your password or not depends a great deal on how accessible your computer is to others. If you are the only user and no one else has access to your computer, the situation is very different than when the same computer can be used by others.

Do Not Remember
If you choose not to let *Windows* remember your password, you will have to type it in each time you want to connect to the Internet. This is recommended if you want to make certain that no one else can use your Internet connection.

Do Remember
If you are the only person who uses your computer and you are reasonably certain no one else will use it, you can choose the convenience of allowing the computer to remember the password for you.

Do you want the computer to remember your password?

Check the box ☑ Remember this password

If you do **not** want the computer to remember your password:

Make sure this box is <u>not</u> checked

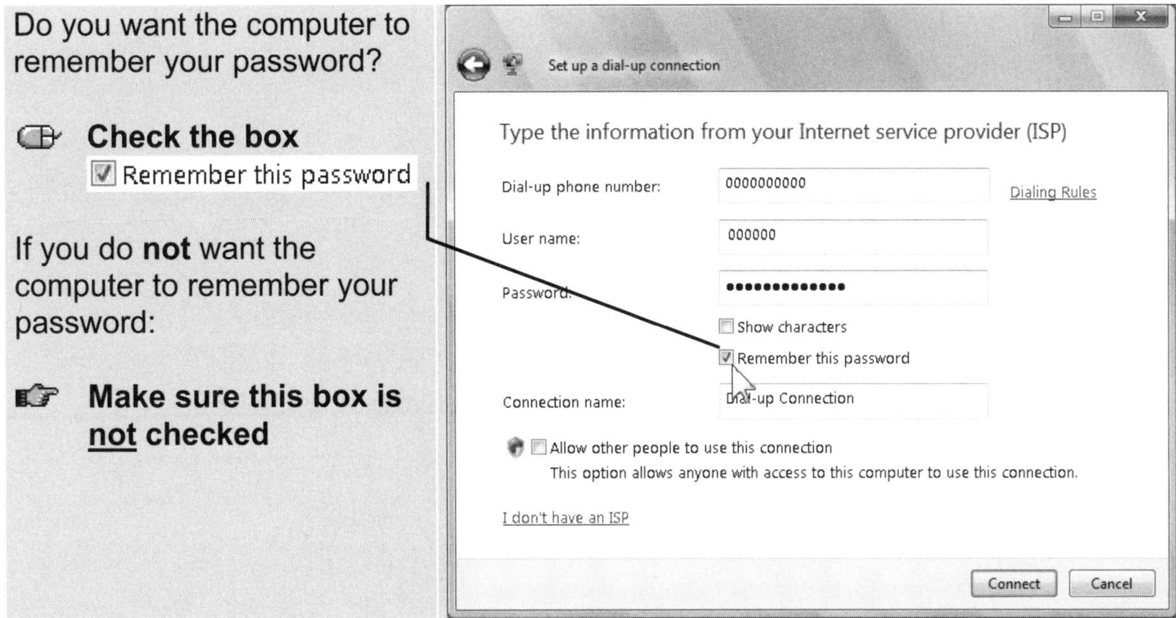

Windows Vista offers the possibility to allow other users access to your computer with this same dial-up connection. This means that other people with a different account can view and use the connection you are about to set up.

Do you want to allow other users access to this dial-up connection?

Check the box ☑ Allow other people to use tl

If you do **not** want the computer to remember the password:

Make sure this box is <u>not</u> checked

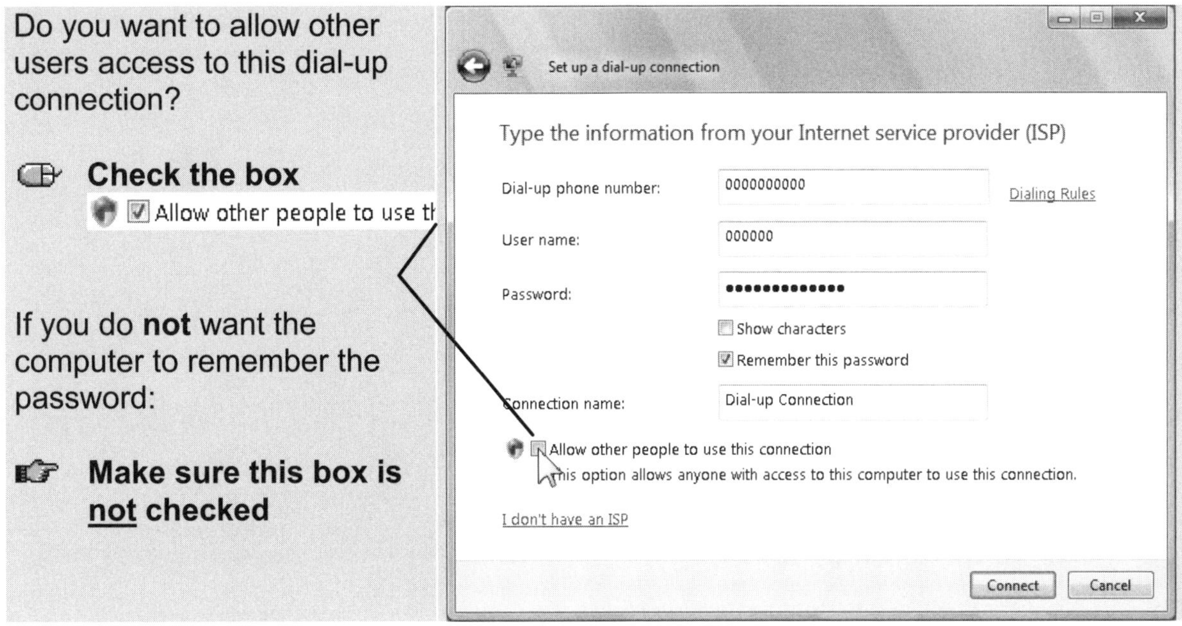

Please note:

As soon as you check the box ☑ Allow other people to use this connection, your screen goes dark and *Windows* will ask you again for your permission to continue. Click the *Continue* button if you want to apply this setting.

Now you can try the connection:

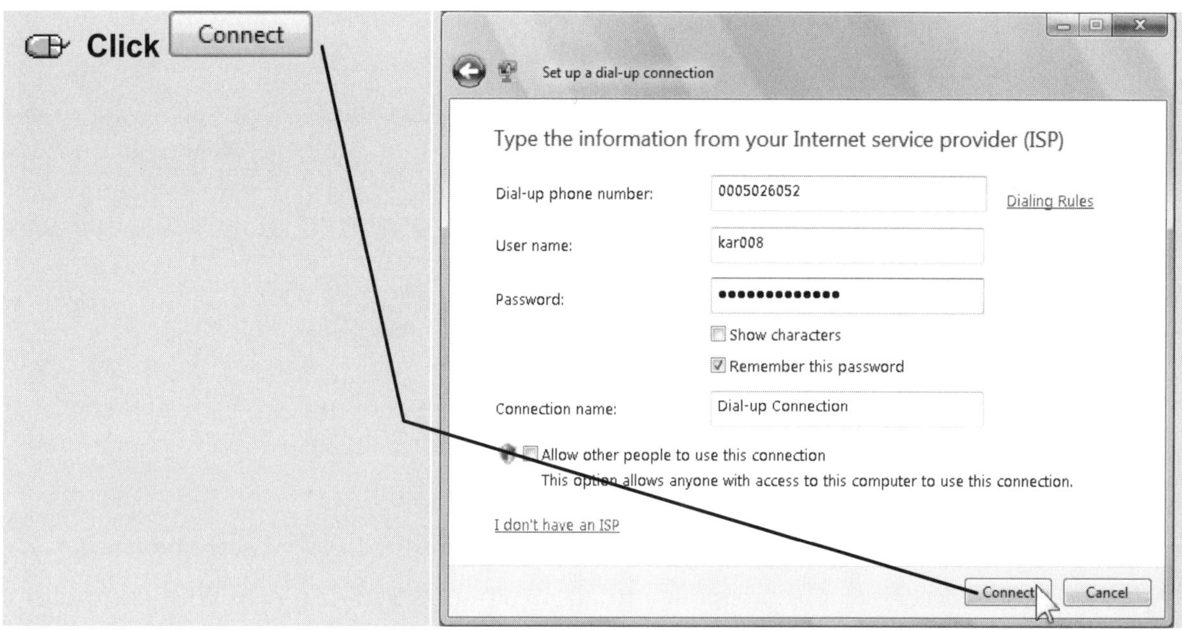

The connection is being made:

After that, your password is verified and the connection is tested.

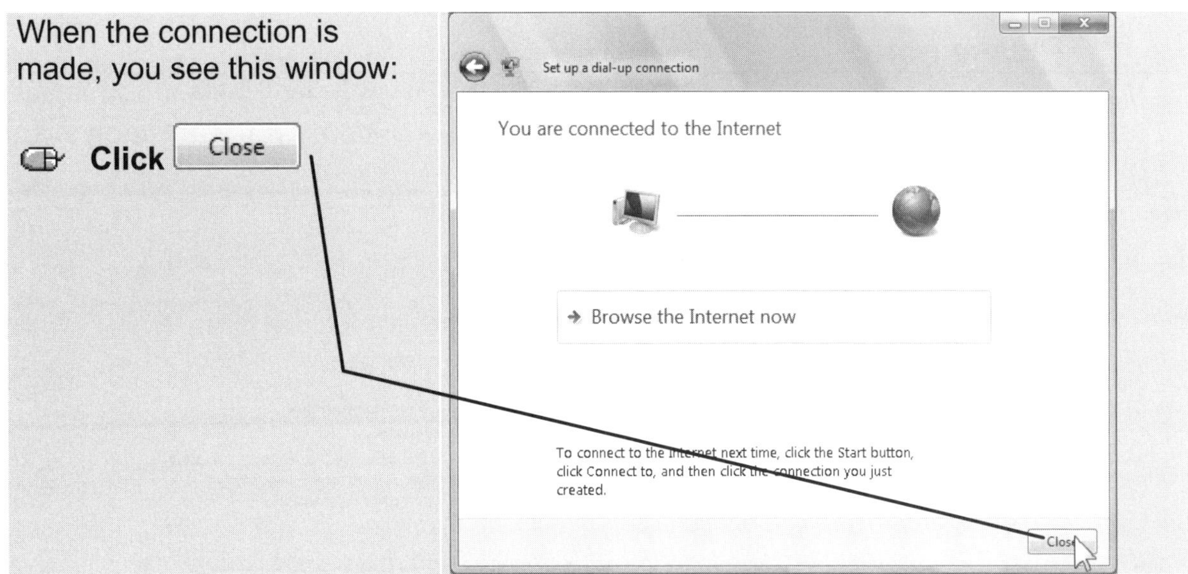

Now you see the window *Set Network Location*. The first time that you connect to a network, you must choose a network location. This automatically sets the appropriate firewall settings for the type of network that you are going to use.

If you want to be able to connect to different networks (for example, a network at home, or at a local coffee shop, or at work), choosing a network location can help ensure that your computer is always set to an appropriate security level.

There are three network locations: *Home*, *Work*, and *Public location*.

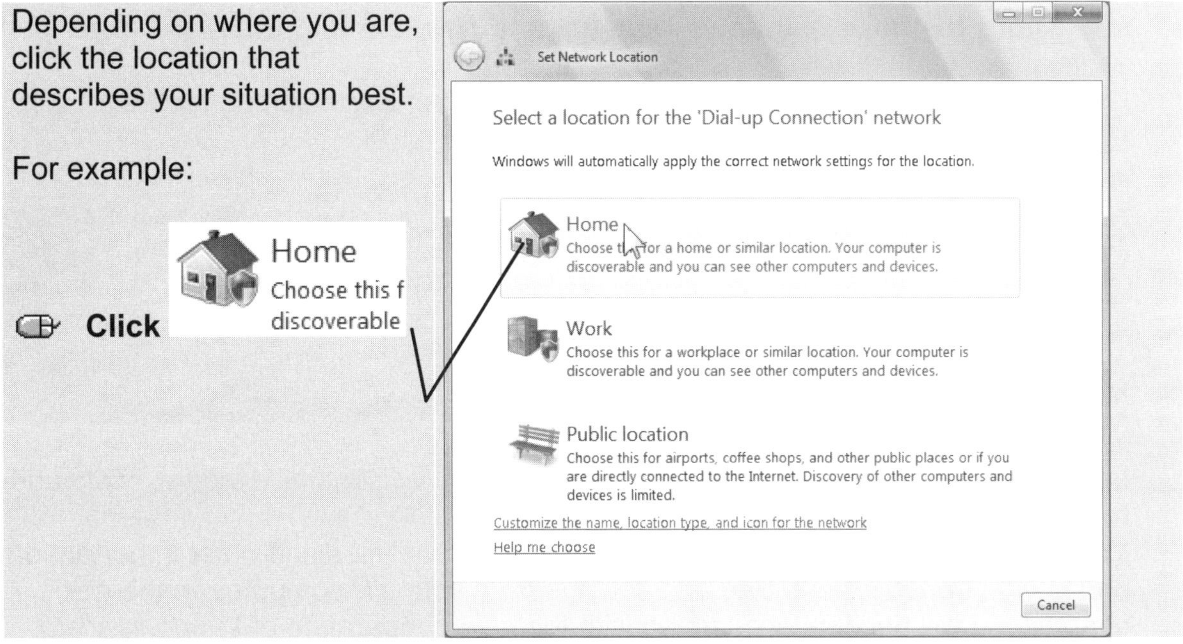

Please note:

As soon as you choose one of the locations, your screen goes dark and *Windows* asks your permission to continue. Click the *Continue* button if you want to give your permission and apply this setting.

The settings are now configured.

Click Close

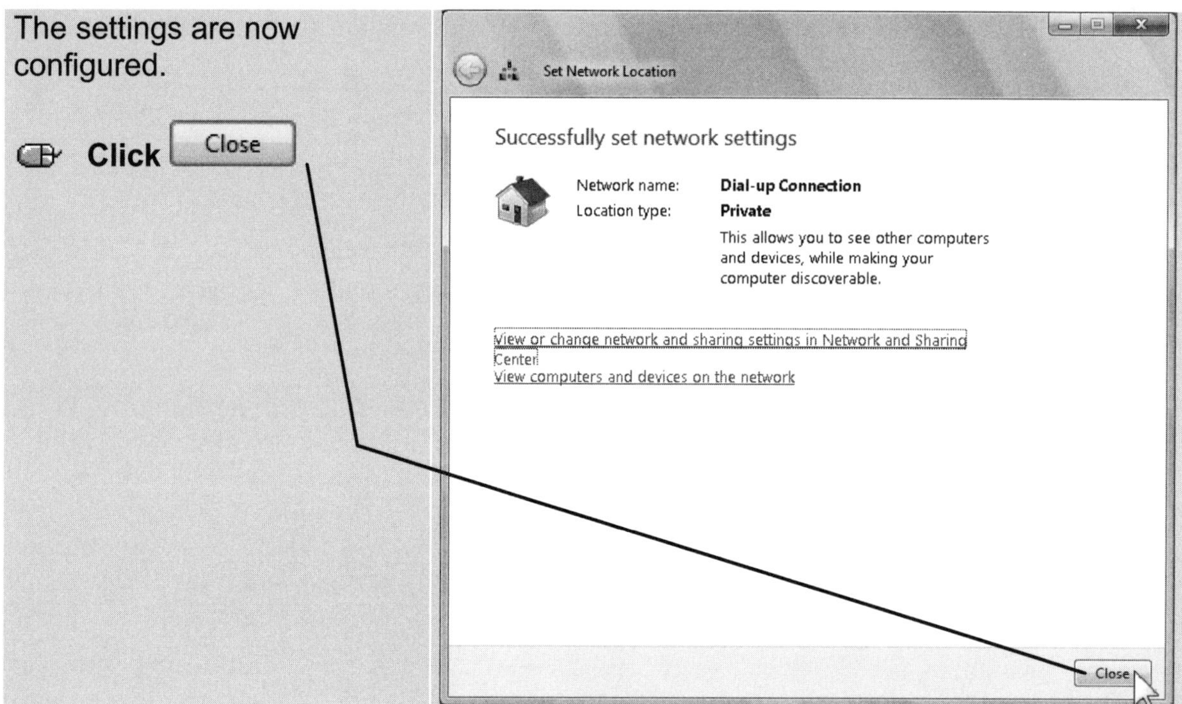

Close the folder windows *Network* and *Network and Sharing Center* 32

Once your dial-up connection is established, you can begin surfing the web.
If you want to do this later, simply click disconnect:

Right-click

Click Disconnect from

Click Dial-up Connection

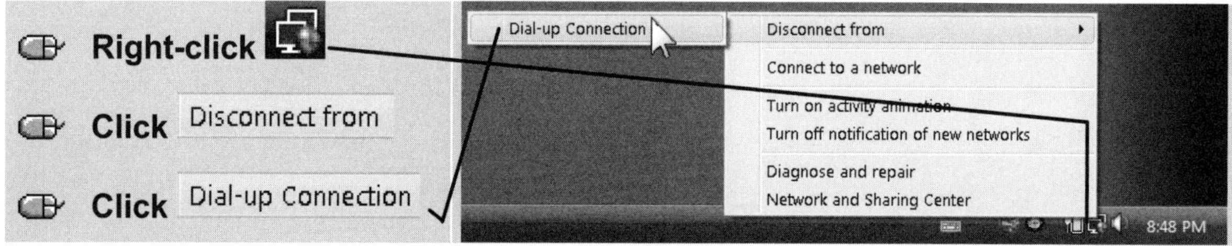

In this chapter you have learned about the different editions of *Windows Vista* and how to install it.
You have also read about ways to safeguard personal files and other important data and how to transfer these files and settings from your *XP* computer. In the next chapter you will become acquainted with the new appearance of *Windows Vista.*

1.15 Tips

Tip

ReadyBoost

Windows Vista's performance is optimized with a system memory of at least 1 GB. If you have less system memory, for example 512 MB, the feature *ReadyBoost* allows you to use an USB stick to extend your system memory. To be able to do so you need a USB stick with a transfer rate of at least 2,5 MB per second for random 4 KB reads. For writing a speed of 1,75 MB per second is enough. The USB stick must contain at least 256 MB of free space to work with *ReadyBoost*.

Using this new feature is easy. First, you start the computer, then you place the USB stick in one of the USB ports.

Windows displays the *AutoPlay* window. Here you can select the option:

Now *Windows Vista* will test the speed of your USB stick. If your USB stick meets the necessary requirements, you will be able to choose how much capacity (in MB) to allow for temporary storage of *Windows* files.

If you want to read more about this feature, go to the following website:
www.microsoft.com/windows/products/windowsvista/features/details/readyboost.mspx

Tip

Windows Anytime Upgrade

Would you like to switch to a more extensive edition of *Windows Vista*? You do not need to buy new software. Each *Windows Vista* DVD contains all editions of *Windows Vista*. The product key on the packaging decides which edition is installed on your computer.

Using *Windows Anytime Upgrade* you can buy and download a new product key to upgrade your edition of *Vista*. You can install this upgrade from the same *Windows Vista* disc. The software you download after purchasing the upgrade, contains a product key. This new product key decides which edition of *Windows Vista* you can install from this disc.

You can start *Windows Anytime Upgrade* from the *Welcome Center* you see when you start *Vista*:

Click 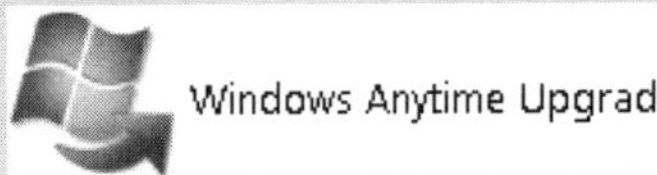

Click 

In this window you can select the option

Upgrade to Windows Vista Ultimate

to start the upgrade process. This process consists of two steps:

1. Buying the *Windows Vista* upgrade online.
2. Performing the *Windows Vista* upgrade.

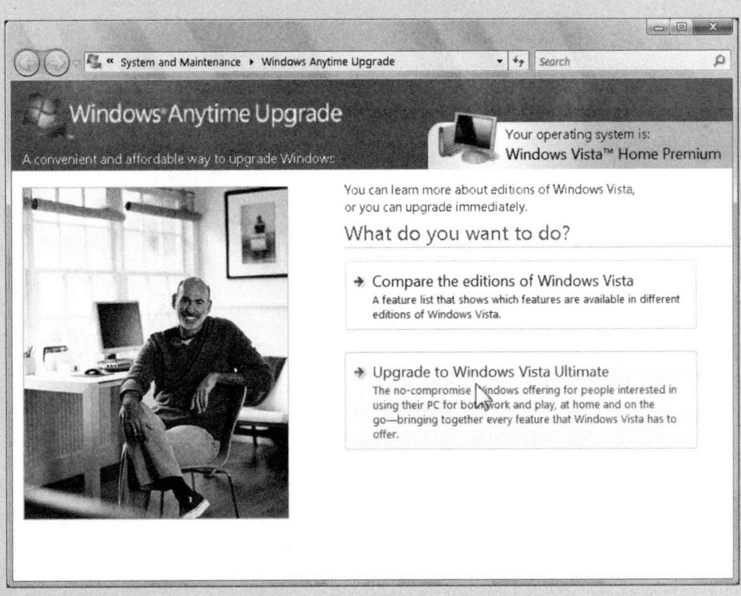

- Continue reading on the next page -

Please note: To be able to perform an upgrade to a more extensive edition of *Windows Vista* you need a DVD with the complete version of the *Vista* software, that carries the *Vista* logo and the text 'Windows Anytime Upgrade'.

It is possible that you do not have the *Windows Vista* DVD. For example when you bought a computer with a pre-installed edition of *Windows Vista* or when you used an upgrade package for *Windows XP*. If you do not have the disc, you can order a 'Windows Anytime Upgrade' disc on the same website where you buy the upgrade.

When you click Begin upgrade process, *Windows Anytime Upgrade* will take you to the store where you can buy the upgrade.

If you do not already have a disc, you can add one to your order (shipping charges will apply).

Do you have a Windows® Anytime Upgrade disc?* Yes No

A Windows Anytime Upgrade disc may have been included with your computer at time of purchase. Look for the Windows Anytime Upgrade logo on your disc.

A Windows Anytime Upgrade disc may be needed to complete the upgrade process. If you do not already have a disc, you can add one to your order (shipping charges only apply).

Tip

Downloading drivers

It is possible that a device like a printer, scanner or webcam no longer functions after switching to *Windows Vista*. In that case you can check the website of the manufacturer of the device to see if the *Vista* version of the device driver is available for download. Look for terms like *support*, *drivers* or *downloads.*

Using the name or the type of the hardware you can check for available drivers.

Always make sure that the driver is suitable for *Windows Vista*!

Here is an example of a page on the *Hewlett Packard* website where a new driver for a laser printer can be found:

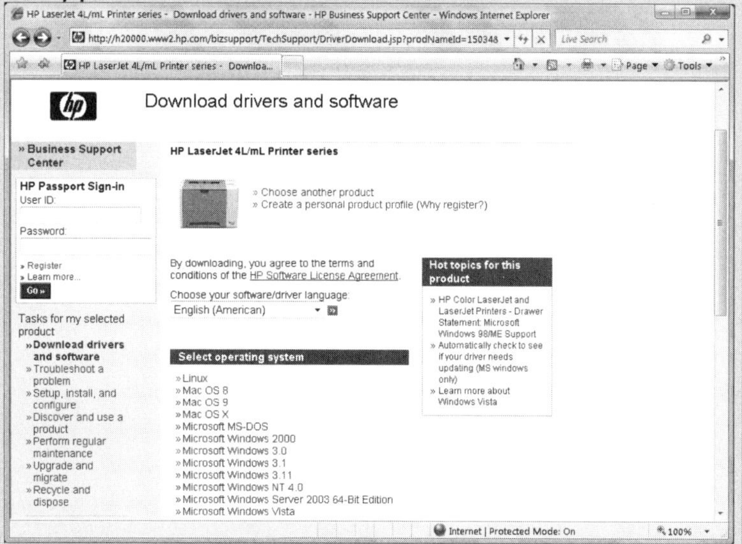

Tip

Downloading updates or patches

Unfortunately, not all of the programs you used on your *XP* computer will work flawlessly in *Vista*. Often this problem can be resolved by downloading an update or patch for the program from the manufacturer's website. A patch is a small piece of software that can be used to make your program compatible with *Vista*. Look for terms like *support* or *downloads.*

On the website of this software manufacturer you see the item

Follow the instructions on the website to install the patch.

Please take into account that software manufacturers will probably not offer updates or patches for older programs. Usually they will take the opportunity to launch a new version of the program and thereby generate more sales.

If this is the case, the only way you will be able to use a familiar software on your *Vista* computer is by purchasing the new version.

2. Getting to Know Windows Vista

Even if you are an experienced *XP* user, switching to *Windows Vista* will take some time getting used to. The overall appearance has changed. Some features and windows can be found in a different location and new features and programs have been added.

In this chapter you will become acquainted with the new *Vista* desktop and other familiar parts of the operating system. Some of the new striking features found in *Vista* will also be introduced.

In this chapter you will get to know the following new and improved features:

- the *Welcome Center*;
- the desktop and *Windows Sidebar*;
- the *Start menu* and the *Search Box*;
- window previews and *Flip 3D*;
- closing *Windows*.

Please note:

Windows Vista can be customized in many ways, just like its predecessor *Windows XP*. It is possible the settings on your computer are different than the settings of the computer that was used to make the screenshots for this book. In that case some windows may look different. This will not interfere however with any of the tasks you need to perform.

Tip

Working with a touchpad
Did you buy a laptop and are you having trouble getting used to working with a touchpad? If this is the case, please read the information on the webpage **www.visualsteps.com/laptopvista**

2.1 Starting Windows Vista

Turn on your computer

After a short time, you see the first screen. Which screen that is, will depend on the settings of your computer. Has a user account, either password protected or not, been created? Then you will see the *Welcome Screen* with the icon of the user account. In that case you can continue as follows:

Click the icon of your account, type the password if necessary and click

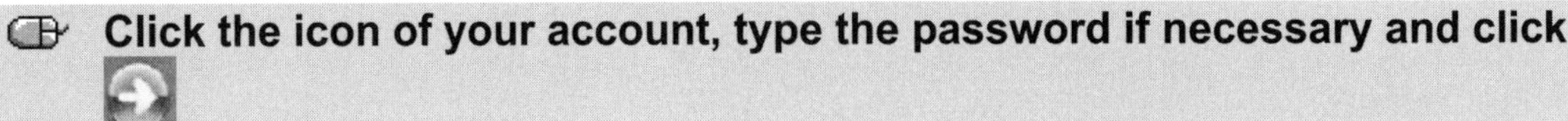

Now the next screen of *Windows Vista* appears. In most cases this will be the *Vista* desktop. It is also possible that you first see a window for a particular software that has been installed on your computer by your computer supplier. For example, a program to write a recovery DVD. Usually programs like this will come in the form of a wizard, a helper program that guides the user step by step through a routine.

Read the information on your screen and perform the requested tasks, if necessary

If necessary, refer to the manual or documentation supplied with your computer

2.2 The Welcome Center

You see the *Windows Vista* desktop.

By default the *Welcome Center* window is the first window to appear on the desktop:

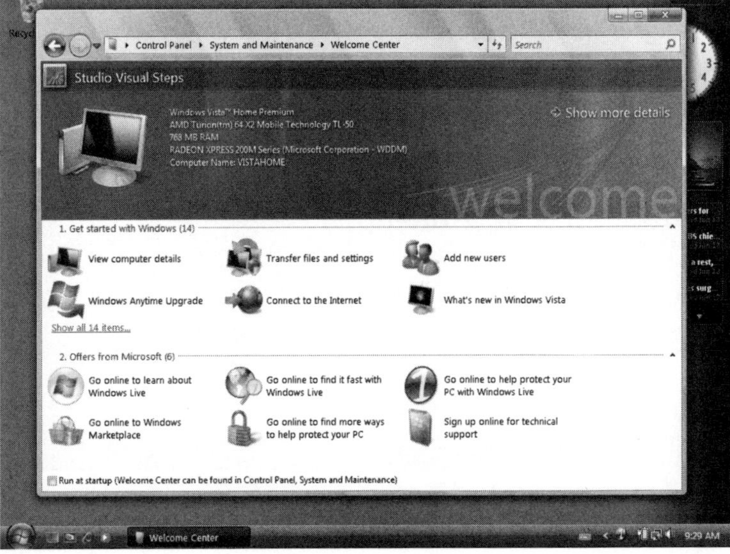

HELP! I do not see the Welcome Center

If you do not see the *Welcome Center*, you can open the window yourself.

Click successively (in the bottom left corner of your screen), All Programs, Accessories, Welcome Center

The *Welcome Center* shows you links to information on a range of different subjects. The *Welcome Center* gives you direct access to several useful options. If you leave the option Run at startup in the bottom left corner checked, this window will be shown each time you start your computer.

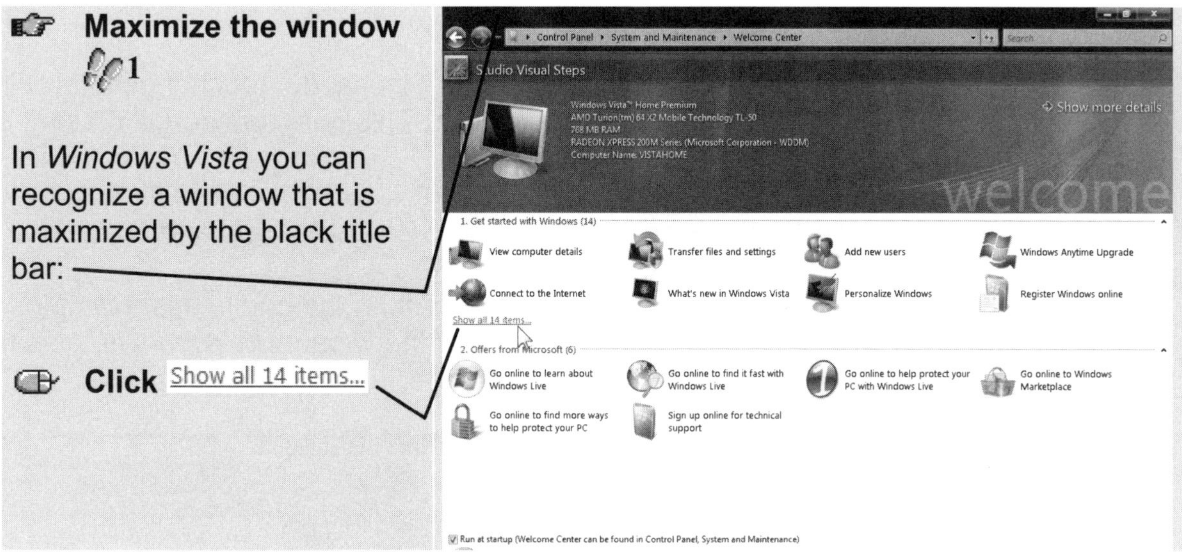

Maximize the window

1

In *Windows Vista* you can recognize a window that is maximized by the black title bar:

Click Show all 14 items...

Now you see all the items in the window. For example, this is how you can access information about the new features in *Windows Vista*:

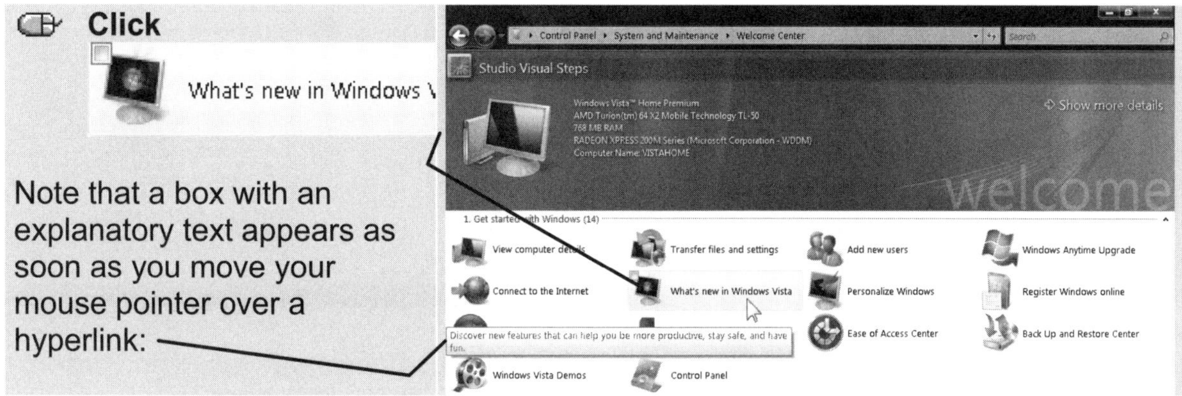

Click What's new in Windows Vista

Note that a box with an explanatory text appears as soon as you move your mouse pointer over a hyperlink:

Windows Vista offers extra help in various forms, like boxes with explanations and other visual cues. This is very handy if you want to be informed of where you will go before clicking an item.

In the top half of the window you can read information about the new features:

To see more information:

Click **See more new features**

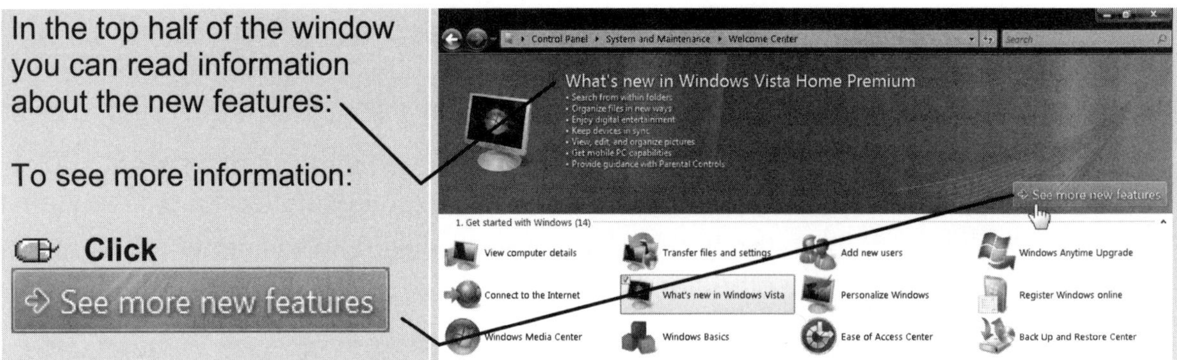

Note that the clickable parts of a window, like text or icons, do not change into visible 'buttons' until you place the mouse pointer on them. This phenomenon is present in many of the windows or *dialog boxes* in *Vista.*

On top of the *Welcome Center* window, the window *Windows Help and Support* appears, with the article *What's new in Windows Vista*.
In your screen this window may be larger or smaller than the one in this example. Just like in *Windows XP*, you can adjust the size of the window in *Windows Vista* by dragging the edges or corners of the window's frame.

You can quickly navigate to a section in the article by clicking one of these hyperlinks:

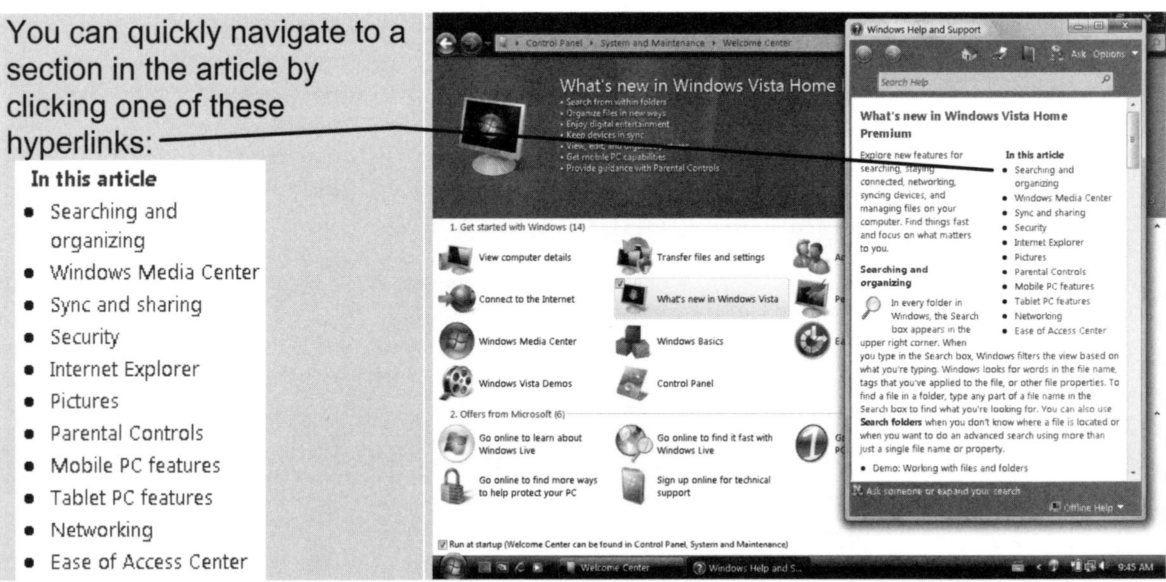

Minimize the windows *Welcome Center* and *Windows Help and Support*

2

Both windows have been reduced to taskbar buttons on the taskbar at the bottom of your screen:

2.3 The Desktop

Now you see the desktop. It may look different on your computer than in this example. In *Windows Vista* you can customize what is displayed on the screen.

In this example you see the *Recycle Bin*:

At the bottom you see the taskbar with the new shape of the *Start button* :

On the right the *Windows Sidebar* is opened with various so-called 'gadgets':

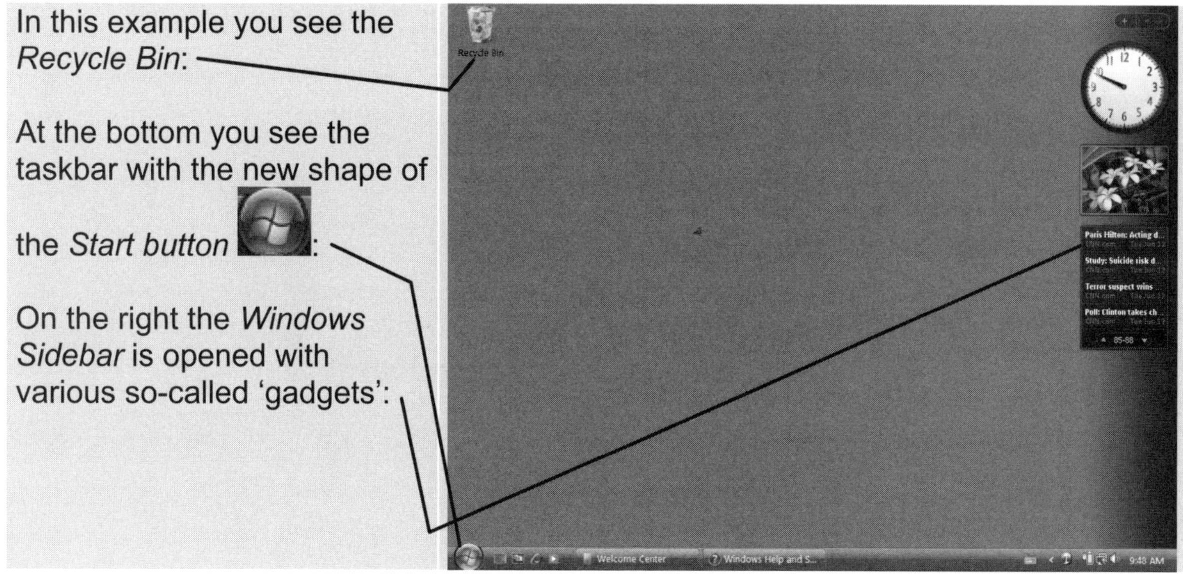

2.4 Windows Sidebar

Windows Sidebar is a remarkable extra 'toolbar' containing various mini-programs also known as *gadgets*. In this example you see three gadgets: a clock, a slideshow of images and *Feed Headlines* (short news items).

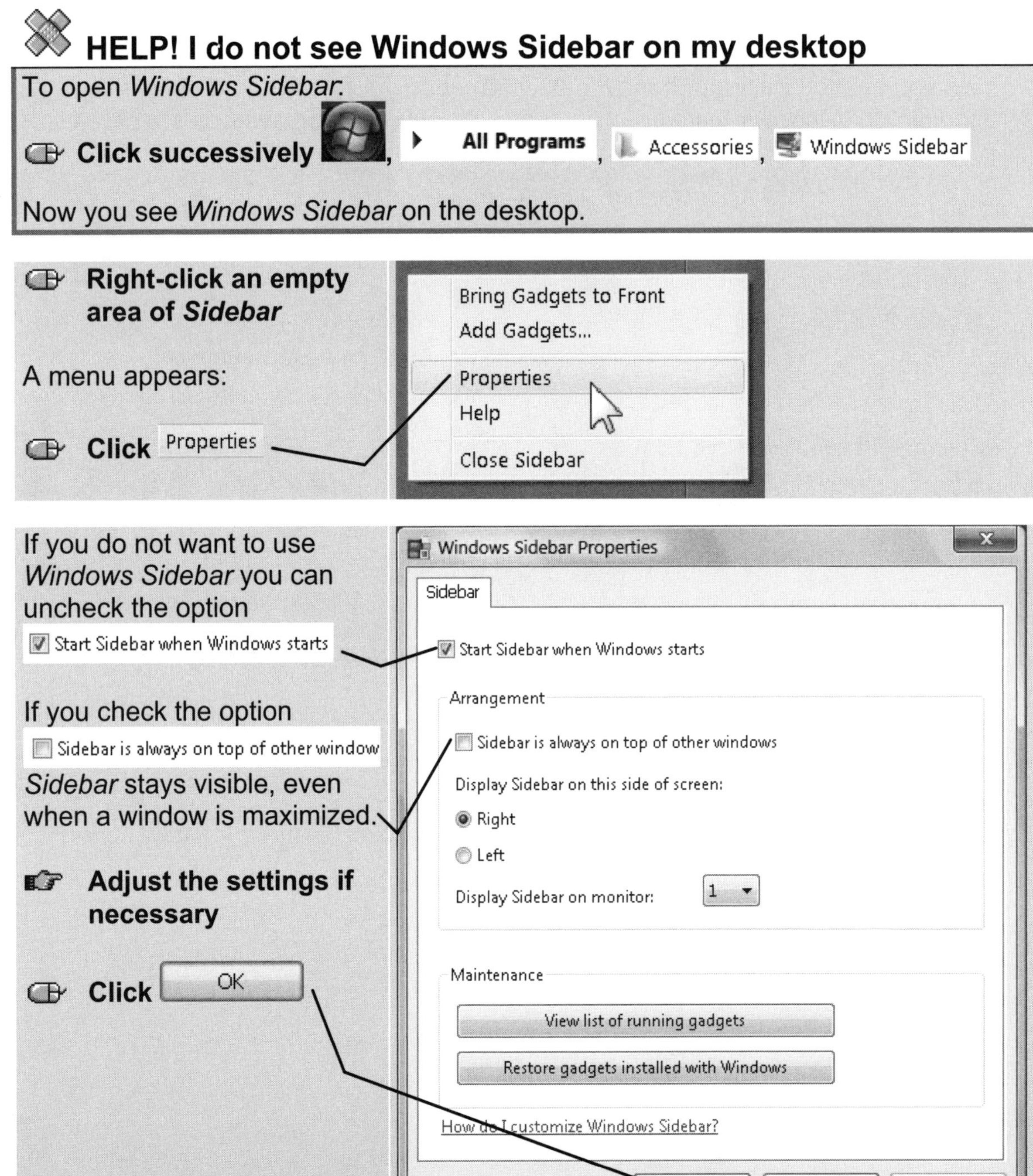

HELP! I do not see Windows Sidebar on my desktop

To open *Windows Sidebar*:

Click successively [Start], All Programs, Accessories, Windows Sidebar

Now you see *Windows Sidebar* on the desktop.

Right-click an empty area of *Sidebar*

A menu appears:

Click Properties

If you do not want to use *Windows Sidebar* you can uncheck the option Start Sidebar when Windows starts

If you check the option Sidebar is always on top of other window *Sidebar* stays visible, even when a window is maximized.

Adjust the settings if necessary

Click OK

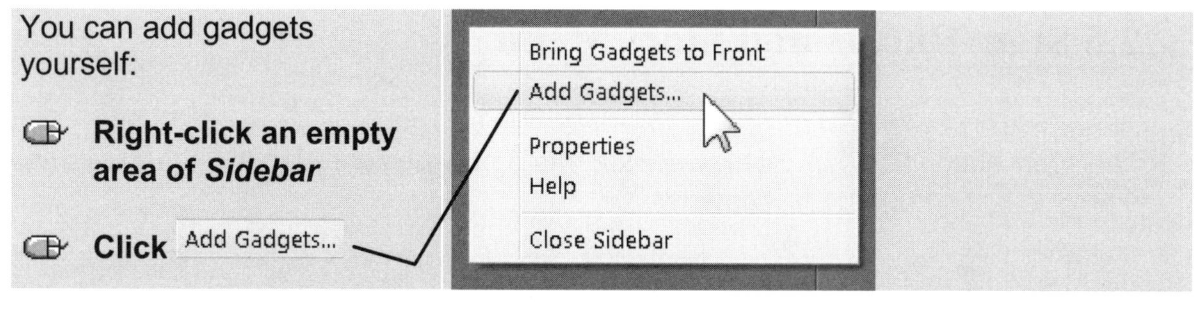

You can add gadgets yourself:

- **Right-click an empty area of *Sidebar***
- **Click** Add Gadgets...

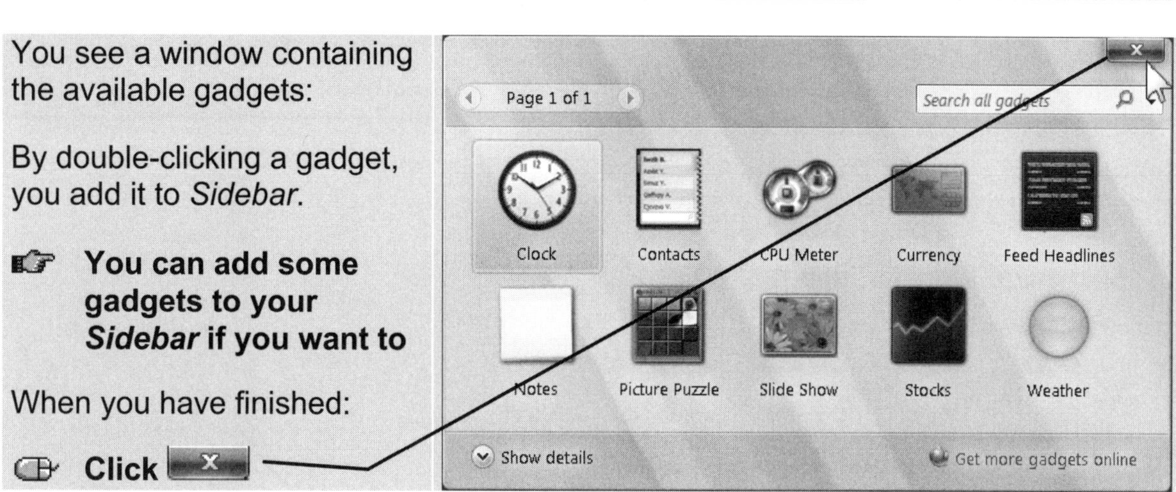

You see a window containing the available gadgets:

By double-clicking a gadget, you add it to *Sidebar*.

- **You can add some gadgets to your *Sidebar* if you want to**

When you have finished:

- **Click** ✕

Some gadgets have various display options. The clock for example is available in eight different designs. When you right-click a gadget a menu appears containing various options for that gadget. When you click Options you see various possibilities.

Would you like to know more about the possibilities of *Windows Sidebar*? In *Windows Help and Support* you can find a lot of information. Read the Tip at the end of this chapter.

2.5 Start Button and Start Menu

The *Start button* in *Windows Vista* has a new design. Also the *Start menu* has a new shape compared to *Windows XP*.

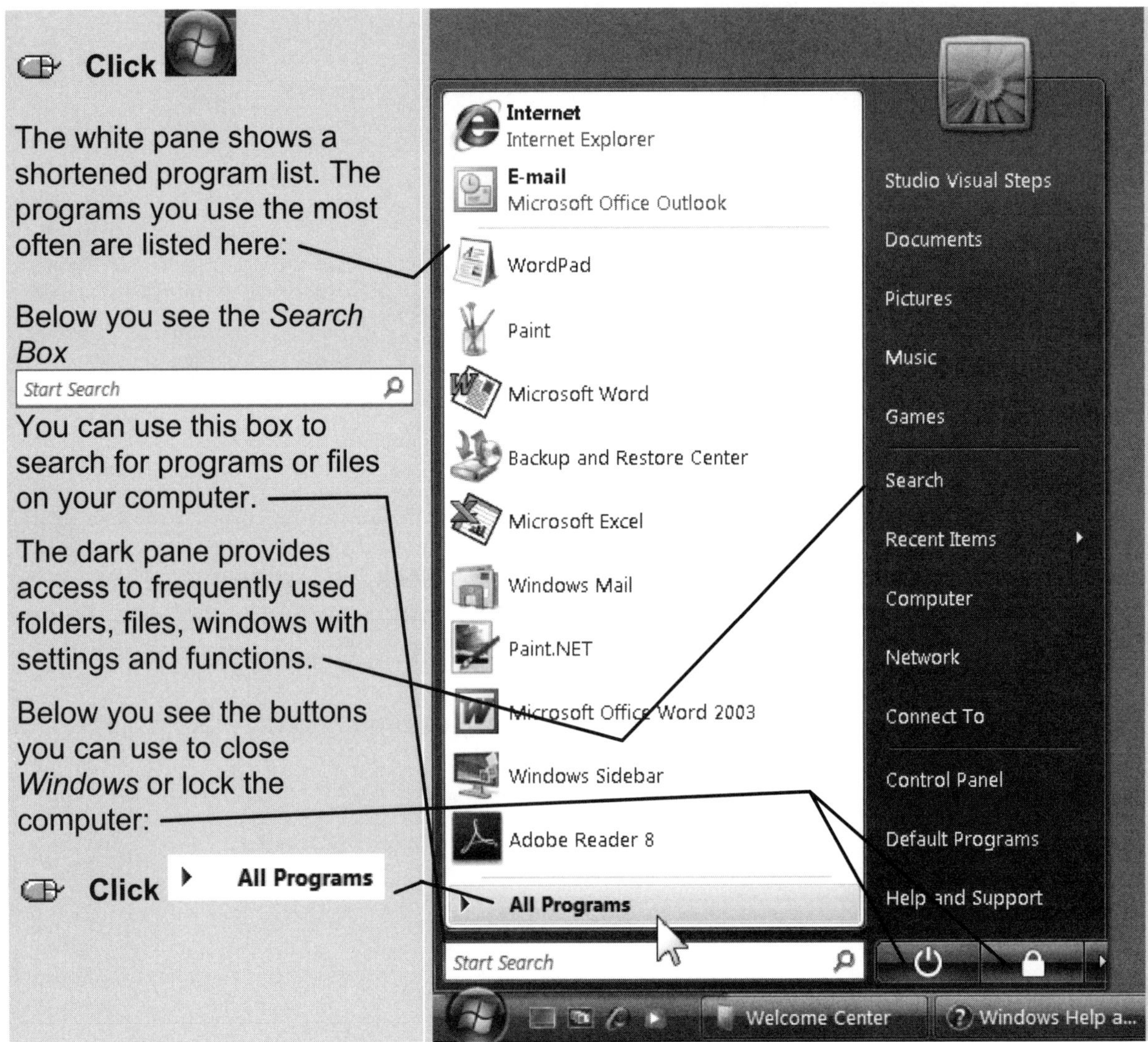

Click

The white pane shows a shortened program list. The programs you use the most often are listed here:

Below you see the *Search Box*

Start Search

You can use this box to search for programs or files on your computer.

The dark pane provides access to frequently used folders, files, windows with settings and functions.

Below you see the buttons you can use to close *Windows* or lock the computer:

Click **All Programs**

In the same white pane a list appears, containing all programs that have been installed on your computer.

2.6 The Search Box

The search function in *Windows Vista* has improved a lot compared to *XP*. The *Search Box* is one of the easiest ways to find items on your computer. The exact location of these items is not important.

The *Search Box* searches all programs and all folders in your *Personal Folder* (which contains *Documents, Pictures, Music,* desktop and other frequently used locations). Your e-mail messages, saved express messages, appointments and contacts are searched as well.

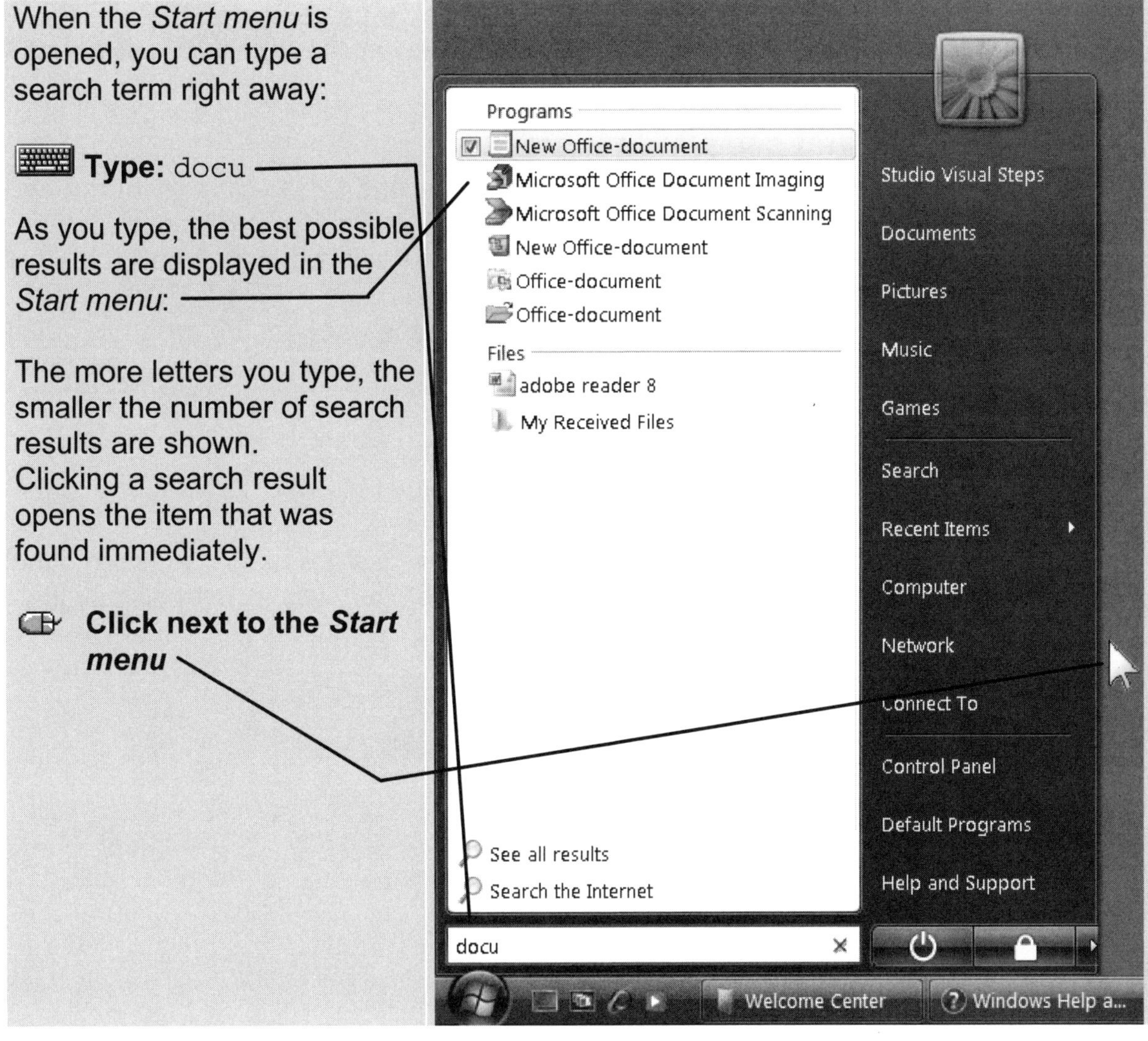

When the *Start menu* is opened, you can type a search term right away:

Type: docu

As you type, the best possible results are displayed in the *Start menu*:

The more letters you type, the smaller the number of search results are shown. Clicking a search result opens the item that was found immediately.

Click next to the *Start menu*

2.7 Window Previews

Your taskbar contains two taskbar buttons of previously opened, minimized windows. *Vista* has a useful feature that allows you to preview these windows without having to enlarge them first.

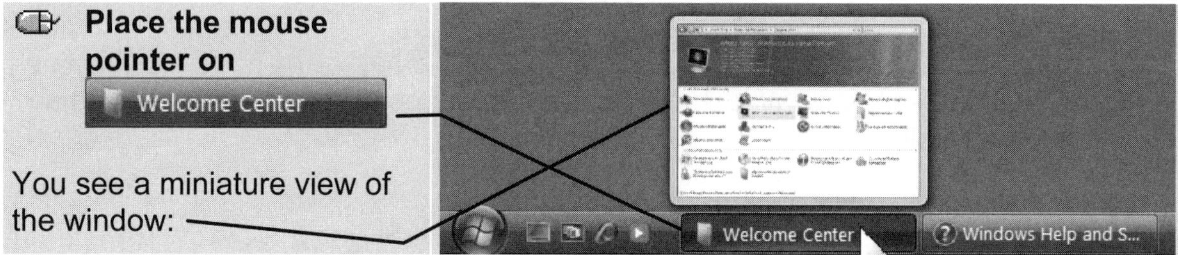

HELP! I do not see window previews

This option is only available in *Vista Home Premium* and *Vista Ultimate*. Furthermore, *Windows Aero* should be turned on. This feature of *Vista* only functions properly if your computer contains a suitable graphics card. The same thing is true for the *Flip 3D* feature you will read about in the next section.
If you do not see a window preview, a text box with the name of the program or file is displayed above the taskbar button.

2.8 Windows Flip 3D

In the advertisements for *Windows Vista*, *Flip 3D* images are used very often. On the left side of the taskbar you find the button *Switch between windows* to display this special effect:

All windows are shown in a 3D stack:

You can 'flip' through the windows using the scrollwheel of the mouse or the arrow keys on the keyboard.

Click a window

The window is enlarged and you can continue working.

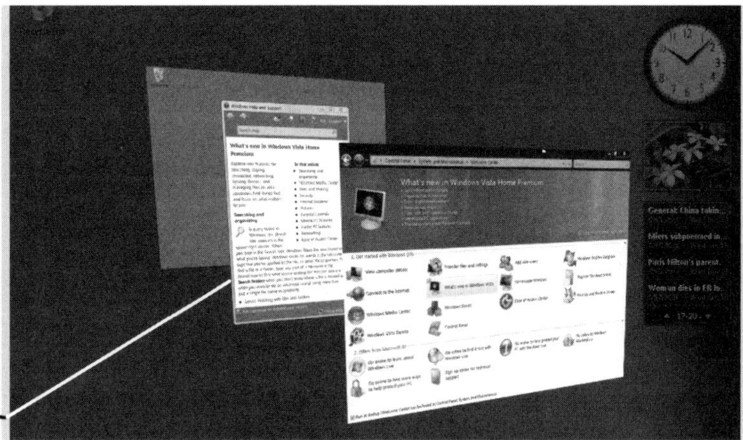

If your PC does not have *Flip 3D* you see this window:

Click an icon

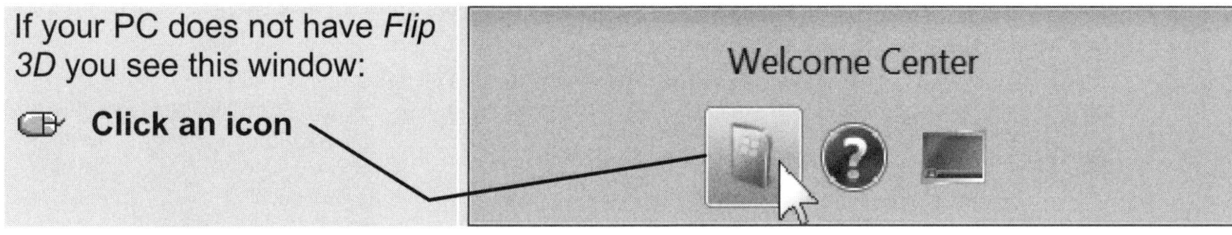

Close all windows

2.9 Turning Off or Shutting Down Your Computer

When you are done using your computer, go to the *Start button*:

Click

Click

Your screen will turn black immediately. Your computer is now 'asleep'. In this sleep mode the computer uses only a very small amount of power. To wake your computer:

Press the power button of your computer

Within seconds the desktop or the *Welcome Screen* appears.

Tip

Some laptops switch to sleep mode simply by closing the lid. Once the lid is opened the computer *wakes up*. Refer to the documentation supplied with your laptop to see if this is the case for your type of laptop.

Putting your computer to sleep is the fastest way to turn it off, and the best option for resuming work quickly. Sleep saves all open documents and programs, and allows the computer to quickly resume full power operation (typically within several seconds) when you want to start working again.

There are certain times when you should shut down instead. For example when you have to unplug the computer to be able to move it to another location.
Shutting down can be done like this:

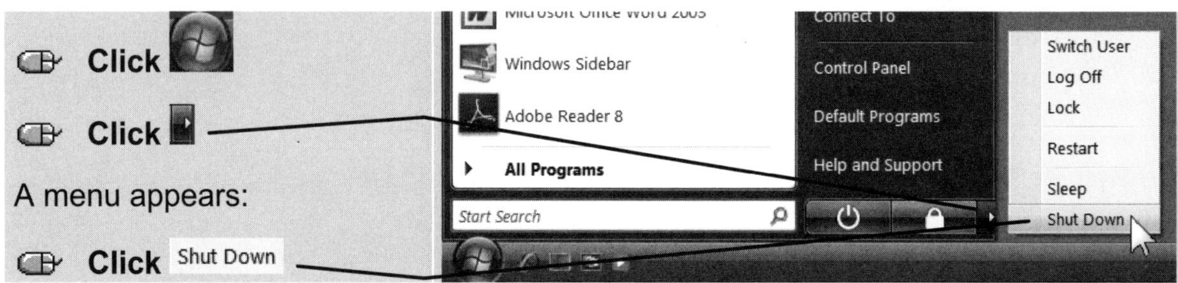

Now *Windows* and the computer are shut down completely. Remember that you have to save your work and close all programs yourself when you use this option.

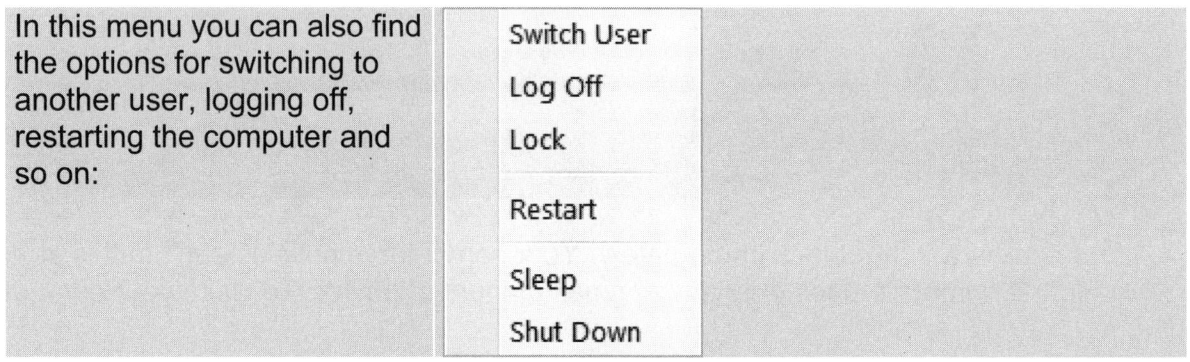

In this chapter you have been introduced to the new appearance of *Windows Vista* and some of its useful features.
In the next chapter you will learn how to work with the improved *Folder window* in *Vista*.

2.10 Background Information

The Power button

The *Power button* in the *Start menu* can change its appearance. The form tells you what will happen when you click the button:

Sleep
When you click this button, your computer goes to sleep immediately. *Windows* saves your work automatically.

Sleep

Shut down
This shuts down your computer. Remember to save your work before closing any open programs. You see this button if you have set your computer to always shut down when the *Power button* is clicked.

Shut down

Install updates and shut down
The button will take this form when there are *Windows* updates ready to be installed. When you click the button, *Windows* installs the updates and then shuts down your computer when the installation is complete.

Install updates and shut down

2.11 Tips

 **Tip**

Circle

The spinning circle  is the *Vista* replacement of the familiar hourglass in *XP*. The circle indicates that the computer is busy performing a task.

 **Tip**

Windows Aero

Would you like more information on *Windows Aero* and *Flip 3D*? In *Windows Help and Support* you can find an article on turning *Aero* on and off.

 **Tip**

Classic view

Do you have trouble getting used to the new design of *Windows Vista*?
Then consider switching to the classic view. In the classic view *Windows* looks and behaves just like it did in earlier versions. In *Windows Help and Support* you can find more information about changing *Windows* to Classic view.

Tip

Windows Help and Support

Windows Help and Support is the very extensive, built-in Help-system for *Windows*. This system quickly provides you with answers to frequently asked questions and gives suggestions to solve problems and instructions for performing tasks. When you are connected to the Internet, you will always get the latest versions of all Help-subjects.

 **Click** , Help and Support

 **Maximize the window** 1

- Continue reading the next page -

Blue text in an article is a hyperlink you can click. Hyperlinks that have already been clicked, turn lilac. Clicking a green word displays a text box with a definition of this word.

Searching for articles on specific subjects you want to have more information about is definitely worth the trouble.

The *Search Box* is a useful tool to find specific information. Type your search term and then click .

For beginners and somewhat advanced computer users the video demonstrations are very clarifying (type the search term **demo** in the *Search Box*):

These narrated video demonstrations are designed to introduce you to personal computing and the *Windows Vista* operating system.

The videos are shown in *Windows Media Player.*

Notes

Write down your notes here.

3. Working With the Folder Window

When you switch from *Windows XP* to *Windows Vista* you will also have to get used to the new folder windows. This chapter will introduce you to some of the convenient features such as the more intuitive lay-out. There are various ways to navigate through your files and folders. For example using the address bar and the *Navigation Pane*. In the *Preview Pane* you can preview files without having to open them first. In the *Details Pane* you can quickly view and edit the properties associated with files.

The search feature in *Windows Vista* also has a number of improvements. In this chapter you will get to know the *Search Box* and the other search features in the *Folder window*. To be able to find a file quickly, the search results can be filtered in various ways. A search you might want to use again, can be saved.

Another improvement is the possibility to check mark files and folders in a *Folder window*. This feature makes it very easy to move or copy multiple files at the same time.

In this chapter, you will learn how to:

- open your *Personal Folder*;
- change the folder view;
- use the buttons *Back* and *Forward*;
- work with the *Navigation Pane*;
- use the different features of the address bar;
- preview a file in the *Preview Pane*;
- change the file properties in the *Details Pane*;
- use the *Search Box*;
- filter search results;
- create an advanced search;
- save a search;
- find and open a saved search;
- create a new folder;
- select multiple files using the check boxes;
- drag and drop files;
- drag and copy files;
- undo your actions.

3.1 Opening Your Personal Folder

Your *Personal Folder* contains common folders like *Documents*, *Pictures*, *Music*, *Contacts* and other folders. The *Personal Folder* is labeled with the same name as your user account in *Windows Vista.* The button you use to open your *Personal Folder*, is located in the top right corner of the *Start menu*. Take a look:

Turn on your computer

Click the icon of your account, type the password if necessary and click

Close the *Welcome Center*

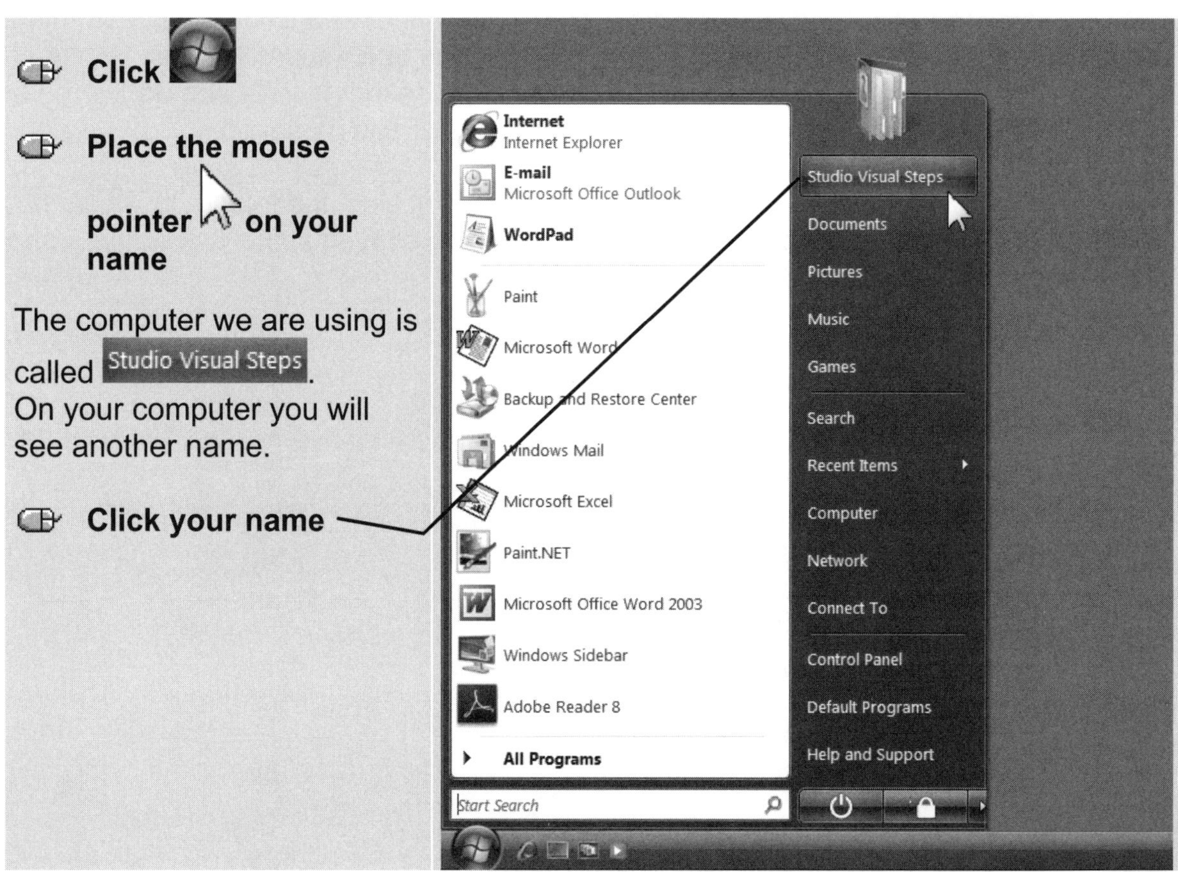

Click

Place the mouse pointer on your name

The computer we are using is called Studio Visual Steps.
On your computer you will see another name.

Click your name

Note that text in any window can change into a hyperlink or button Studio Visual Steps as soon as you move the mouse pointer over it. You will see this phenomenon often in *Vista.*

You see a window with the content of your *Personal Folder*. It contains the folders made for you by *Windows Vista*:

This window is called a *Folder window.*

The content of the *Personal Folder* can be slightly different on every computer.

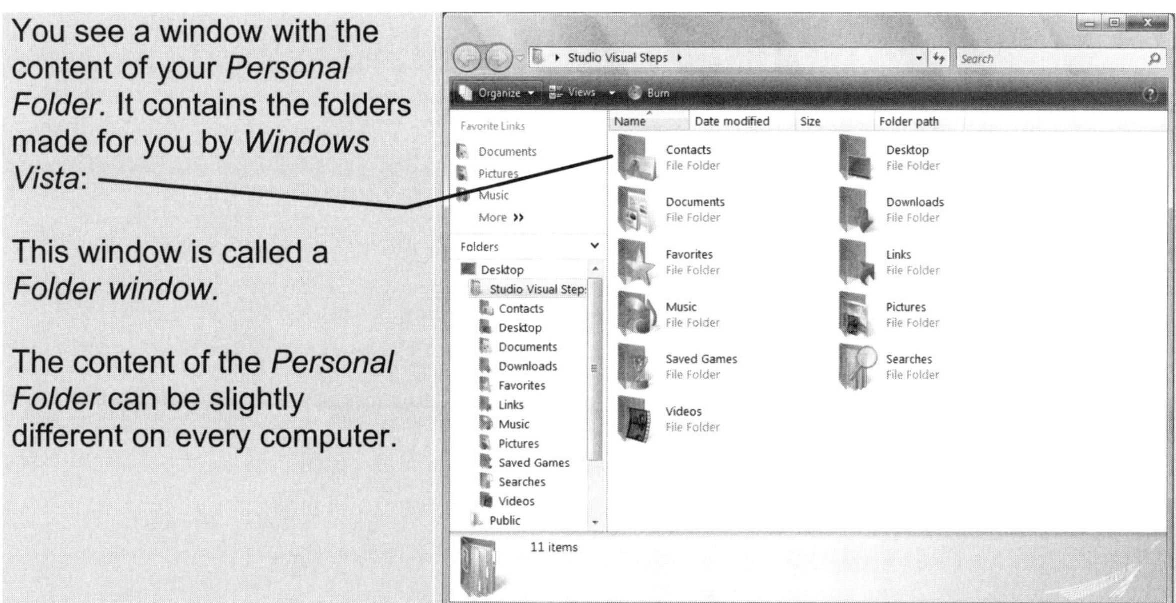

HELP! Where are the folders in the left pane?

If the left pane of your window does not show folders like those in the previous figure:

Click Folders

Now you see the *Folder list* in the left pane of the window.

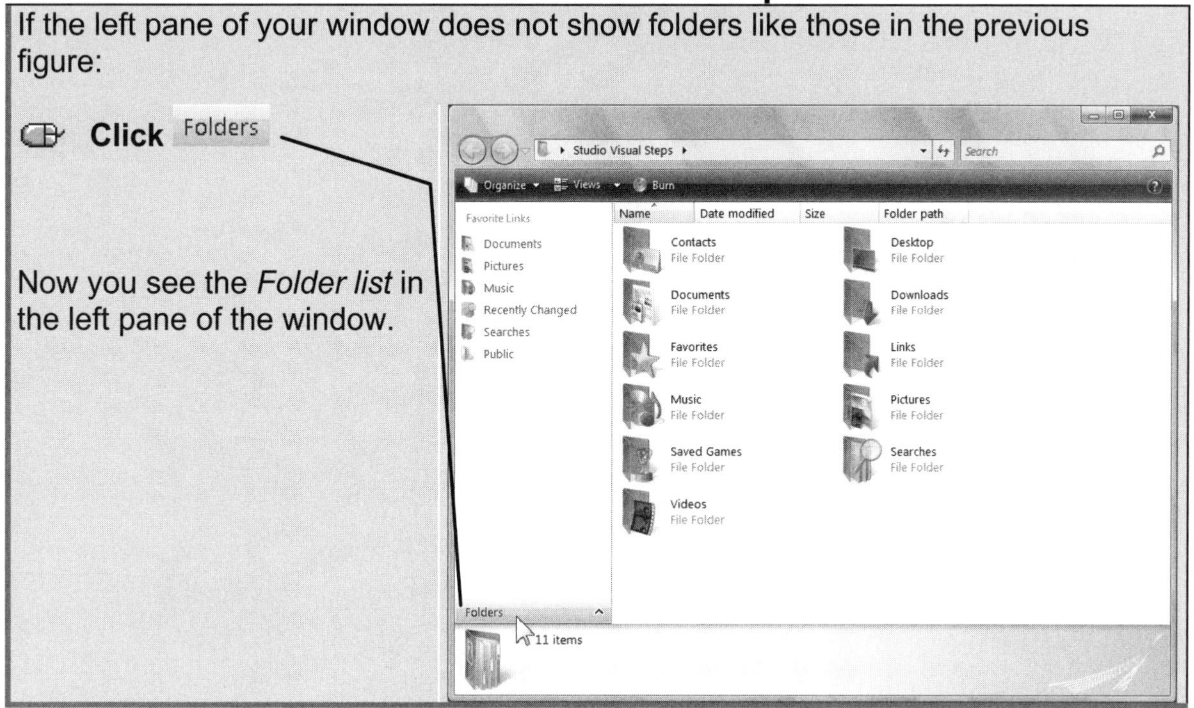

3.2 Changing the Display of the Folder Window

There are several ways to display your folders in the *Folder window*. Maybe the window looks different on your screen. Change the display settings as follows:

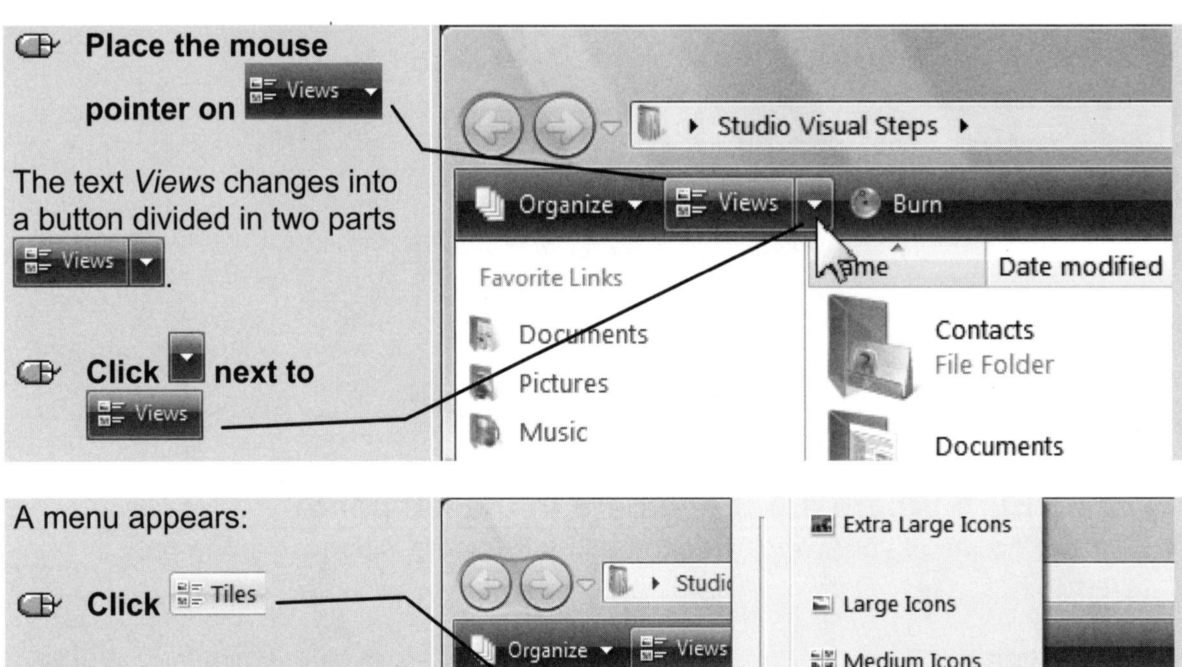

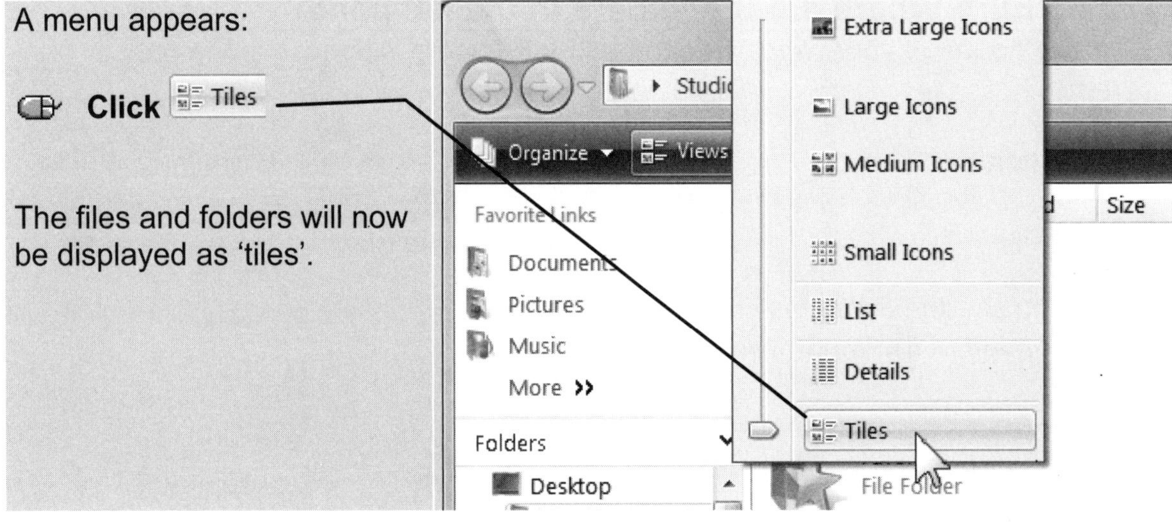

You can apply other settings to change the display of the *Folder window*:

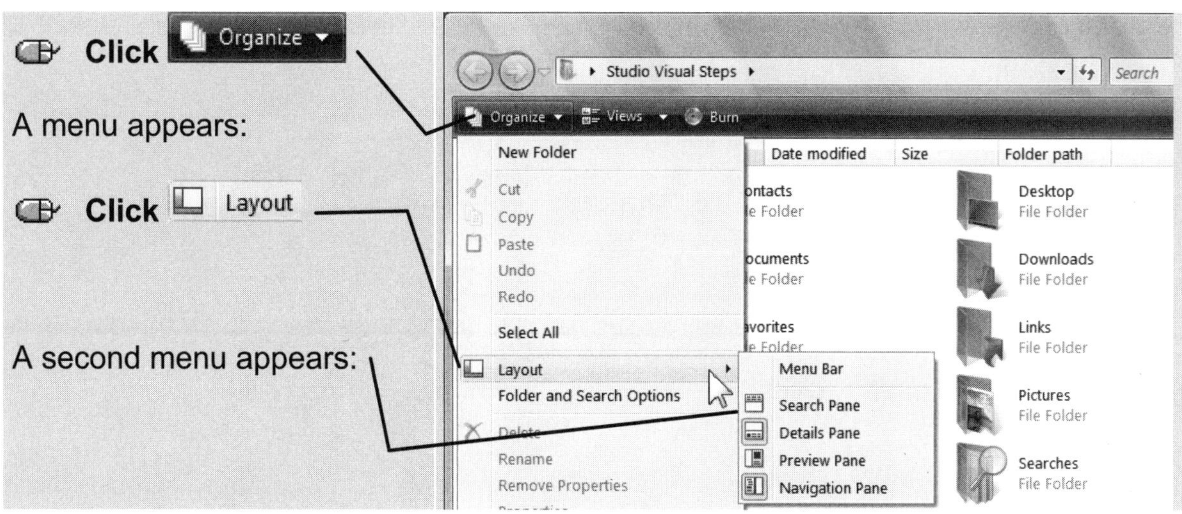

In this second menu only the options Details Pane and Navigation Pane are active. If an option is active, it is highlighted with a light blue box around the icon. If the icon is not highlighted, you can activate the option by clicking it.

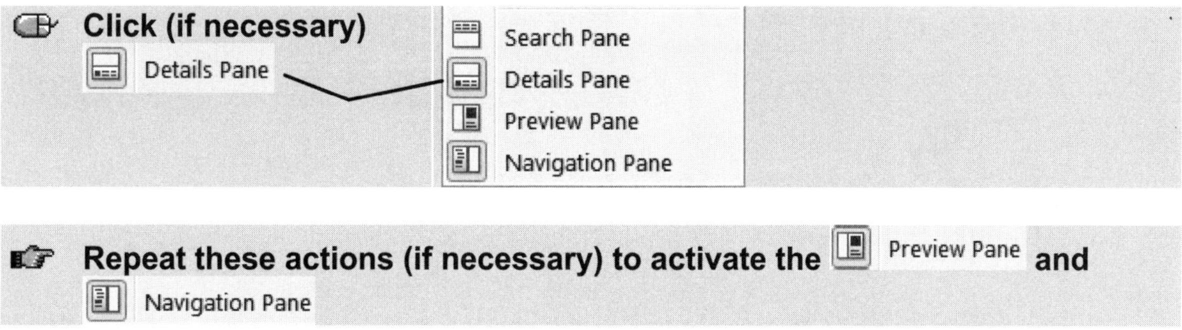

Deactivating an option is done in the same way, by clicking the highlighted option in the list.

Repeat these actions (if necessary) to deactivate the option Search Pane

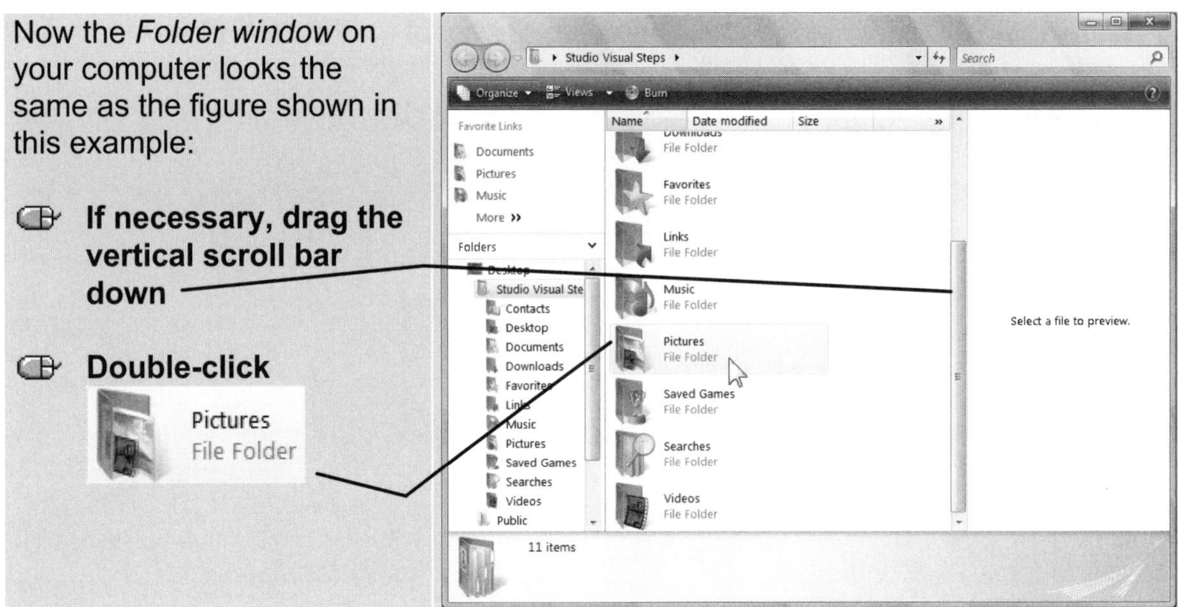

Now the *Folder window* on your computer looks the same as the figure shown in this example:

If necessary, drag the vertical scroll bar down

Double-click Pictures File Folder

You see the content of your *Pictures* folder. It is possible that you have already stored some photos in there. This folder contains a shortcut to the folder *Sample Pictures* that *Vista* has placed on your computer:

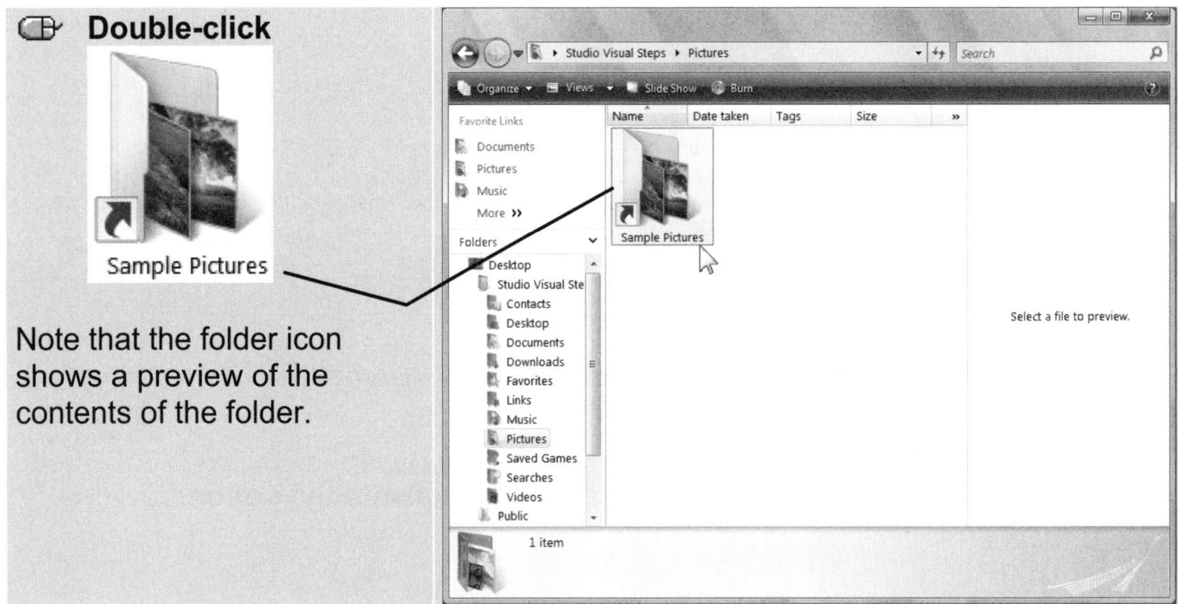

Double-click Sample Pictures

Note that the folder icon shows a preview of the contents of the folder.

3.3 The Different Parts of the Folder Window

In addition to showing the contents of the folder, a *Folder window* has specific areas that are designed to help you navigate around the folders on the hard disk of your computer, and in general to work with files and folders more easily.

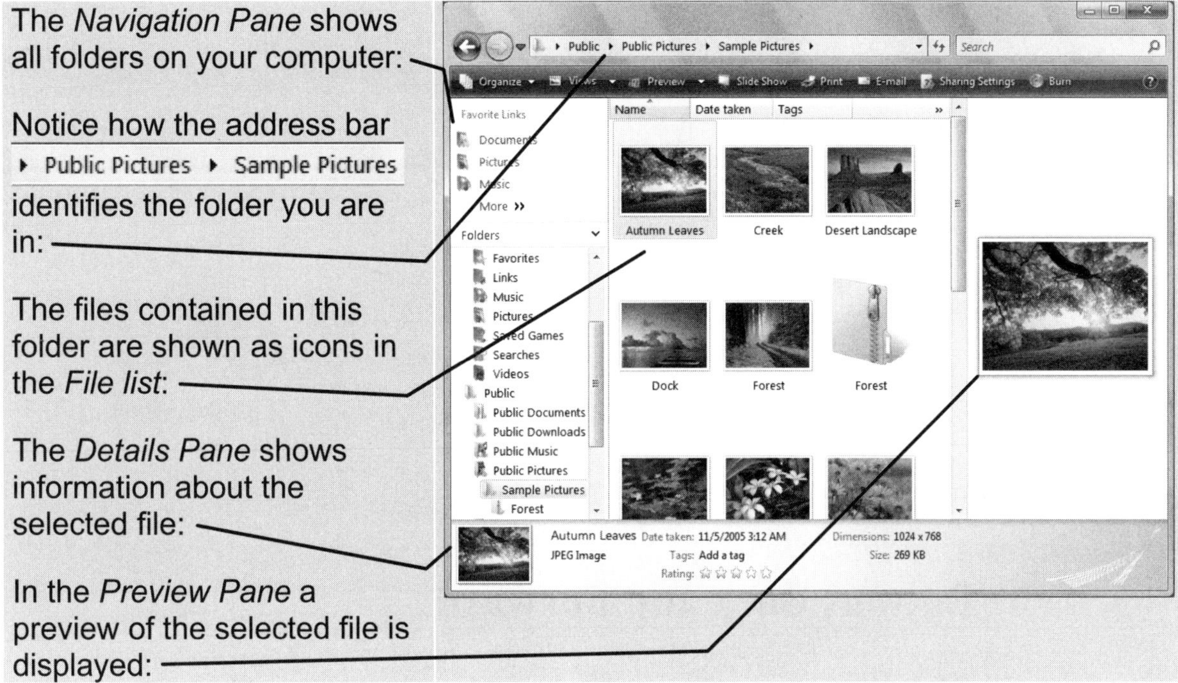

In the next sections you will take a closer look at the different parts of the *Folder window*.

3.4 Favorite Links

The *Navigation Pane* on the left hand side of the *Folder window* has two parts: the *Favorite links* and the *Folder list.*

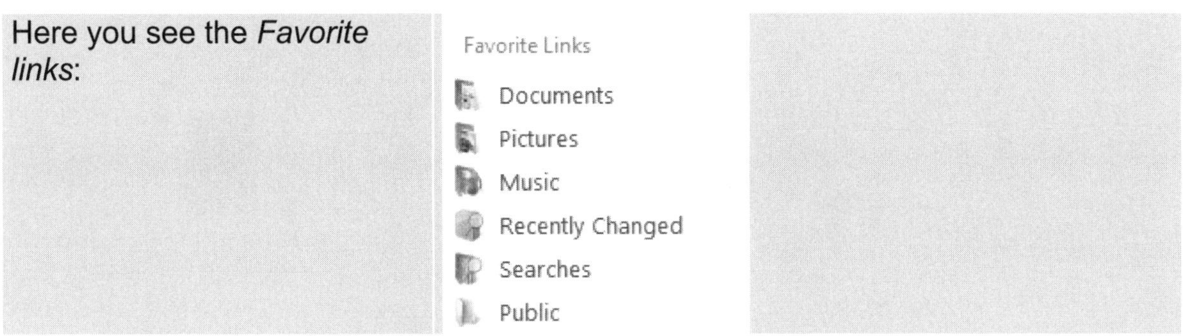

When you click one of these links, the contents of the corresponding folder are displayed in the *File list*.

For example, click Music

You see the contents of the folder *Music*. The contents of this folder is possibly different on your computer:

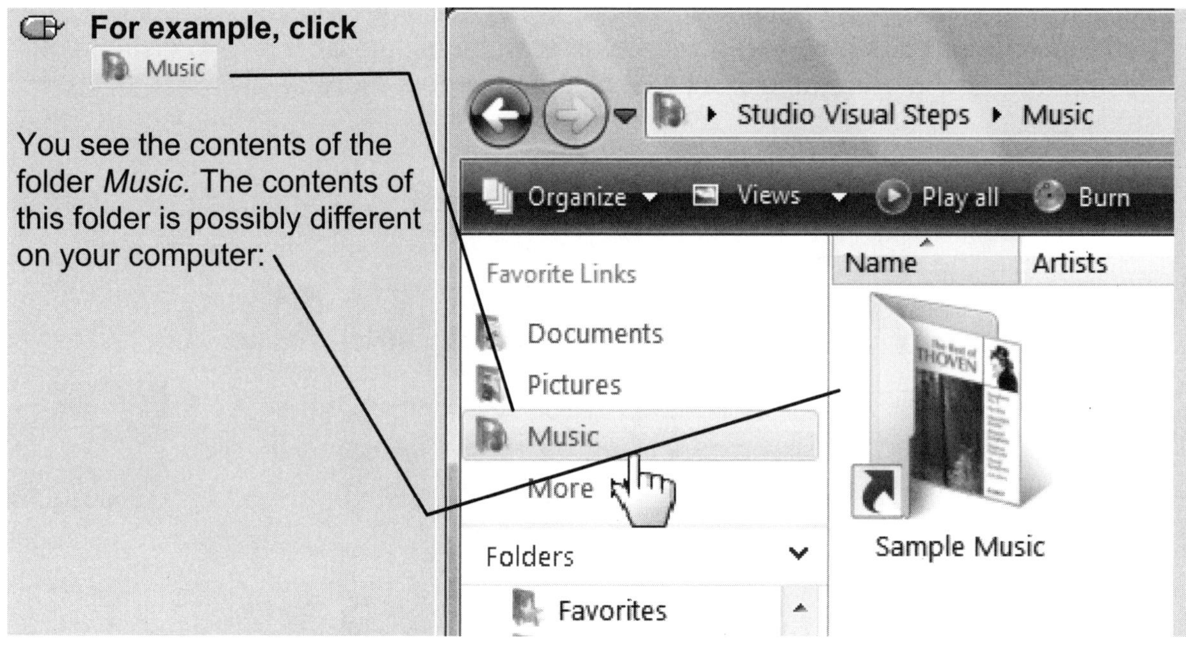

3.5 The Buttons Back and Forward

The buttons can be used to quickly navigate between previously opened folders. To return to the previous folder:

Click

The folder *Sample Pictures* is opened again.

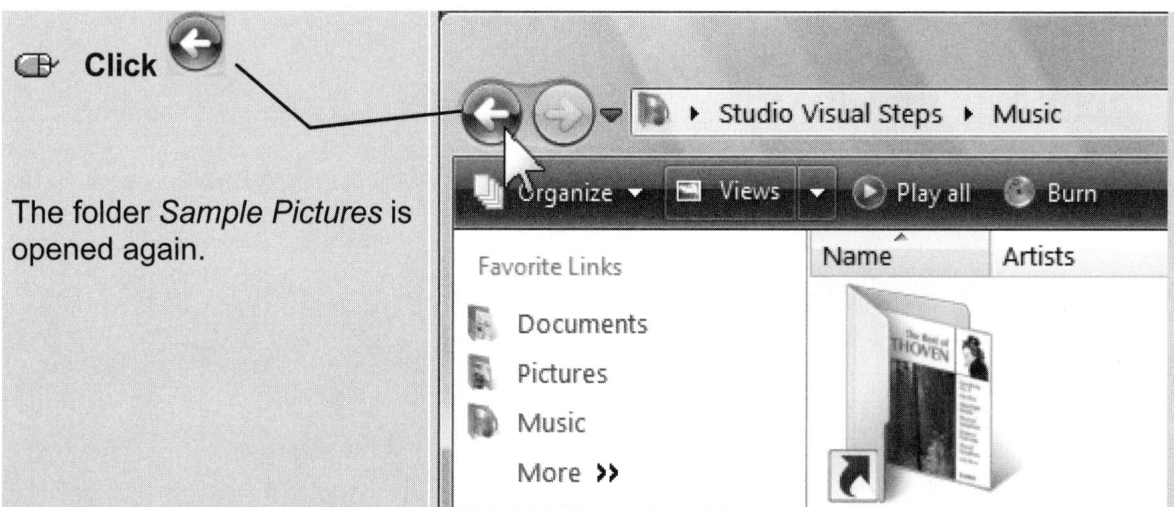

It will be obvious that the button can be used to return to the folder you opened after the current folder. If you opened multiple folders in a row, you can use the buttons to switch between the folders. But there is even a quicker way!

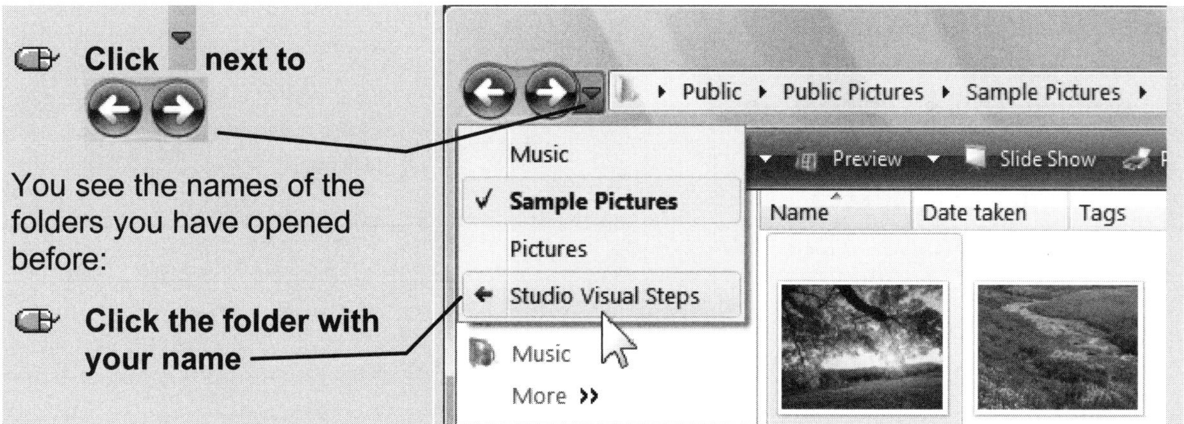

Click next to

You see the names of the folders you have opened before:

Click the folder with your name

Now, you see the contents of your *Personal Folder* again.

3.6 Working with the Folder List

In the *Folder list* in the *Navigation Pane* you see all folders on the hard disk of your computer. You can use the *Folder list* to navigate directly to each folder or subfolder.

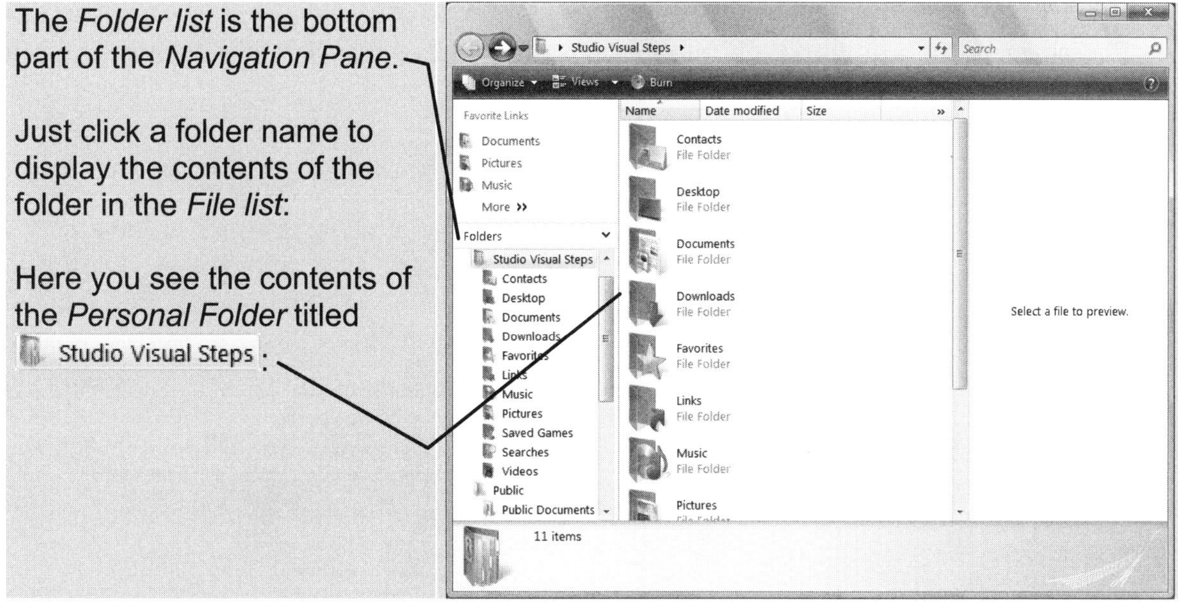

The *Folder list* is the bottom part of the *Navigation Pane*.

Just click a folder name to display the contents of the folder in the *File list*:

Here you see the contents of the *Personal Folder* titled Studio Visual Steps :

Place the mouse pointer on the folders in the *Folder list*

Small arrow icons appear next to some folders.

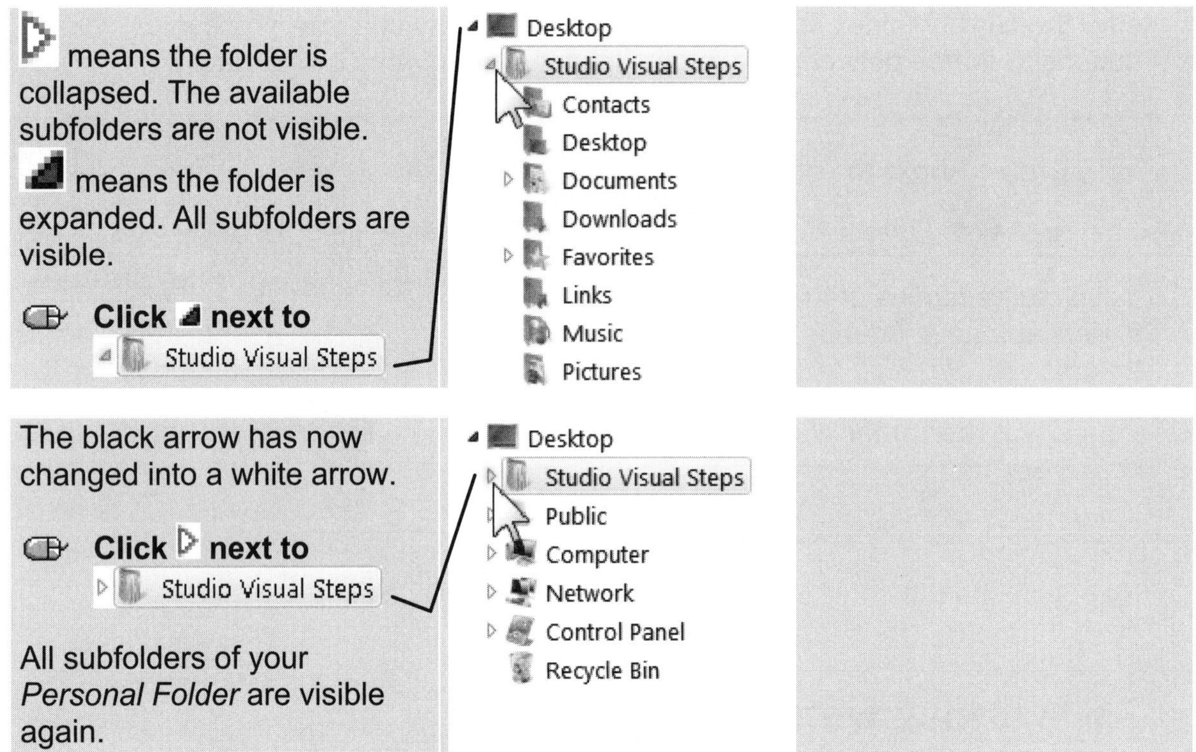

3.7 The Address Bar

The address bar shows which folder is opened. At the moment this is your *Personal Folder*: Studio Visual Steps.

You can use the address bar to quickly navigate to another folder. To open one of the subfolders of your *Personal Folder*:

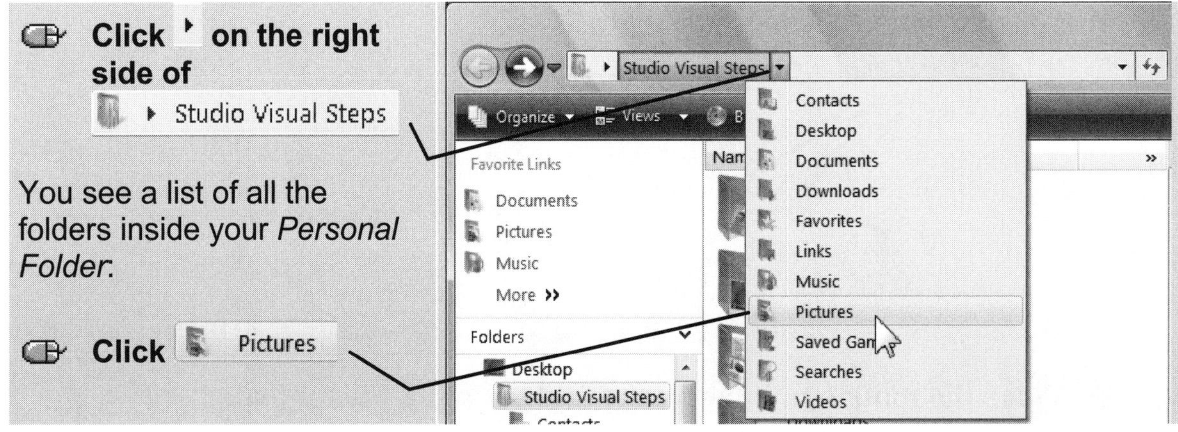

You see the contents of your folder *Pictures* again. The address bar now looks like this: ▸ Studio Visual Steps ▸ Pictures.

The folder names on the address bar are also buttons you can use to open another folder:

The *Personal Folder* Studio Visual Steps is opened again. Another part of the address bar gives access to even more locations on the hard disk of your computer:

You see the *Control Panel* where you can adjust all kinds of settings in your computer. This window looks different than a *Folder window*, but some elements are still the same. Just like in a *Folder window* you can return to the folder *Pictures* like this:

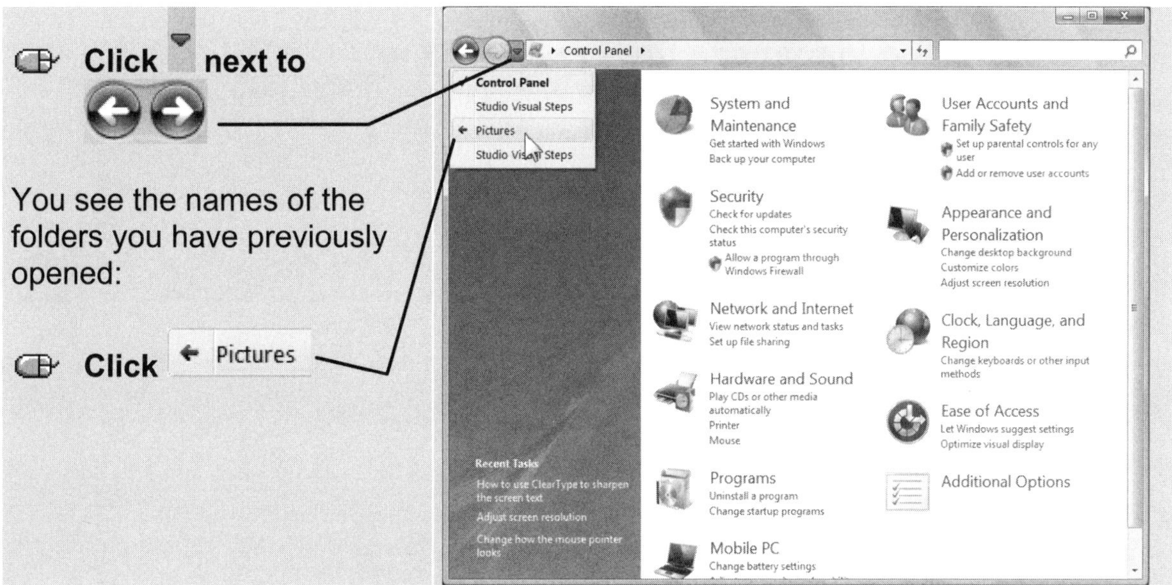

The folder *Pictures* is now open. You use the shortcut in the *File list* to open the folder *Sample pictures*:

Double-click Sample Pictures

3.8 The Preview Pane

In the *Preview Pane* you can preview a selected file. Just click the file to do so:

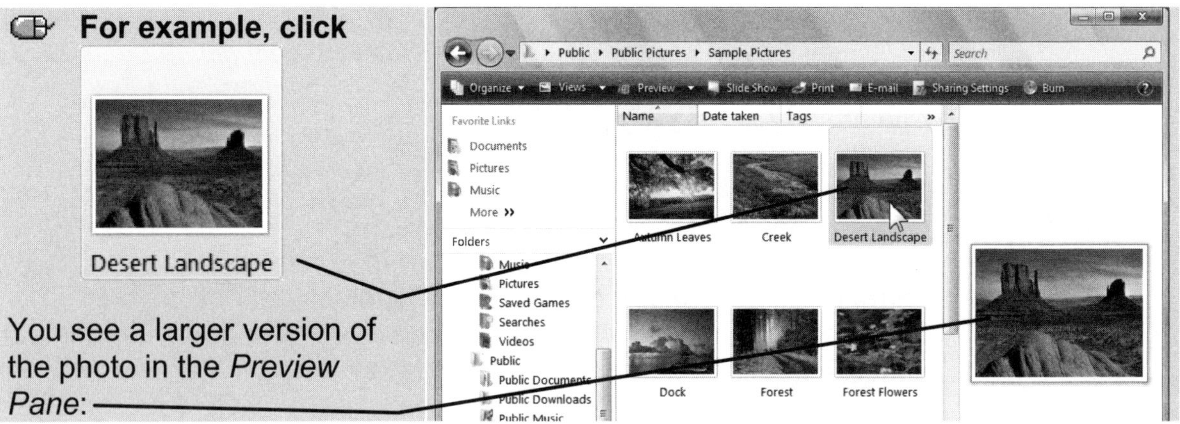

For example, click Desert Landscape

You see a larger version of the photo in the *Preview Pane*:

HELP! I no longer see the Preview Pane

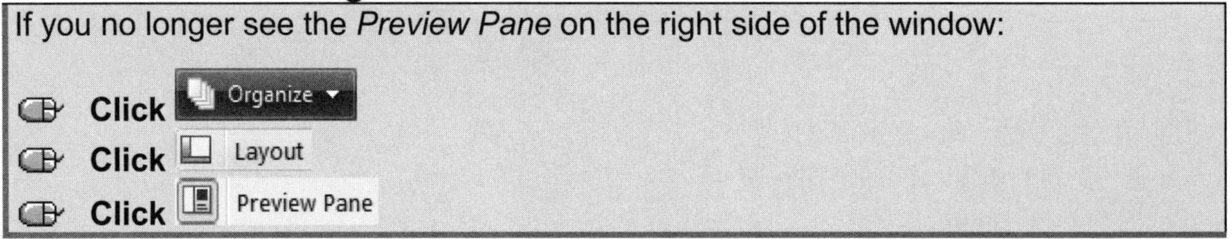

If you no longer see the *Preview Pane* on the right side of the window:

Click Organize

Click Layout

Click Preview Pane

 **Tip**

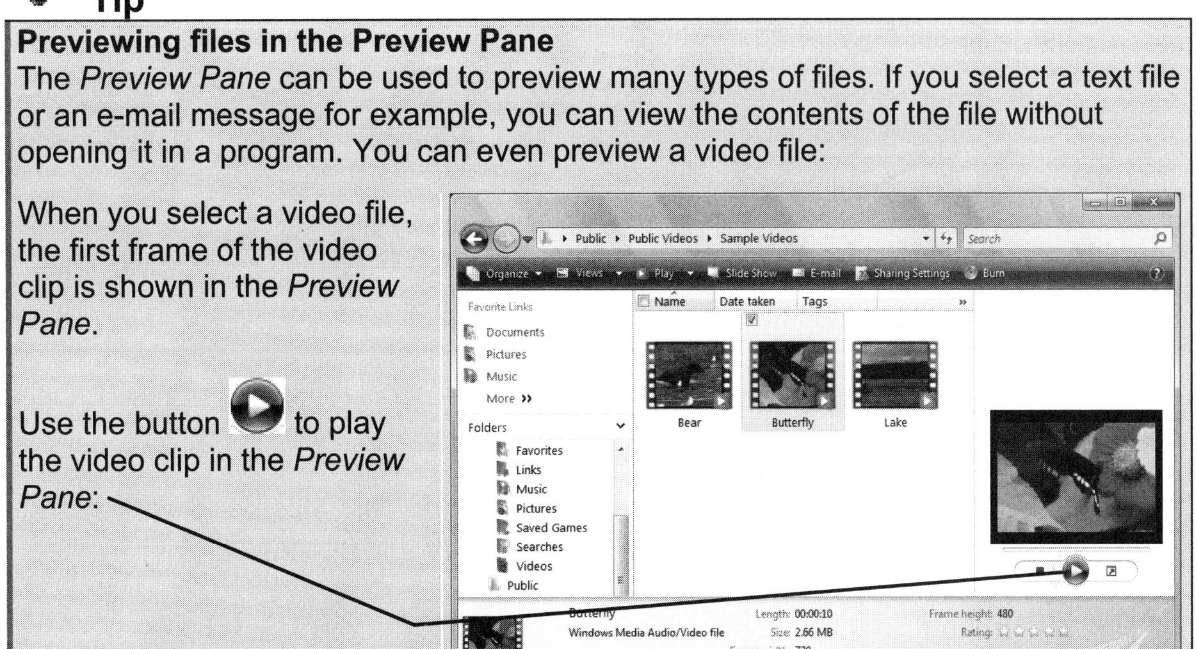

Previewing files in the Preview Pane
The *Preview Pane* can be used to preview many types of files. If you select a text file or an e-mail message for example, you can view the contents of the file without opening it in a program. You can even preview a video file:

When you select a video file, the first frame of the video clip is shown in the *Preview Pane*.

Use the button to play the video clip in the *Preview Pane*:

3.9 The Details Pane

In the *Details Pane* at the bottom of the *Folder window* you see the properties associated with the selected file:

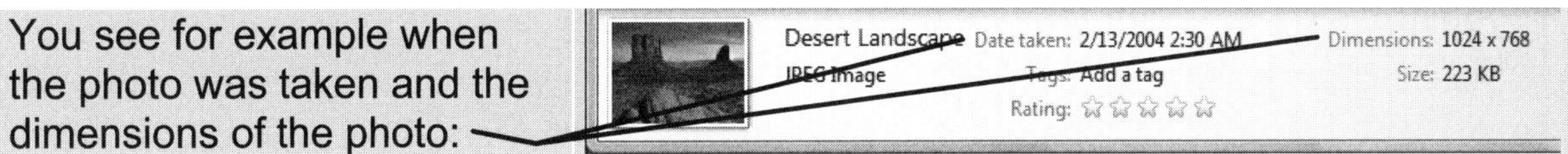

You see for example when the photo was taken and the dimensions of the photo:

In the *Details Pane* you can change several items. For example, here is how to change the date:

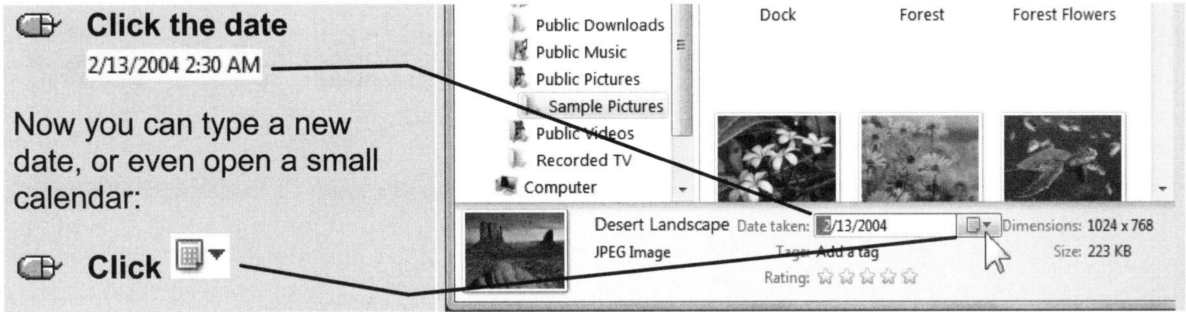

Click the date 2/13/2004 2:30 AM

Now you can type a new date, or even open a small calendar:

Click

In the calendar you can select a new date by clicking it. For example, choose the next day:

Click 14

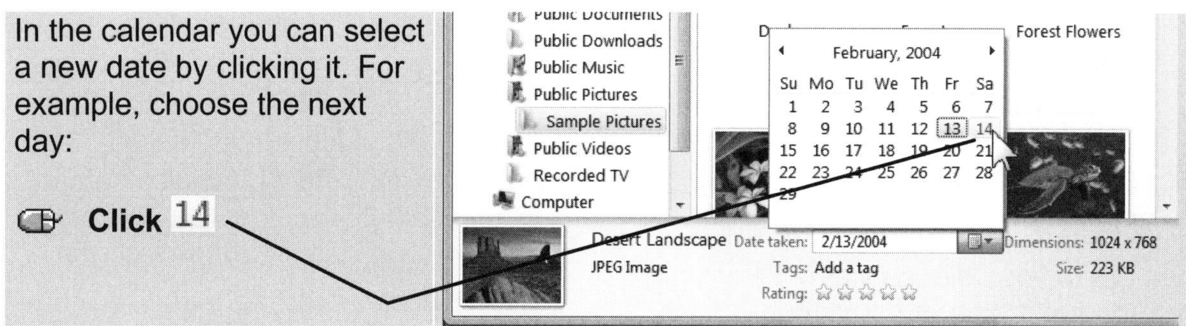

To save the changes you made:

Click Save

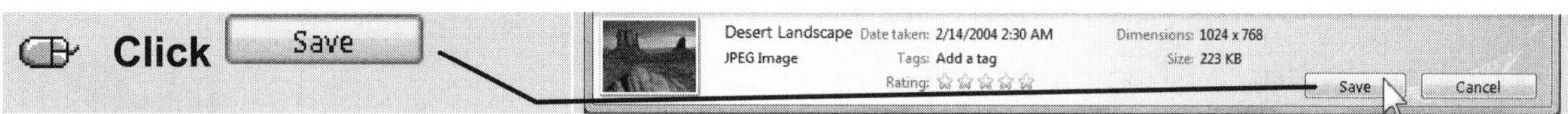

You can also change the *rating* and *tags* of a file. You can rate your files by giving them a certain number of stars. This is how you give this photo a five star rating:

Click the fifth star

Click Save

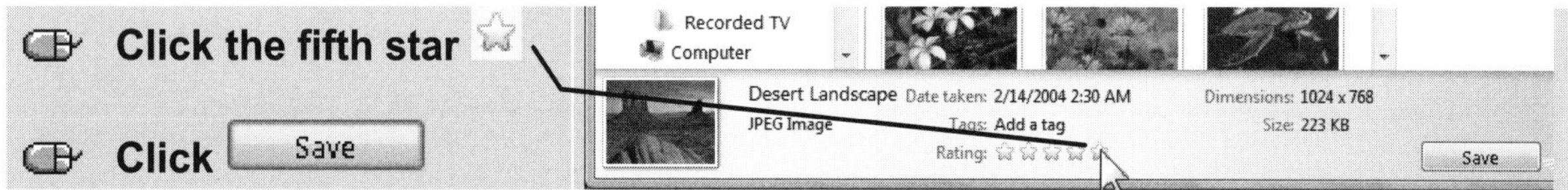

This is a useful way to make a distinction between your favorite and not-so-favorite photos.

Another way to organize your photos is by using *tags*. A tag is a word or short phrase applied to a photo. The photo of the desert in this example does not have a tag yet, you see Add a tag. If someone else uses the computer the photo may already have tags.

You can add a tag to a photo yourself:

Click Add a tag

Type: `Holiday`

Press Enter

Now the photo has a tag:

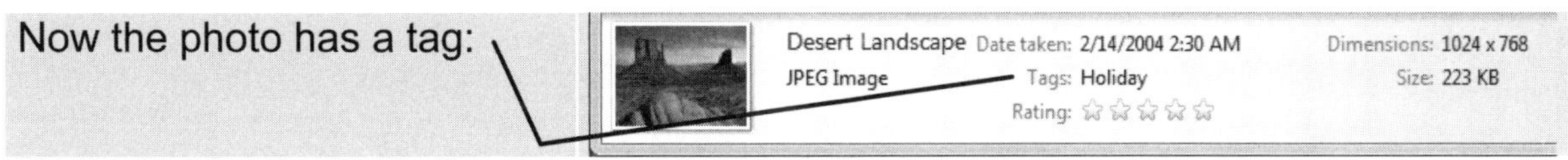

You will encounter the ratings and tags again in the next section where you take a closer look at the search feature of the *Folder window*.

3.10 Using the Search Box

The search feature in *Windows Vista* has been greatly improved.

In the *Folder window* you find a *Search Box* in the top right corner:

You can use this *Search Box* to filter the files and subfolders that are displayed in the *File list*.

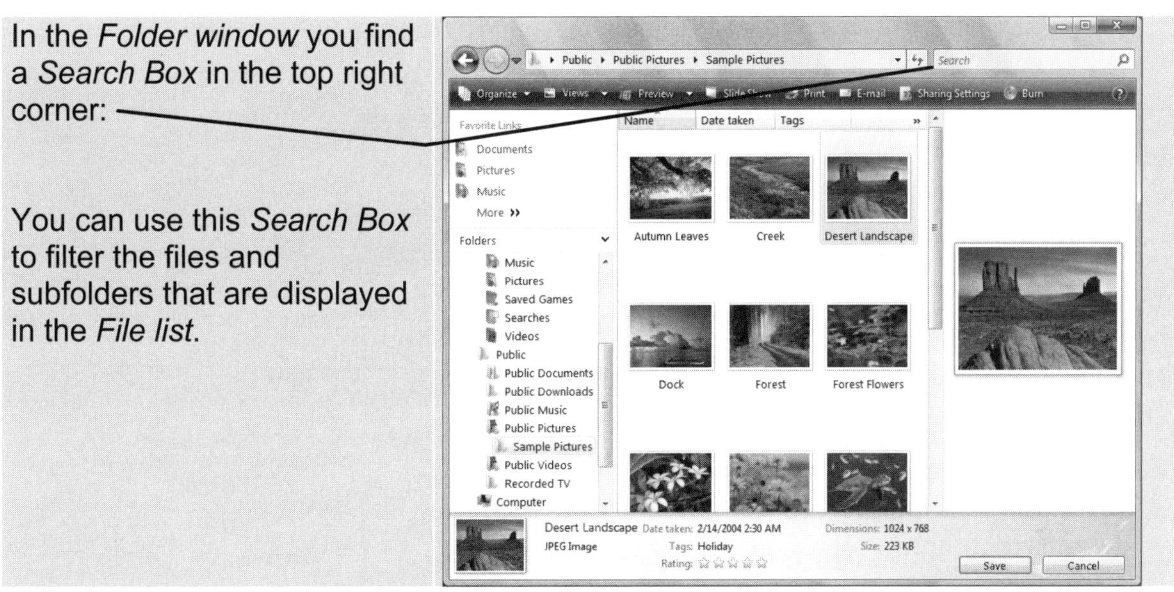

Click in the *Search Box*

Type:
`hol`

As you type, the *File list* is searched for items that contain the letters 'hol'. The photo you gave the tag 'holiday' is the only item that is shown:

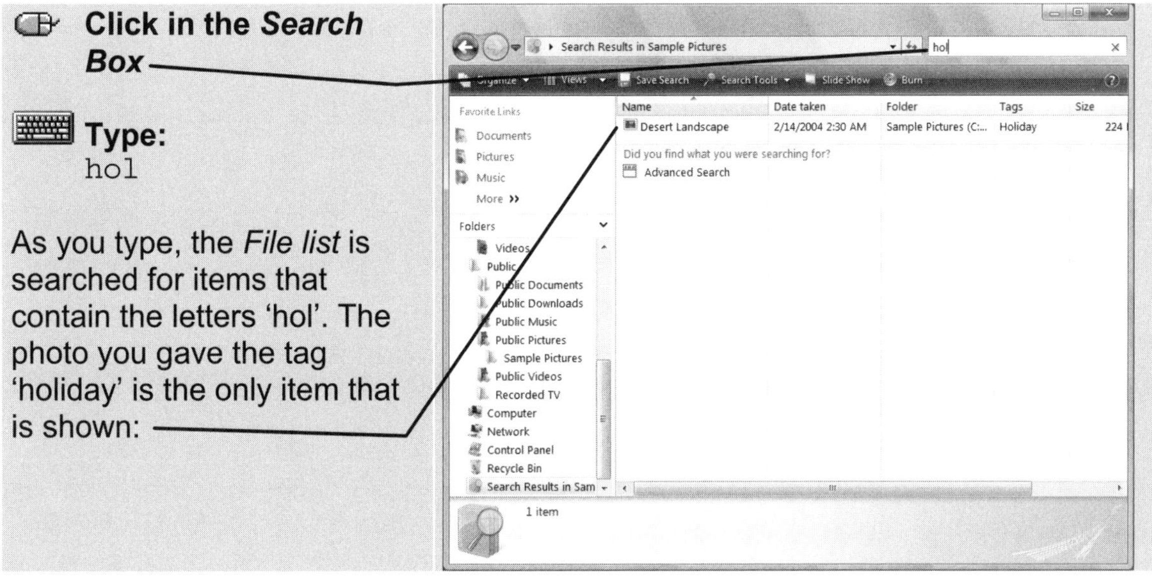

You see that the search feature not only looks for file names. Properties such as tags are also searched.

HELP! My search results are displayed differently

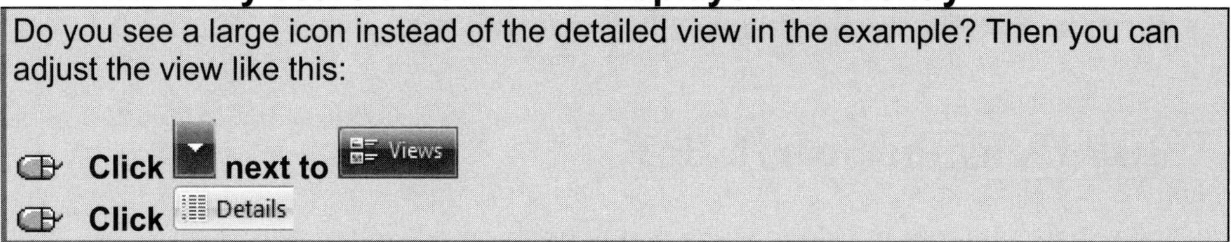

Do you see a large icon instead of the detailed view in the example? Then you can adjust the view like this:

Click [▼] **next to** Views

Click Details

If you shorten the search term, the search result changes right away:

Press ← Backspace **twice**

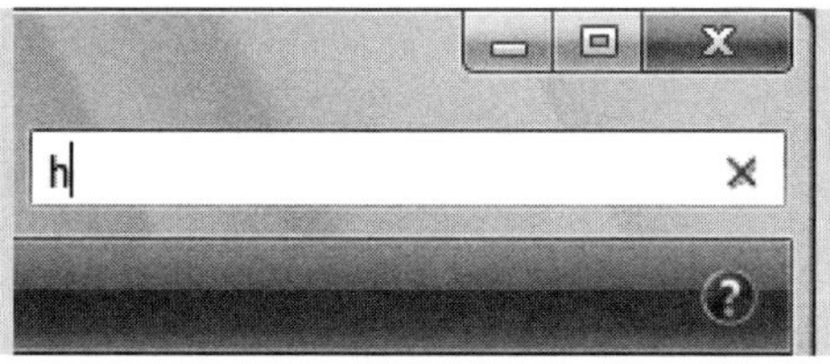

Now the search feature looks for files containing the letter **h**. The search result now consists of three files:

Depending on the tags used on your computer you will see more or less files in the search result:

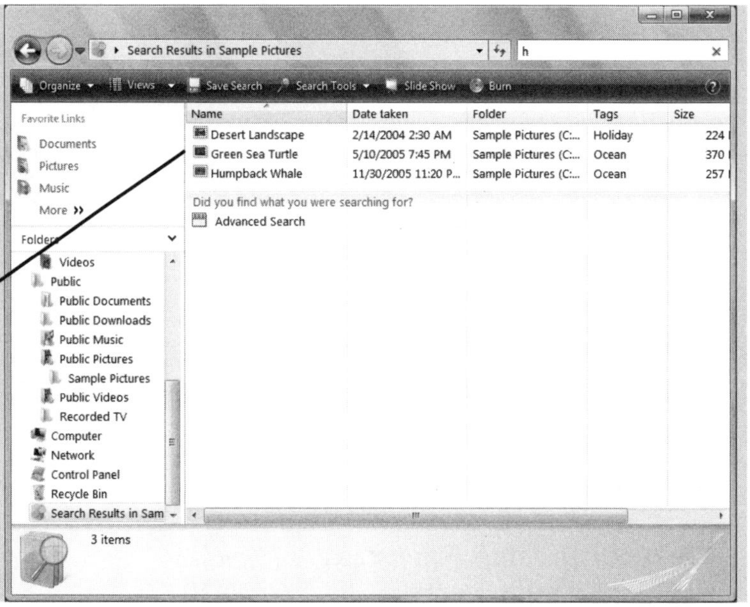

3.11 Filtering Search Results Using the Column Headers

When your search has resulted in a long list of files, you can filter it. You do this by using the *column headers*. This is how you can filter all photos with the tag 'holiday' from the search result:

- **Click ▾ next to Tags**
- **For example, click a check mark for ☑ Holiday**

When this tag is not available:

- **Choose a different tag**

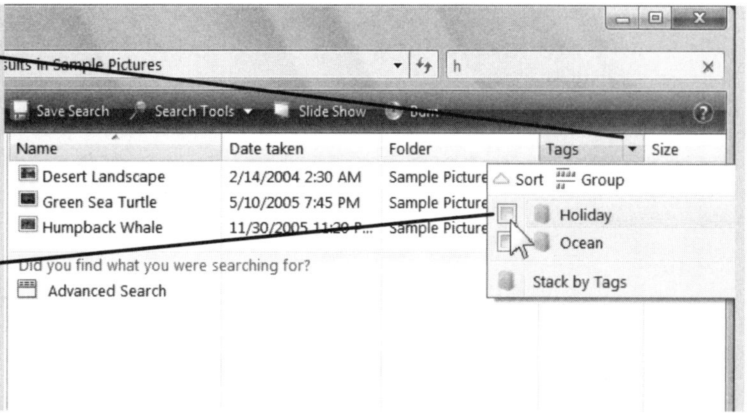

- **Click the empty area below the search results**

The menu is closed.
You see the filtered search results:

The search results on your computer may be different from those in the example.

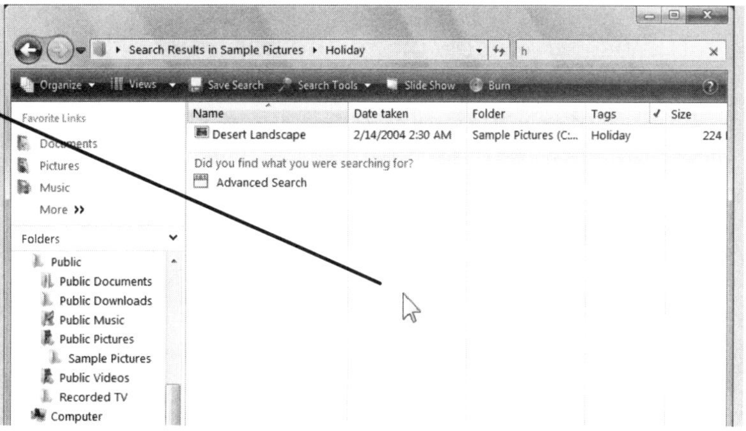

Tip

Tags
When you have a large collection of digital photos, you can use tags to organize your photos. Each photo may contain several tags. For example, you can give a photo you took of a nice tree during your holiday in France the tags 'Holiday France' and 'Nature'. A photo you took of your grandchild during the same holiday, can be given the tags 'Holiday France' and 'Grandchildren'. If you do this consistently for all your photos, it will be much easier to find a photo in the future because you can display all the pictures that have a particular tag by entering the word in the *Search Box*.

Tags may also be used in the new program *Windows Photo Gallery*. You can read more about this program in chapter 9.

Tip

Other filter options
You can filter the search results even further using the other column headers:

- **Name**: here you can choose the first letter of the file name A-E, F-L, M-R and S-Z.
- **Date taken**: here you can choose a specific date, or the photos without a date instead.
- **Folder**: if the search results are found in several subfolders, you can chose which folder(s) to display in the search results.
- **Size**: here you can choose photos with a file size between 10 KB - 100 KB and 100 KB - 1 MB.
- **Rating**: here you can choose the number of stars.

3.12 Filtering Search Results Using the Search Pane

The *Folder window* offers another way to filter search results. You can use the *Search pane* to choose which types of files you want to display in the search results. This is how you display the *Search Pane*:

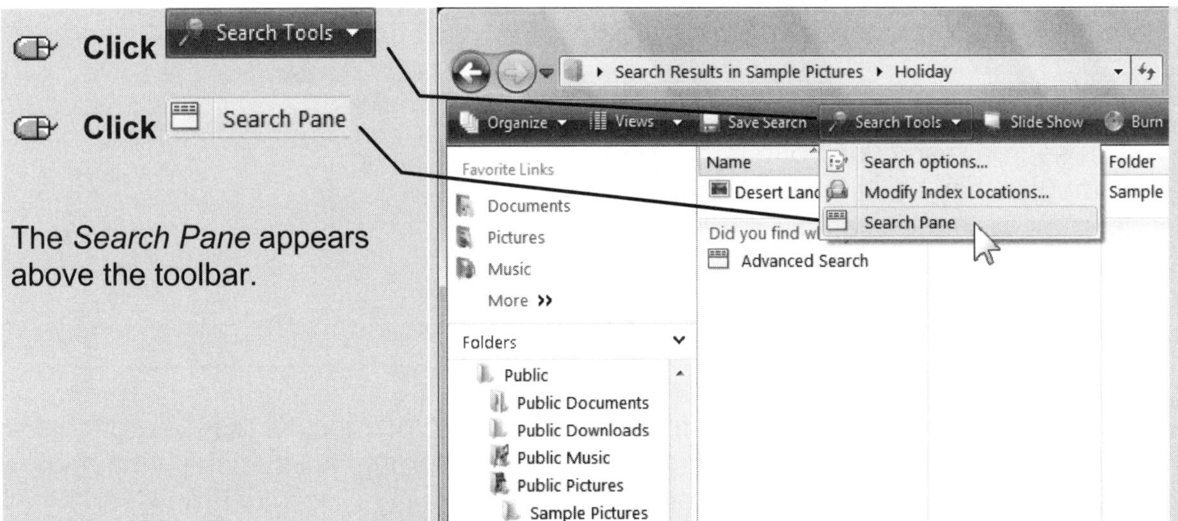

In the *Search Pane* you can choose between these file types:

When you click a button in the *Search Pane*, only files of that type are displayed in the search results.

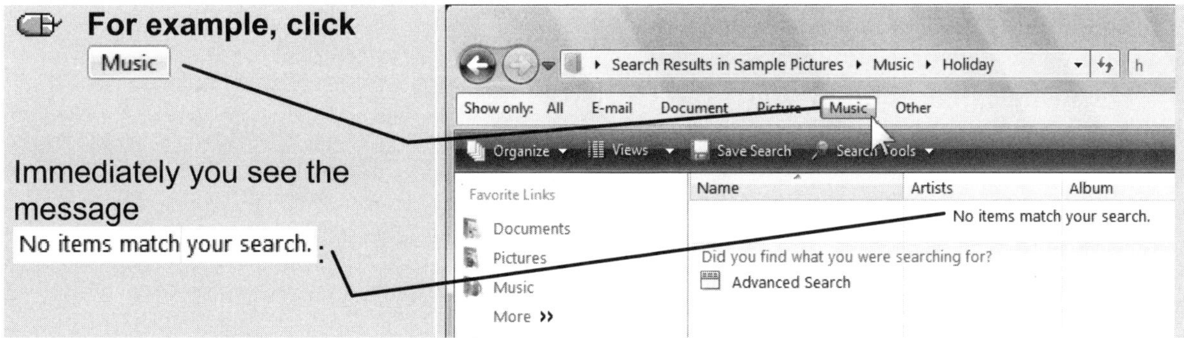

The search results you are trying to filter only contain photos, so no music files are found.

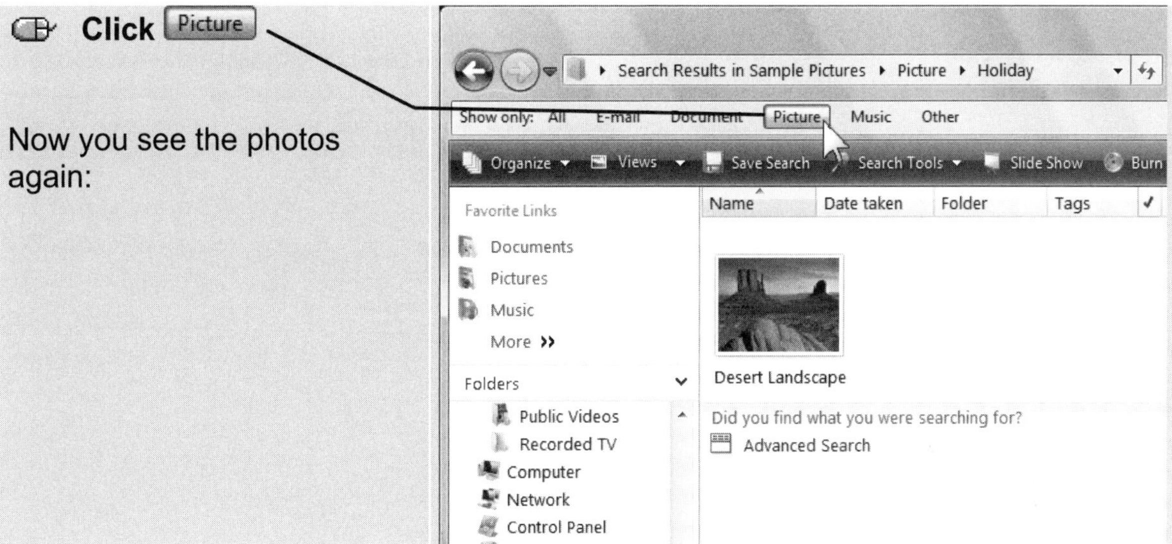

When you are finished searching, you can return to your *Personal Folder*. Here is another way to do that:

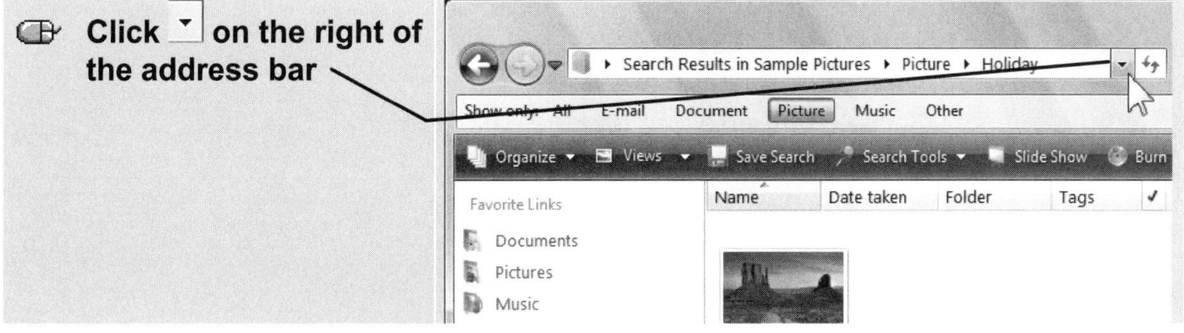

A list with previously visited locations appears.

Click the name of your *Personal Folder*

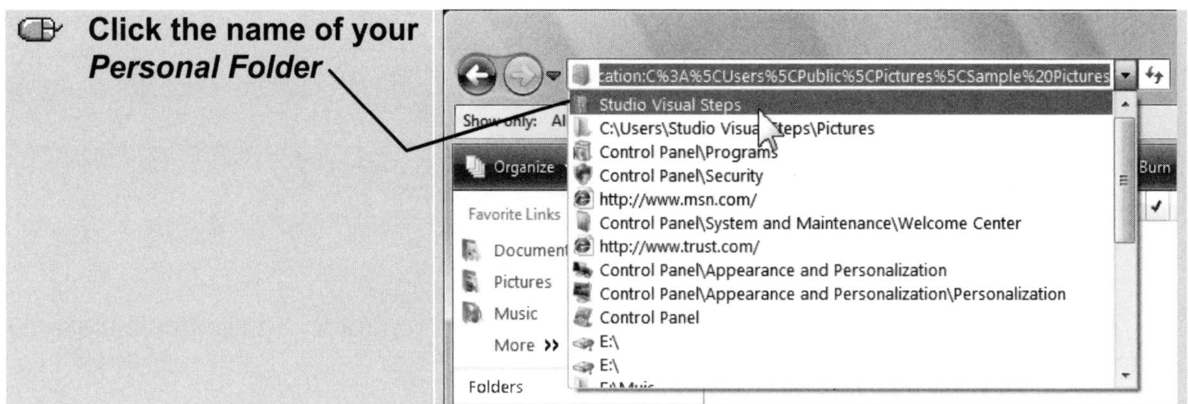

You see your *Personal Folder* again:

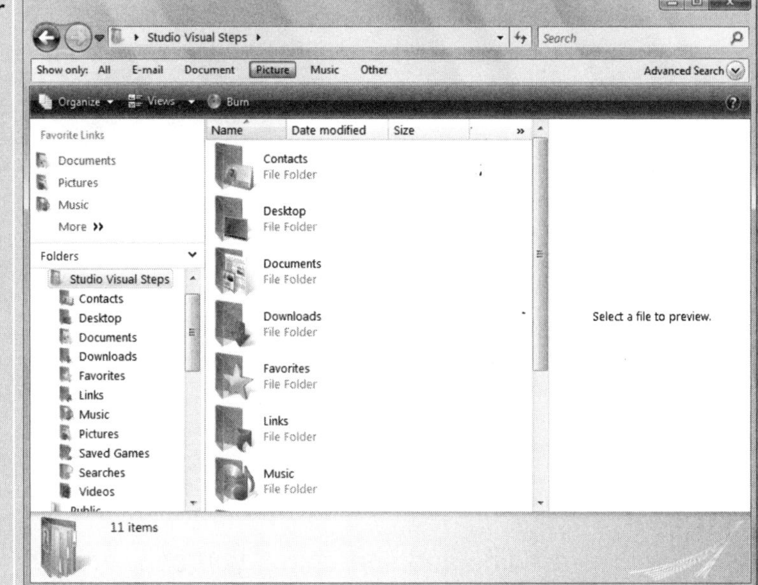

3.13 Advanced Search

You can also select *Advanced Search* in the *Search Panel*. Like this:

Click

You see a new pane:

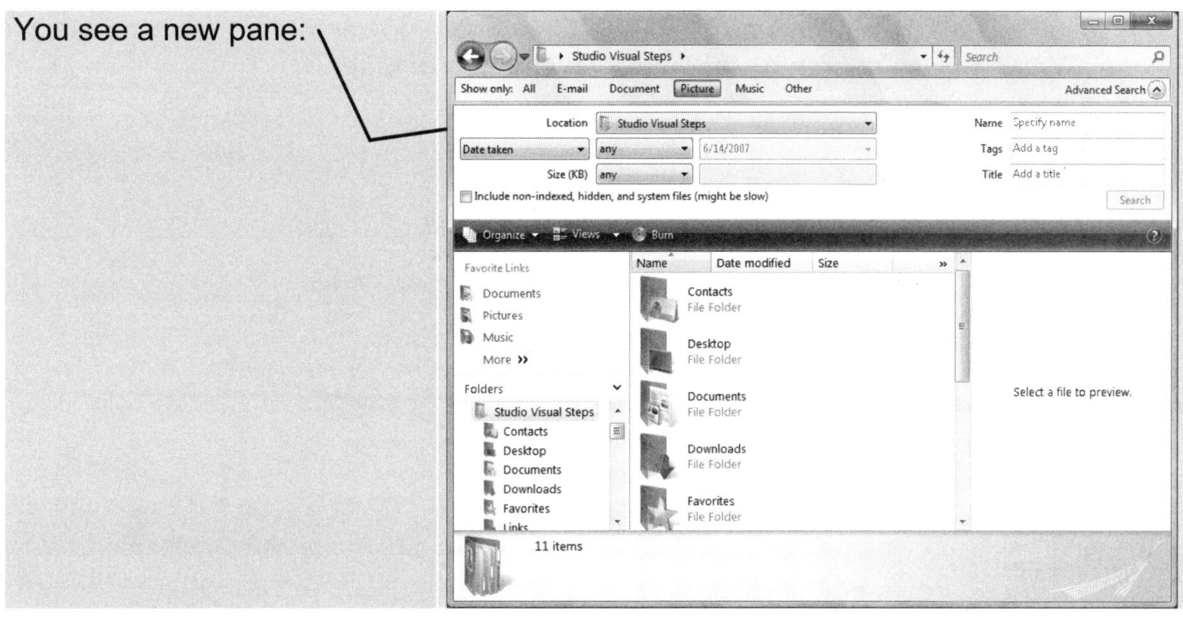

In this pane you can search for example by the date the photo was taken or the size of the file:

Vista assumes you are looking for a photo because Picture is still selected:

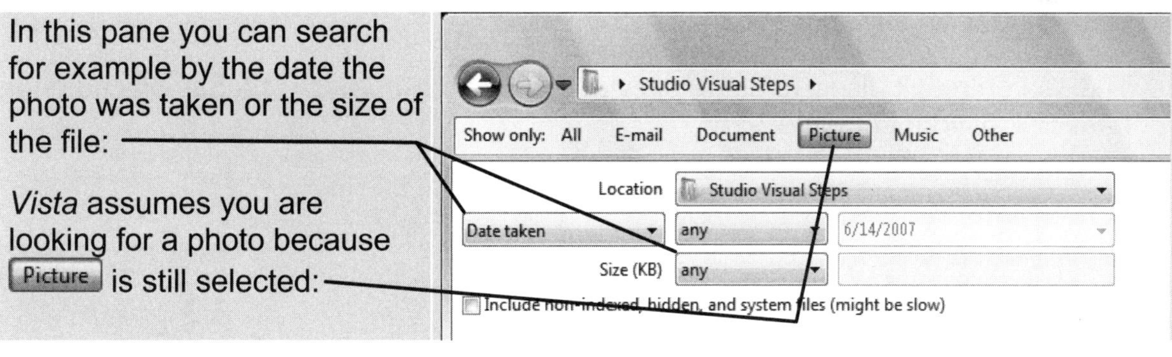

Click All

Now you can search for all types of files, not just photos. If you are not sure where a file is located, you can search the entire computer:

Click Studio Visual Steps next to Location

Click Computer

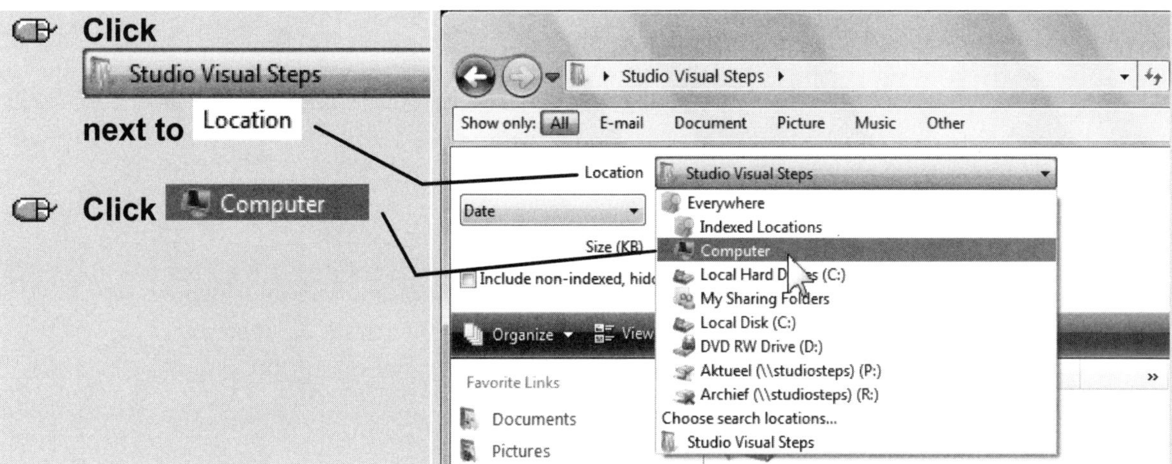

If you know the date a file was created of changed, you can enter that information as well. You can also search by the name and the tag of a file:

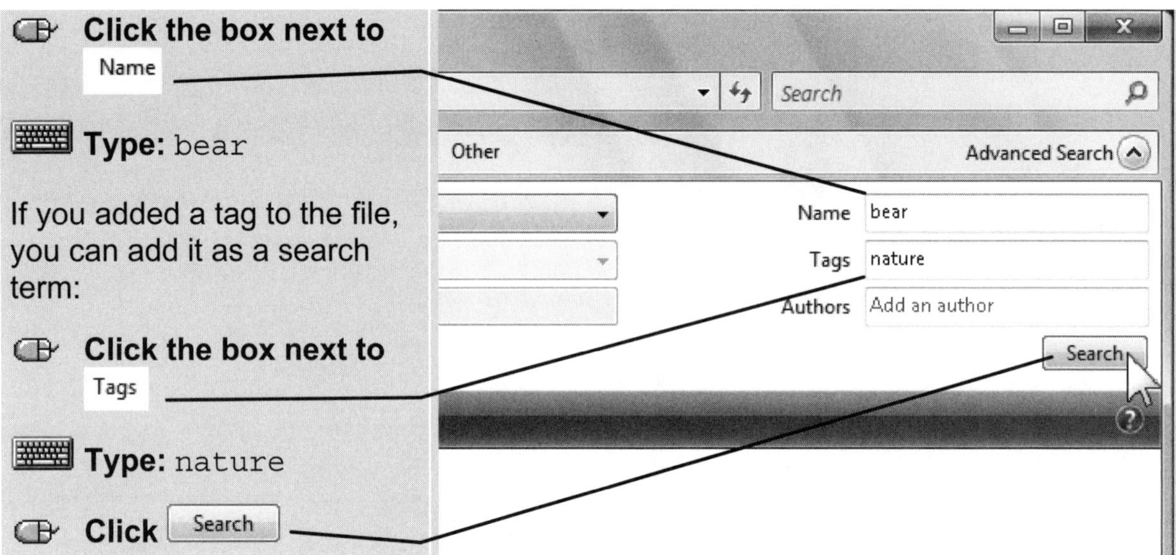

The search result displays a sample video file that *Windows Vista* has placed on the hard disk of your computer.

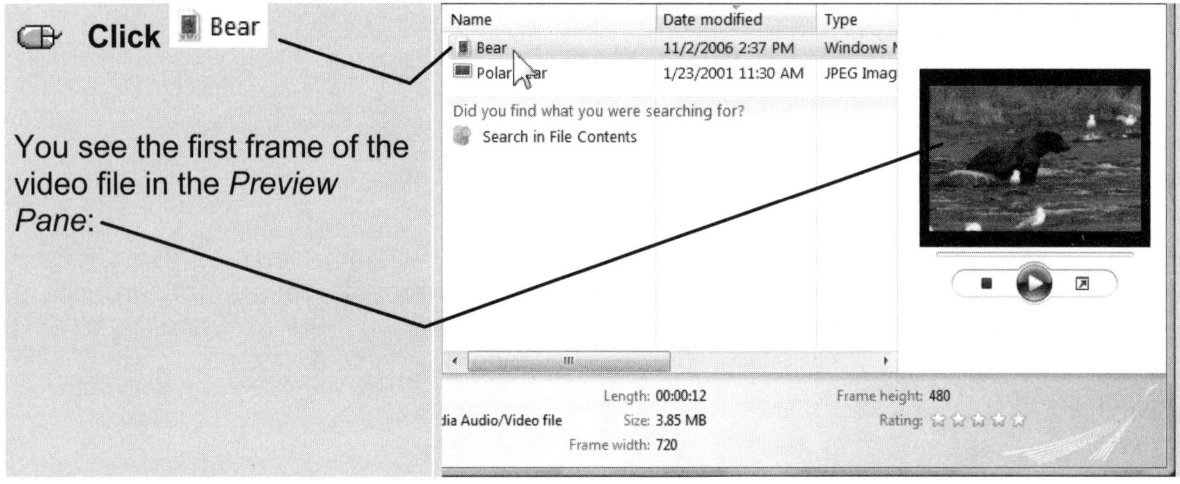

3.14 Saving a Search

Windows Vista gives you the opportunity to save a search. This way you can perform the same search without having to enter the different search criteria all over again. Try that with the current search:

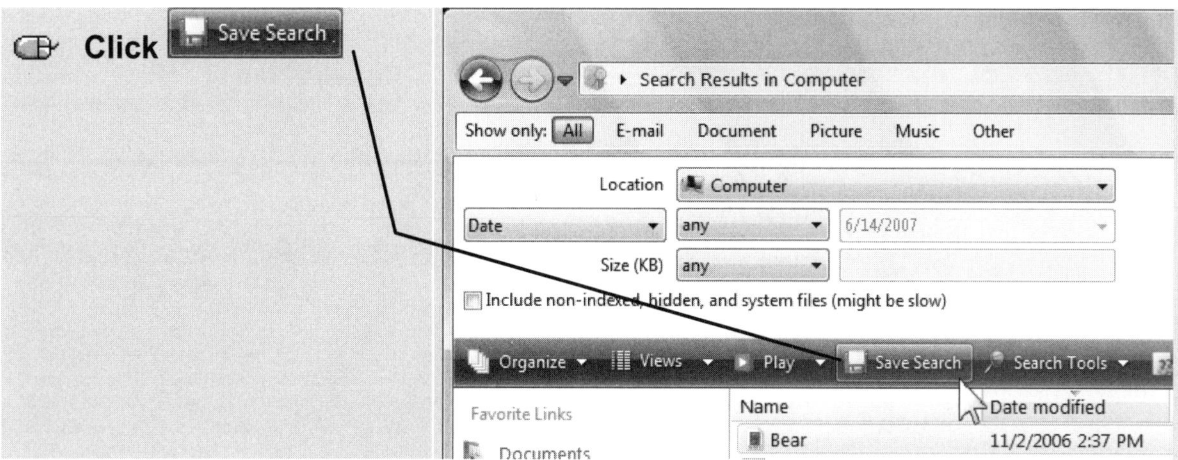

A window appears where you can give the search a name.

The search has been added to the subfolder *Searches* in your *Personal Folder*. The search is performed again and the address bar now looks like this:

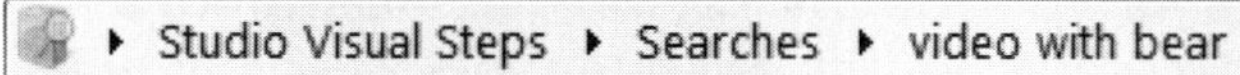

3.15 Running a Saved Search

Your search has been saved in the folder *Searches*. To verify that:

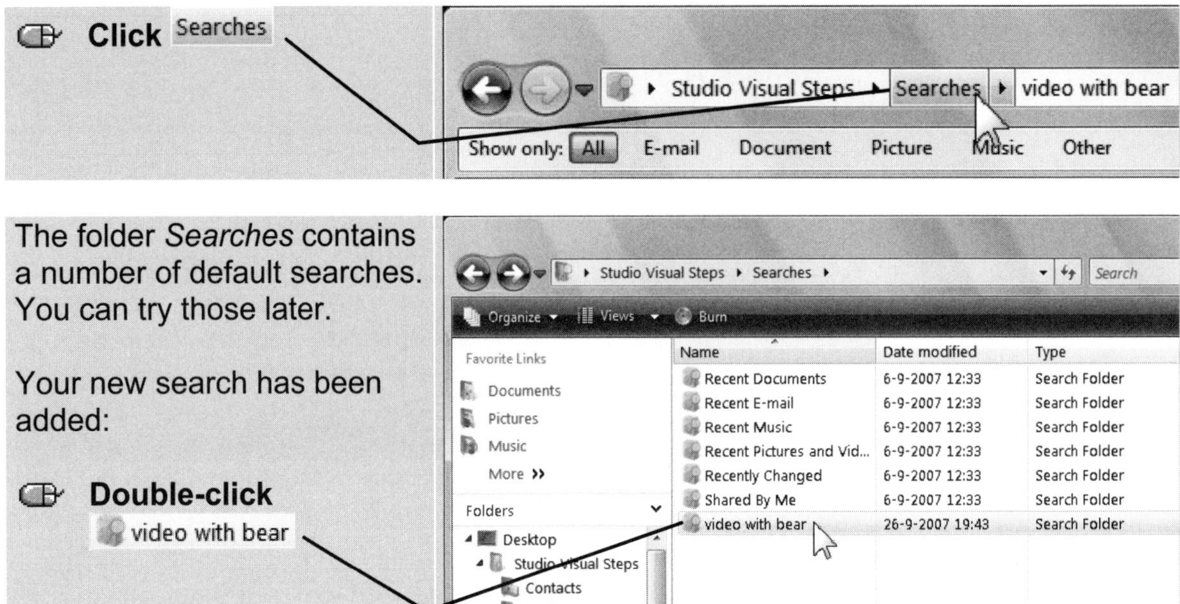

Click Searches

The folder *Searches* contains a number of default searches. You can try those later.

Your new search has been added:

Double-click video with bear

HELP! My search results look different

If you cannot see the detailed display like in the example above:

Click next to Views

Click Details

Please note:

A saved search can be opened whenever you want. When you add or remove files and folders that correspond to the search criteria, the search result will change.

You see the search result again. Since you did not add or remove any files, the search result is still the same:

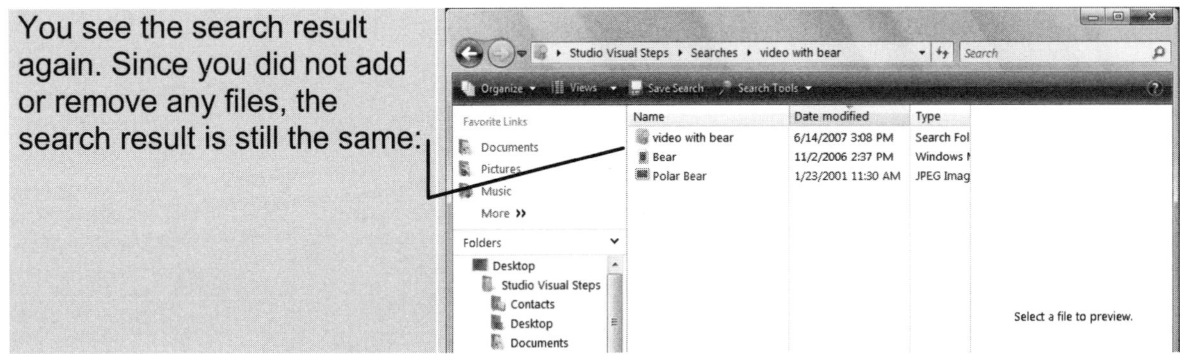

Tip

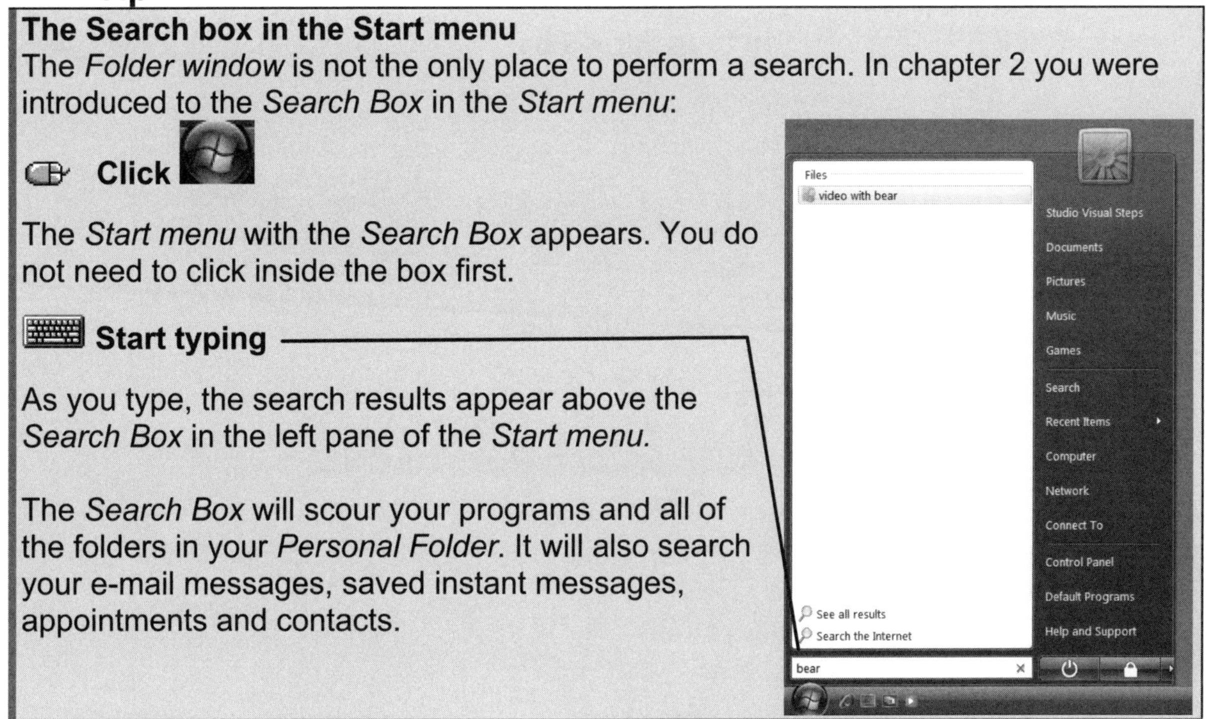

The Search box in the Start menu

The *Folder window* is not the only place to perform a search. In chapter 2 you were introduced to the *Search Box* in the *Start menu*:

Click

The *Start menu* with the *Search Box* appears. You do not need to click inside the box first.

Start typing

As you type, the search results appear above the *Search Box* in the left pane of the *Start menu.*

The *Search Box* will scour your programs and all of the folders in your *Personal Folder*. It will also search your e-mail messages, saved instant messages, appointments and contacts.

3.16 The Changing Buttons on the Toolbar

In *Windows XP* you were used to menu bars that always look the same. Perhaps you have noticed that in *Windows Vista* the toolbar in the *Folder window* changes its appearance. After your last search the toolbar looks like this:

When you click the video file that was found, the toolbar changes:

Click Bear

Now the toolbar looks like this:

The contents of the toolbar are constantly adapted to the most obvious tasks for the selected file or folder.

For example, the video file can be played right away with the Play button.

As soon as you open a folder containing photos, the toolbar changes again:

Click Studio Visual Steps in the address bar

Double-click Pictures and then Sample Pictures

Now the toolbar looks like this:

With the button Slide Show you can view the photos in the opened folder as a full-screen slideshow.

3.17 Making a New Folder

Folders can be used as a tool to organize your files. Saving your photos in several subfolders, for example, is a handy way to organize your collection. In *Windows Vista* you can make a subfolder in the folder *Sample Pictures* like this:

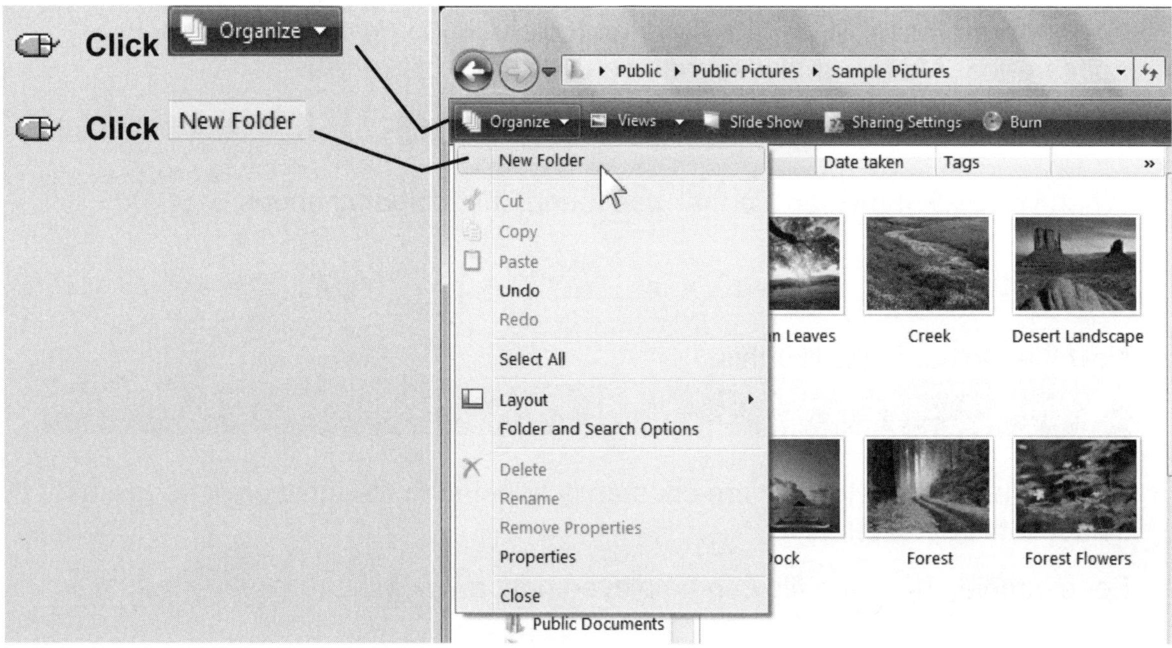

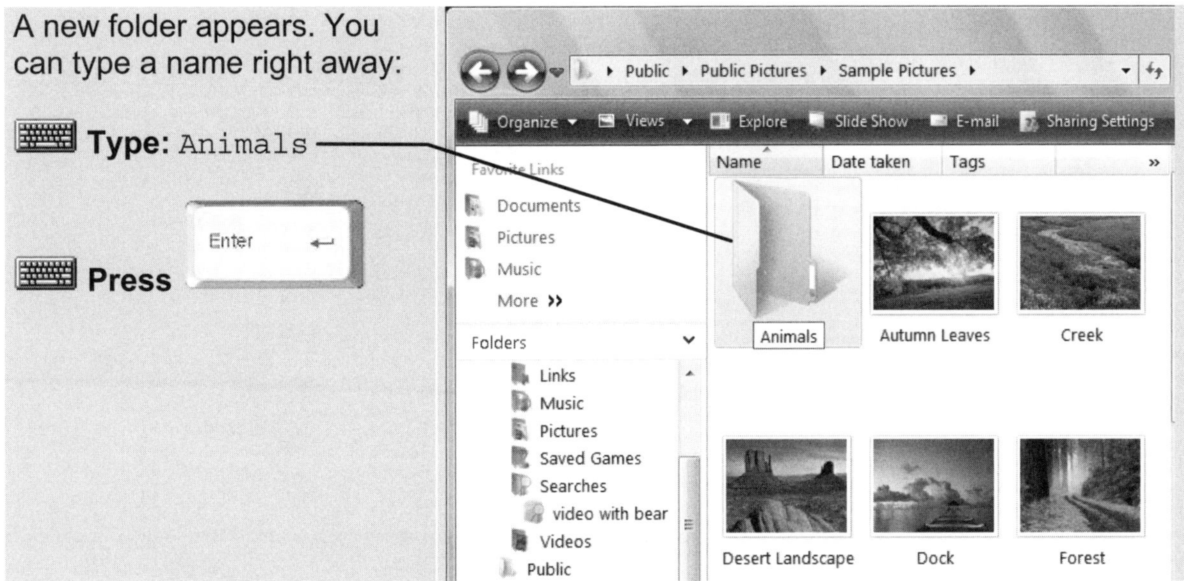

The folder *Animals* can be used to store your photos of animals. You can 'cut' the files and 'paste' them in the new folder the way you used to do in *Windows XP*. But you can work faster when you select multiple files using the check boxes. These files can be dragged to the new folder. In the next two sections you can read how to do that.

3.18 Selecting Files and Folders Using Check Boxes

You start by changing the display of the *File list* to ensure your window looks the same as the windows in the following examples:

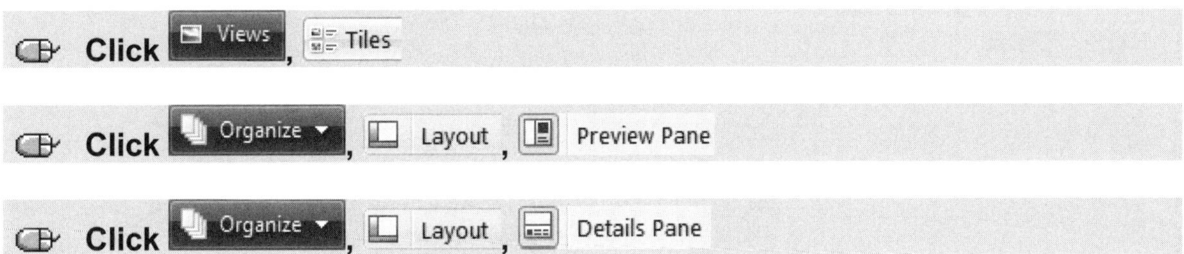

The files and folders in the *Folder window* are now displayed as 'tiles', without the *Preview Pane* and the *Details Pane.*

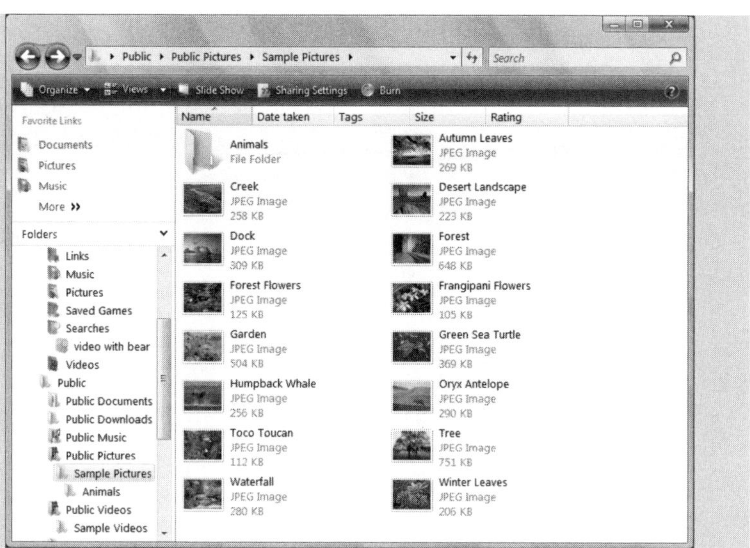

Windows Vista contains a new feature that allows you to quickly select multiple files and/or folders by using check boxes. This feature can be activated like this:

- **Click** Organize, Folder and Search Options
- **Click the tab** View
- **Drag the vertical scroll bar down**
- **Check mark the option** Use check boxes to select items
- **Click** OK

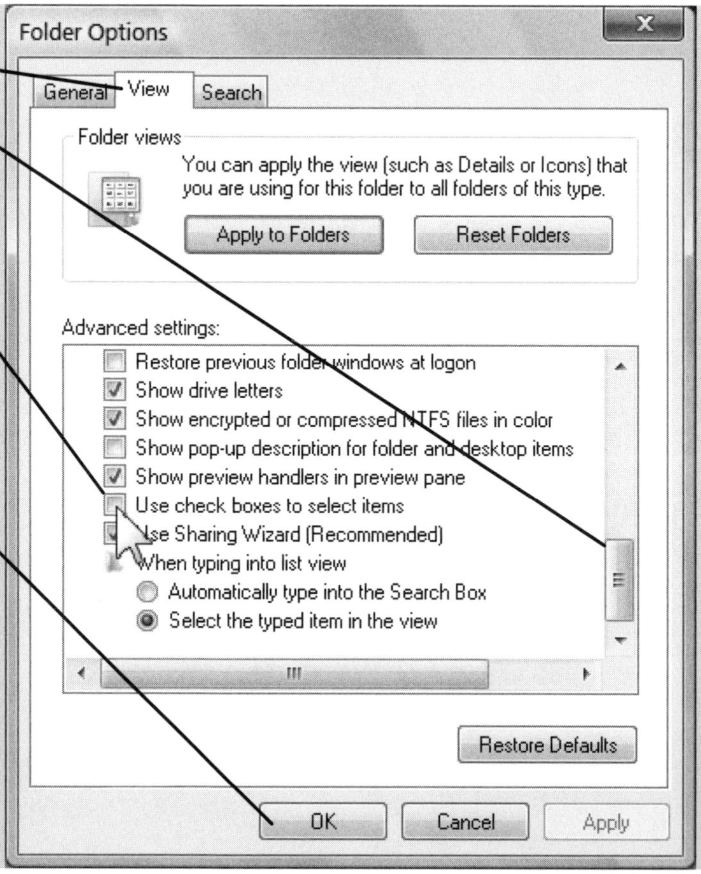

The feature is now activated.

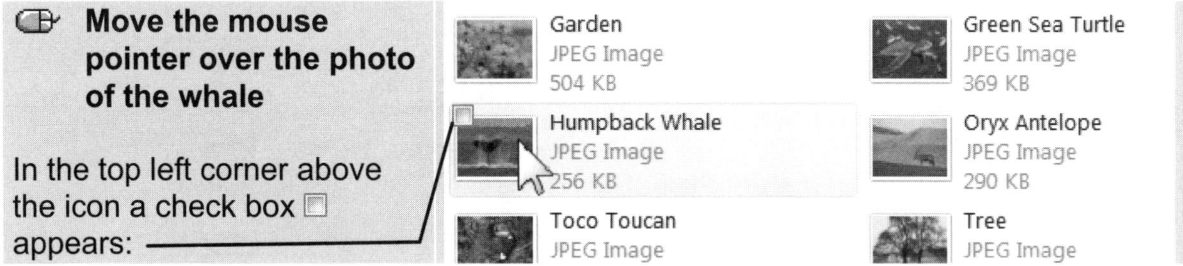

A check mark placed in the check box will automatically select that file.

Both files have now been selected. Folders can be selected the same way.

3.19 Dragging and Dropping Files

Dragging and dropping is the fastest way to move the two selected files.

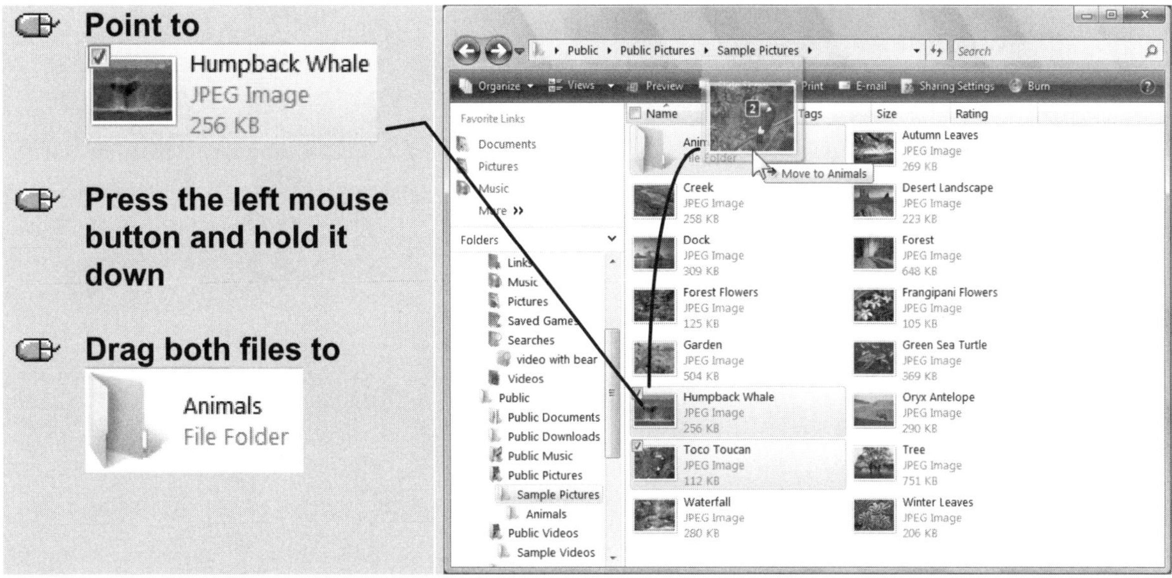

2 shows that two files are being moved:

When you see this box → Move to Animals appear:

Release the mouse button

The files have been moved to the folder Animals File Folder .

3.20 Drag and Copy Files

You can also copy files when you drag them.

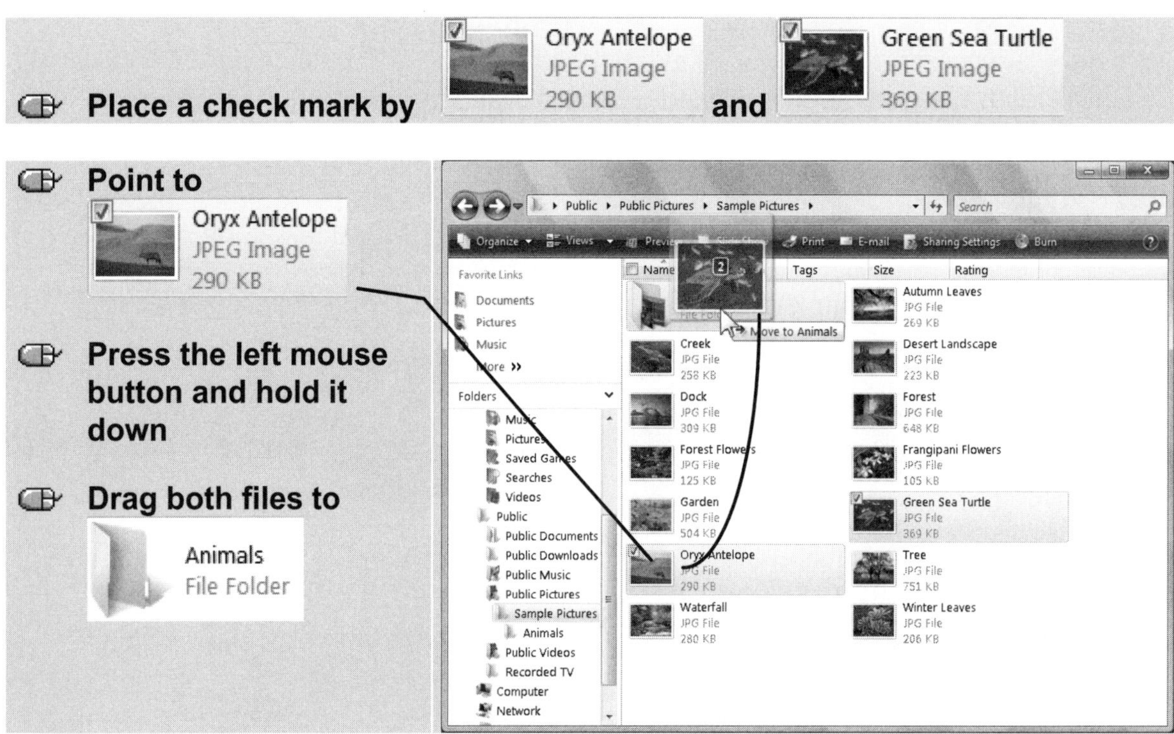

Place a check mark by Oryx Antelope JPEG Image 290 KB **and** Green Sea Turtle JPEG Image 369 KB

Point to Oryx Antelope JPEG Image 290 KB

Press the left mouse button and hold it down

Drag both files to Animals File Folder

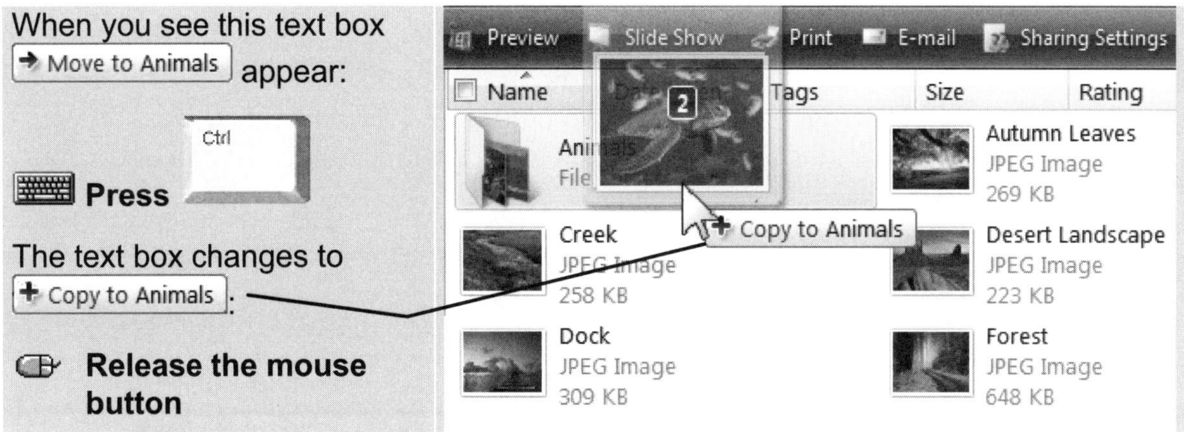

When you see this text box ➔ Move to Animals appear:

Press Ctrl

The text box changes to ✚ Copy to Animals:

Release the mouse button

Not only files can be copied this way, but also complete folders.

Tip

Dragging while holding the right mouse button down

When you drag a file or folder to another location while holding the **right mouse button** down, you see this menu when you release the mouse button:

Copy Here
Move Here
Create Shortcuts Here
Cancel

Click the desired action

Please note:

When you drag a file or folder to another (partition of the) hard disk, *Vista* assumes that you want to copy the file.

When you drag a file or folder to a location on the same (partition of the) hard disk, *Vista* assumes that you want to move the file.

3.21 Undoing Your Actions

You have moved two files and copied two other files to the folder *Animals.* If you prefer to return the folder *Sample Pictures* to its original state, you can undo your actions.

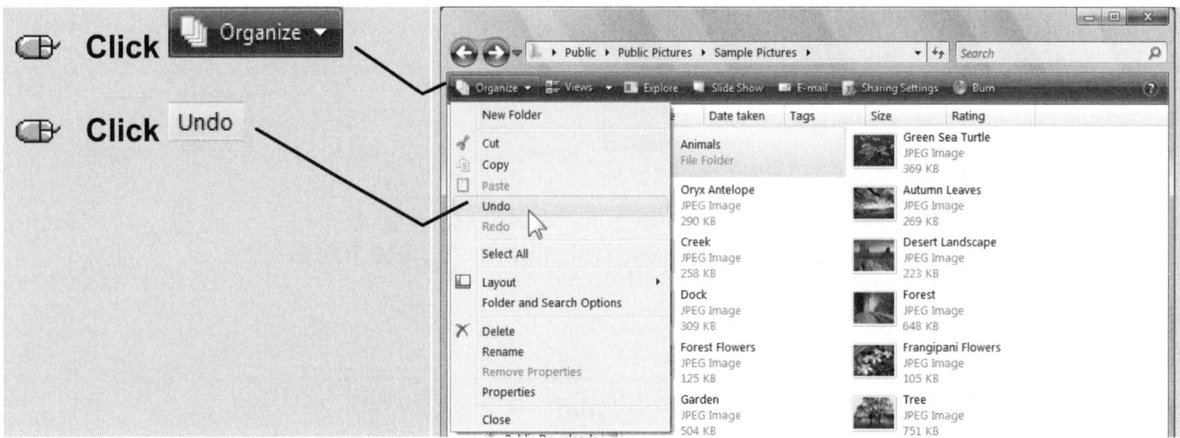

Click Organize

Click Undo

Windows asks if you want to permanently delete the two copied files.

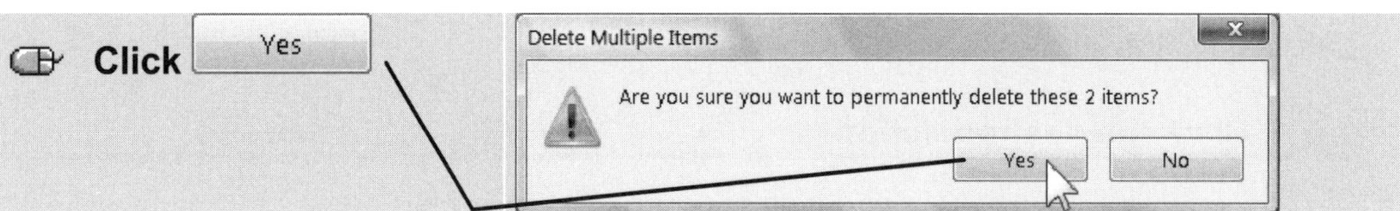

Click Yes

You can also undo the previous action, moving the two files:

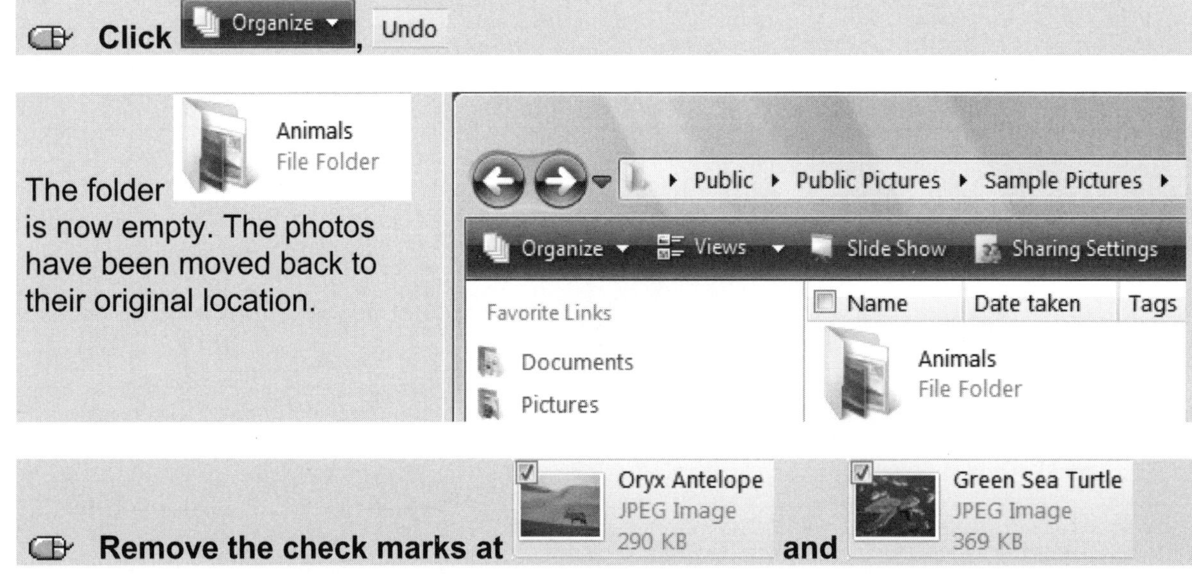

Click Organize, Undo

The folder Animals File Folder is now empty. The photos have been moved back to their original location.

Remove the check marks at Oryx Antelope JPEG Image 290 KB **and** Green Sea Turtle JPEG Image 369 KB

3.22 Deleting Files and Folders

Files and folders you no longer need can be deleted. That way you keep your file system manageable. You can remove the empty folder *Animals* like this:

Click a check mark for

Now you can delete the empty folder:

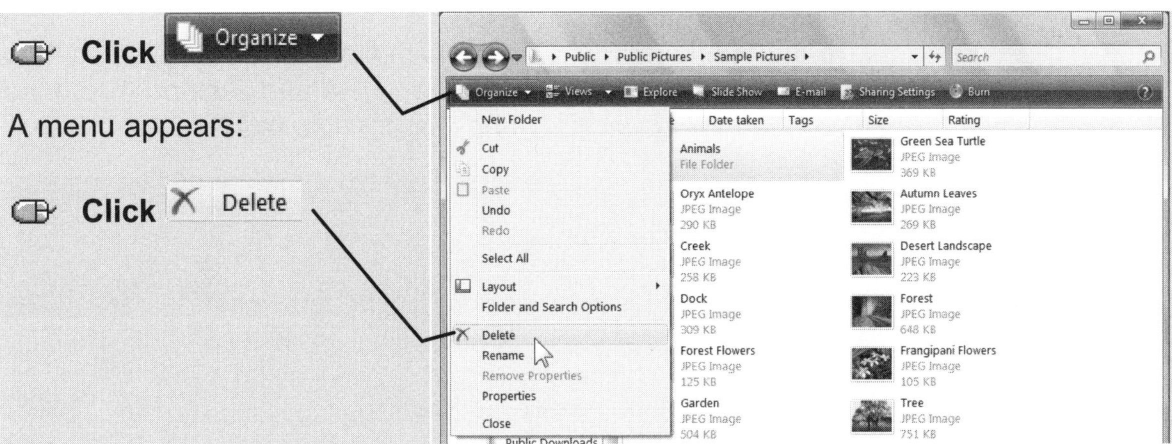

Click Organize

A menu appears:

Click Delete

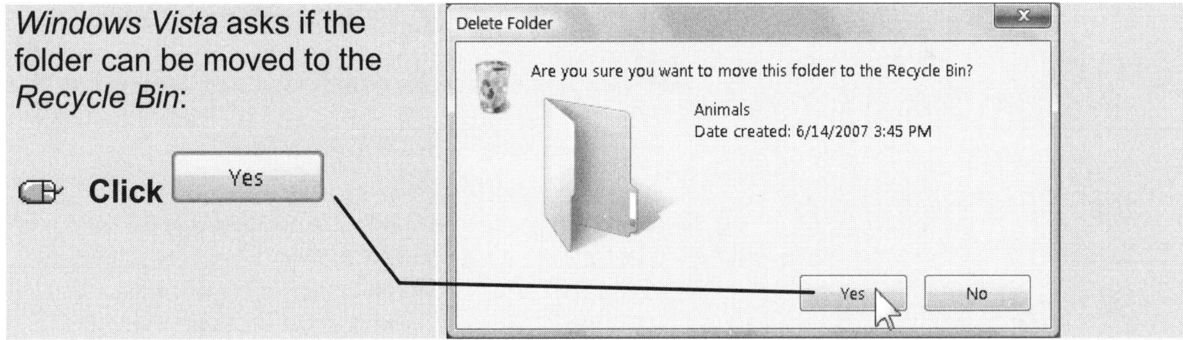

Windows Vista asks if the folder can be moved to the *Recycle Bin*:

Click Yes

The folder 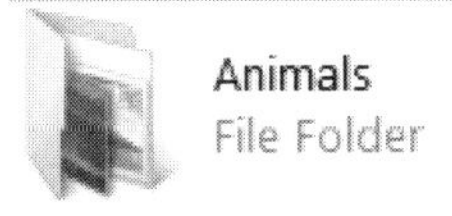

has disappeared from the *Folder window*.

Please note:

Files and folders that have been deleted are not lost forever. As a kind of safety catch, they are put in the *Recycle Bin* first. They will permanently be removed when you empty the *Recycle Bin*. As long as a file is in the *Recycle Bin*, you can retrieve it later if you need it.

 **Please note:**

Only delete your own files
Be careful when deleting files. Only delete files that you have made yourself. If you did not create a file, it is better not to delete it.
Never delete files or folders if you do not know what they are used for.
Never delete files or a folder of programs that you do not use. Program files must be deleted in a different way.

3.23 Using Help and Support

You can find extensive information about working with files and folders, using the different search methods and much more in *Windows Help and Support*. From the *Folder window* you can open *Windows Help and* Support like this:

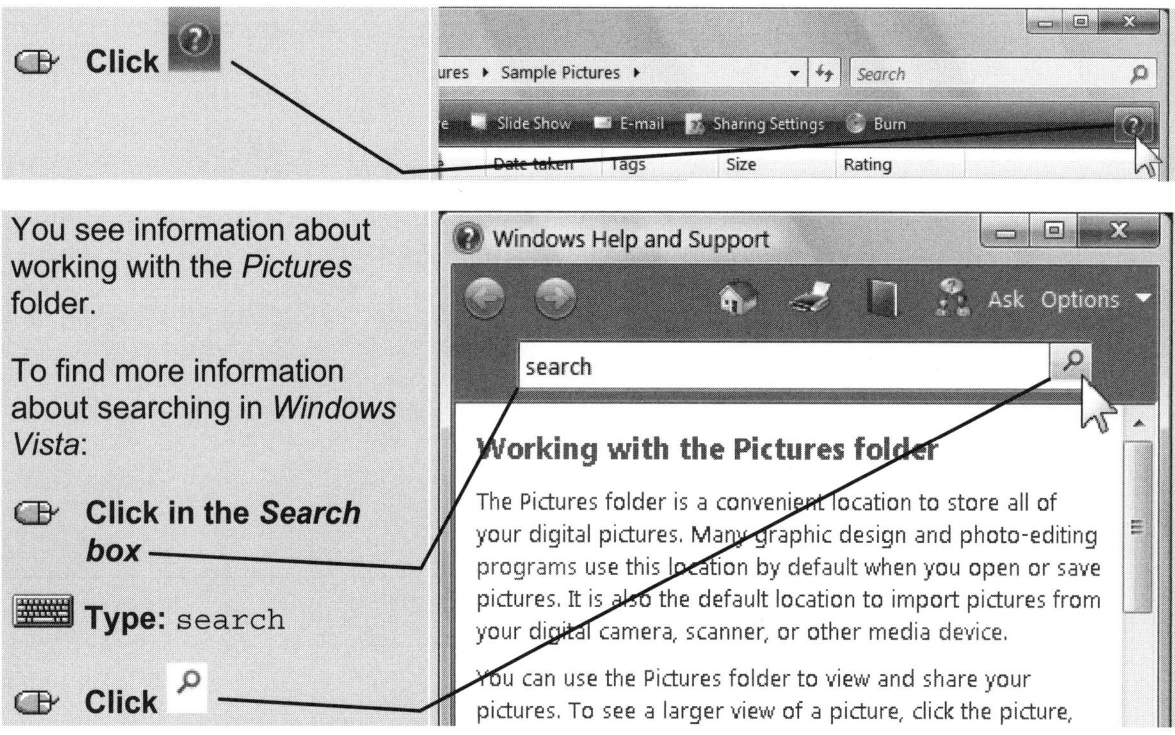

Click

You see information about working with the *Pictures* folder.

To find more information about searching in *Windows Vista*:

Click in the *Search* box

Type: `search`

Click

You see several articles that have something to do with the word 'search'. For example, read the article Tips for finding files.

Close the *Folder window*

In this chapter you have learned how to work with the *Folder window* in *Vista*. In the next chapter you will find information about backups, system recovery and burning CDs and DVDs.

3.24 Tips

Tip

Windows Vista demos

In the previous chapter you read about the video demonstrations in *Windows Help and Support*. There is also a demonstration available about working with files and folders. You can watch this demo now:

Click , Help and Support

At the top of the window:

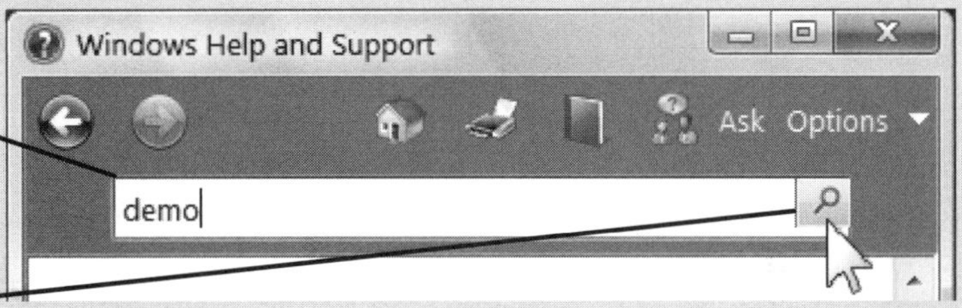

Type: `demo`

Click

In the search results:

Click Demo: Working with files and folders

In the next window:

Click → Watch the demo

The program *Windows Media Player* opens and the demo starts playing:

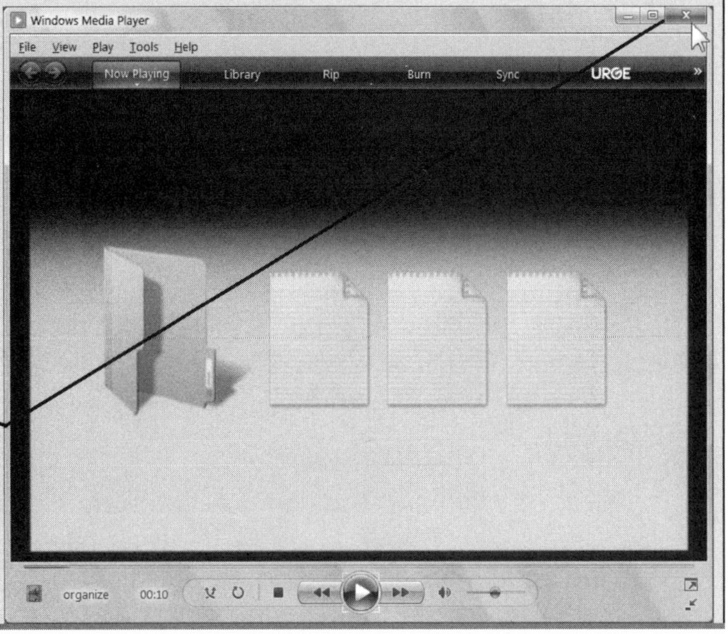

Watch the demo

To close *Windows Media Player*:

Click X

 **Tip**

The Search folder

There is another way to search files: the *Search folder*.

Using the *Search folder* is a good idea when:

- You do not know where a file or folder is located.
- You want the search results to include files from more than one folder, such as *Pictures* and *Music*.
- You want to search by using more than a single file name or file property.

To open the *Search folder*:

Click Search **in the *Start menu***

Start typing in the *Search Box*

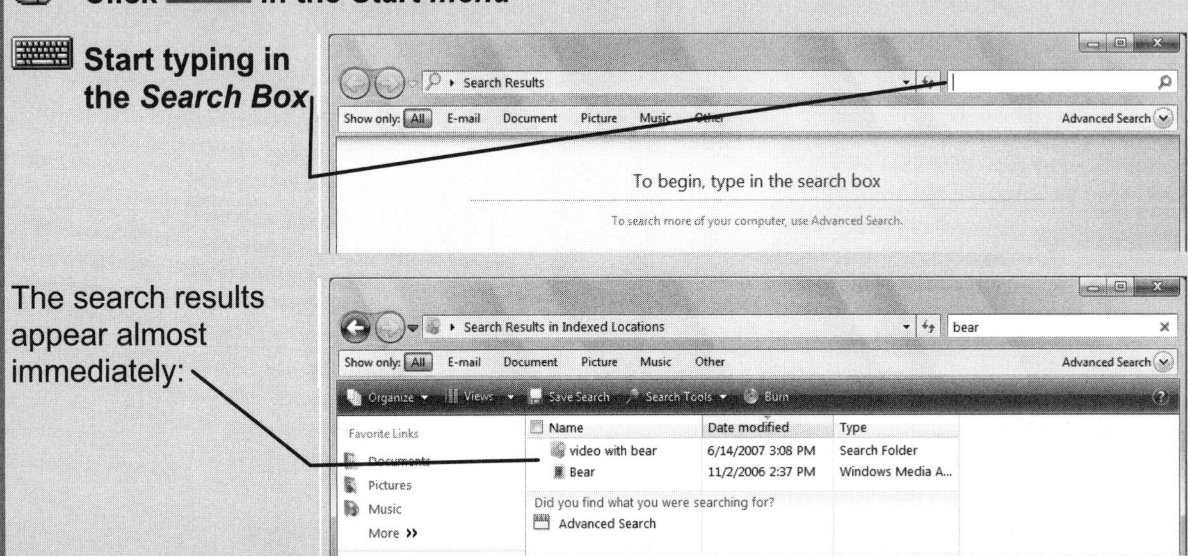

The search results appear almost immediately:

In the address bar you see Search Results in Indexed Locations. This means that only files in the *index* of *Windows* have been searched. The index contains detailed information on the files on your computer. The index is used by *Windows* to increase the search speed.

By default, the most common files on your computer are indexed. Indexed locations include all of the files in your *Personal Folder* (such as *Documents*, *Pictures*, *Music*, and *Videos*), as well as e-mail and offline files. Program files and system files are not indexed.

In *Windows Help and Support* you can read more about the index.

Use the search term 'index'. In the article Improve Windows searches using the index: frequently asked questions you can read more about adding locations or file types to the index.

Tip

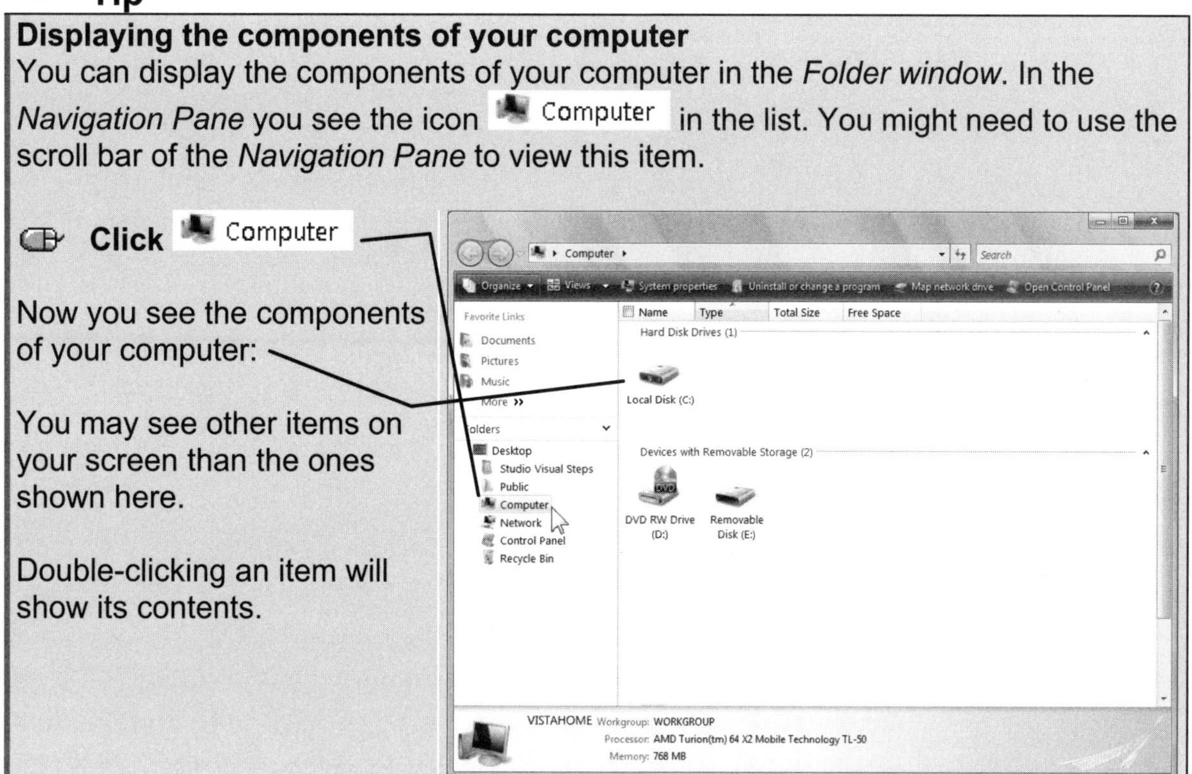

Displaying the components of your computer

You can display the components of your computer in the *Folder window*. In the *Navigation Pane* you see the icon Computer in the list. You might need to use the scroll bar of the *Navigation Pane* to view this item.

Click Computer

Now you see the components of your computer:

You may see other items on your screen than the ones shown here.

Double-clicking an item will show its contents.

Notes

Write down your notes here.

4. Backups, System Restore and Writing CD/DVD

Making backups (copies) of files has become increasingly important for computer users. More and more people store crucial information on their computer. Not only business projects or financial records, but also photos and videos. These days, most cherished memories and unforgettable moments are recorded with digital photo and video cameras.

Important advice: be sure to make regular backups of your files, because some day your computer may stop working. Maybe it will happen soon, because of a short-circuit in your computer or an aggressive virus attack. It may not happen until years from now, but eventually normal wear and tear will take its toll. When this happens, it is always unexpected. You probably will have no time left to rescue your data.

Microsoft recognizes the importance of good backup procedures. That is why *Windows Vista* has been equipped with new features to enable easy backups of large amounts of data. The possibilities to write data to CD or DVD have been extended and improved, for example with the introduction of a new file system.

In this chapter you will be introduced to the various possibilities *Windows Vista* offers to safeguard your data.

In this chapter you will learn:

- what a complete PC backup and a recovery CD are;
- how to create a complete PC backup;
- how to create a full backup;
- how to select the necessary files;
- how to set up an automatic backup;
- how to create and restore a system restore point;
- the difference between the file systems *Mastered* and *Live File System*;
- how to format a CD or DVD;
- how to write data to a CD or DVD.

4.1 Windows Complete PC Backup

Windows Vista Ultimate contains the program *Windows Complete PC Backup.* You can use this program to create a complete backup of your computer. Do you have *Vista Home Basic* or *Home Premium*? Then you can just read through this section.

Windows Complete PC Backup creates a backup image, which contains copies of your programs, system settings, and files. You can use this backup image to restore the contents of your computer if your hard disk crashes or your computer suddenly stops working. A complete backup is also known as a *recovery CD.*

To be able to create a *Windows Complete PC Backup* image, your hard disk must be formatted to use the *NTFS File System.* In *Windows Help and Support* you can find more information on this subject.

Open the *Control Panel* 3

Click Back up your computer

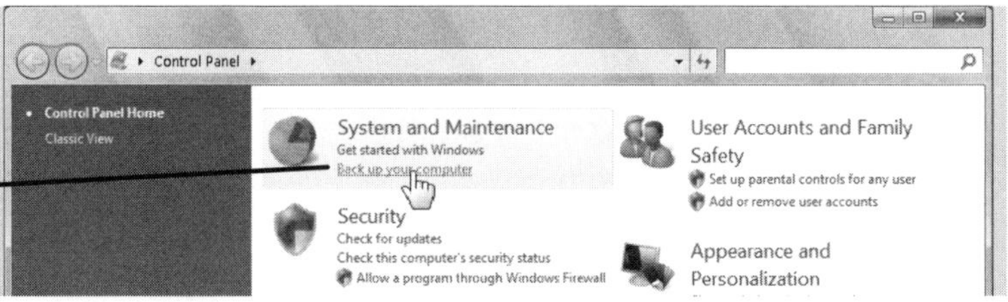

You see the window *Backup and Restore Center*.

In *Windows Vista Ultimate* you see this window with the option to create a *Complete PC Backup*:

Click Back up computer

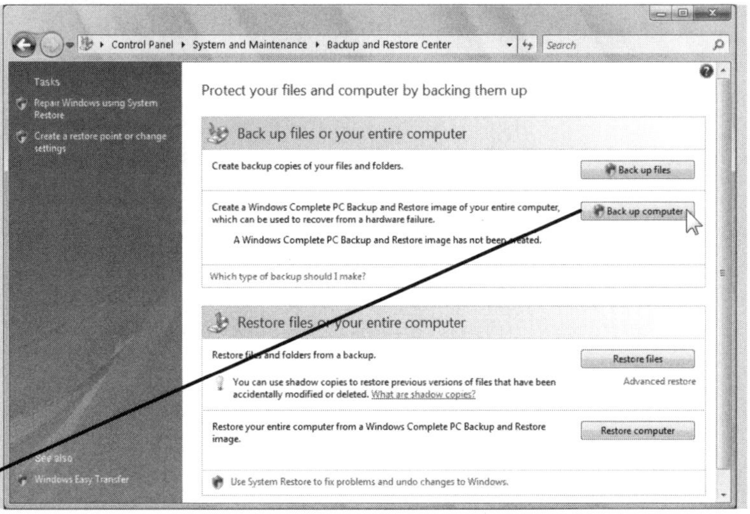

Your screen goes dark. You see the window *User Account Control* where you need to give your permission to continue.

Then you see the next window:

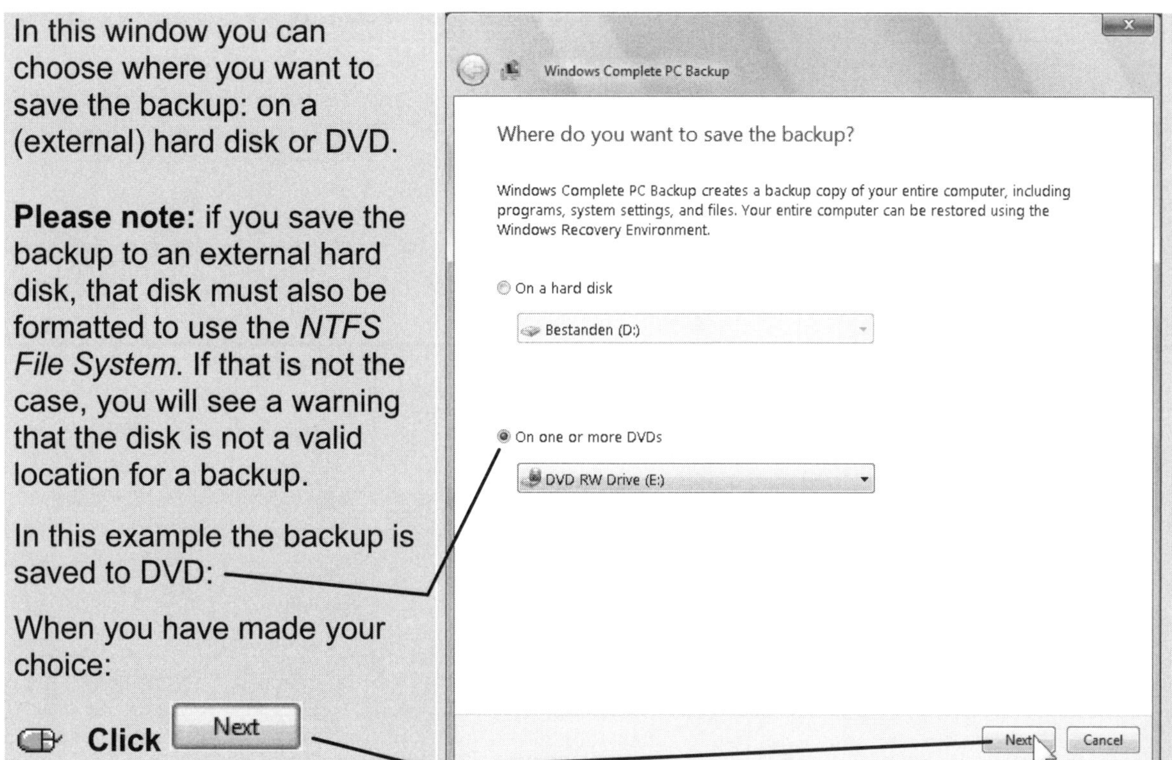

In this window you can choose where you want to save the backup: on a (external) hard disk or DVD.

Please note: if you save the backup to an external hard disk, that disk must also be formatted to use the *NTFS File System*. If that is not the case, you will see a warning that the disk is not a valid location for a backup.

In this example the backup is saved to DVD:

When you have made your choice:

Click Next

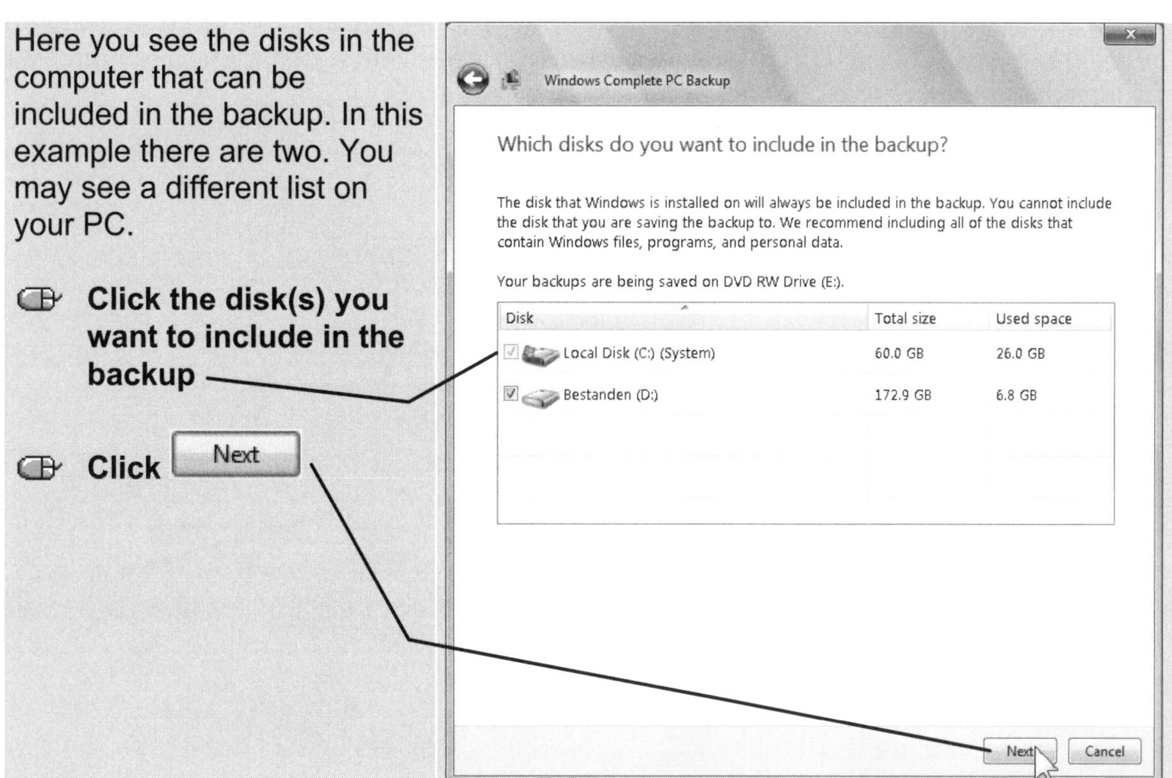

Here you see the disks in the computer that can be included in the backup. In this example there are two. You may see a different list on your PC.

Click the disk(s) you want to include in the backup

Click Next

In the next window you see how many DVDs you need for the complete backup. In this example the backup will take five to nine DVDs:

If you want to start creating the backup, click Start backup.

If you want to cancel the backup, click Cancel.

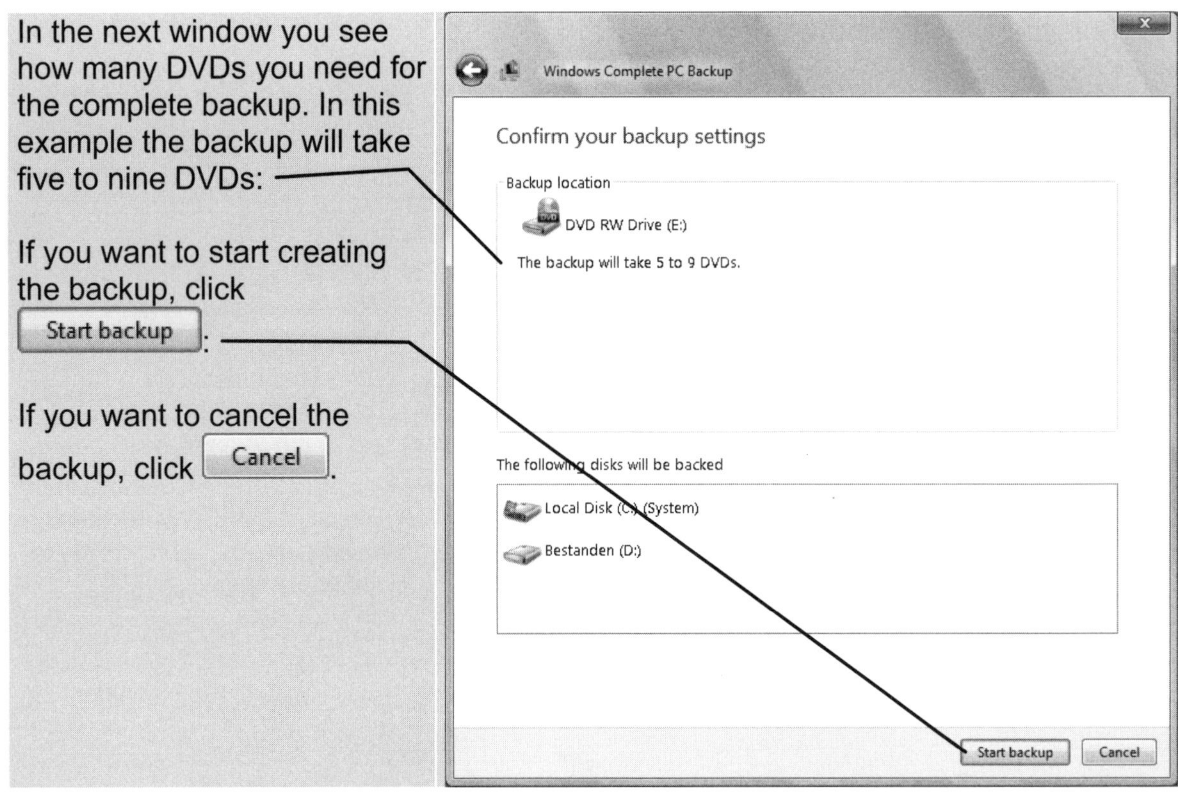

When you start the backup, a number of windows will guide you through this procedure. Follow the instructions in each window. At the end of the procedure you will have a number of DVDs or an external hard disk with a complete backup of your current system. Store this backup in a secure place.

If you ever need to restore the backup you can start the procedure from the *Backup and Restore Center*.

You can use the button Restore computer:

You will be guided through the procedure by a number of windows. Follow the instructions in each window.

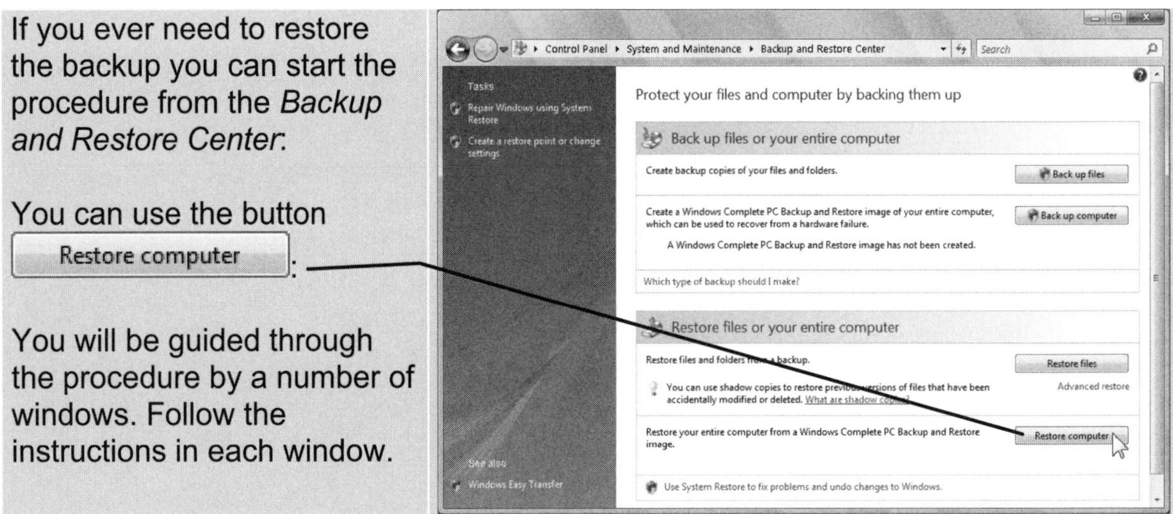

 **Please note:**

When you restore your computer from a *Windows Complete PC Backup* image, it is a complete restoration. You can not select individual items to restore, and all of your current programs, system settings, and files will be replaced.
It is important to make regular backups to secure your recent work, your photos etcetera. In the next sections you can read how to do that.

Windows Vista Home Basic and *Home Premium* do not facilitate a complete PC backup. However in some cases this is done automatically using a separate program that has been added by the computer manufacturer. This program will appear when you start the computer for the first time.
In that case follow the instructions in each window and store the backup in a secure place.

 **Close all windows**

4.2 Back Up and Restore Files

In the *Backup and Restore Center* of *Vista* you can create a backup of your own files.

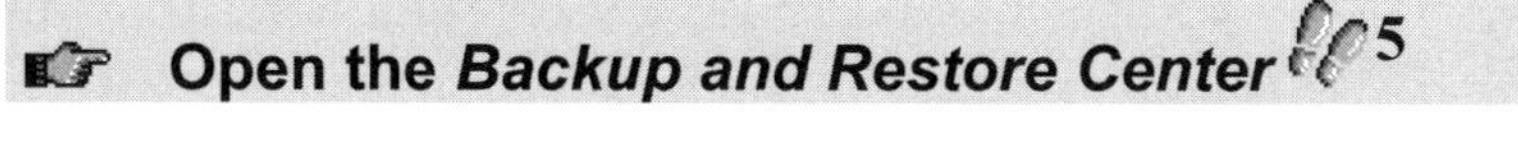

Open the *Backup and Restore Center* 5

Here you see the *Backup and Restore Center* in *Vista Home Premium.* The option *Complete PC Backup* is missing in this edition.

But it is possible to back up files and folders. This option is also available in *Vista Ultimate*.

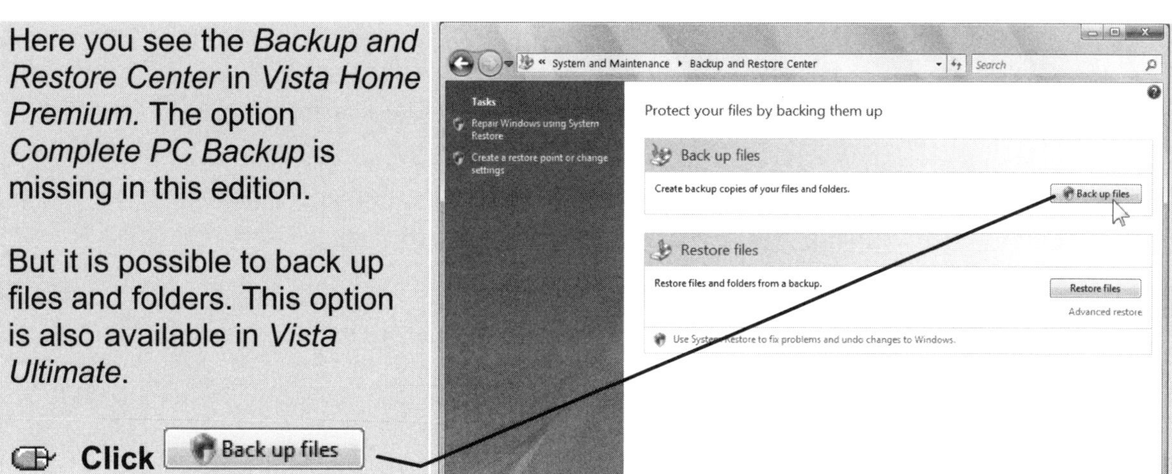

Click

Your screen goes dark. You see the window *User Account Control* where you need to give your permission to continue.

Click

HELP! I see an error message

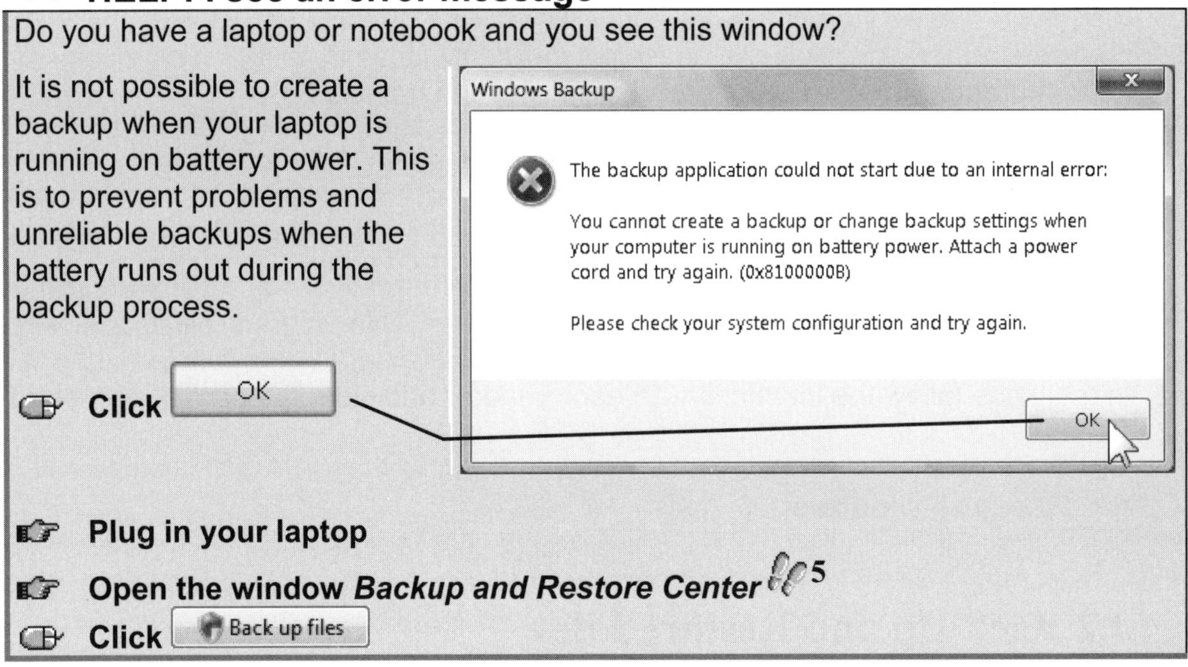

Do you have a laptop or notebook and you see this window?

It is not possible to create a backup when your laptop is running on battery power. This is to prevent problems and unreliable backups when the battery runs out during the backup process.

- **Click** OK

- **Plug in your laptop**
- **Open the window *Backup and Restore Center*** 5
- **Click** Back up files

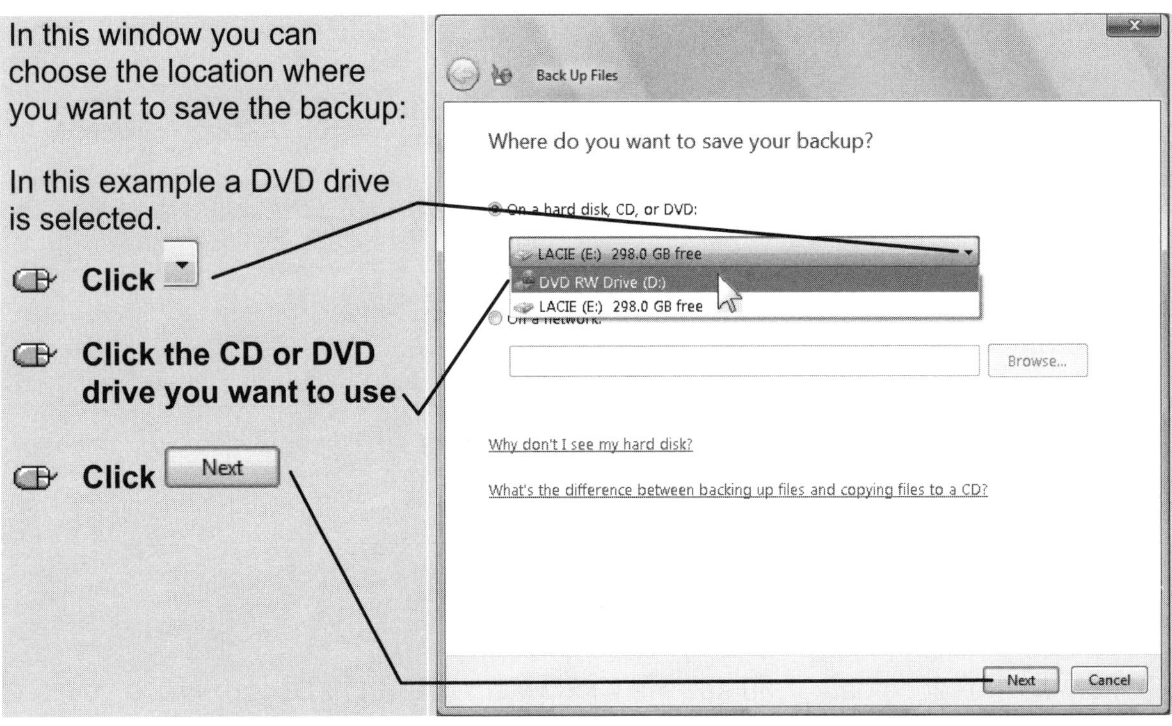

In this window you can choose the location where you want to save the backup:

In this example a DVD drive is selected.

- **Click** ▾
- **Click the CD or DVD drive you want to use**
- **Click** Next

Which location?

The available locations to save a backup depend on the setup of your computer. Take the following into account:

- It is not possible to save the backup to the same hard disk you are trying to back up. It is also not possible to save the backup to the hard disk *Windows Vista* is installed on. That makes sense, because in case of computer problems you will not be able to use both your original files and your backup.
- You can save a backup to another hard disk in your computer.
- If the hard disk has been divided in several partitions, it is possible to back up to another partition. It is not advisable to use this as your only backup, because it is still the same hard disk. In case of problems you will be unable to use this disk. Combine this method with regular backups to another location.
- You can not back up files to a USB stick. USB sticks are meant for temporary storage and are not suitable for backups.
- Backing up files to diskettes or tape drives is also not possible.

The most suitable storage media for backups are external hard disks, CDs or DVDs.

Here you see the disks in the computer that can be included in the backup. In this example there are two. You may see a different list on your PC.

Click the disk(s) you want to include in the backup

Click Next

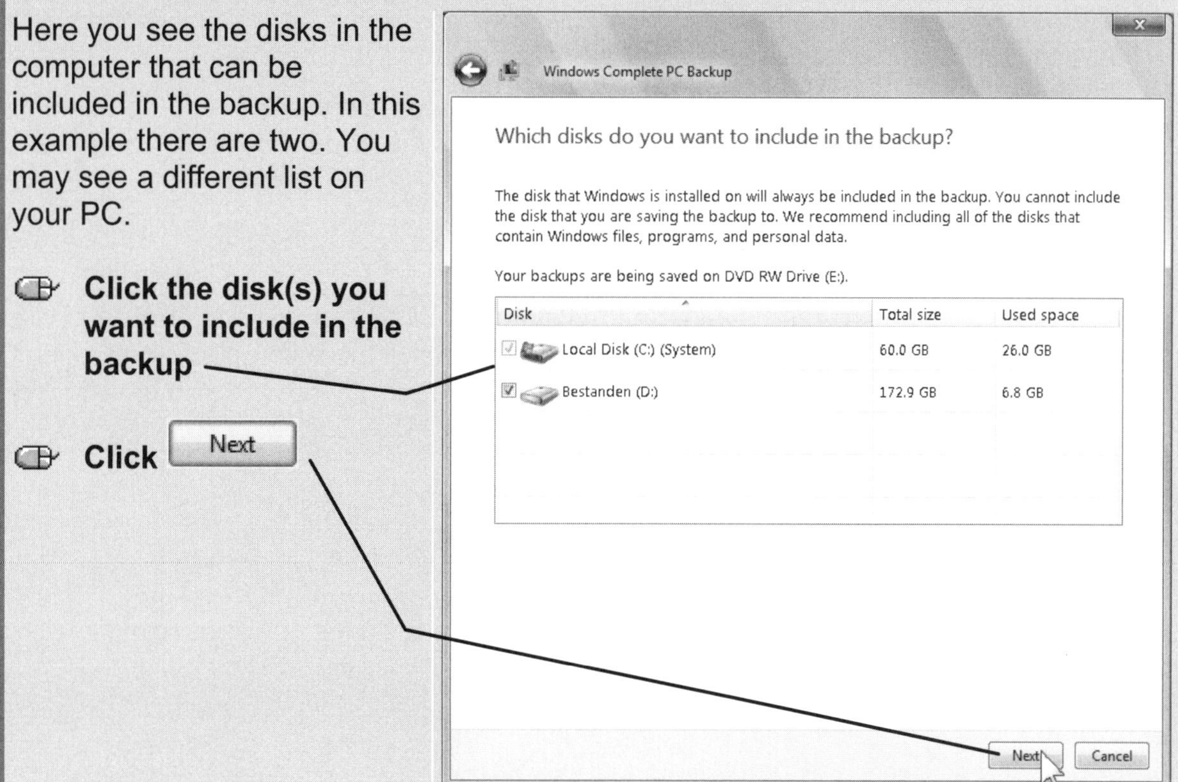

The wizard shows which file types will be included in the backup, regardless of where they are located on the hard disk:

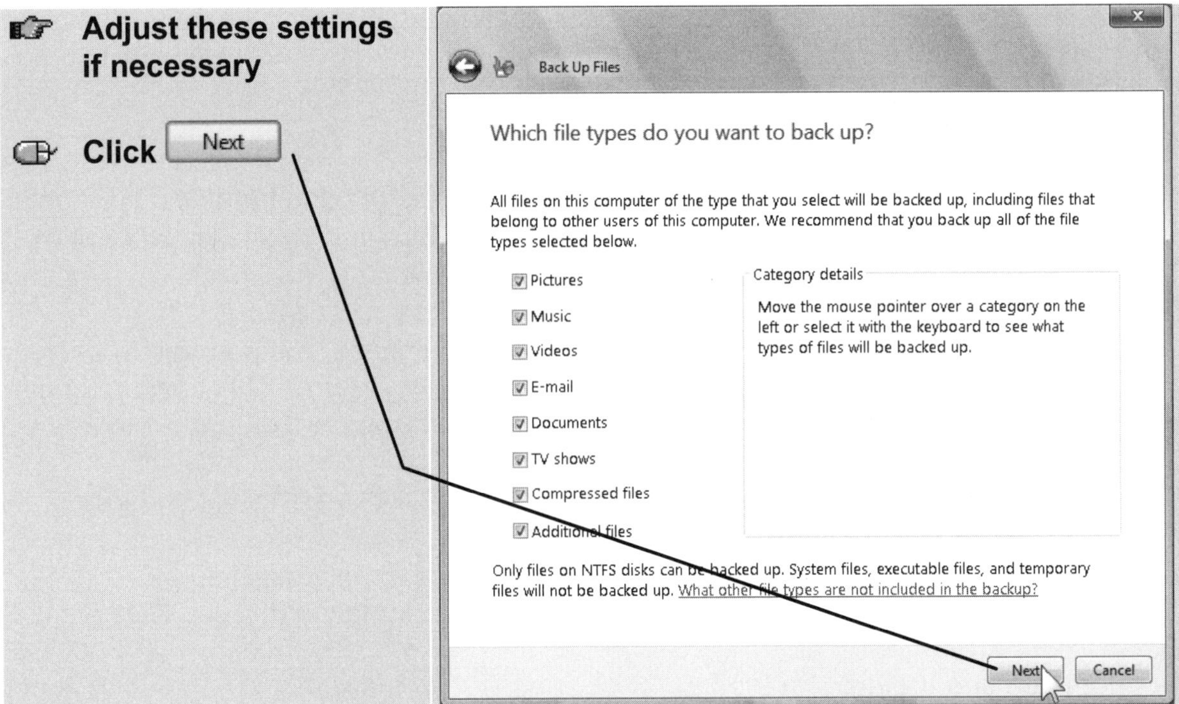

Backups should be created on a regular basis. In the next window you can select how often you want to create a backup. How often you should back up your files depends on how important they are and how often they change.

 **Please note:**

Automatic backups are not available in *Windows Vista Home Basic*. The next window will not be shown in this edition. You will have to make the backup yourself using the *Backup and Restore Center*. *Windows Vista* will frequently remind you to create a backup.

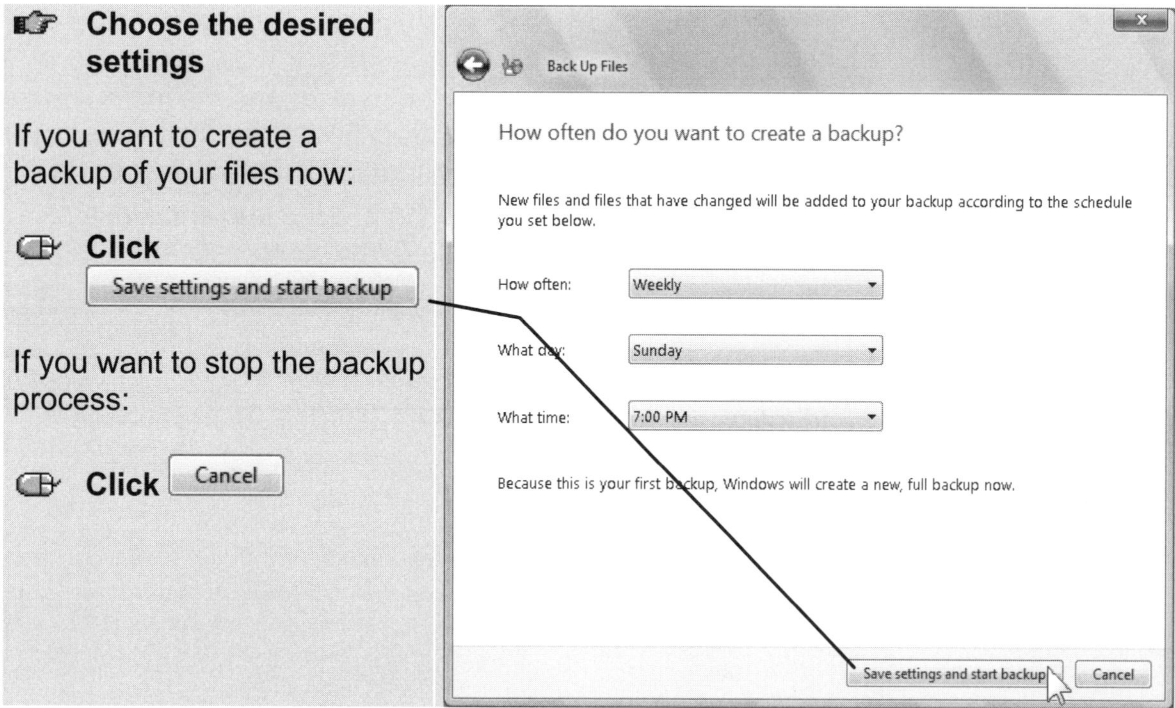

When you start the backup, you will be guided through the procedure by a number of windows. Follow the instructions in each window. If necessary, the DVD will be formatted during the procedure. While the backup is in progress you can continue to work on the computer. Do not turn off the computer during the backup procedure.

If it is necessary to interrupt the backup process, click Stop backup. When you open the *Backup and Restore Center* again, you can continue the process at the point where it was interrupted the last time. This will also happen when you have to interrupt the backup process because you have run out of the amount of CDs or DVDs necessary to save the files.

When you have made a backup schedule, the backup will be created automatically at the scheduled time. If the computer is not turned on at that time, the backup procedure will be started as soon as the computer is turned on.

The first time you start the backup procedure a new, full backup is created. The next time you can choose to limit the backup to the files that have been modified or added since the last backup. This is called an incremental backup and saves a lot of time and disk space.

Please note:

A full backup is not the same as the complete PC backup that was described in the previous section. In a full backup, *Windows* and all programs and settings are not backed up.

 **Tip**

To avoid having to store a lot of backup disks (the full backup and the incremental backups) it is advisable to create a full backup on a regular basis. Then you only need to store those disks and the incremental backup disks that follow. You can create a new full backup when you click Change settings in the *Backup and Restore Center*. There you can change the backup schedule for the automatic backups as well.

When it is necessary to restore a backup, you choose Restore files in the *Backup and Restore Center* and follow the instructions of the wizard. You can choose:

- which files and folders you want to restore;
- where you want to restore the files and folders;
- if you want to replace the original files.

☞ **Close all windows**

4.3 System Restore

Backing up your files helps to protect them from being lost or changed in the event of computer problems or accidental deletion. Sometimes, the installation of a program or a driver can cause an unexpected change to your computer or cause *Windows* to behave unpredictably. In that case your files are still intact, but *Windows* is not reliable anymore. Restoring a backup of your files does not solve that problem. Restoring a complete PC backup or recovery CD will make your computer work properly again, but you will lose all of your personal files.

System Restore creates automatic restore points to help you restore your computer's system files to an earlier point in time. These restore points contain information about registry settings and other system information that *Windows* uses. When *Windows Vista* no longer works properly, you can try restoring your computer's system to an earlier date when everything did work correctly. Usually this solves the problem.

System Restore was also available in *Windows XP* and has not changed much. *Windows Vista* creates automatic restore points every day, and also at important moments, for example when you install new programs or devices. At crucial moments you can also create restore points manually if necessary.

☞ **Open the *Backup and Restore Center*** 5

Click Create a restore point or change settings

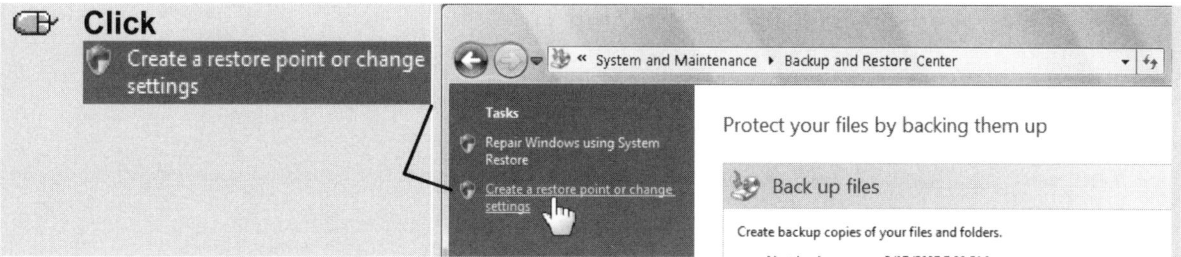

Your screen goes dark. You see the window *User Account Control* where you need to give your permission to continue.

Click Continue

Here you see when the last restore point was created:

Click Local Disk (C:) (System)

Usually this is the disk where *Vista* is installed.

Click Create...

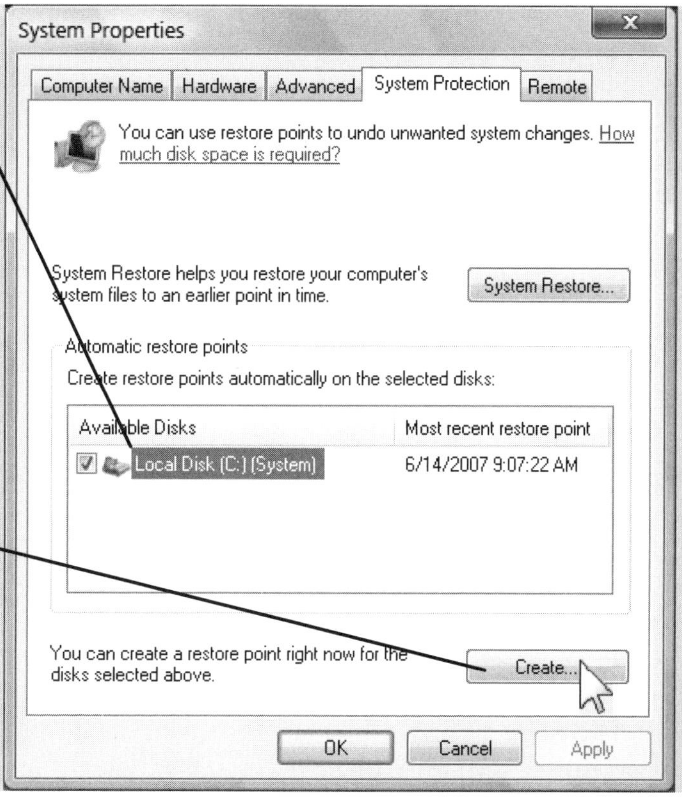

Type a name for the restore point

Click Create

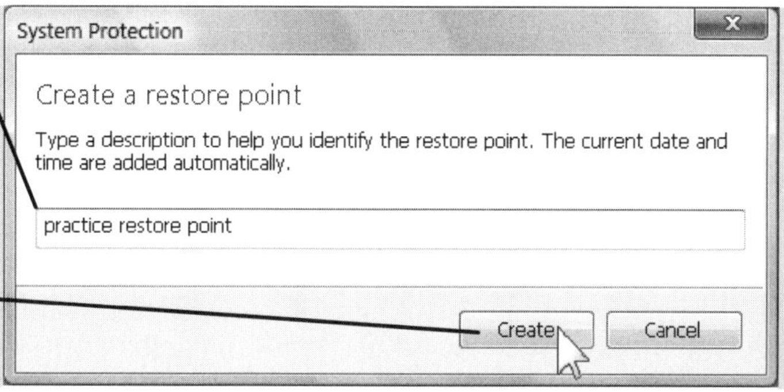

When the restore point has been created:

You see the *Backup and Restore Center* again. Here you can repair *Windows* using *System Restore*.

Please note:

When you use *System Restore* your computer will be restarted. Close all programs and save your work before you start *System Restore*.

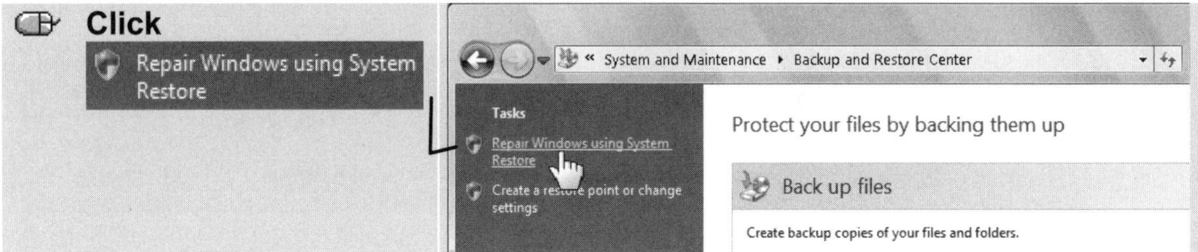

Your screen goes dark. You see the window *User Account Control* where you need to give your permission to continue.

After a few moments the *Wizard System restore* starts:

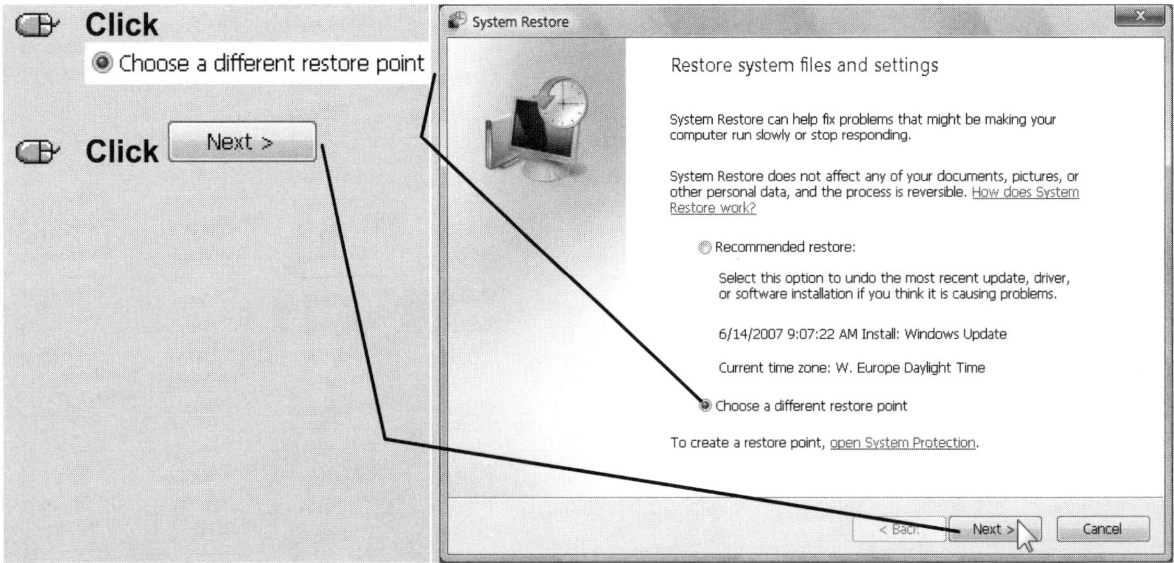

Click the restore point you want to use

Click Next >

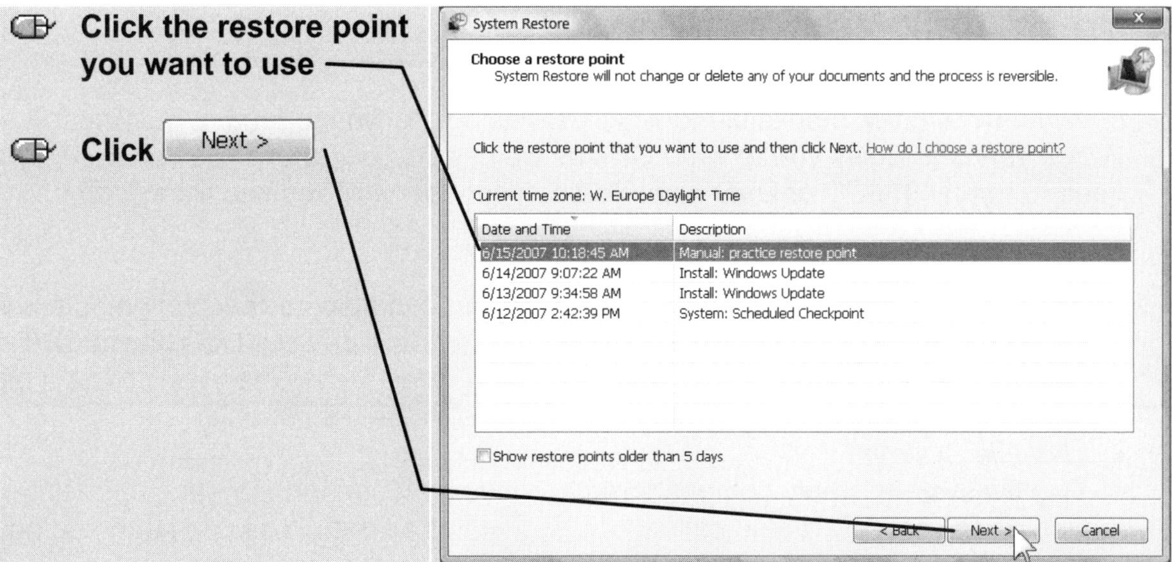

In the next window:

Click Finish

System Restore asks you for a confirmation:

Click Yes

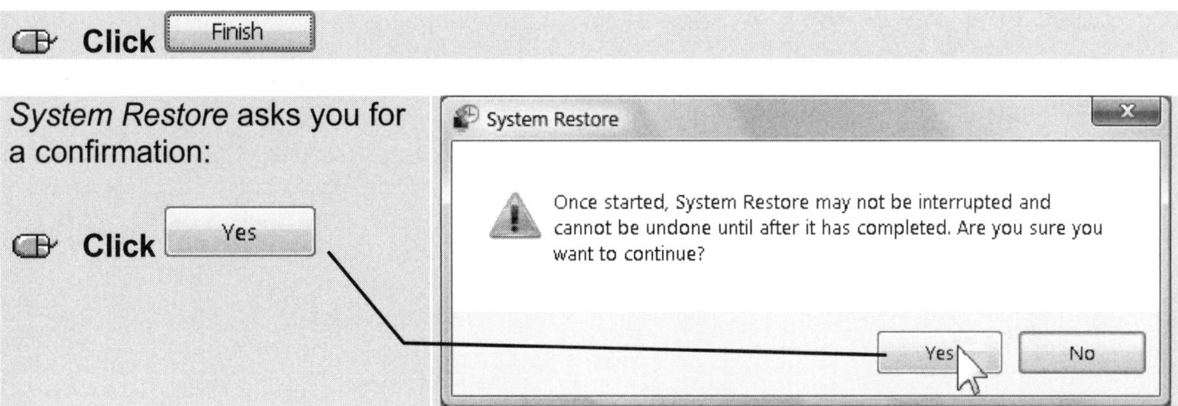

When your system has been restored, *Windows Vista* is restarted. Then you see this message:

Click Close

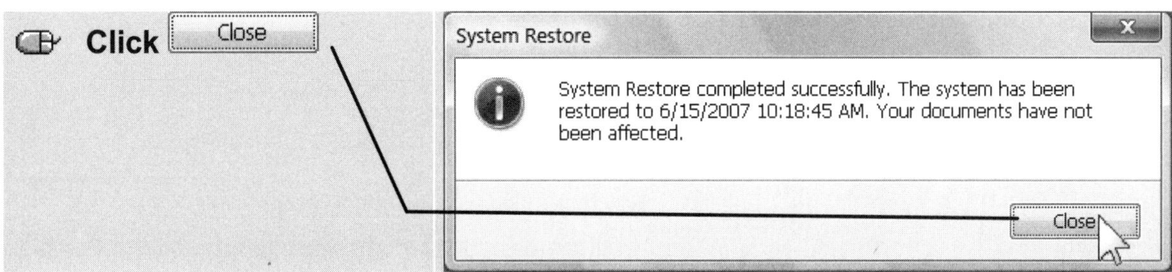

In most cases *Windows* will now function normally again.

4.4 Writing CDs and DVDs

In *Windows XP* it was possible to write CDs using the writing feature in *Windows. Windows Vista* allows you to write CDs as well as DVDs. Before you can do that, you need to format the CD or DVD disc. You can choose between two file systems:

- *Mastered*
  The CD or DVD you write using this file system can also be read in computers with older versions of *Windows* (before *Windows XP*) and devices like CD and DVD players that are able to read digital music and video files. When you create a disc using this file system you need to write all files to the disc at once.
- *Live File System*
  This file system is only compatible with *Windows Vista* and *Windows XP*. Writing files on CD or DVD is also called 'copying' in this system. You can keep adding files to a *Live File System* disk by dragging them to the disc folder.

By default *Windows Vista* selects the *Live File System*, but you can make your own choice when you format the disc.

Insert a new blank CD or DVD in the CD or DVD writer

In this example a DVD is used.

You see the next window:

Click

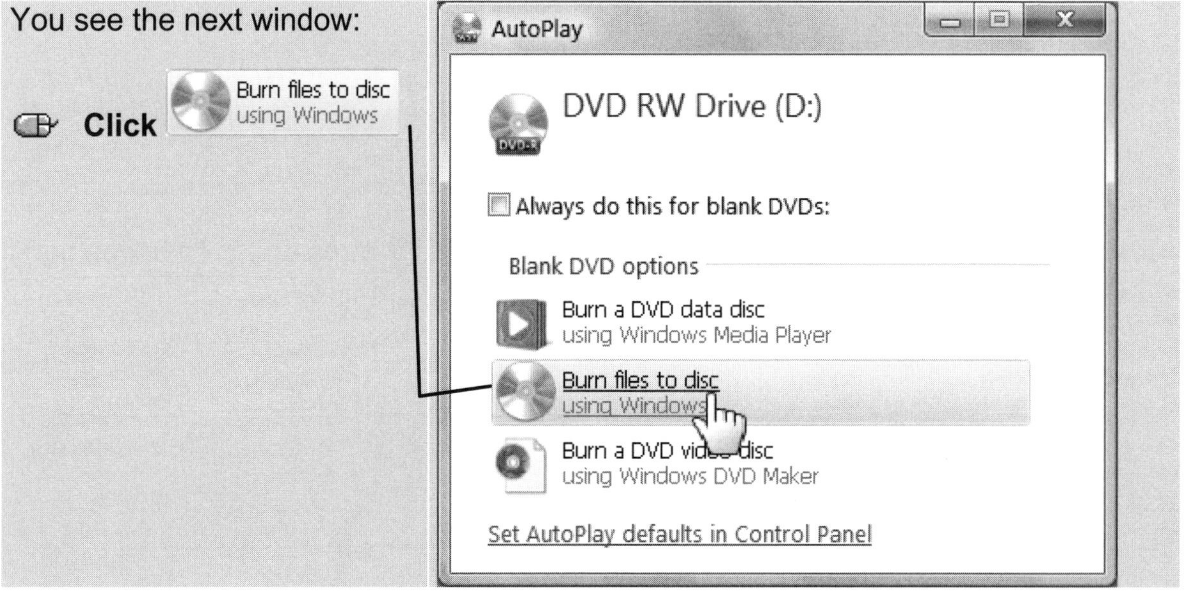

Type a name for this disc

Click next to
Show formatting options

You see the options with short explanations:

To read more about file systems:

Click
Which CD or DVD format should I ch

In the window of *Windows Help and Support* you see an article about the differences between the file systems. Read through the information. Then you can close the window:

The file system *Mastered* corresponds to the file system you used in *Windows XP*. The biggest difference is that you can write DVDs now as well.

The file system *Live File System* is new and works differently:

Click 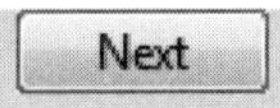
Next

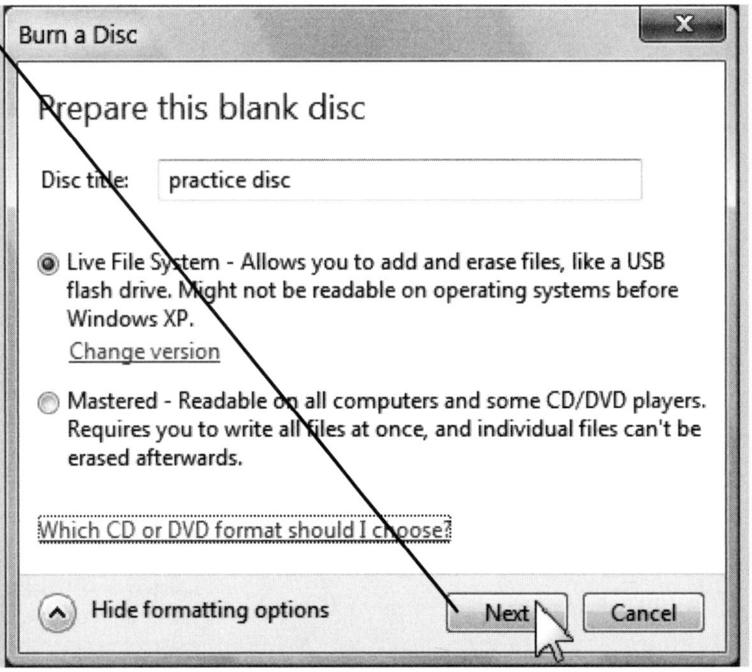
Burn a Disc
Prepare this blank disc
Disc title: practice disc
Live File System - Allows you to add and erase files, like a USB flash drive. Might not be readable on operating systems before Windows XP.
Change version
Mastered - Readable on all computers and some CD/DVD players. Requires you to write all files at once, and individual files can't be erased afterwards.
Which CD or DVD format should I choose?
Hide formatting options
Next
Cancel

During the formatting process you see this window:

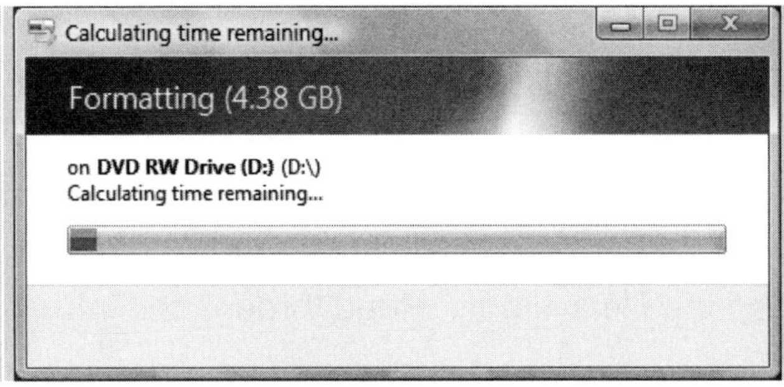
Calculating time remaining...
Formatting (4.38 GB)
on DVD RW Drive (D:) (D:\)
Calculating time remaining...

The folder window is opened. Here you can select the files you want to copy to the formatted disc:

Click
Pictures

Double-click
Sample Pictures

Studio Visual Steps
Pictures
Search
Organize
Views
Slide Show
Burn
Favorite Links
Documents
Pictures
Music
Name
Date taken
Tags
Size
Rating
Sample Pictures
Folders
Desktop
Studio Visual Steps
Contacts

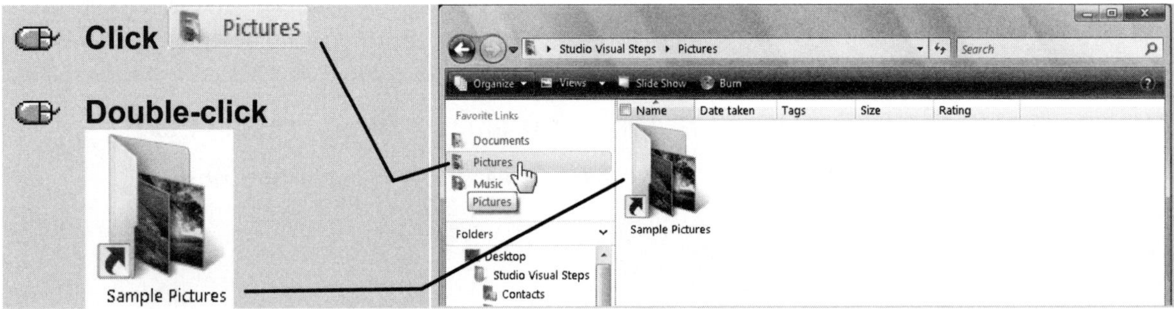

Please note:

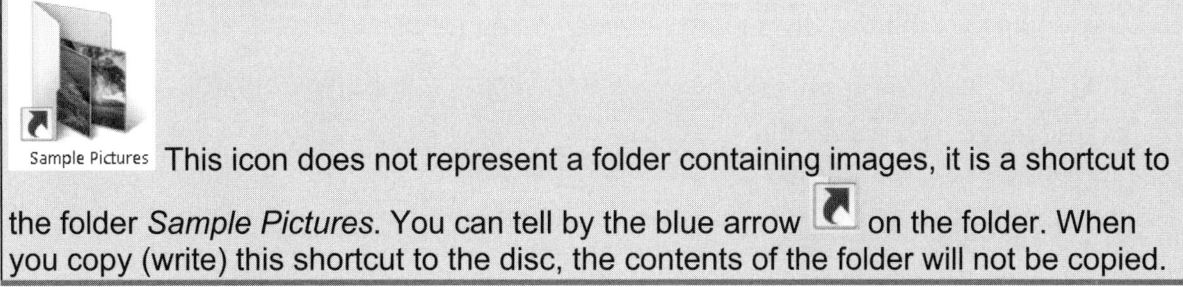

This icon does not represent a folder containing images, it is a shortcut to the folder *Sample Pictures*. You can tell by the blue arrow on the folder. When you copy (write) this shortcut to the disc, the contents of the folder will not be copied.

You see the images in the folder *Sample Pictures*. Now you can select the files you want to copy to the disc:

Tip

If you activated the check box feature in the previous chapter, you can select the images using the check boxes.

Discs formatted with *Live File System* allow you to copy files to the disc at any time, instead of copying (writing) them all at once like you had to do in *Windows XP* and with the *Mastered* file system.

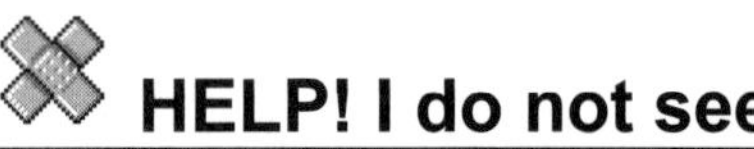

HELP! I do not see Burn

Depending on the display settings of your computer it is possible that you do not see the button Burn when you have selected one or more files or folders.

In that case, click » on the right side of the toolbar to show the button Burn:

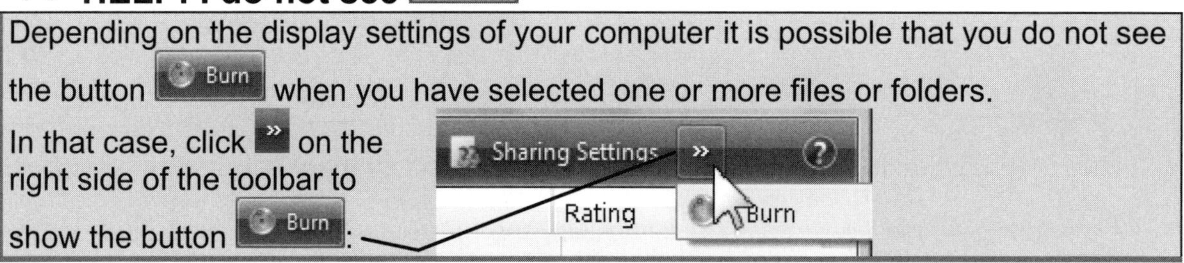

The files are written to the disc right away. You can write a complete folder the same way.

When the copying is done the contents of the disc are displayed:

In the address bar of the folder window you can check from the location of these contents:

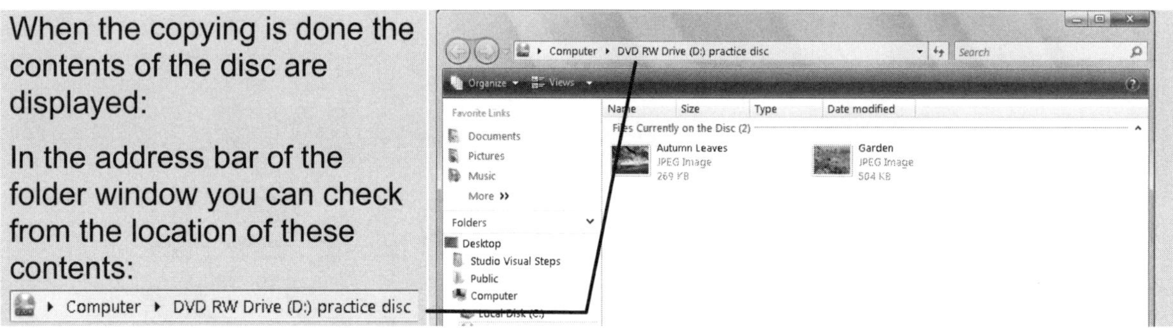

You can add more files to this disc later.

Tip

Formatting a CD Rewritable (CD-RW) or DVD Rewritable (DVD-RW) using the *Live File System* allows you to delete files or folders from the CD or DVD. Just select the file or folder and press Delete or right-click it and select Delete. Rewritable discs are special discs on which files can be copied, erased, and replaced.

Close all windows

Next time, you can add a file or folder to this preformatted disc like this:

Open the *Folder window Pictures*

In this *Folder window* you select the files you want to copy to the disc.

Then you click Burn again:

 **Close the window**

Live File System discs are very convenient. You can copy the selected files right away and as often as you want, just like you can when using a diskette or USB stick. A disadvantage of *Live File System* discs is that they are not compatible with older computers and devices.

Tip

Writing with the Mastered file system

Writing files or folders on a CD or DVD using the *Mastered* file system is done the same way. The only difference is that the files are placed in a queue first. You write the complete list of selected files to the disc at once:

Click Burn to disc

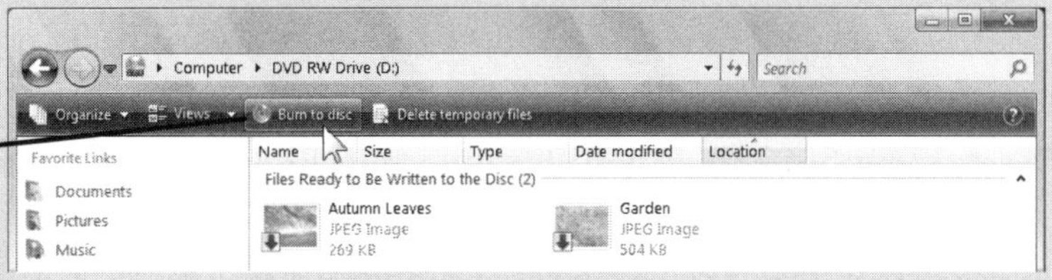

The disc is prepared when you start the writing process:

Click Next

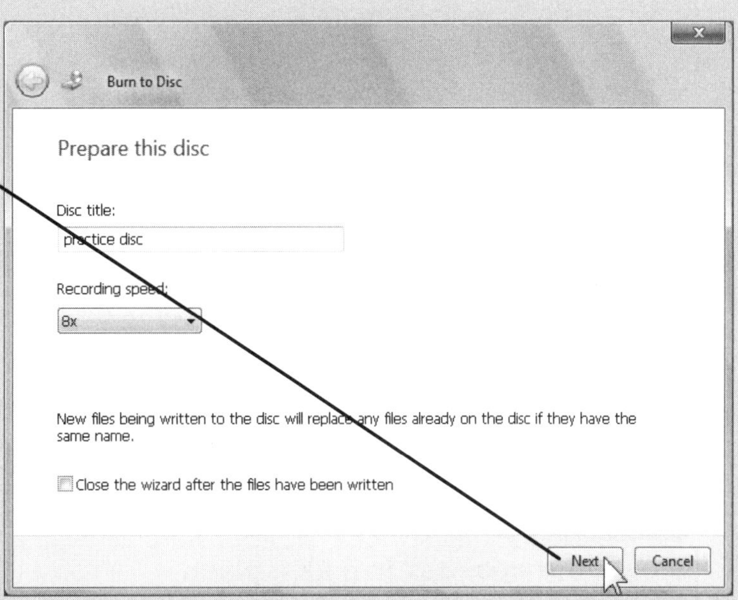

Please note: when you use the *Mastered* file system the data is stored in a temporary folder until you write the disc. Consequently, you will need extra free space on your hard disk when you use this file system, varying between 650 MB for a CD and 8.5 GB for a dual layer DVD.

In the next window you click Yes.

When the writing process is finished, the drawer of your disc writer is opened and you can finish the process by clicking Finish.

In this chapter you have learned to create backups, use *System Restore* and writing CDs or DVDs. In the next chapter you will be introduced to the improved *Ease of Access* feature.

4.5 Background Information

Grandfather - father - son backups
Even if you create backups on a regular basis things can go wrong. You can end up being unable to use your original data as well as your backup. For example when a malfunction occurs during the backup process. Or when you infect the backup with a virus that has not yet been discovered on your computer. Then both your original files as well as the backup will be infected.

To warrant the reliability of your backups, you can save different generations of backups on rewritable discs. This is done as follows:

- You start by making a full backup you call the *grandfather.*
- Some time later, for example a week or a month, you create another full backup on a new set of discs you call the *father*. You also keep the *grandfather*.
- The next time you create a new full backup you call the *son*. You also keep the *grandfather* and *father*.
- Then the next time you create a full backup on the *grandfather* discs, then on the *father* discs and finally on the *son* discs.

When something goes wrong during the backup process, or the backup contains an error or a virus, you can always go back two generations. This increases the chance of having a reliable backup. Do not make the interval between the generations too short, for example use intervals of a week or a month. In between these full backups, you create the regular incremental backups.

Store your backups in a safe place
You can also lose your data as a result of fire or theft. Always keep one set of backup discs outside your own home when you keep important data on your computer. And make sure to renew that backup regularly as well.

Creating a backup or copying files for other uses

You can safeguard your data by creating backups or by copying files to another disc. What is best in your situation depends on the type of data and the things you want to do with the data:

- If you want to create a safety copy of (all) your data that you can use to restore your computer if necessary, it is best to create a backup. A backup file is always compressed and takes up less space.
- If you want to copy data so you can use it on another computer, it is best to copy it to a separate CD or DVD. A backup CD or DVD is not always readable on another computer, especially when that computer works with another version of *Windows*.
- If you want to put a couple of files or folders on a disc, for example to be able to show your holiday photos at work, you need to collect these files yourself and copy them to a CD or DVD.
- It is best to copy data you want to keep for a longer time, like wedding pictures, your bookkeeping or important documents, to a separate CD or DVD. That way these files are easily accessible on any computer you might want to use.

To summarize: backups are made for security reasons. If you want to use the files for activities other than restoring your computer (share, show etcetera) it is better to write a separate CD or DVD. If you want to use the disc in other computers or devices it may be necessary to use the *Mastered* file system.

Audio or video CDs/DVDs

To be able to play music and movies in a CD or DVD player the disc and the files on it should have a specific format. It is best to use special audio or video programs to write CDs or DVDs that can be played in a standalone DVD player.

With *Windows Photo Gallery* you can create a slideshow of your own pictures and write it to a DVD video disc. With *Windows Movie Maker* you can create a movie using your own video files and write it to a DVD video disc. With *Windows Media Player* you can write audio CDs using music files you have stored on your computer. For more information on how to use these programs, see **More Windows Vista for SENIORS**, ISBN 978 90 5905 055 6.

Choosing between Live File System or Mastered
What choice to make, depends on what you want to do with the written CD or DVD disc.

***Live File System* discs:**

- You can copy (write) files by dragging them to the disc.
- Are convenient if you want to leave a disc in your computer's writer and copy files to it at your convenience.
- Are convenient because there is no time-consuming queuing and writing process like you have with *Mastered* discs. Each file is copied to the disc as soon as you drag it to the disc folder.
- When you use a rewritable disc like a CD-RW, DVD-RW or DVD-RAM you can delete separate files or format the disc to free disc space.
- Possibly need to be **closed*** before they can be used on other computers.
- Are only compatible with *Windows XP* and newer versions of *Windows.*

***Mastered* discs:**

- Do not copy files immediately, meaning you need to select the entire collection of files that you want to copy to the disc, and then write them all at once.
- Are convenient if you want to write a large collection of files, such as an audio CD.
- Are compatible with older computers and devices such as CD and DVD players.
- You need a large amount of hard disk space to be able to write a *Mastered* disc (as much as the capacity of the disc you are going to write).

* Before you can use a recordable disc (such as CD-R, DVD-R, or DVD+R) formatted with the *Live File System* format in other computers and devices, you need to **close** the current disc session to prepare the disc for use. By default, *Windows* closes your disc automatically when it is ejected by pressing *the Eject button* on the disc drive. Closing the disc can take a few minutes and requires 20 MB disk space.

After you close a disc session, you can still add additional files to the disc. But you must close each additional session to be able to use the disc on another computer.

Please note: some programs might **finalize** your disc instead of closing the current session. You can not add any additional files to a disc that has been finalized.

Source: *Windows Help and Support*

5. How to Make Working with Your Computer More Pleasant

Just like in *Windows XP* you can change many of the settings in *Vista* to make working with your computer more pleasant. For example, you can adjust the font and the text size to increase readability for all windows, menus and other screen elements.

Perhaps, when you bought a new computer you deliberately chose a larger size monitor, thinking this would mean larger sized windows. But a larger monitor does not necessarily mean larger windows. Fortunately, there are various ways to fine tune the look and feel of *Windows Vista* so it is just the way you want.

You can experiment with new settings, adjust them as often as you like, making it easier for you to use your computer. If you do not like the result, the new settings can be just as easily returned to their original state.

For some adjustments you need to have certain user privileges (administrator rights) on the computer. If you logged on to the computer you are working on now as a *Guest*, your ability to adjust settings will be limited. For settings that require administrator permissions, *Windows* will ask for an administrator password or show a message saying you do not have the correct permissions. If you do not have an administrator password you can just read through that section.

In this chapter you will learn:

- to adjust the DPI setting of the monitor;
- to change the desktop background;
- how to work with the *Ease of Access Center*.

5.1 Change the Size of Text and Icons

Not everybody is happy with the readability of (small or large) monitors. For example the standard size of the text used for menus and buttons may be too small for some people. You can specify a different text size like this:

Make sure you have logged on using an administrator account

If necessary, read the information on this subject in chapter 8.

Open the *Control Panel* 3

Click Ease of Access

Click Optimize visual display

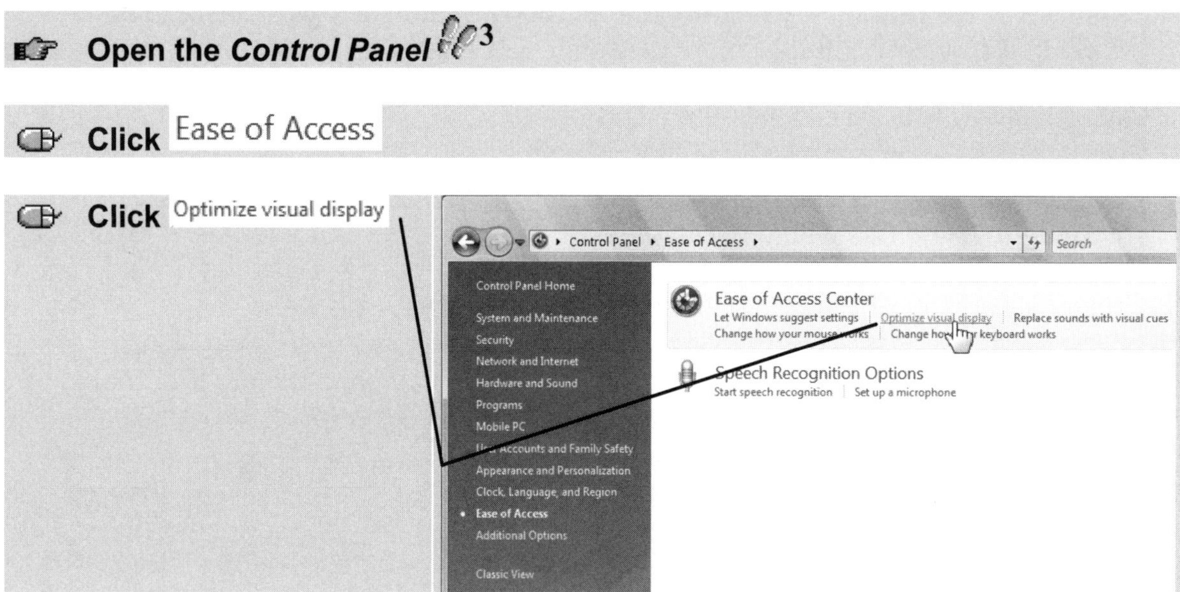

Click Change the size of text and icons

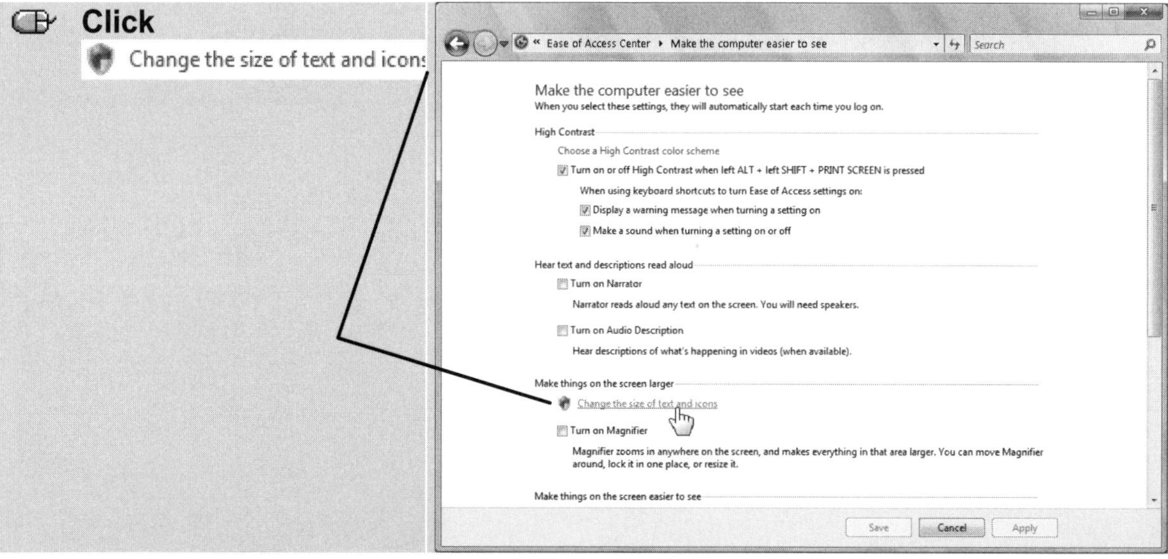

Your screen goes dark and the window *User Account Control* appears. By asking for permission in a separate window, *Windows Vista* prevents unwanted changes to your computer.

Give permission to continue:

Click Continue

User Account Control
Windows needs your permission to continue
If you started this action, continue.
DPI Scaling Control Panel
Microsoft Windows
Details
Continue
Cancel
User Account Control helps stop unauthorized changes to your computer.

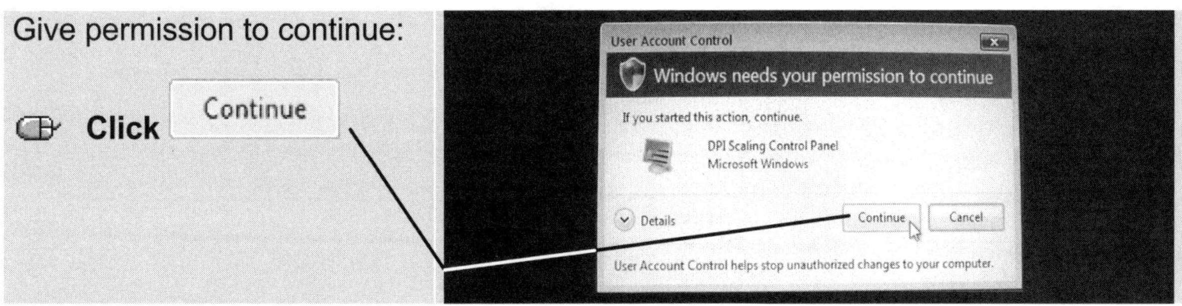

The default scale is 96 DPI (Dots Per Inch):

DPI Scaling
DPI Scaling
Choose a smaller scale to fit more information on the screen or a larger scale to make text more readable. How do I know which DPI to choose?
Default scale (96 DPI) - fit more information
Larger scale (120 DPI) - make text more readable

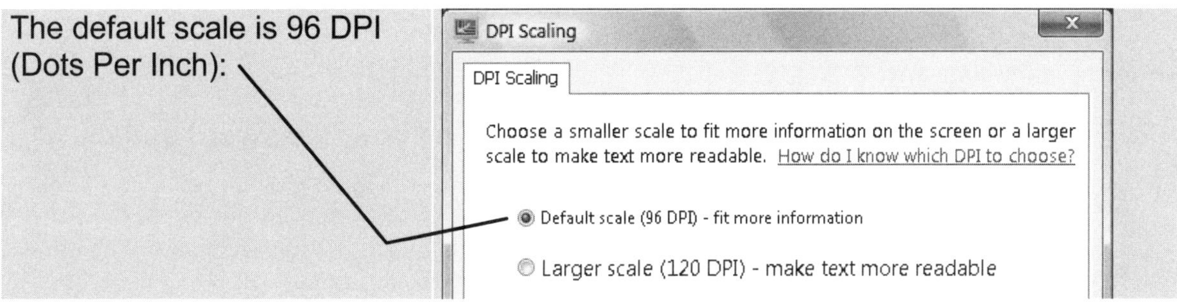

Click Larger scale (120 DPI)

Click OK

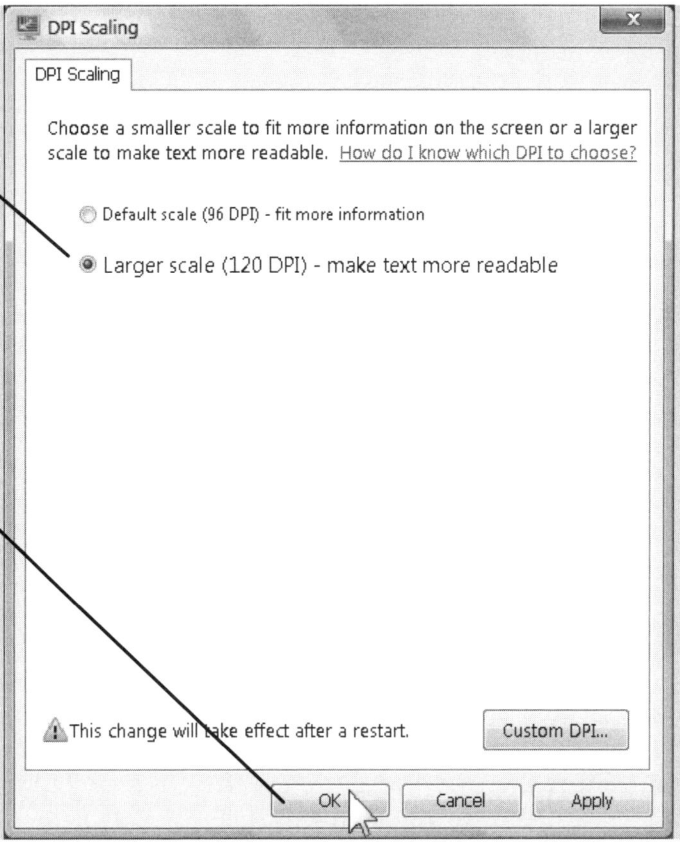

DPI Scaling
DPI Scaling
Choose a smaller scale to fit more information on the screen or a larger scale to make text more readable. How do I know which DPI to choose?
Default scale (96 DPI) - fit more information
Larger scale (120 DPI) - make text more readable
This change will take effect after a restart.
Custom DPI...
OK
Cancel
Apply

To apply these changes you must restart your computer:

Click Restart Now

Close the *Control Panel* 3

Your computer will restart now.

If necessary, click your account name, type your password and click 

Close the *Welcome Center*

Open the *Start menu*

The *Start menu* window has been enlarged. The larger text makes the *Start menu* more readable:

Comparing the different sizes of the *Start menus*:

On the left side you see the *Start menu* in the 120 DPI setting and on the right side in 96 DPI setting:

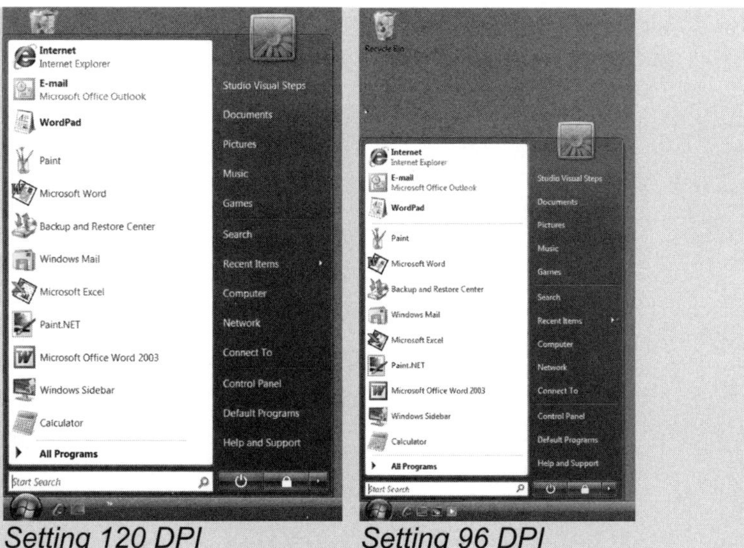

Setting 120 DPI Setting 96 DPI

Would you like to go back to the original setting?

Start the section *Change the Size of Text and Icons* from the beginning and change back to the default settings - 96 DPI

HELP! Part of the image is missing

Nine out of ten programs will work with the larger scale 120 DPI setting. However, it is possible some older programs will not display properly or parts of the program appear off screen. When this happens, you will need to close the program and select the original 96 DPI setting.

Sometimes it is not possible to close a program because the buttons  are not displayed on your screen. You can always close a program by pressing the  Alt and  F4 keys on your keyboard at the same time.

5.2 A Different Background

If you do not like the default *Vista* background on your desktop, you can easily select a different one. Access to this setting and all of the corresponding windows are very user friendly in *Vista*. Take a look now:

Open the *Control Panel* 3

Look for the category  Appearance and Personalization:

Click Change desktop background

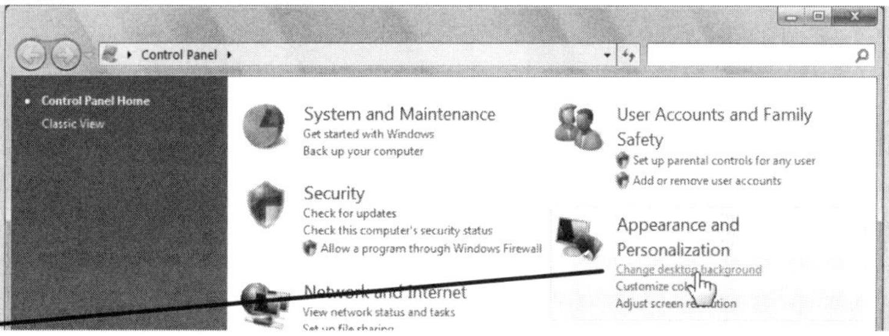

The *Choose a desktop background* window appears:

Drag the scroll bar up and down

You see many pictures.

Click

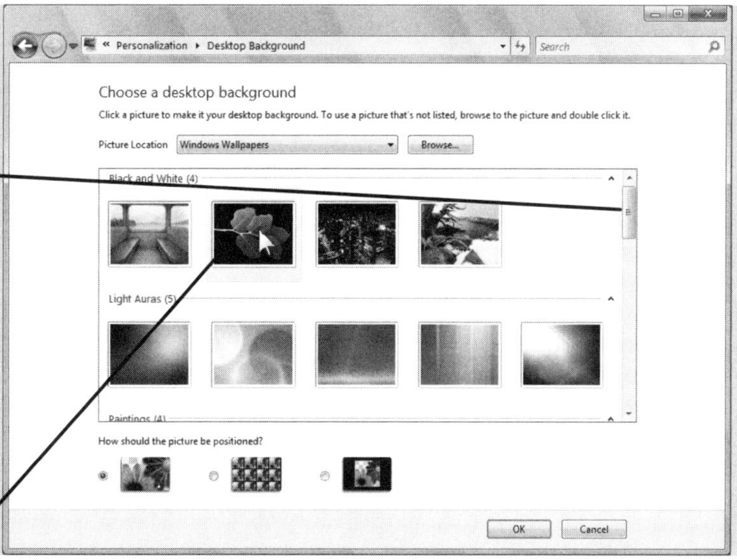

The new background picture is applied instantly:

Next to the *Start button* you find a special icon to display the desktop:

Click

You see the new background:

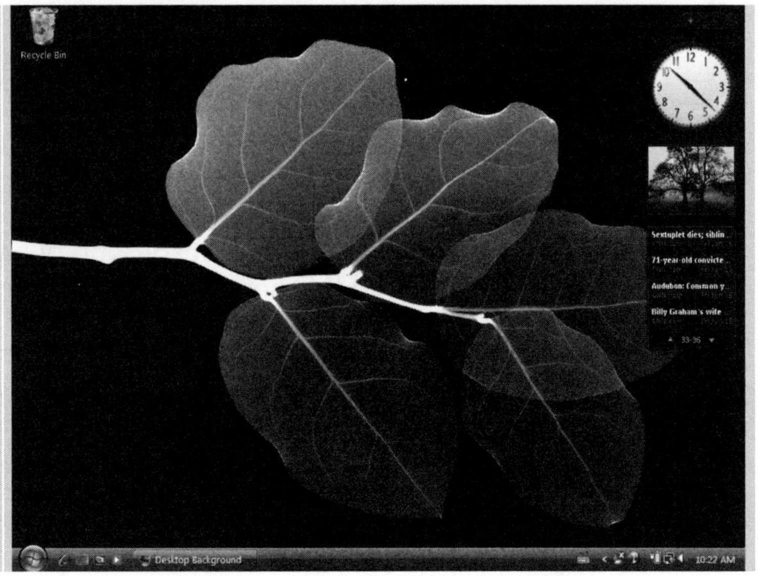

Open the *Choose a background* window using the taskbar button

If the photo that was applied as your desktop background is too distracting for you, you might want to select a solid color instead. You do this as follows:

Click Windows Wallpapers

A menu appears:

Click Solid Colors

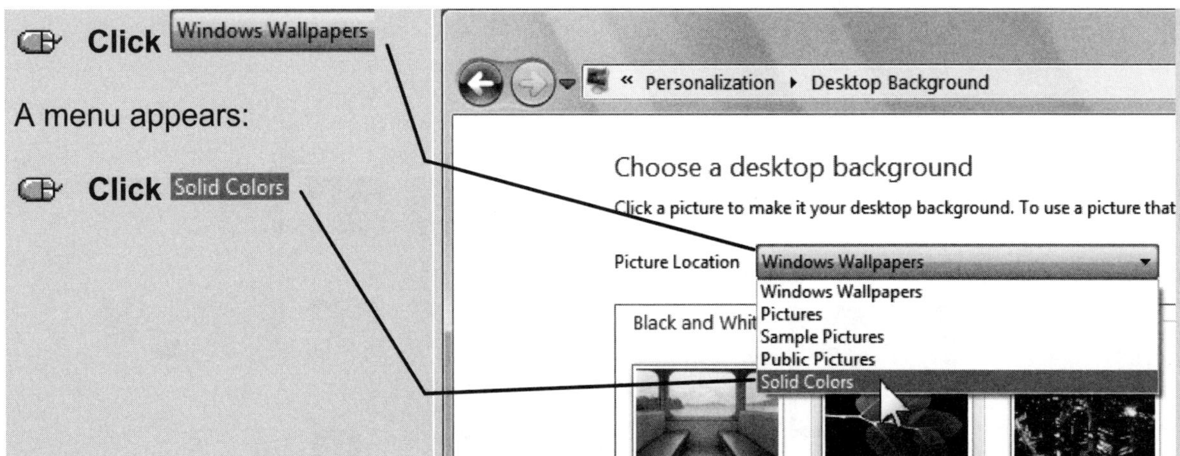

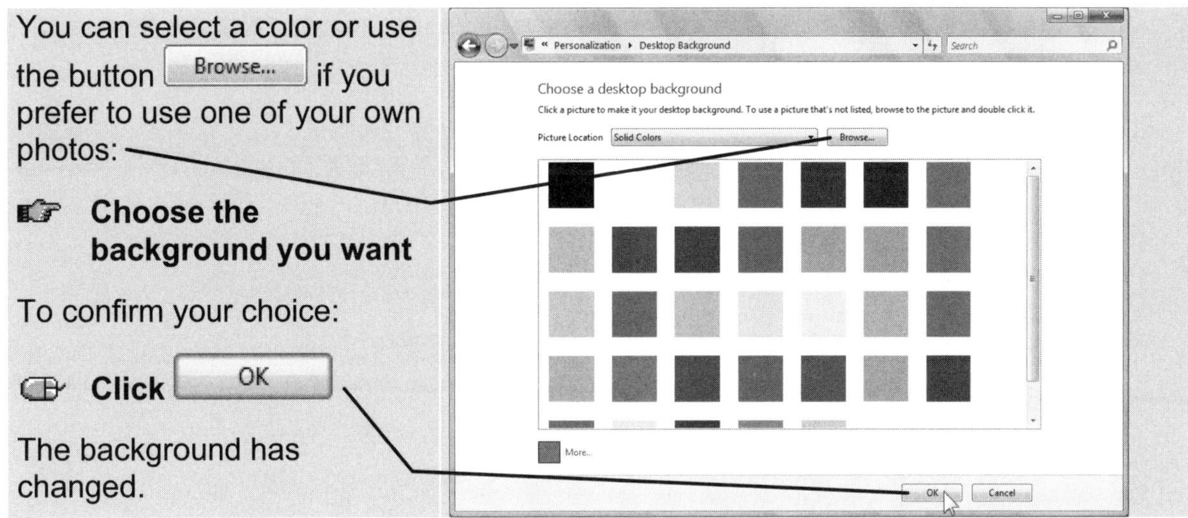

You can select a color or use the button Browse... if you prefer to use one of your own photos:

Choose the background you want

To confirm your choice:

Click OK

The background has changed.

5.3 Ease of Access Center

The *Ease of Access Center* is a centralized location for accessibility settings and programs. Here you can find a questionnaire that you can use to get suggestions for accessibility features that you might find useful. Take a look at it:

The *Control Panel* window is still open.

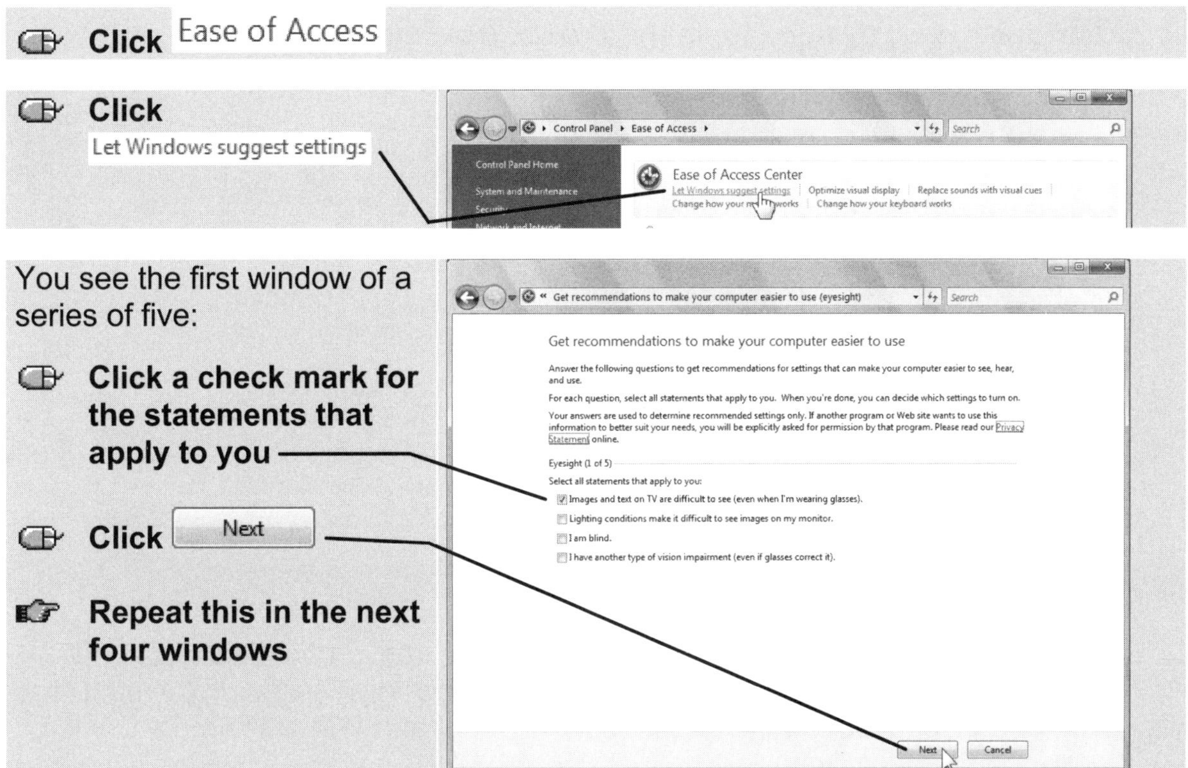

Click Ease of Access

Click Let Windows suggest settings

You see the first window of a series of five:

Click a check mark for the statements that apply to you

Click Next

Repeat this in the next four windows

After the fifth window, *Vista* will give recommendations for possible solutions and settings that might be applicable in your situation.

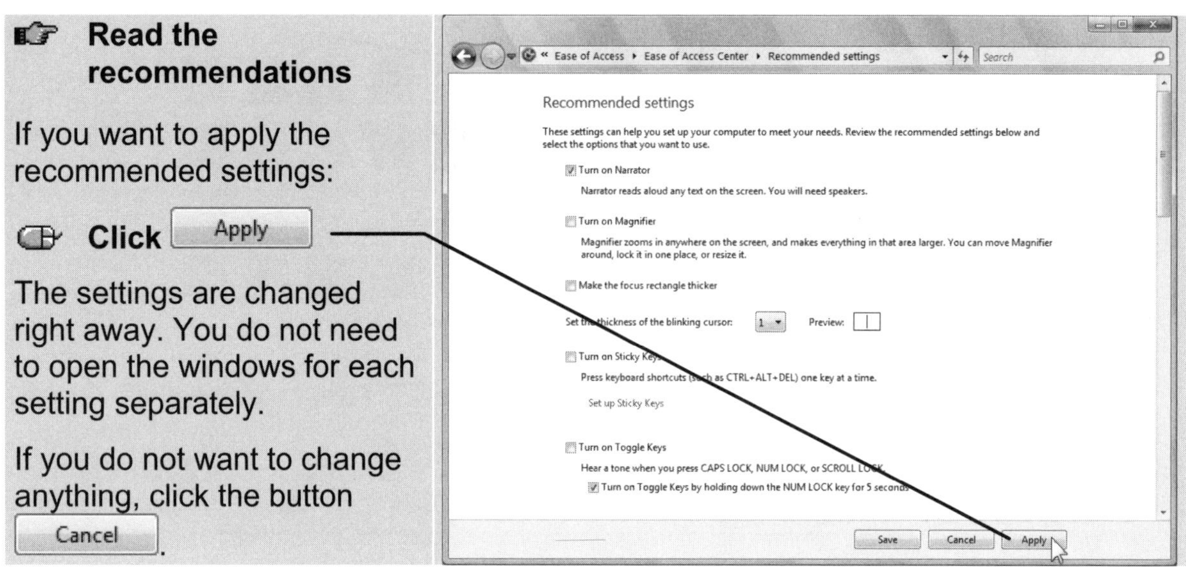

Read the recommendations

If you want to apply the recommended settings:

Click Apply

The settings are changed right away. You do not need to open the windows for each setting separately.

If you do not want to change anything, click the button Cancel.

Close all windows

Open *Windows Help and Support* 4

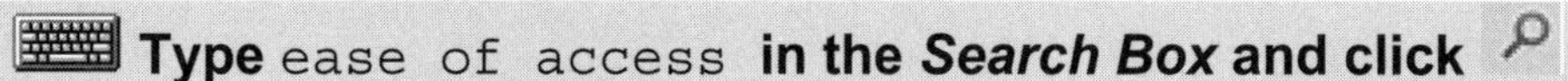

Type `ease of access` **in the *Search Box* and click** 🔍

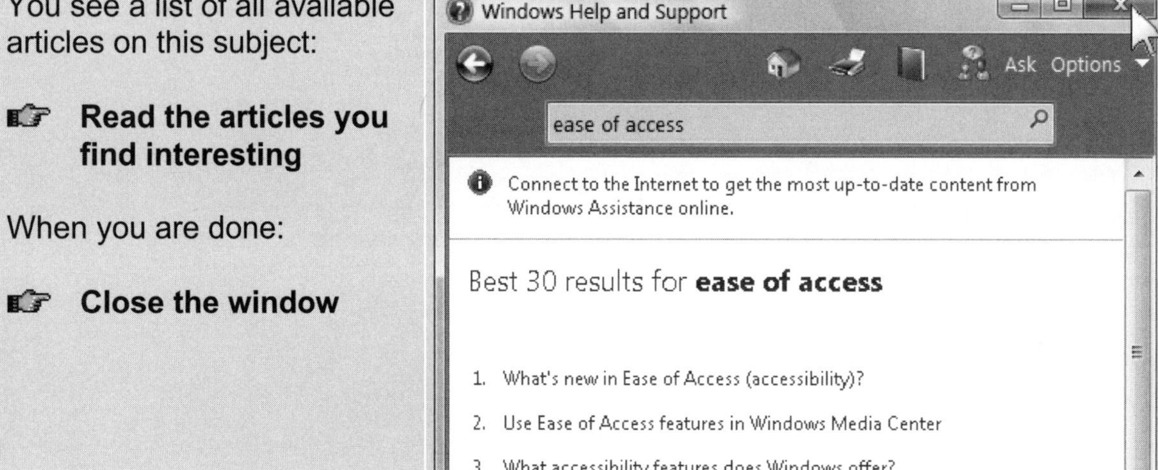

You see a list of all available articles on this subject:

Read the articles you find interesting

When you are done:

Close the window

You have seen how the improved accessibility features in *Windows Vista* offer different ways to easily adjust the computer to fit your own needs. In the next chapter you will be introduced to *Windows Media Player 11* and *Windows Media Center*.

6. Media

Working with media has become increasingly popular in recent years. From digital photo and video editing to playing music on the PC, there are a number of good software programs available, as well as several, easy online applications for you to share your media files with friends and family.

Windows Vista follows this trend with greatly improved media programs. The well known program for playing music and videos *Windows Media Player* has been extended and has become more user friendly. The video editing program *Windows Movie Maker* offers more possibilities, and the ease with which you can import images from a digital video camera is a real plus.

The owners of *Windows Vista Home Premium* and *Windows Vista Ultimate* also have the extensive program *Windows Media Center* at their disposal. Perhaps you already know this program from the popular *Windows Media Center* PCs. *Windows Media Center* is the center for all your digital entertainment: music, photos, video, television and online media can be viewed in this program. *Windows Media Center* has been integrated in *Windows Vista* and offers a more user friendly interface than its predecessors.

In this chapter you are going to:

- explore *Windows Media Player 11*;
- rip (copy) music;
- write an audio CD in *Windows Media Player*;
- explore *Windows Media Center*;
- view a slide show;
- play a video;
- view online media;
- write CDs or DVDs in *Windows Media Center*;
- explore *Windows Movie Maker*.

Please note:

Windows Media Center is not available in the edition *Windows Vista Home Basic.*

6.1 Open Windows Media Player

In previous versions of *Windows*, the program *Windows Media Player* was the default program for playing music and video. *Windows Vista* offers the latest version: *Windows Media Player 11*. This is how you open *Windows Media Player*.

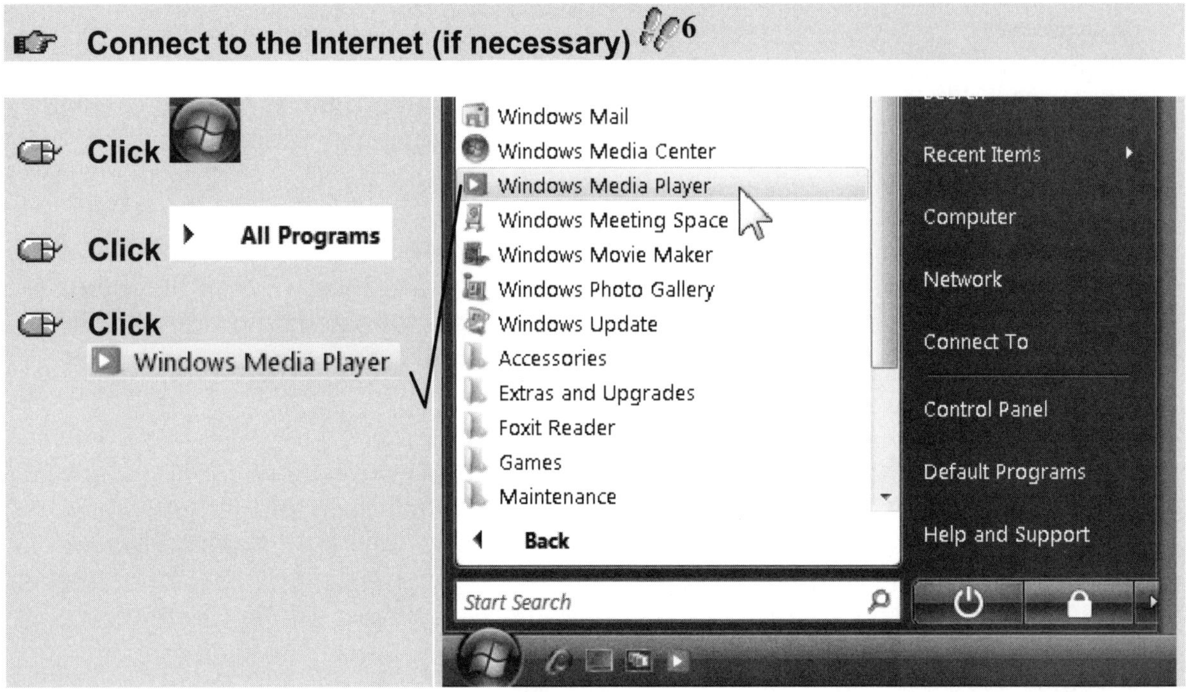

When you start *Windows Media Player* for the first time, you will need to configure some initial settings for the program. You can always change these settings later in *Windows Media Player*.

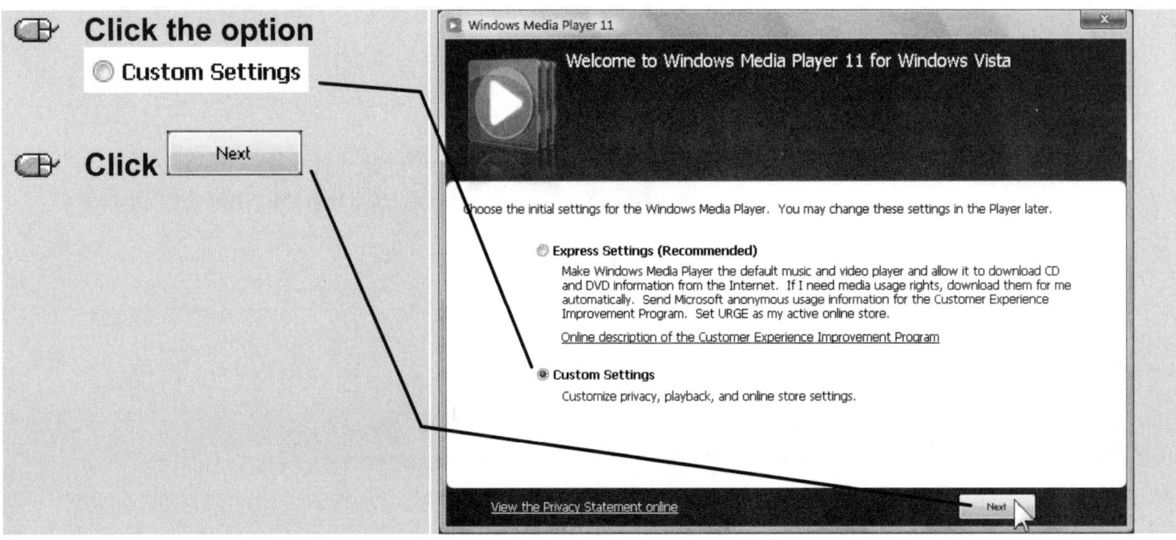

You see a window where you can enter various privacy settings:

Download and display media information from the Internet:

Allow data to be sent from *Media Player* to *Microsoft* and providers of music:

Save information about the media you have played:

For more information, click More information about these privacy options.

Click Next

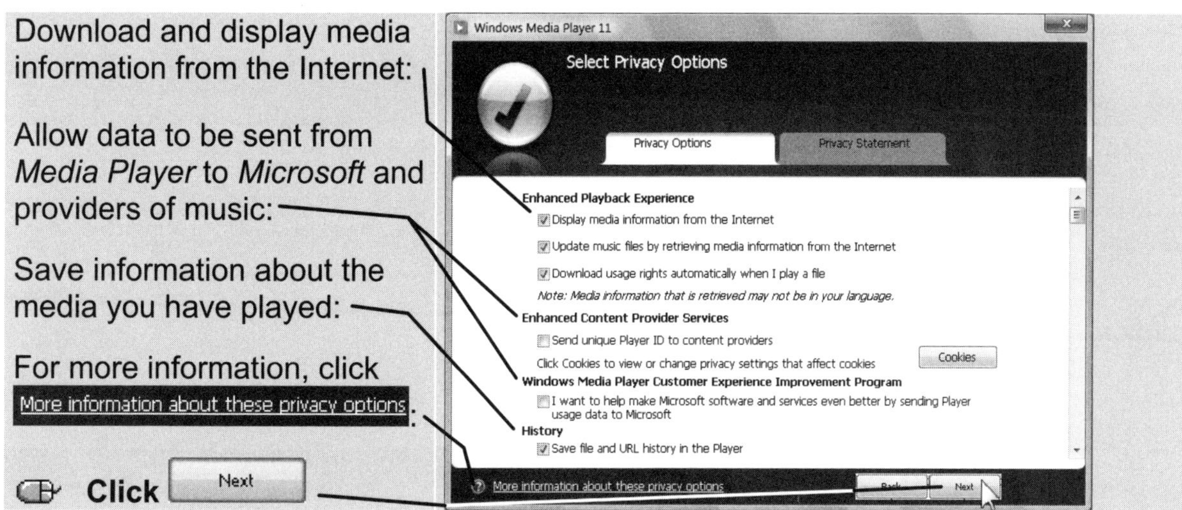

Now you see a window with installation options:

You can choose whether or not you want to add shortcuts to the desktop and the *Quick Launch* toolbar:

Click Next

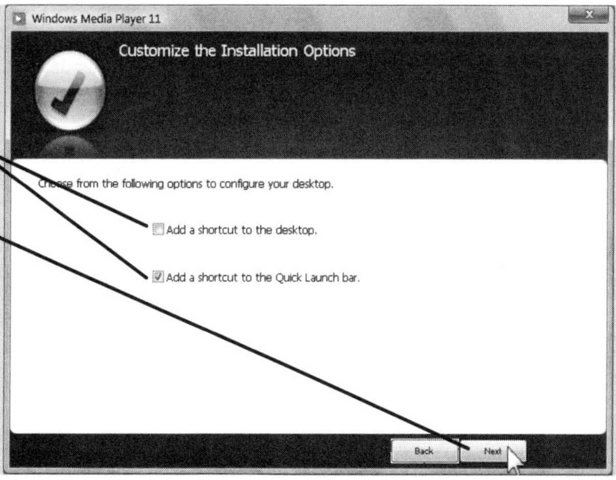

You can make *Windows Media Player* the default media player:

Click the option Make Windows Media Player 11

You can choose the default file types that will always be played by *Windows Media Player*.

Click Next

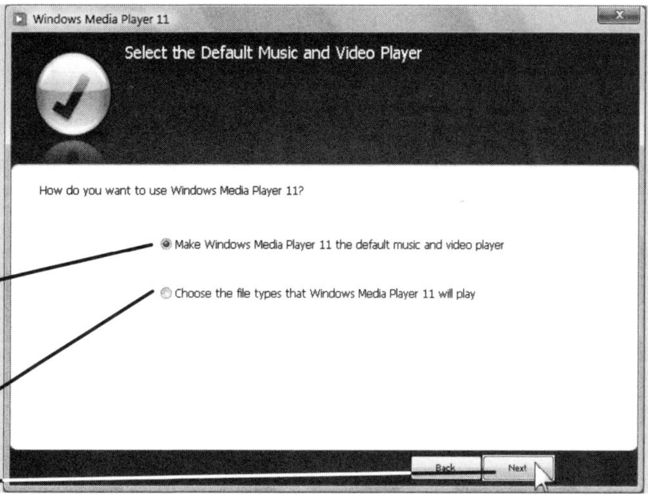

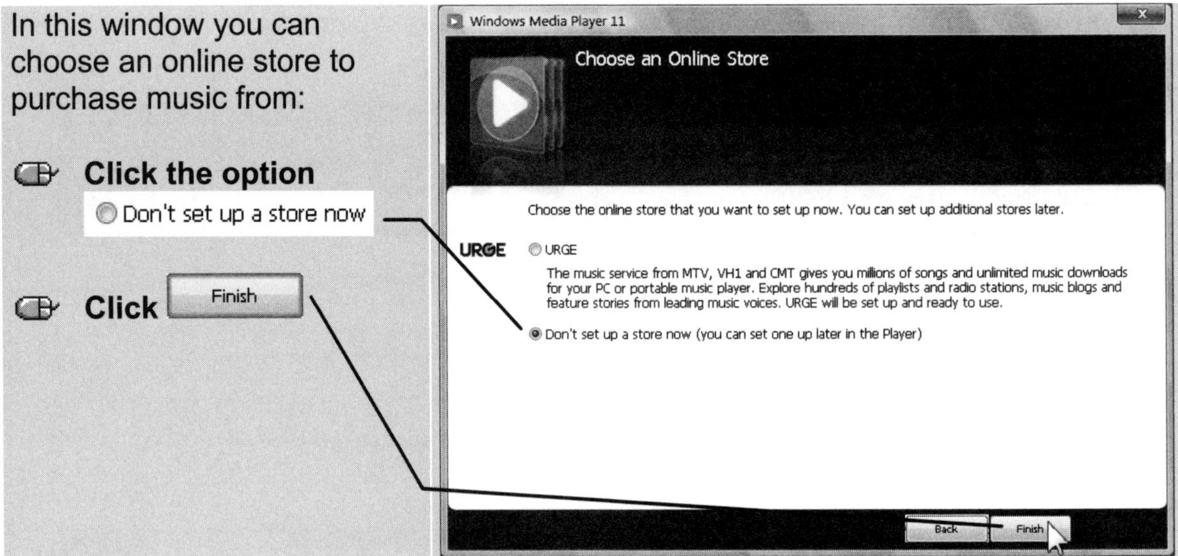

In this window you can choose an online store to purchase music from:

Click the option Don't set up a store now

Click Finish

You have successfully adjusted the initial settings for the program:

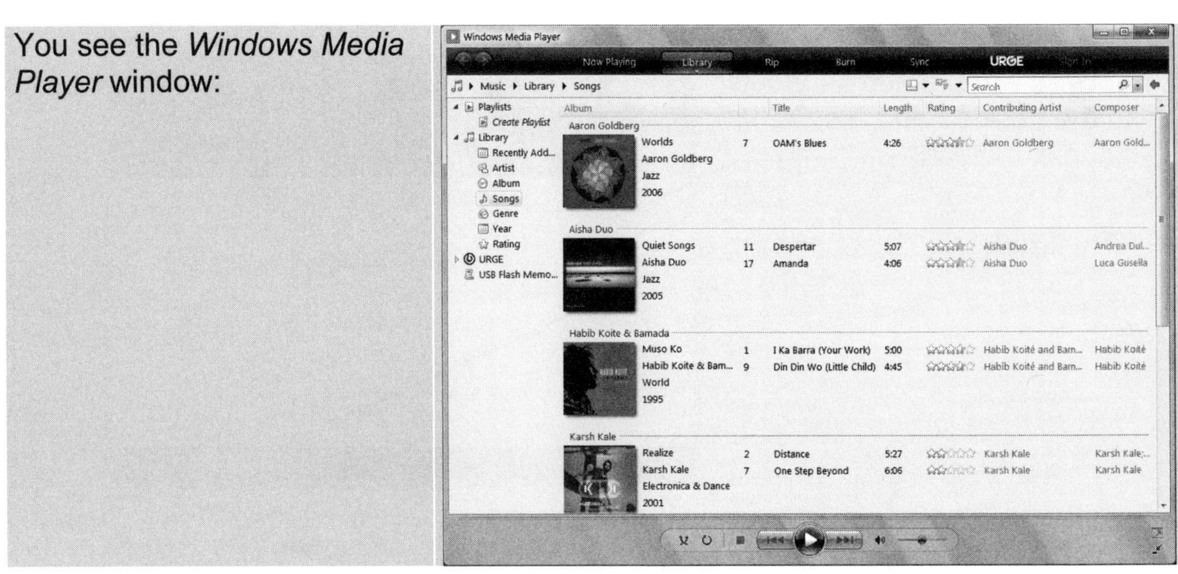

You see the *Windows Media Player* window:

Tip

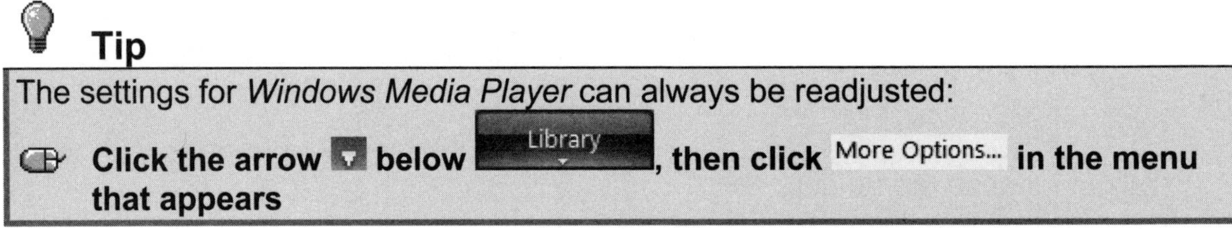

The settings for *Windows Media Player* can always be readjusted:

Click the arrow below Library**, then click** More Options... **in the menu that appears**

6.2 Windows Media Player 11

Windows Media Player 11 is the latest version of *Windows'* default media player. You can use it to organize your media files, rip (copy) music files from audio CDs and write audio CDs.

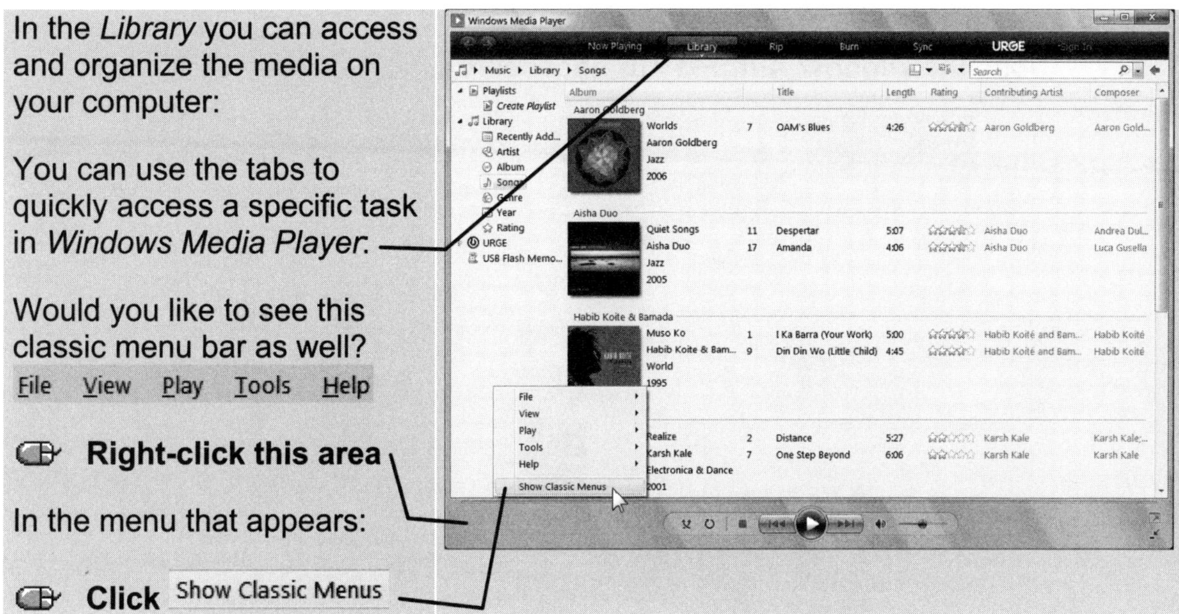

In the *Library* you can access and organize the media on your computer:

You can use the tabs to quickly access a specific task in *Windows Media Player*.

Would you like to see this classic menu bar as well?

File View Play Tools Help

Right-click this area

In the menu that appears:

Click Show Classic Menus

The tabs have the following functionality:

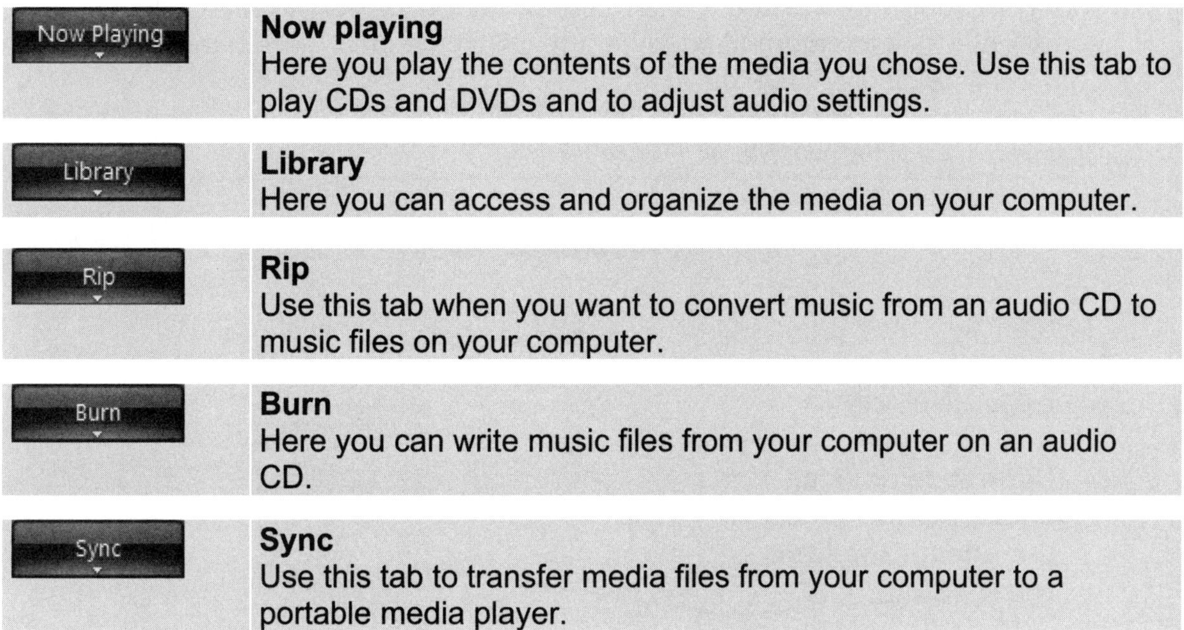

Now playing
Here you play the contents of the media you chose. Use this tab to play CDs and DVDs and to adjust audio settings.

Library
Here you can access and organize the media on your computer.

Rip
Use this tab when you want to convert music from an audio CD to music files on your computer.

Burn
Here you can write music files from your computer on an audio CD.

Sync
Use this tab to transfer media files from your computer to a portable media player.

To access the settings for each of the tabs, click the arrow ▾ below the tab.

6.3 Ripping a Music File

Ripping is another name for converting the music on an audio CD to music files on the computer. This is very easy in *Windows Media Player*:

Insert an audio CD in the CD or DVD drive of your computer

Close the window *AutoPlay* (if necessary)

Click Rip

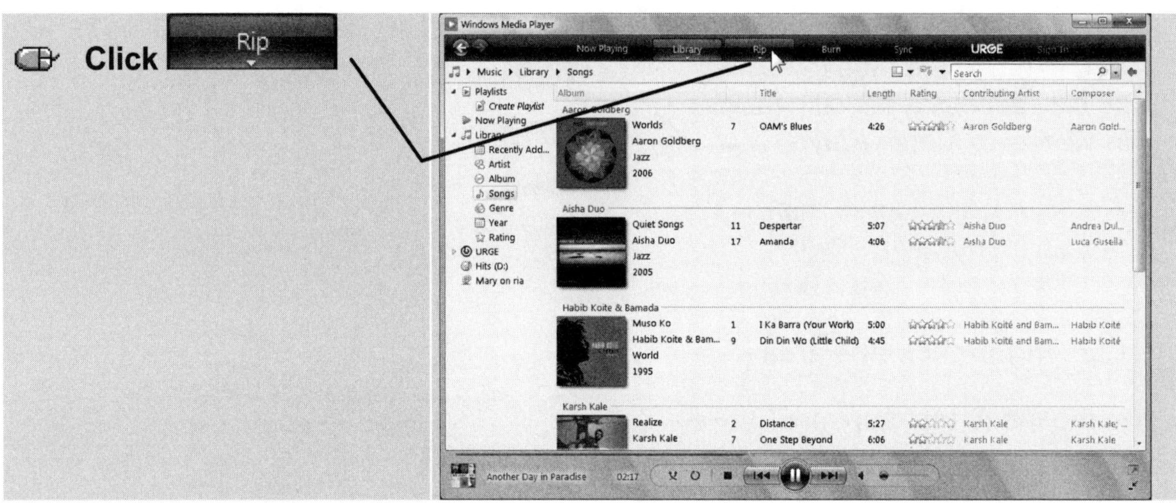

Please note:

If your computer is connected to the Internet, *Windows Media Player* will automatically look for information about the CD in the drive. When the information is found, it will be displayed in the window.
If you don't receive any information from the Internet, it is possible that your firewall program blocks *Windows Media Player*.

You see the tab *Rip*:

In case the ripping started automatically:

Click Stop Rip

Click to remove all check marks, except the one for the first track

Click Start Rip

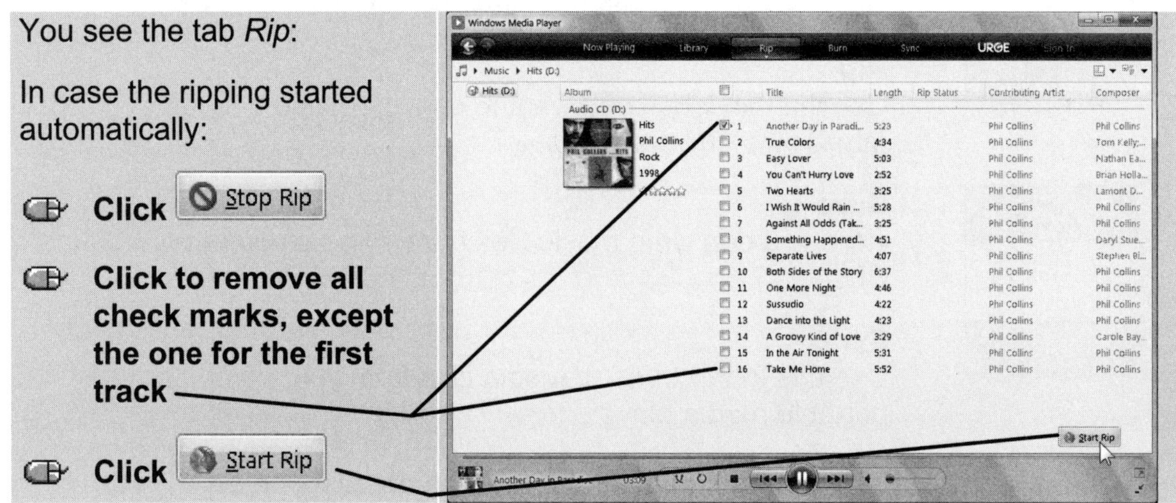

The selected track is now ripped from the CD to the hard disk:

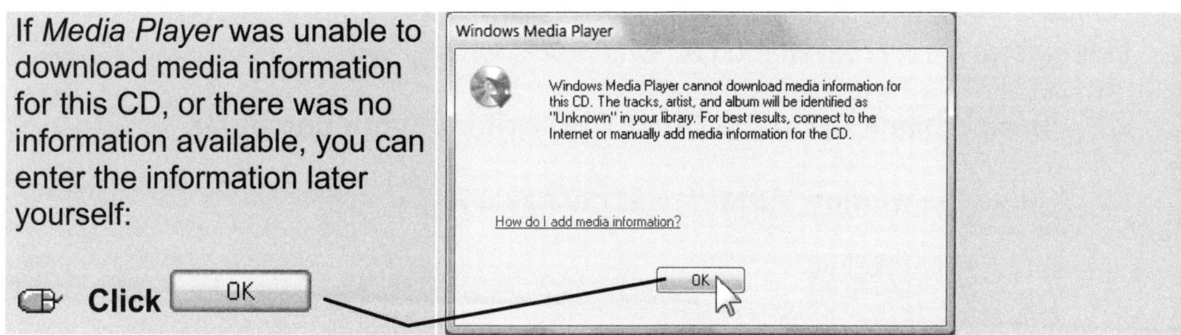

If *Media Player* was unable to download media information for this CD, or there was no information available, you can enter the information later yourself:

Click OK

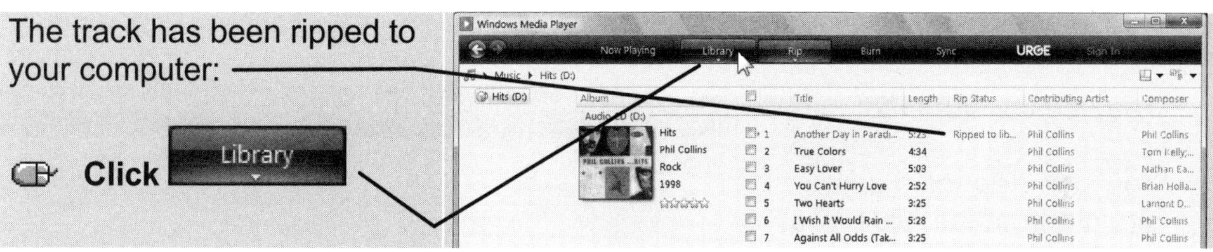

The track has been ripped to your computer:

Click Library

HELP! The track was not ripped

Sometimes *Windows Media Player* does not succeed in ripping a track. The Rip Status will be shown as Stopped.

In that case you can click Start Rip again, or take the audio CD out of the drawer, clean it, insert the CD again and click Start Rip.

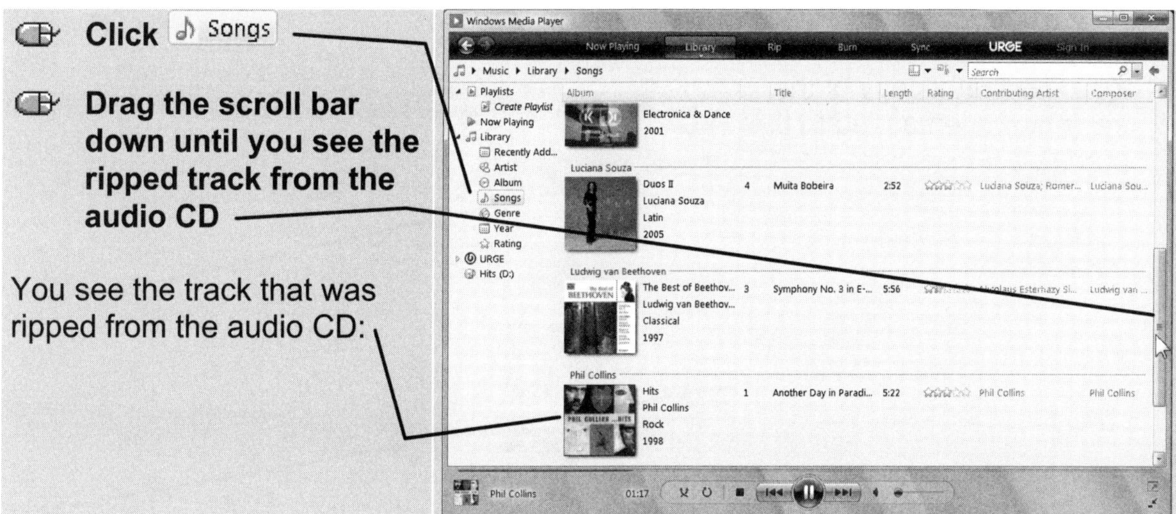

Click Songs

Drag the scroll bar down until you see the ripped track from the audio CD

You see the track that was ripped from the audio CD:

From now on, you can play this song right from your computer.

Take the audio CD out of the CD or DVD drive of your computer

6.4 Writing an Audio CD

In *Windows Media Player* you can write audio CDs:

Insert a blank CD in the CD or DVD writer of your computer

Close the window *AutoPlay* (if necessary)

Click Burn

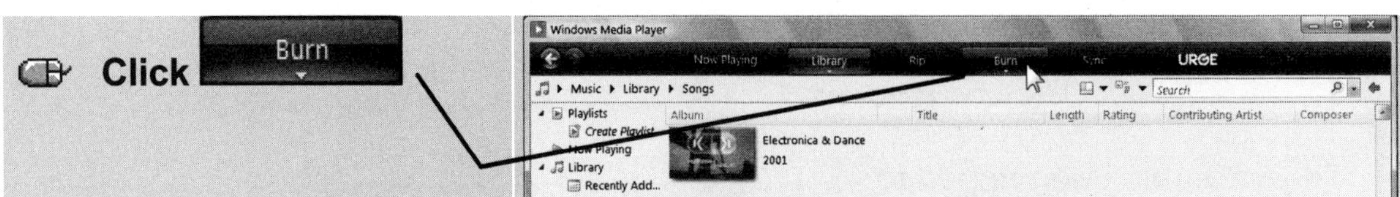

You see the *Burn* tab:

You can drag the media straight from the *Library* to the CD:

Drag the track you just ripped to the burn list

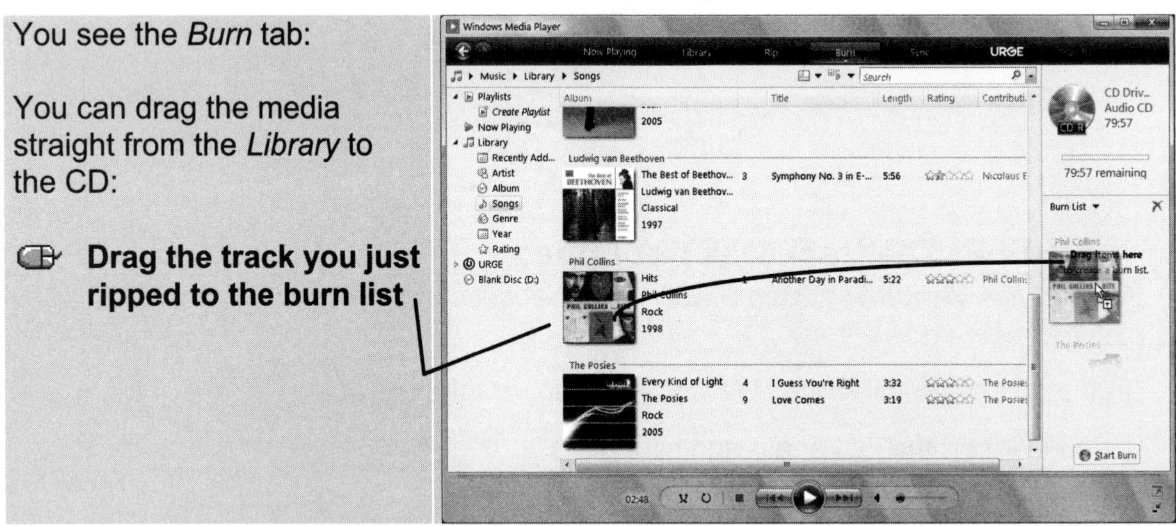

You see that a copy of the track has been added to the burn list:

Click Start Burn

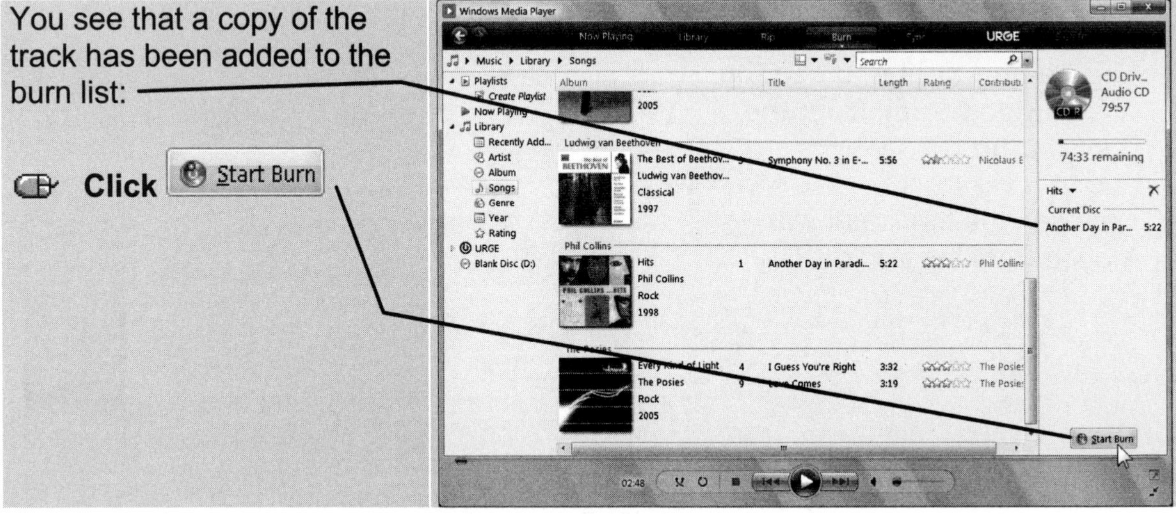

The audio file will now be written on the CD.

Please note:

The *Windows Vista* sample music files can not be written on CD. When you try to do that, only a shortcut to the file is placed on the CD.

When the writing process has finished, you see this window:

You can use the same method to write several music files on a CD.

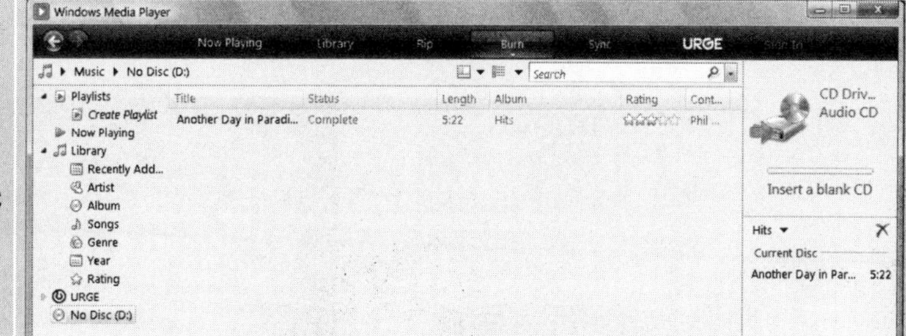

Take the CD you have written out of the CD or DVD writer of your computer

Close the *Windows Media Player* window

6.5 Opening Windows Media Center

Windows Media Center is the central point for all your media in *Windows Vista*. You can use it to listen to digital music, download online media, watch slide shows of your photos and write CDs and DVDs. If your computer is equipped with a TV tuner card you can use *Windows Media Center* to watch and record live television on your computer. A TV tuner card is a graphics card that is capable of receiving television signals, for example using your cable connection.

Please note:

Windows Media Center is only available in the editions *Windows Vista Home Premium* and *Ultimate*.

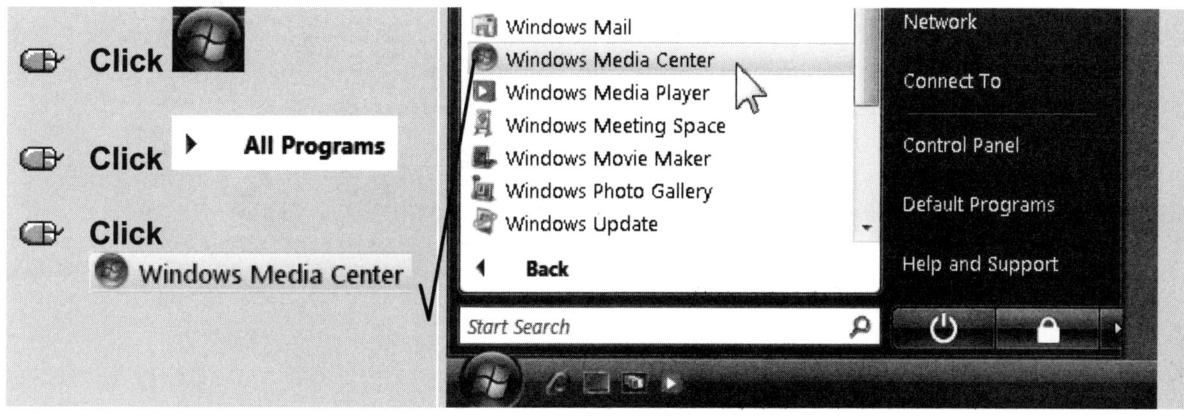

When you start *Windows Media Center* for the first time, you will need to configure some initial settings for the program. You can always change these settings later in *Windows Media Center*.

The most convenient choice is the default setup option 'Express setup' that allows information for your media and improvements for the program to be downloaded:

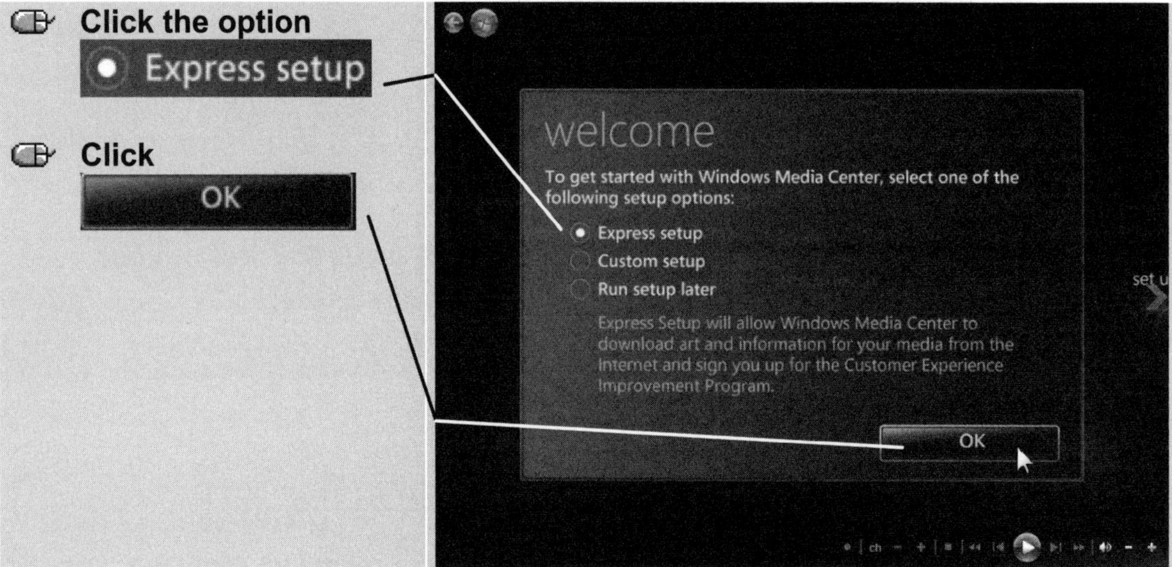

You have now successfully adjusted the initial settings for the program:

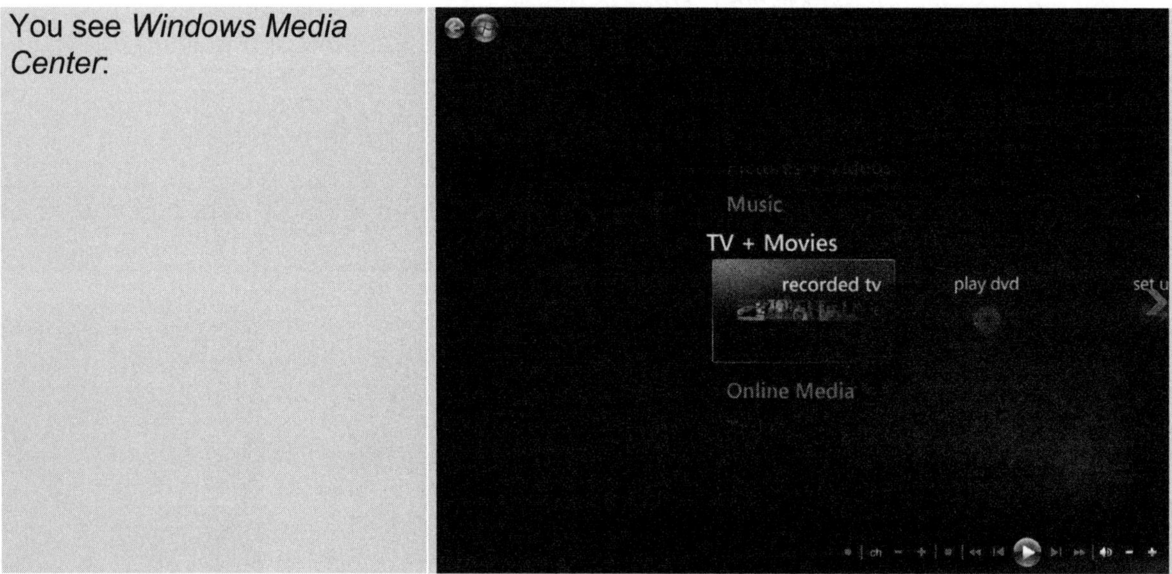

6.6 Exploring Windows Media Center

Windows Media Center looks different than any other program you have become accustomed to in *Windows*. *Media Center* is displayed full screen by default and is not viewed in a window. This is because the program can also be used on a television. In that case *Media Center* is operated with a remote control. The program looks a lot like a DVD menu because of that:

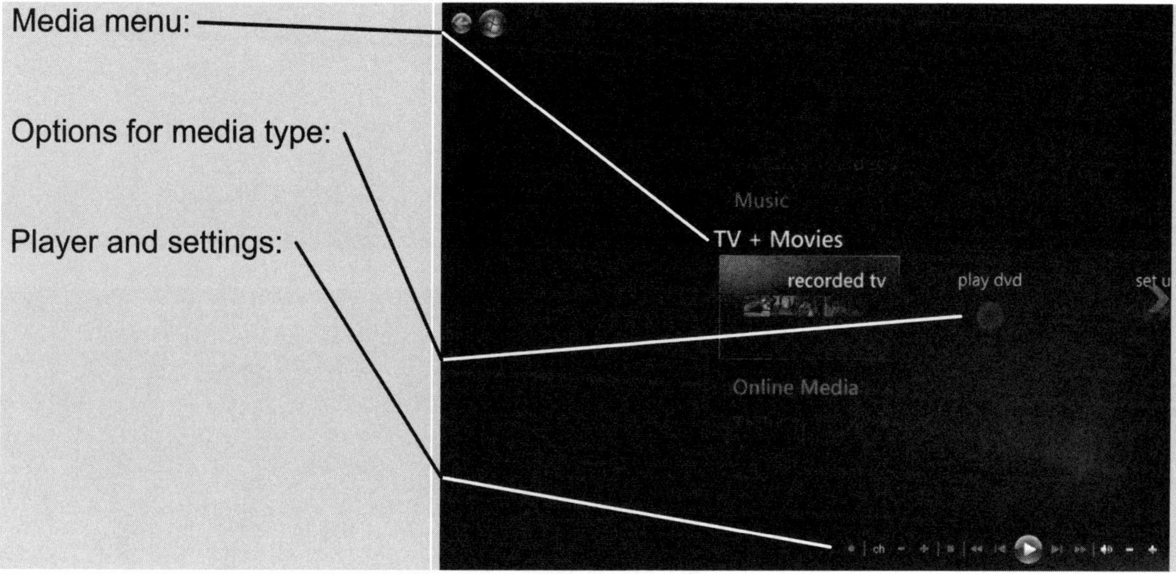

You can scroll through the various media types as follows:

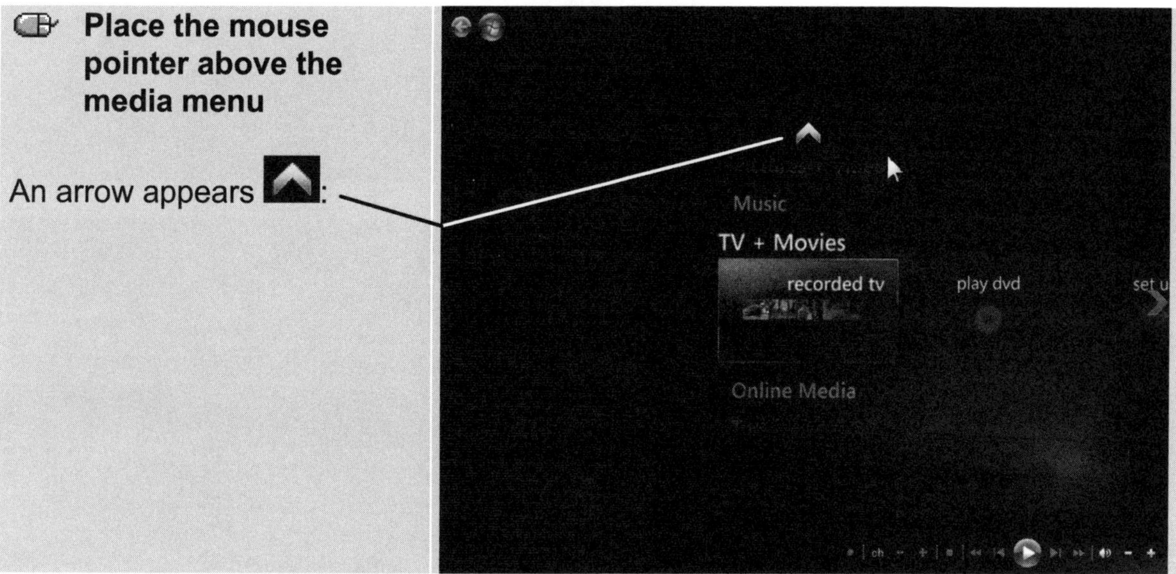

The menu begins to scroll automatically in an upward direction. Watch for a moment how the different options scroll by:

You can also click one step at a time with your mouse.

Move the mouse pointer to the right to make the arrow disappear

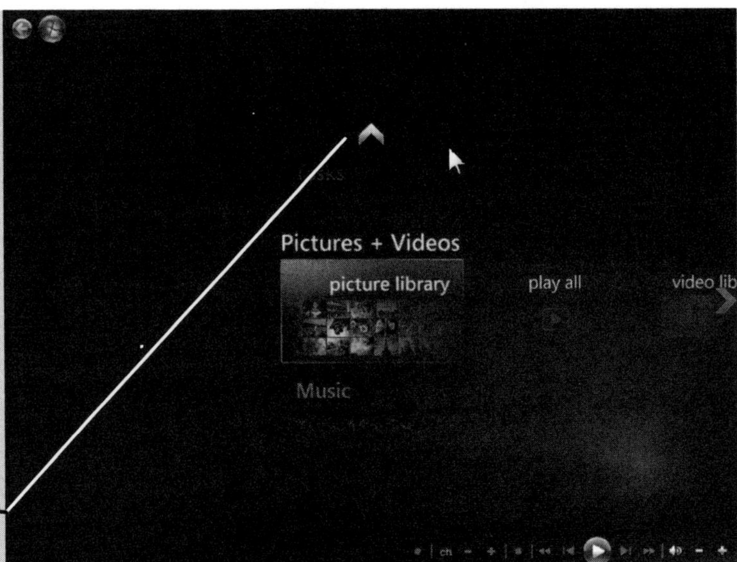

If the scrolling has not already stopped, it will now:

Another media type has been selected:

When you place the mouse pointer below the menu, you can scroll in the other direction:

Scroll or click until you see the media type Pictures + Videos

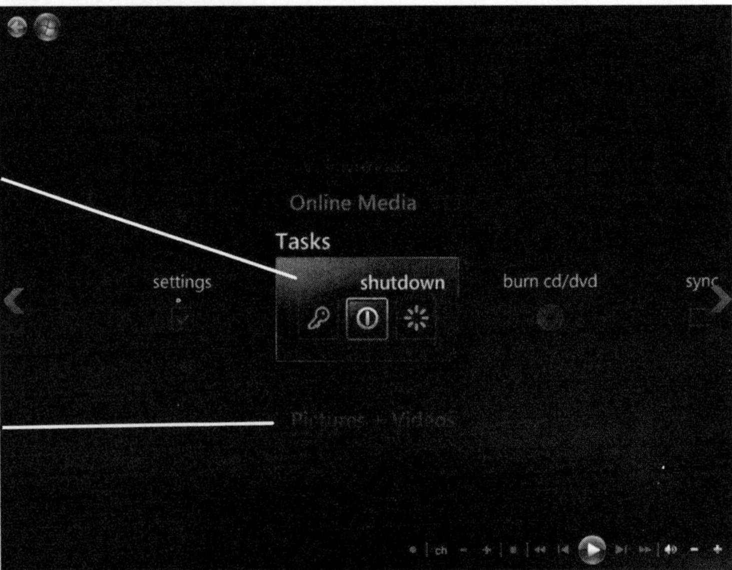

Place the mouse pointer on

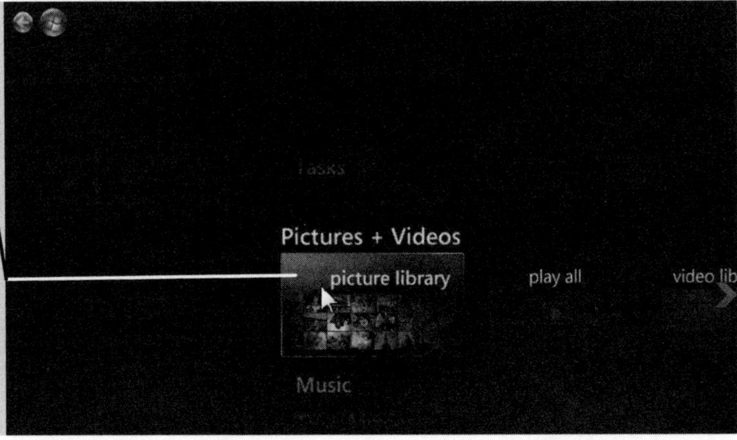

A selected media type usually has options of its own. These are found on the left and right side of the media type. You can scroll through these options as well:

Place the mouse pointer next to the arrow on the right side of the screen

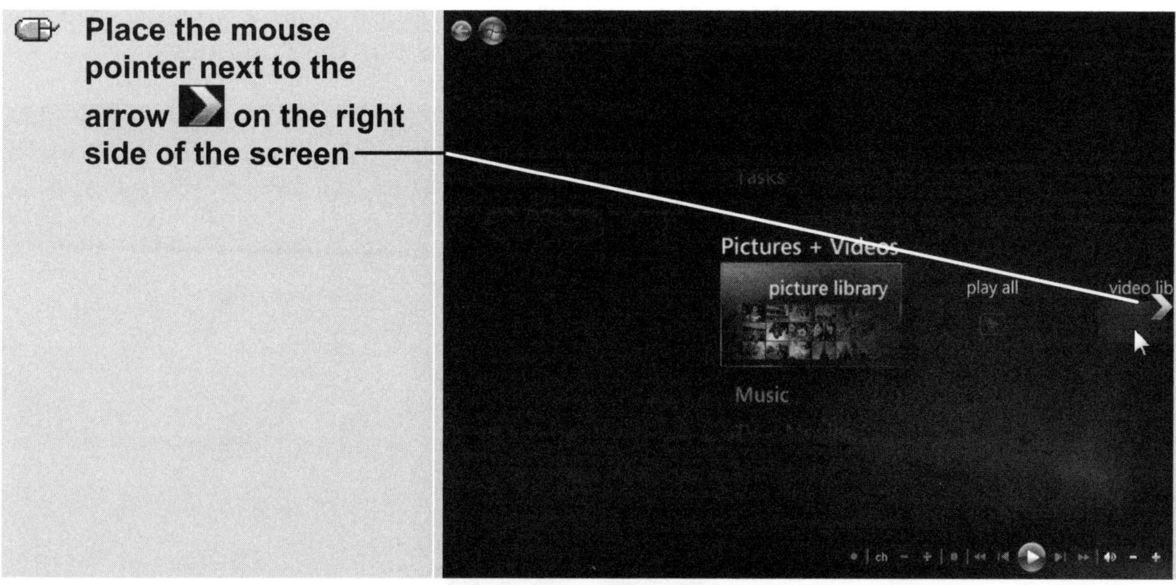

You see the other options:

When you place the mouse pointer next to the other arrow, you scroll in the opposite direction:

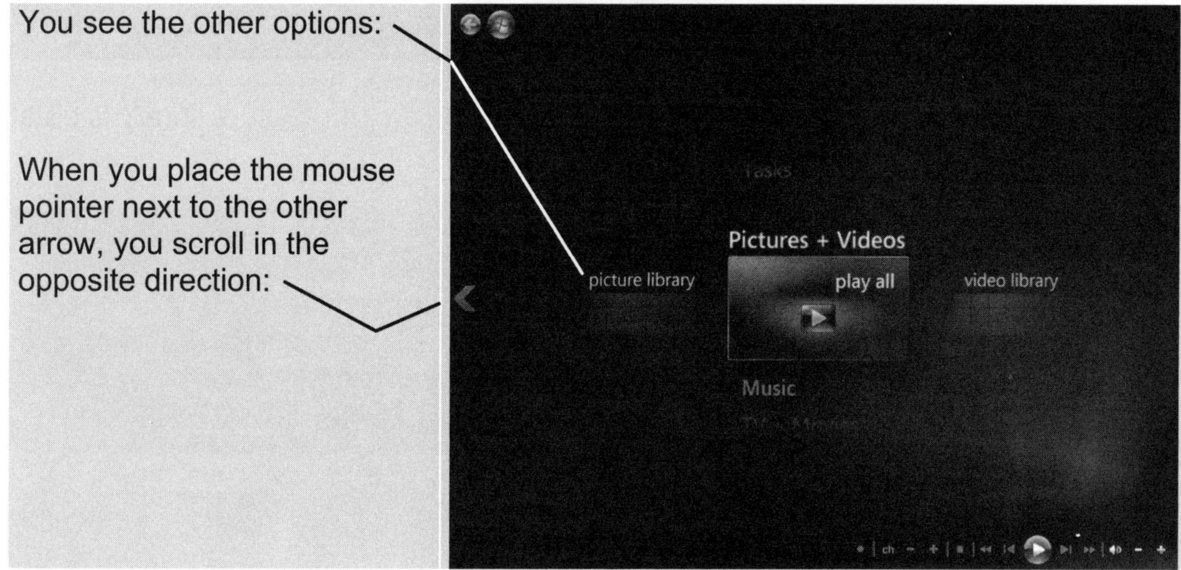

Tip

The *Windows Media Center* settings can be adjusted in this location:

Click **on the left side of media type**

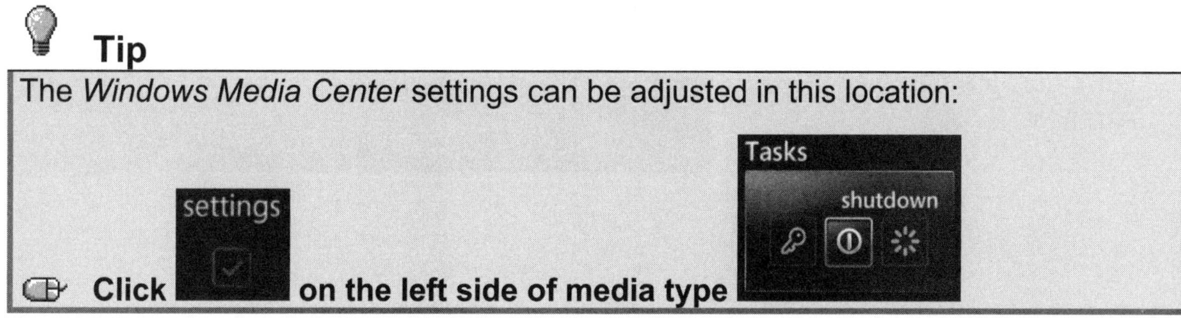

6.7 Playing a Slide Show

You can work with many different media types in *Windows Media Center*. One of the possibilities is viewing a slide show using the photos on your computer:

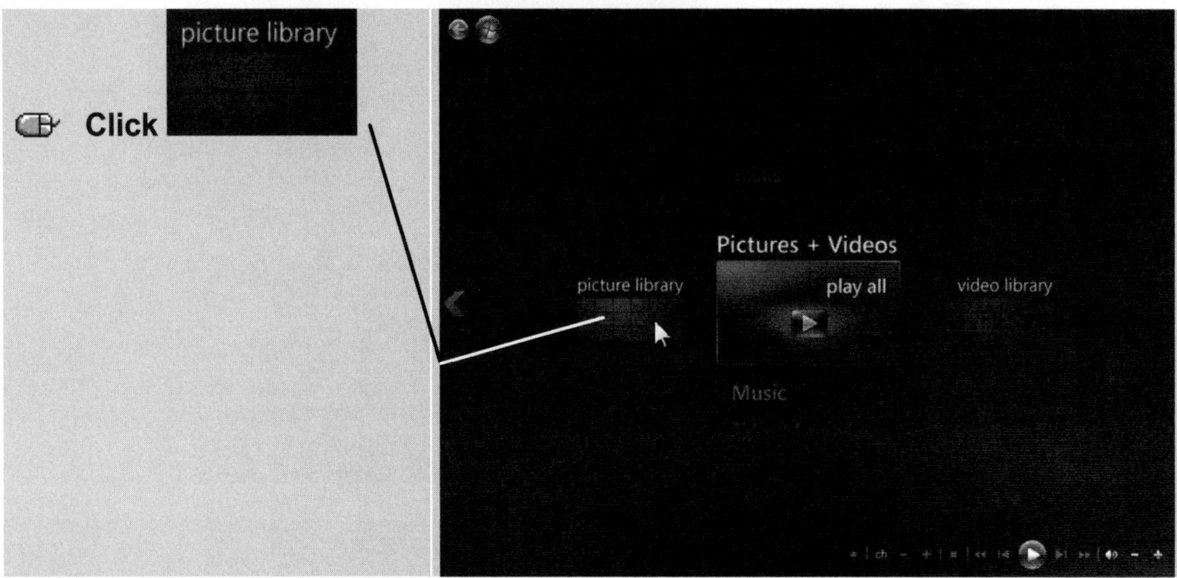

When you open the page *picture library* for the first time, the picture library is created automatically:

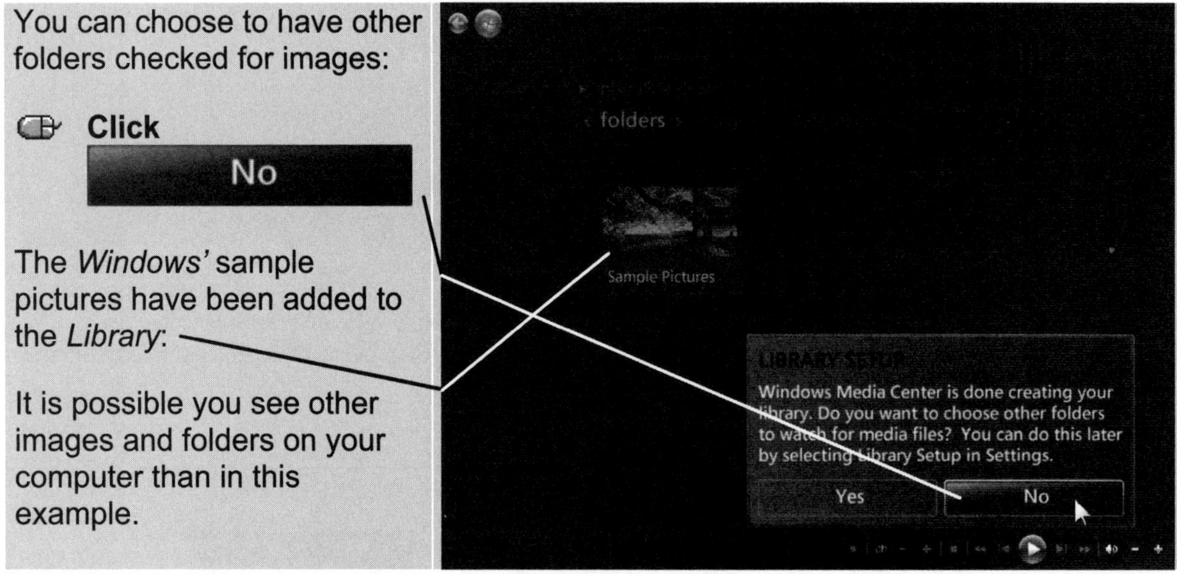

You can view these photos in a slide show:

Click **play slide show**

You see the slide show:

To stop the slide show:

Click

Click

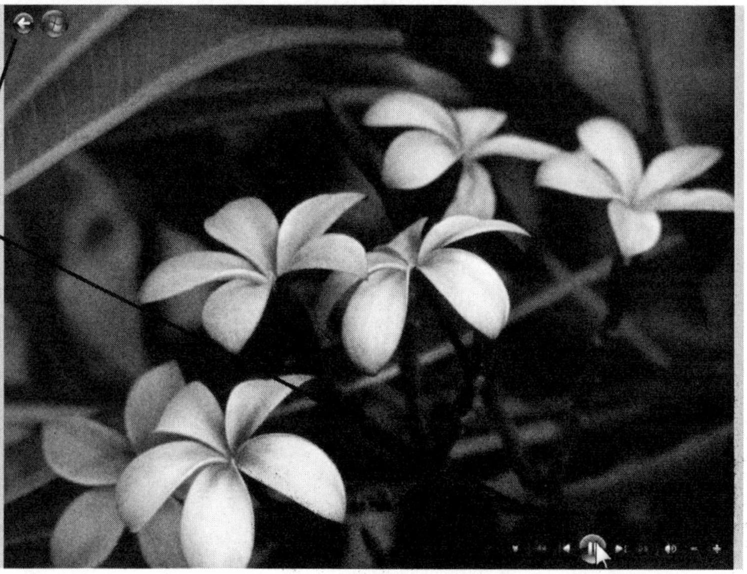

You return to the page *picture library*:

Click

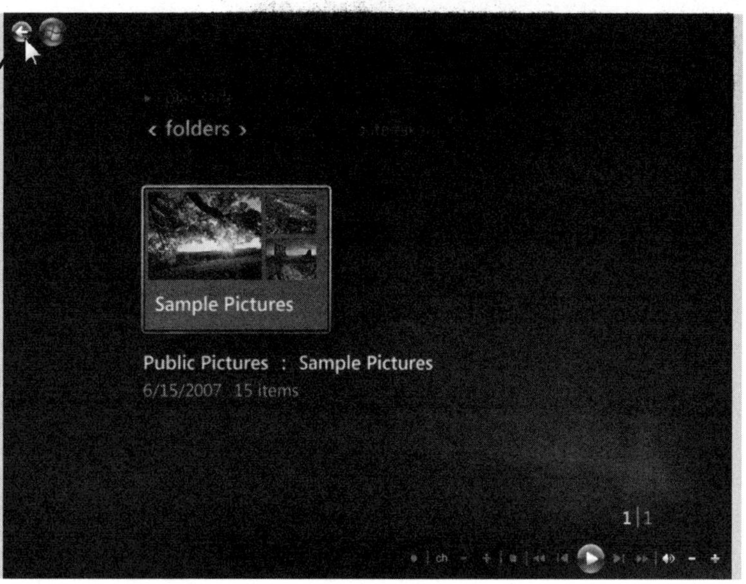

Tip

You can create, extend and edit your own slide shows using *Windows Photo Gallery*. Read chapter 9 for more information.

6.8 Playing a Video

You can also play videos in *Windows Media Center*:

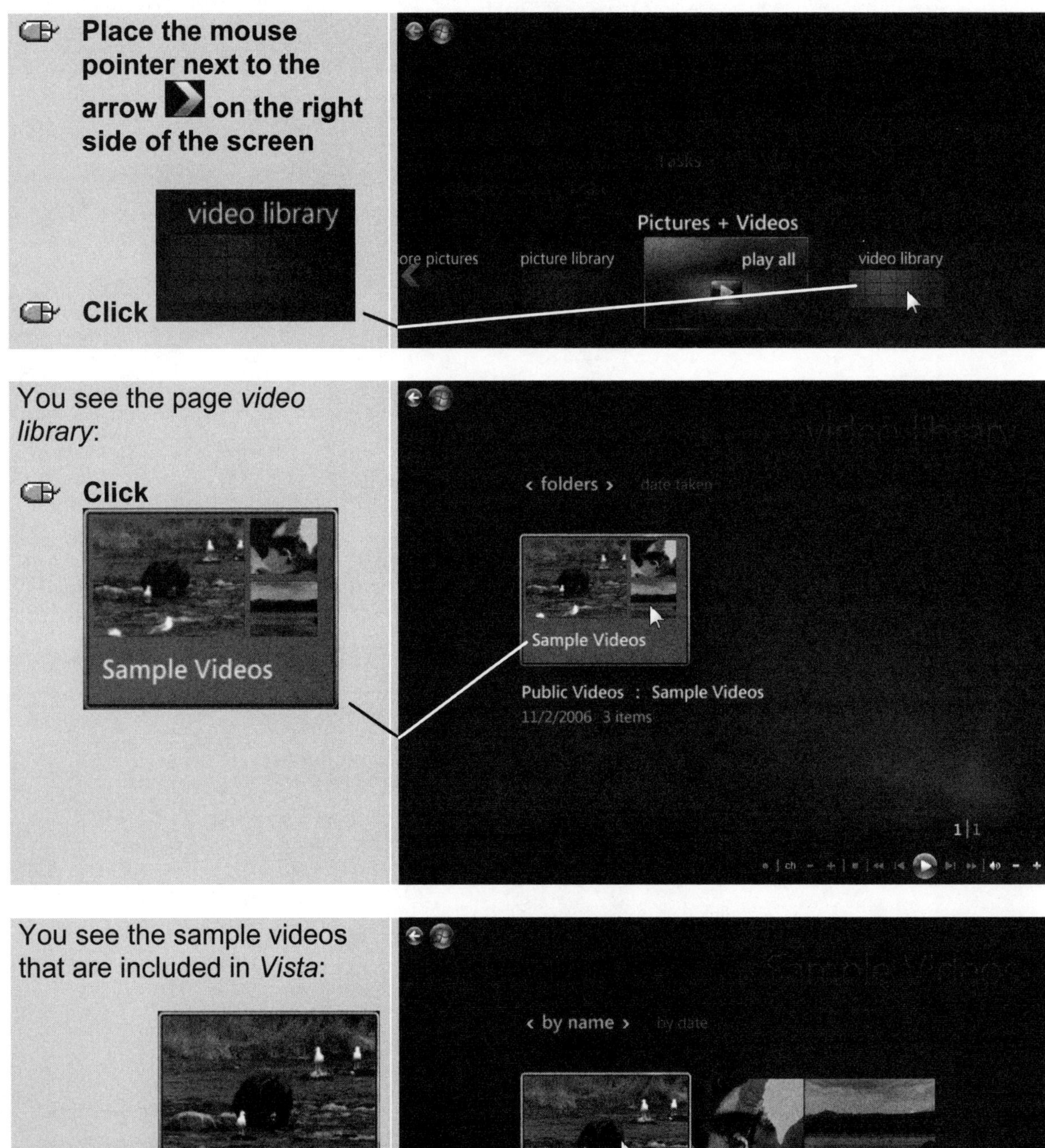

Click three times in the top left corner of the screen

6.9 Watching Online Video

Windows Media Center is not limited to playing content residing on your computer. You can also use *Media Center* to play media hosted from the Internet and perform all kinds of tasks online. For example listening to Internet radio, online banking, downloading music or watching television shows.

 **Please note:**

You need a high speed Internet connection like DSL of cable to be able to watch online video. If you have that kind of connection, but are unable to connect to the Internet in *Windows Media Center*, check the settings of your firewall program. It is possible that *Windows Media Center* is being blocked by your firewall.

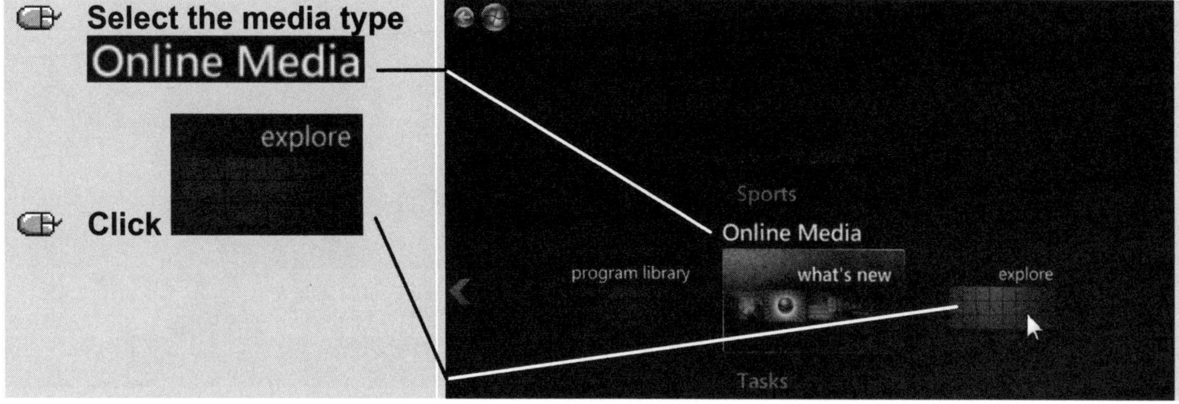

Click

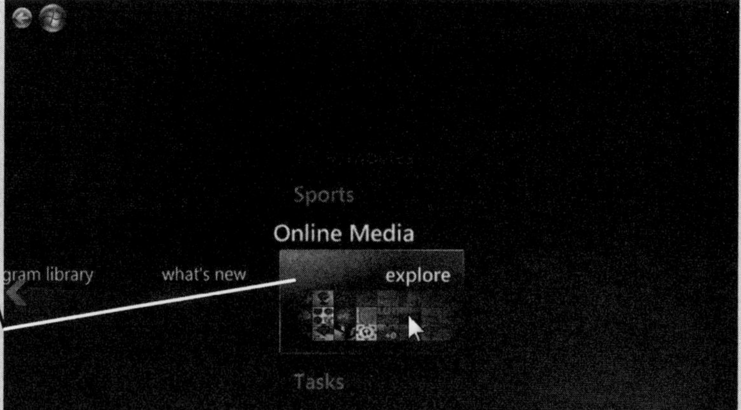

Now you can choose an online option:

When you place the mouse pointer at the edge of the screen you can scroll through the options:

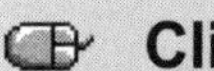
Click

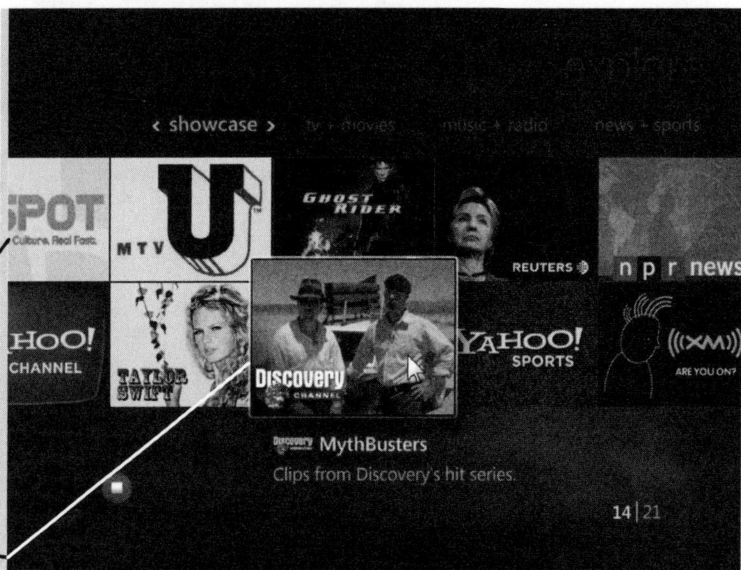

You can choose video previews from several TV programs broadcasted by 'Discovery Channel':

Click the video preview you want to see

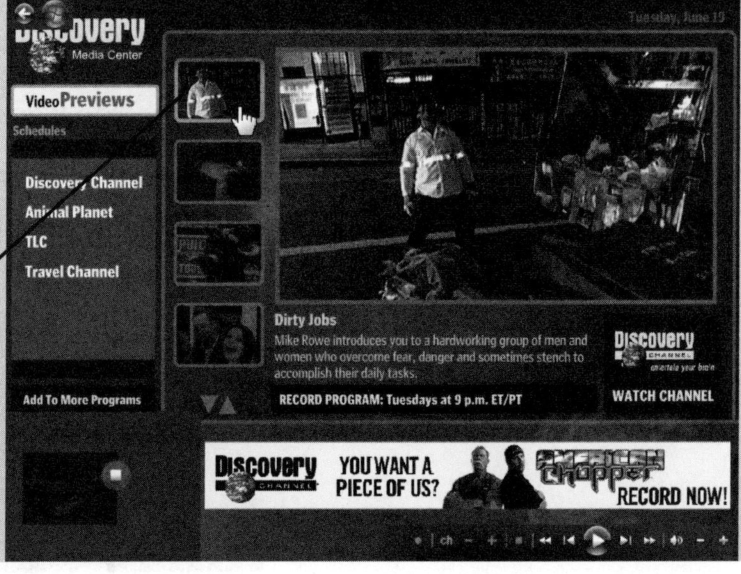

You see the preview of the program you chose:

Click

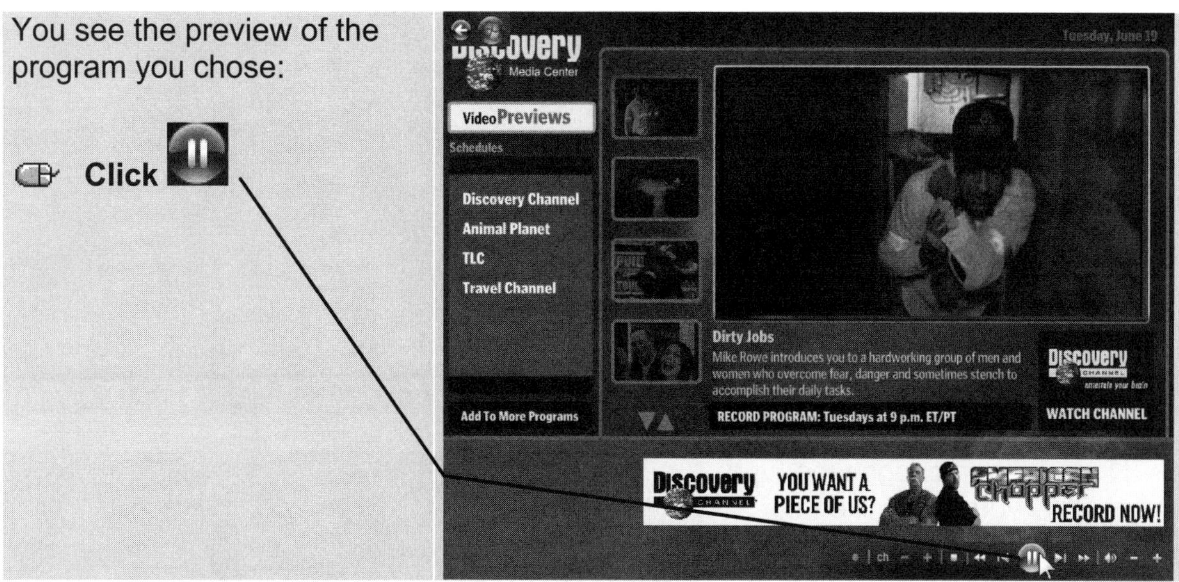

Click twice in the top left corner of your screen

6.10 Writing CDs and DVDs in Windows Media Center

In *Windows Media Center* you can write different kinds of media to CD and DVD:

Select the media type Tasks

Click burn cd/dvd

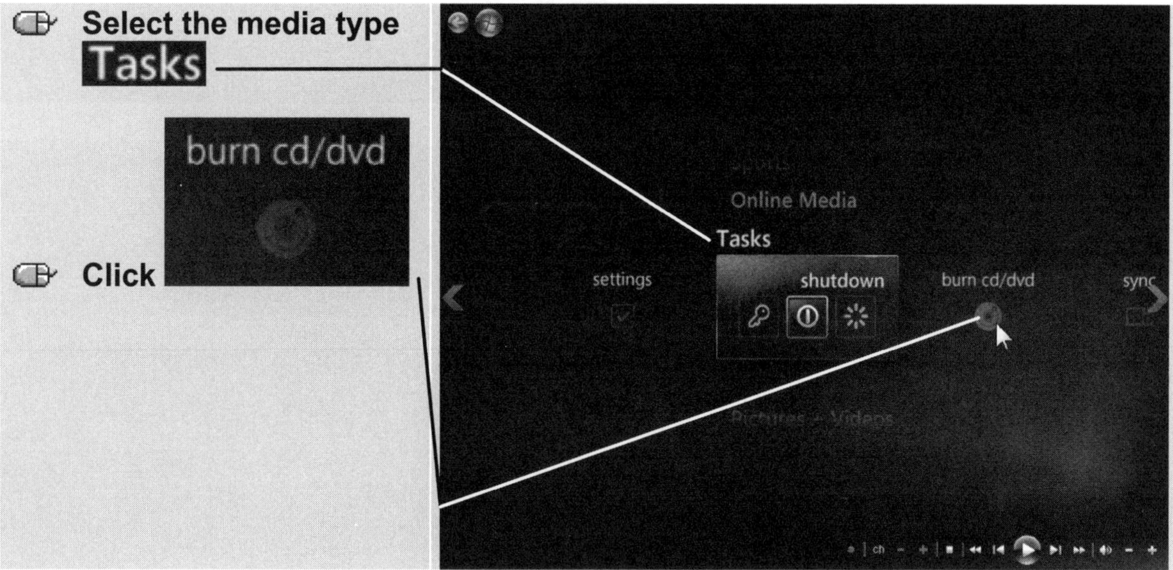

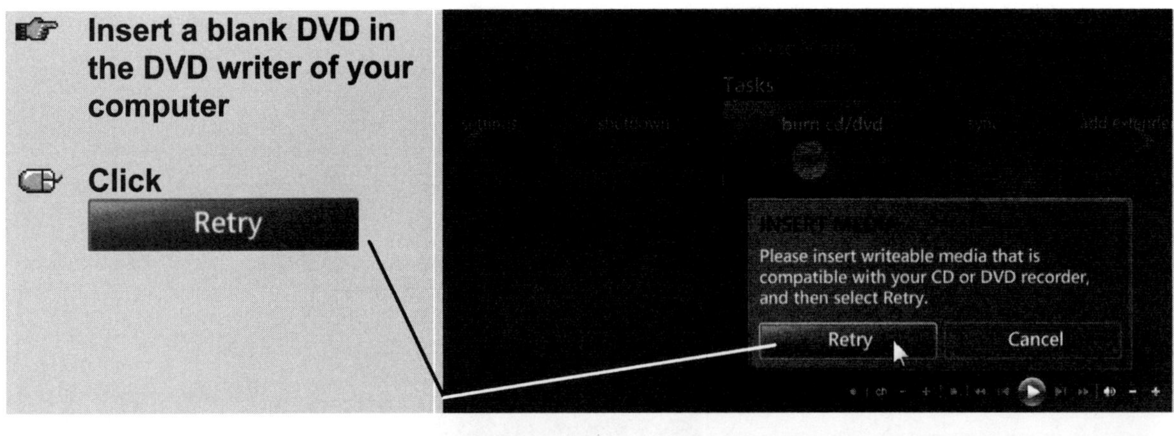

Insert a blank DVD in the DVD writer of your computer

Click Retry

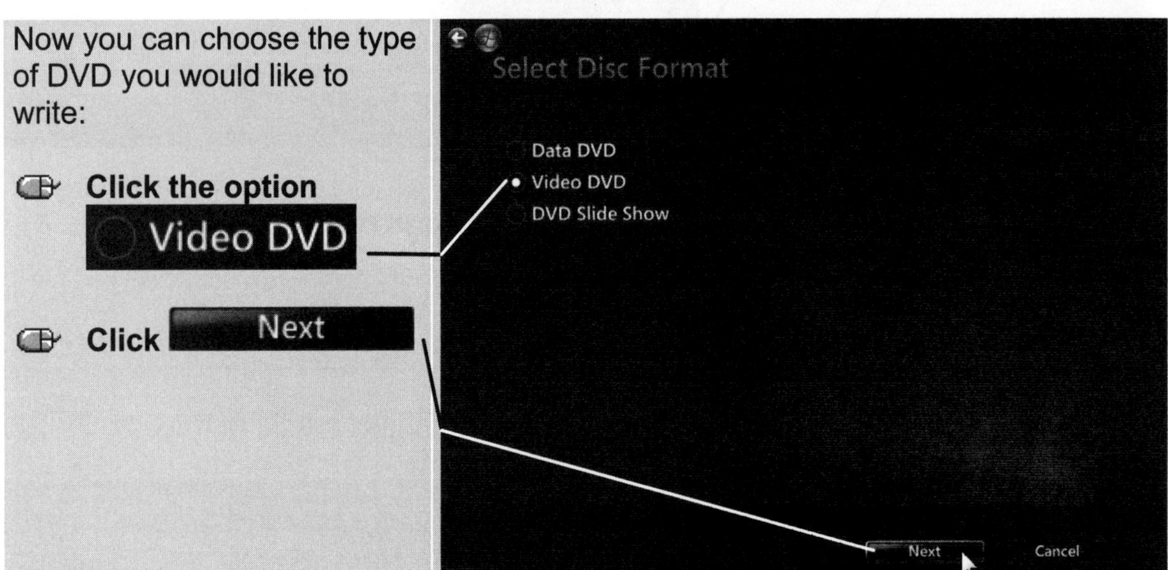

Now you can choose the type of DVD you would like to write:

Click the option Video DVD

Click Next

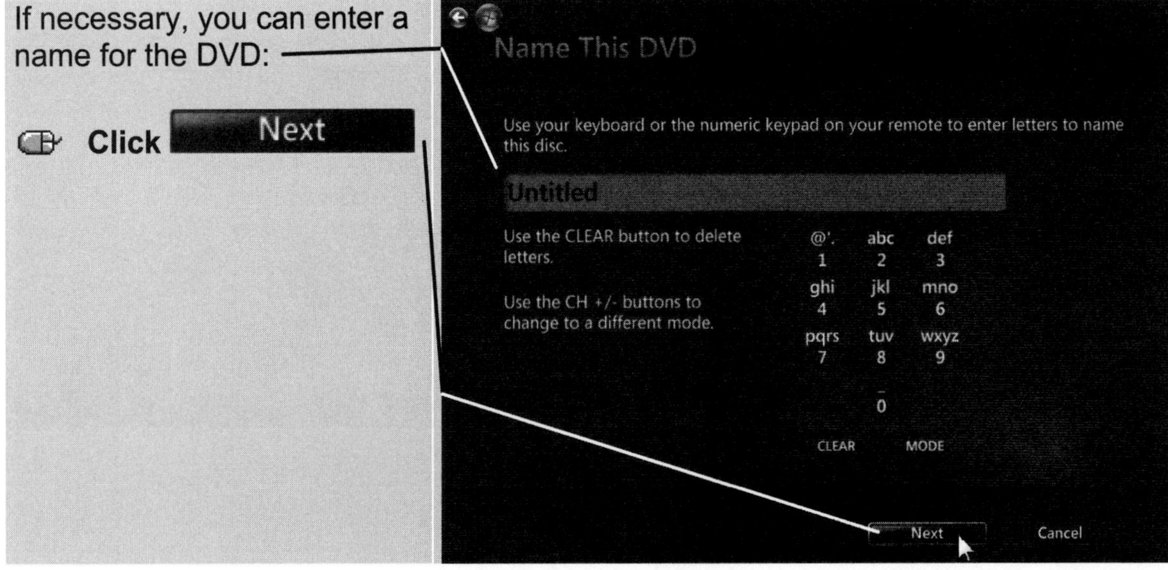

If necessary, you can enter a name for the DVD:

Click Next

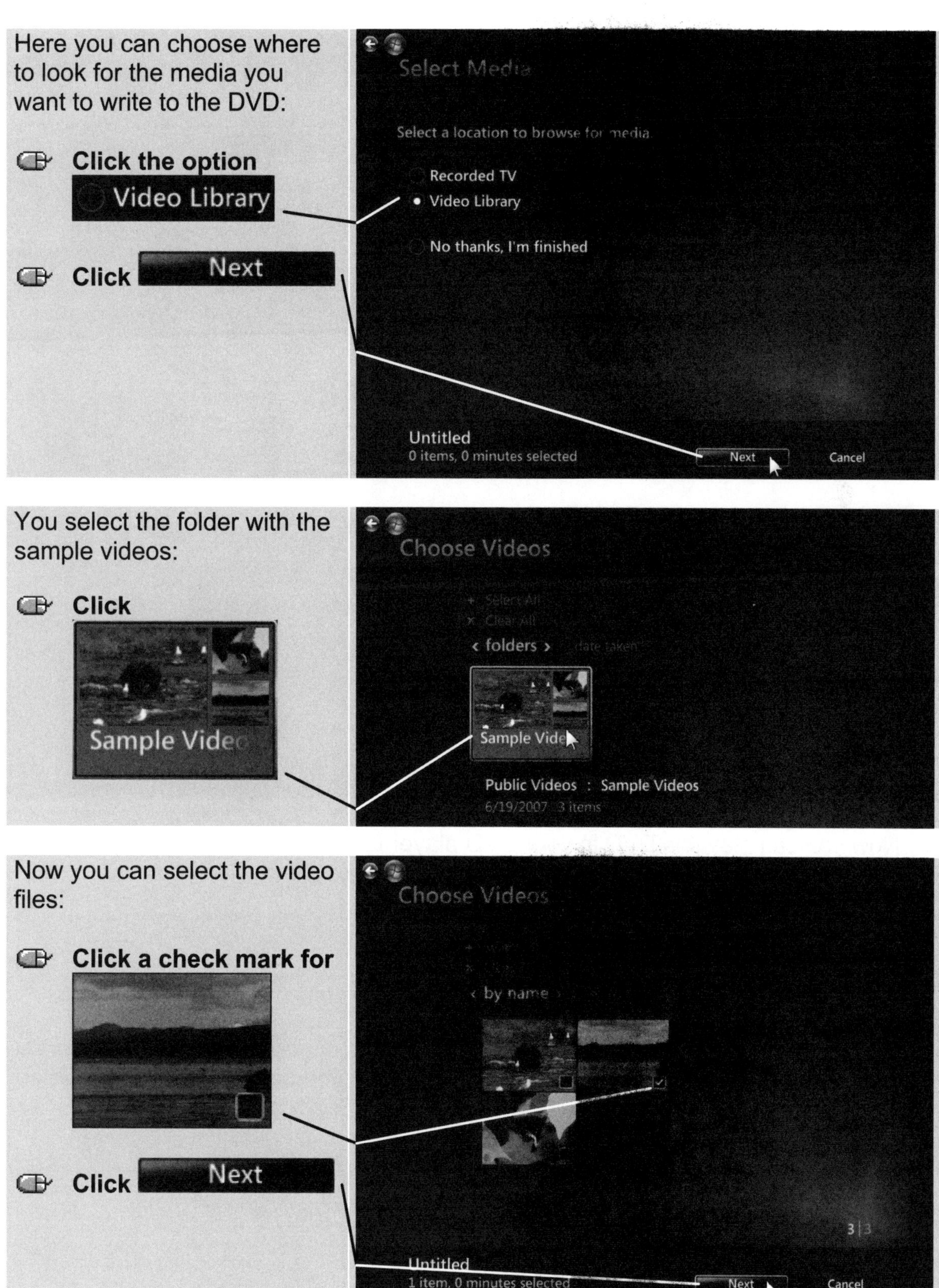
Here you can choose where to look for the media you want to write to the DVD:
Click the option
Video Library
Click
Next
Select Media
Select a location to browse for media
Recorded TV
Video Library
No thanks, I'm finished
Untitled
0 items, 0 minutes selected
Next
Cancel
You select the folder with the sample videos:
Click
Sample Vide
Choose Videos
‹ folders ›
Sample Vide
Public Videos : Sample Videos
6/19/2007 3 items
Now you can select the video files:
Click a check mark for
Click
Next
Choose Videos
‹ by name ›
3 | 3
Untitled
1 item, 0 minutes selected
Next
Cancel

Now you can write the video DVD:

Click **Burn DVD**

If you really want to write this DVD:

Click **Yes**

After a while the files are written to the disc:

Click **Done**

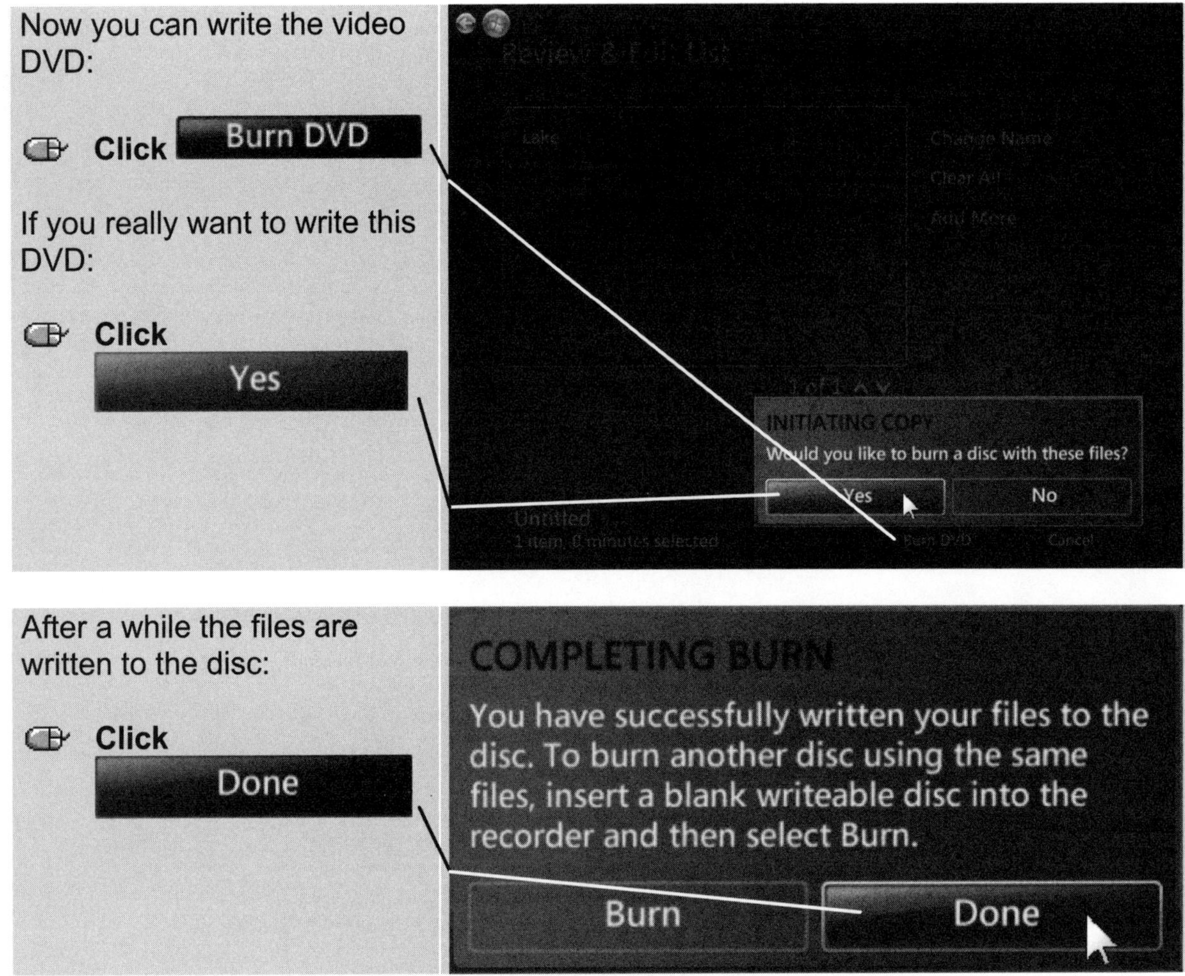

Now you can play this DVD in your DVD player for example. You can use the same method to write CDs and DVDs containing data, music and slide shows.

Take the DVD you just wrote out your computer

Close the *Windows Media Center* window

Would you like to know more about the possibilities of your computer and *Windows Media Center* combined with your television? Then you can read the extensive series of articles that can be found in *Windows Help and Support* on this subject.

6.11 Windows Movie Maker

Windows Vista also has its own program for digital video editing: *Windows Movie Maker*. You can use this program to simply and quickly edit your own movies, using titles, transitions and menus. This is how you open the program:

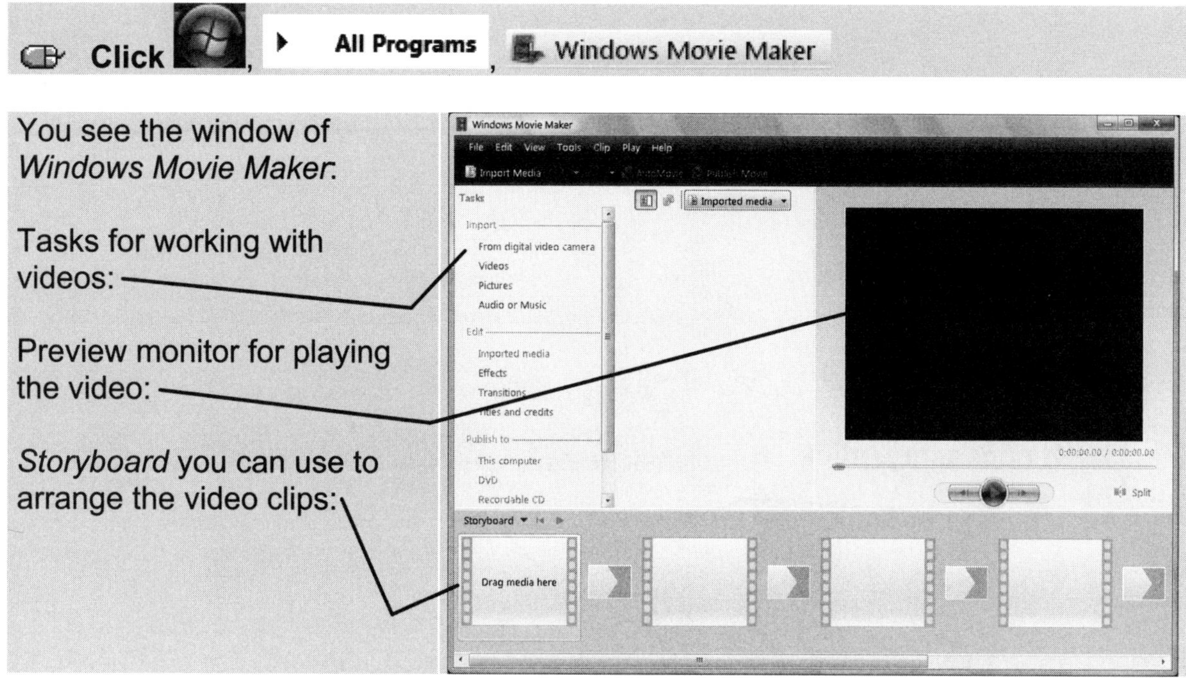

You are going to import one of the sample videos available in *Vista*:

HELP! I can not open Movie Maker

If you can not open *Windows Movie Maker*, your graphics card probably does not have enough memory. In that case you can download *Windows Movie Maker 2.6* from the *Microsoft* website. On the website **www.visualsteps.com/switchtovista/news** you can find a PDF file with information about downloading *Windows Movie Maker 2.6*.

Click **Import Media**

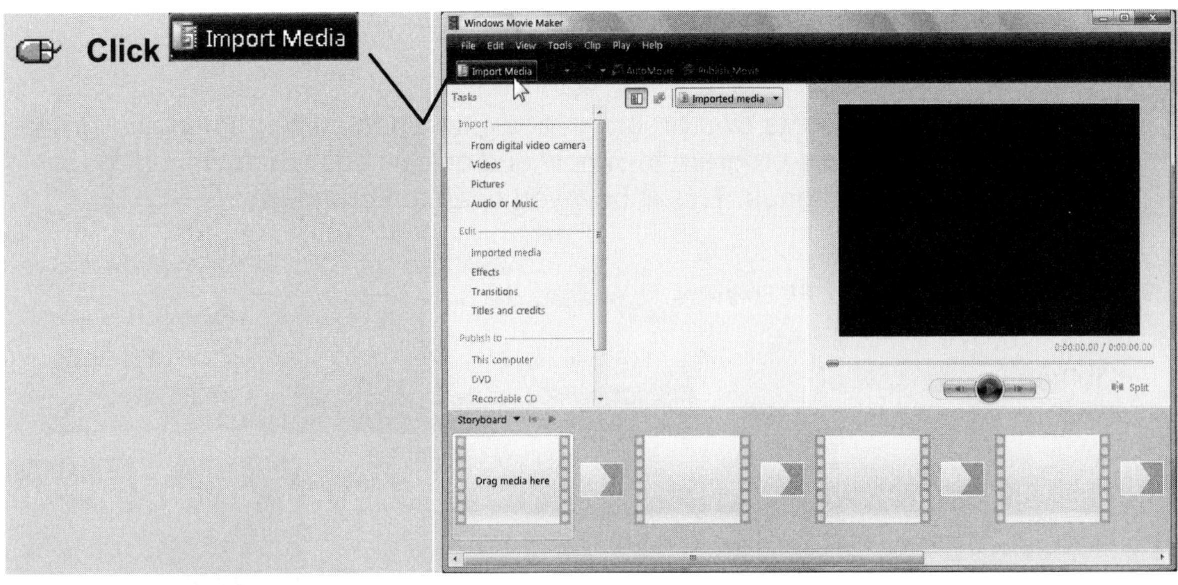

You see this window:

If necessary, click Videos

Double-click Sample Videos

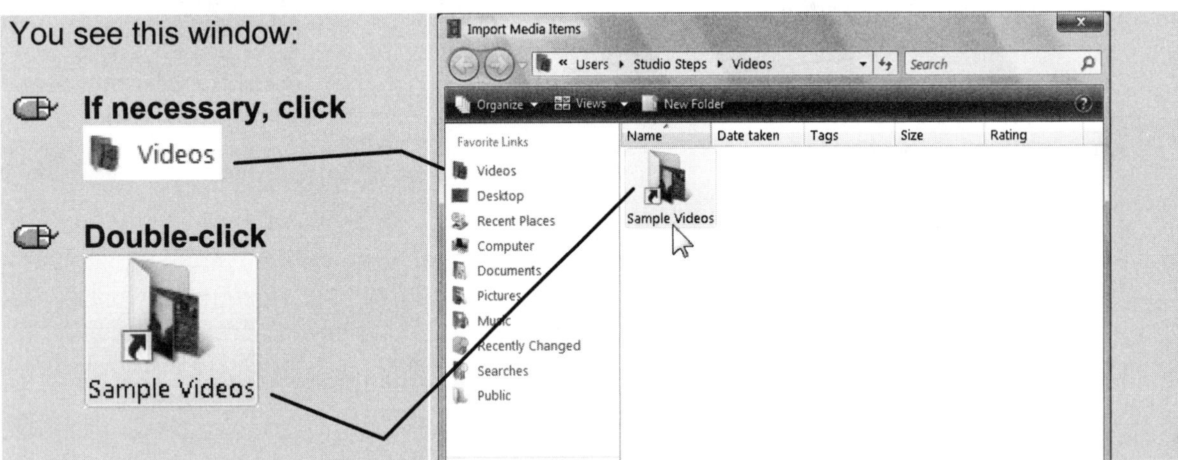

The *Windows Vista* sample videos appear in the *File list*:

Click Bear

Click Import

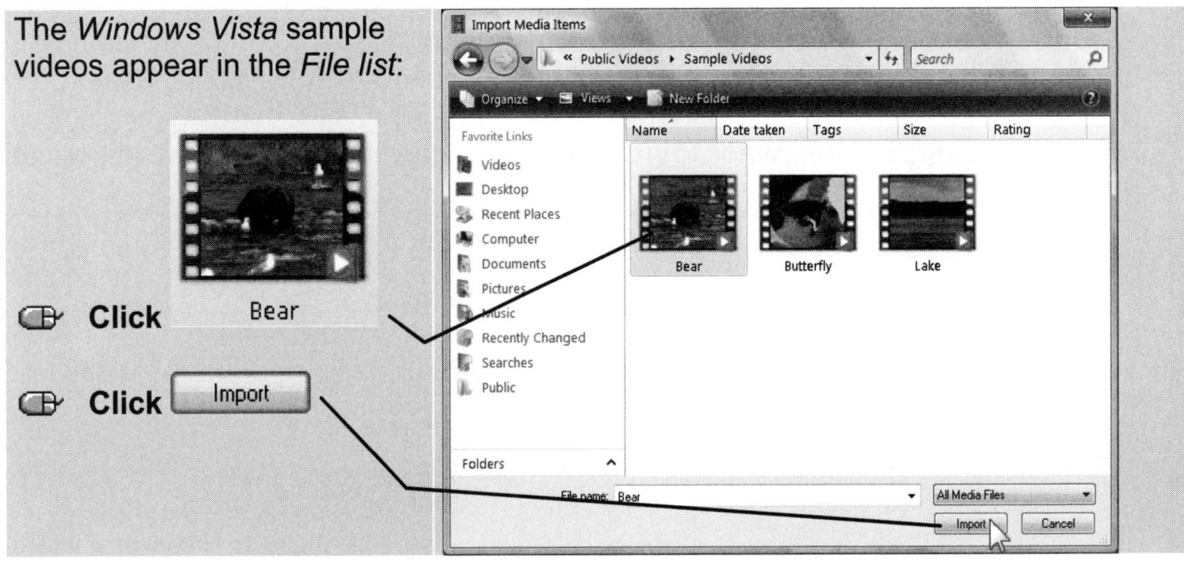

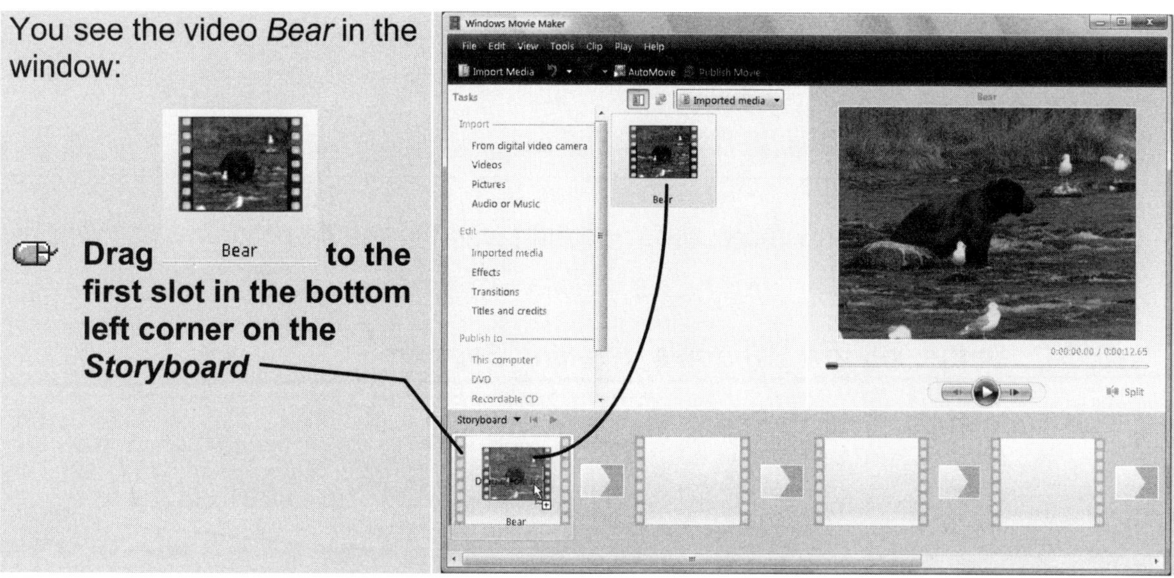

You see the video *Bear* in the window:

- **Drag** Bear **to the first slot in the bottom left corner on the *Storyboard***

- **Use the same method to import the video file *Lake* and drag it to the second slot on the *Storyboard***

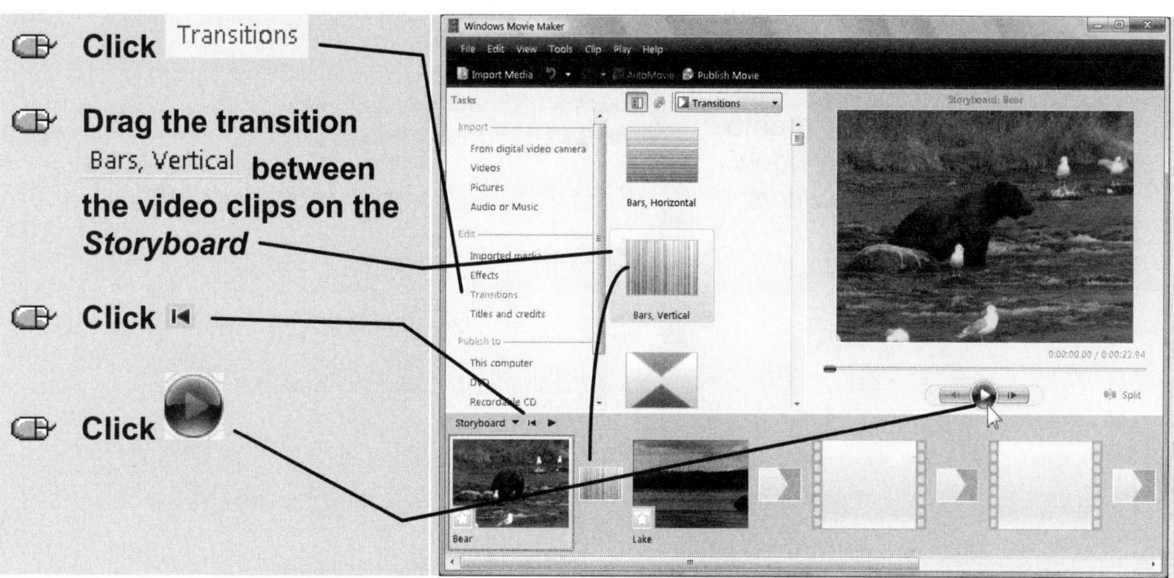

- **Click** Transitions
- **Drag the transition** Bars, Vertical **between the video clips on the *Storyboard***
- **Click** ⏮
- **Click** ▶

The edited movie is played with the transition you added. In *Windows Movie Maker* you can quickly edit movies by dragging clips and adding transitions. These movies can be written on DVD or sent by e-mail. Click Publish Movie on the *Movie Maker* toolbar to open a wizard that will guide you through the procedure in a number of windows. Follow the instructions in each window.

- **Close the *Windows Movie Maker* window**

In this chapter you have been introduced to the media programs in *Windows Vista.*

6.12 Tips

 Tip

Help and Support
If you would like to know more about working with the media programs in *Windows Vista*:

Open the window *Windows Help and Support* 4

Type in the *Search Box*: Windows Media Player

Click

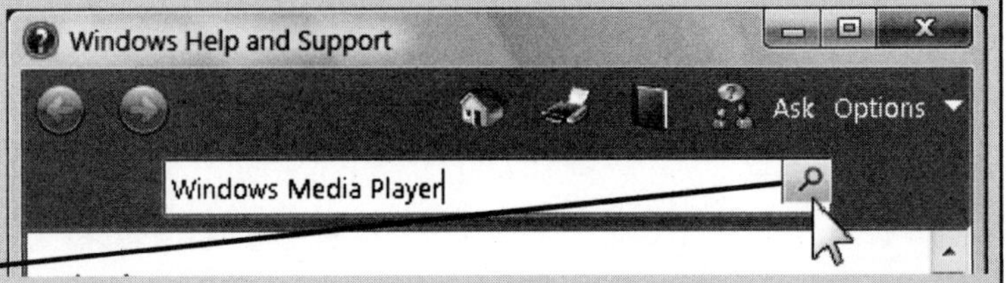

You see a list of articles containing extensive information on *Windows Media Player*.

You can use the same method to find articles about *Windows Media Center* and *Windows Movie Maker*.

 Tip

Find more information about the media programs in *Vista* by going to the *Windows Help and Support* section at www.microsoft.com. You can also learn more about the media programs in *Windows Vista* using the step by step method of Visual Steps in our book ***Photos, Video and Music with Windows Vista for SENIORS*** (ISBN: 978 90 5905 065 5). For more information: **www.visualsteps.com**.

7. Internet and E-mail

To surf the Internet, *Windows Vista* comes equipped with *Internet Explorer 7*. In this chapter you will be introduced to the most important new features of *Internet Explorer 7*. Learn how to use the new version quickly and easily even when you are quite comfortable using version 6 on your old computer.

One of the most important changes is the new appearance. Some of the familiar buttons and bars have been moved or even have disappeared. Also a couple of new features have been added to follow new trends on the Internet, like RSS feeds with the latest headlines from your favorite websites.

Windows Vista has also replaced its e-mail management program *Outlook Express* with a new program called *Windows Mail*. This program has enhanced security for banning junk e-mail and avoiding phishing attempts. For managing your contact lists, the old address book has been replaced with a new application called *Windows Contacts*.

To be able to use this chapter you need a working Internet connection. You can read chapter 1 section 1.14 *Setting Up a Dial-Up Connection* for more information.

In this chapter you will find information on the following subjects:

- the new appearance of *Internet Explorer 7*;
- working with tabs;
- searching using the *Instant Search Box*;
- changing the default search engine;
- RSS feeds;
- the *Favorites Center*;
- setting up e-mail accounts in *Windows Mail*;
- managing unwanted e-mail;
- saving your contacts list.

7.1 A New Appearance

You can find *Internet Explorer* in the *Start menu*:

Internet Explorer 7 has a clean new design:

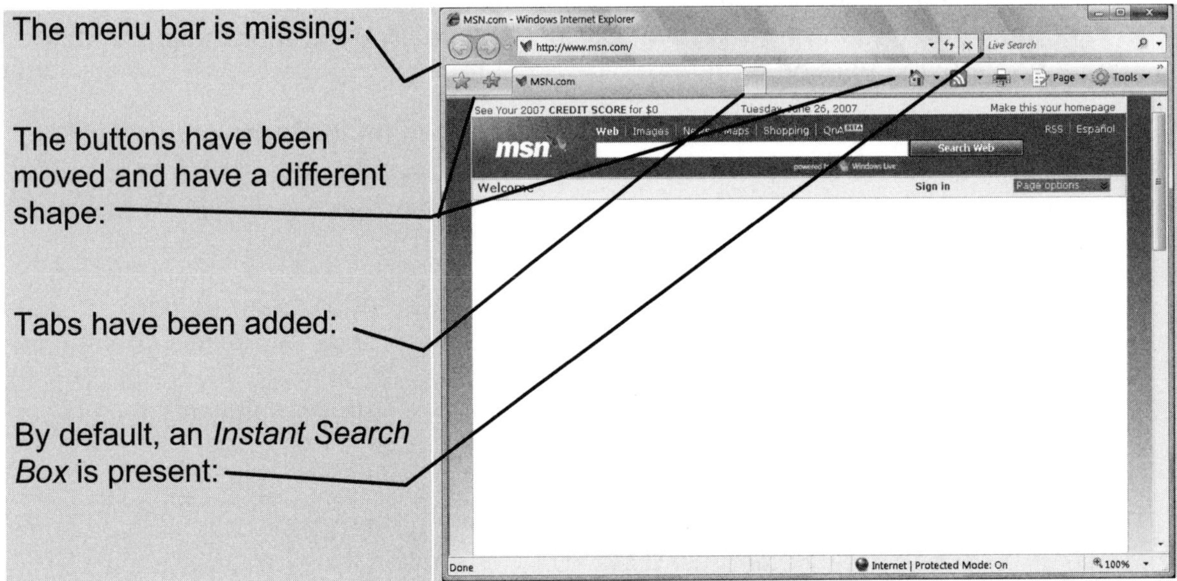

Getting used to the new set up should not be too difficult. Some people might miss the menu bar from earlier versions of *Internet Explorer.* You can display it like this:

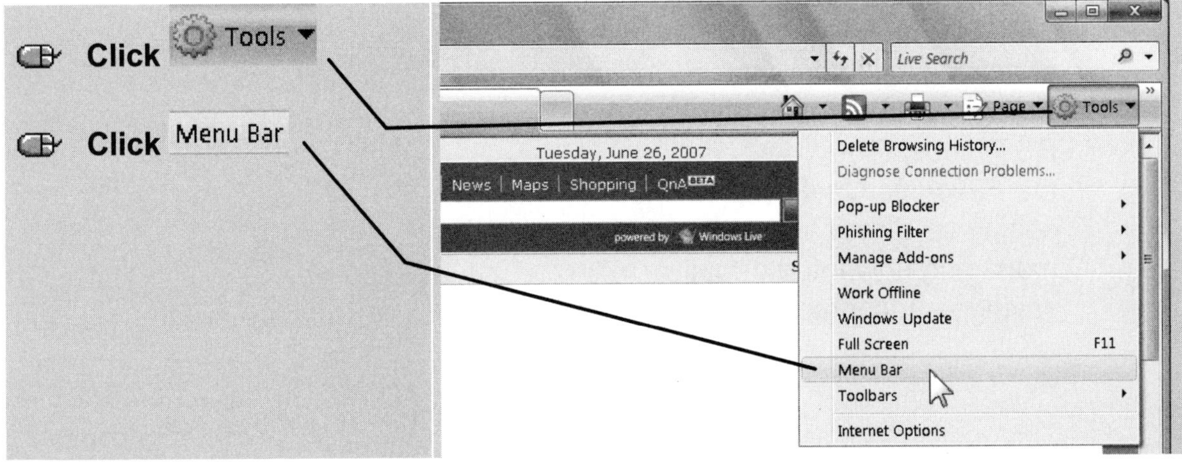

The menu bar is now displayed in its usual spot right below the title bar. If you do not need the menu bar you can hide it like this:

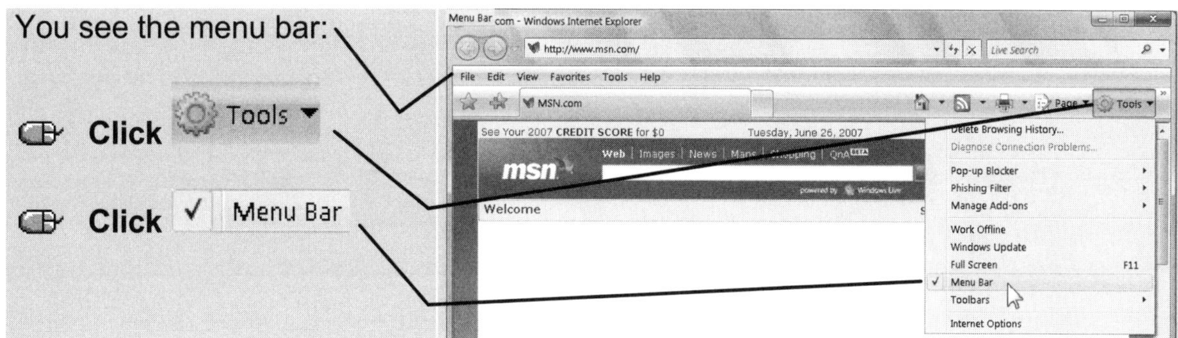

Tip

A quick way to display the menu bar is by pressing the Alt key. The menu bar will appear immediately in your browser window. Just press it again to hide it.

7.2 Working with Tabs

Internet Explorer 7 has a wonderful new feature that allows you to open multiple websites in a single browser window. This is called *tabbed browsing*. You can start by opening a new, blank tab:

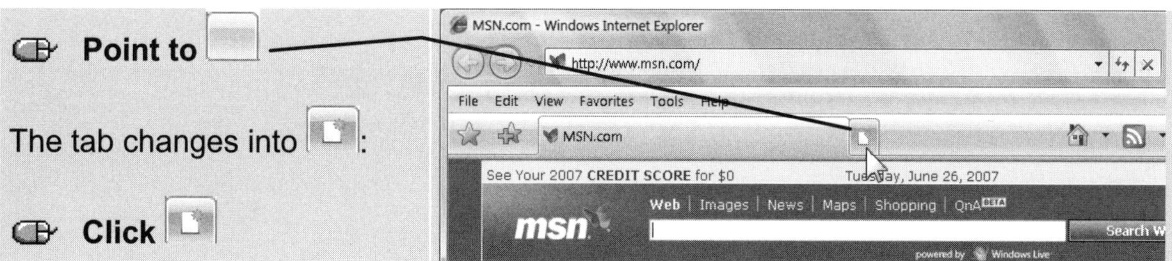

In the new tab you will see a webpage with information about tabs. The web address about:Tabs is blue, so you can type a new address right away:

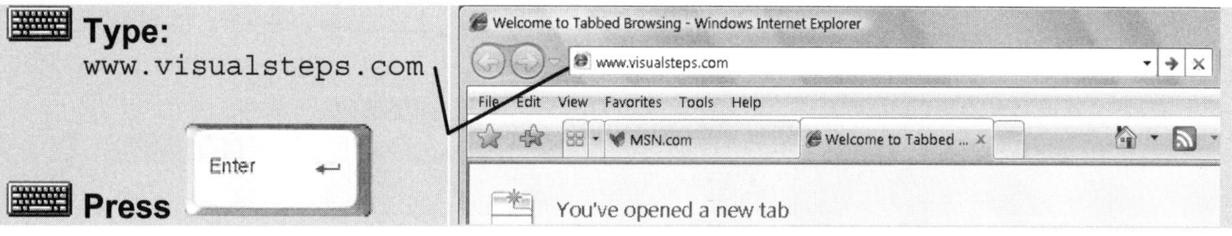

After a short while, you see the website on the new tab. You can switch between tabs by clicking the tab you want to display. You can also close a tab:

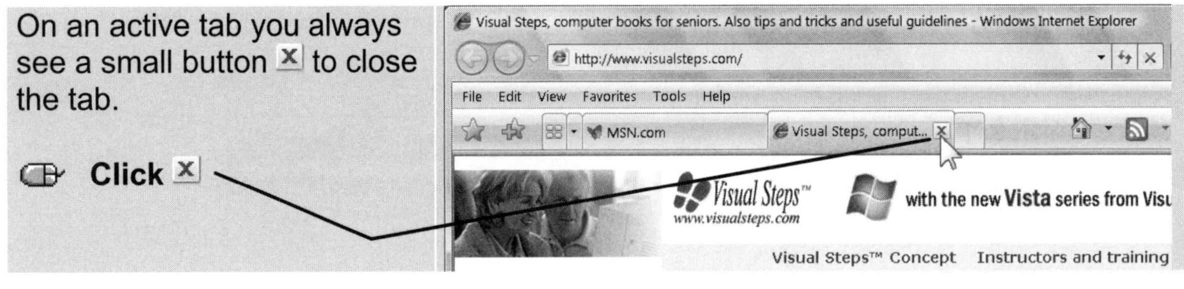

On an active tab you always see a small button ☒ to close the tab.

Click ☒

Tip

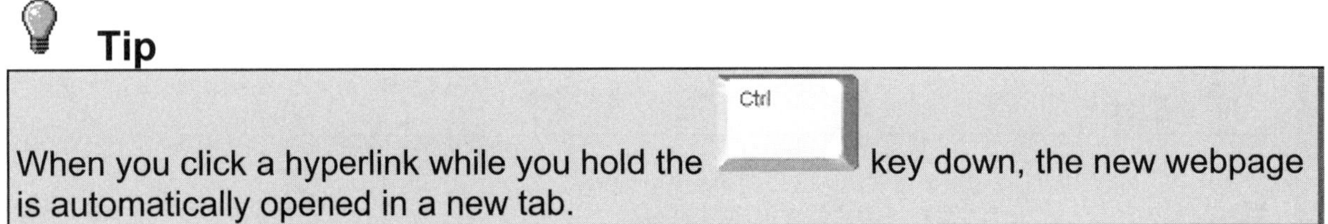

When you click a hyperlink while you hold the Ctrl key down, the new webpage is automatically opened in a new tab.

7.3 The Instant Search Box

In *Internet Explorer 7* you do not need to start a search engine to start a search. You can type your search term in the *Instant Search Box*:

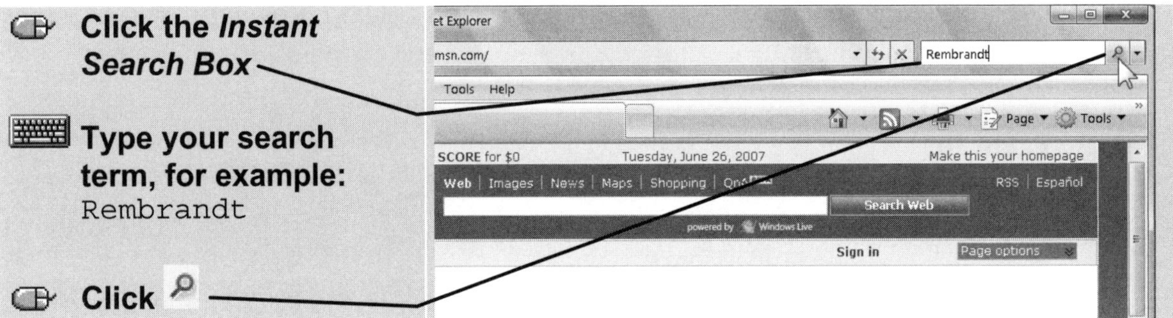

Click the *Instant Search Box*

Type your search term, for example: `Rembrandt`

Click 🔍

The search results will appear in the window. *Live Search* is the default search engine, but you can also replace it with your favorite search engine:

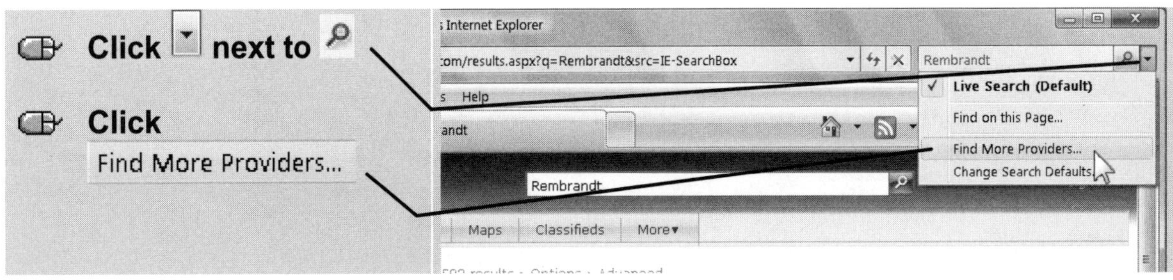

Click ▾ next to 🔍

Click Find More Providers...

You can select any of the additional search providers shown on this webpage.

Click the search engine you want to use, for example *Google*

The window *Add Search Providers* appears:

Click 

The search provider has been added.

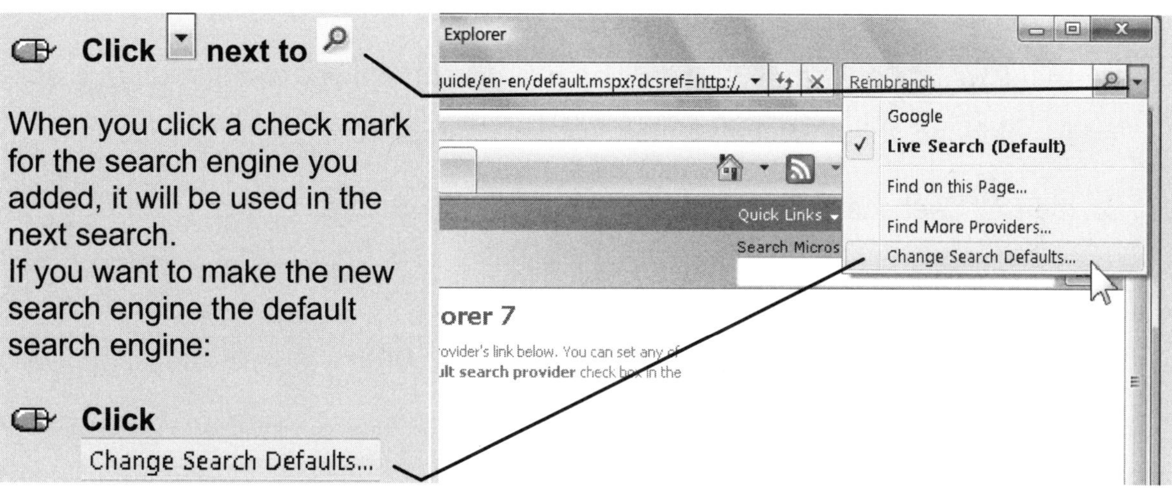

Click ▾ **next to** 🔍

When you click a check mark for the search engine you added, it will be used in the next search.
If you want to make the new search engine the default search engine:

Click Change Search Defaults...

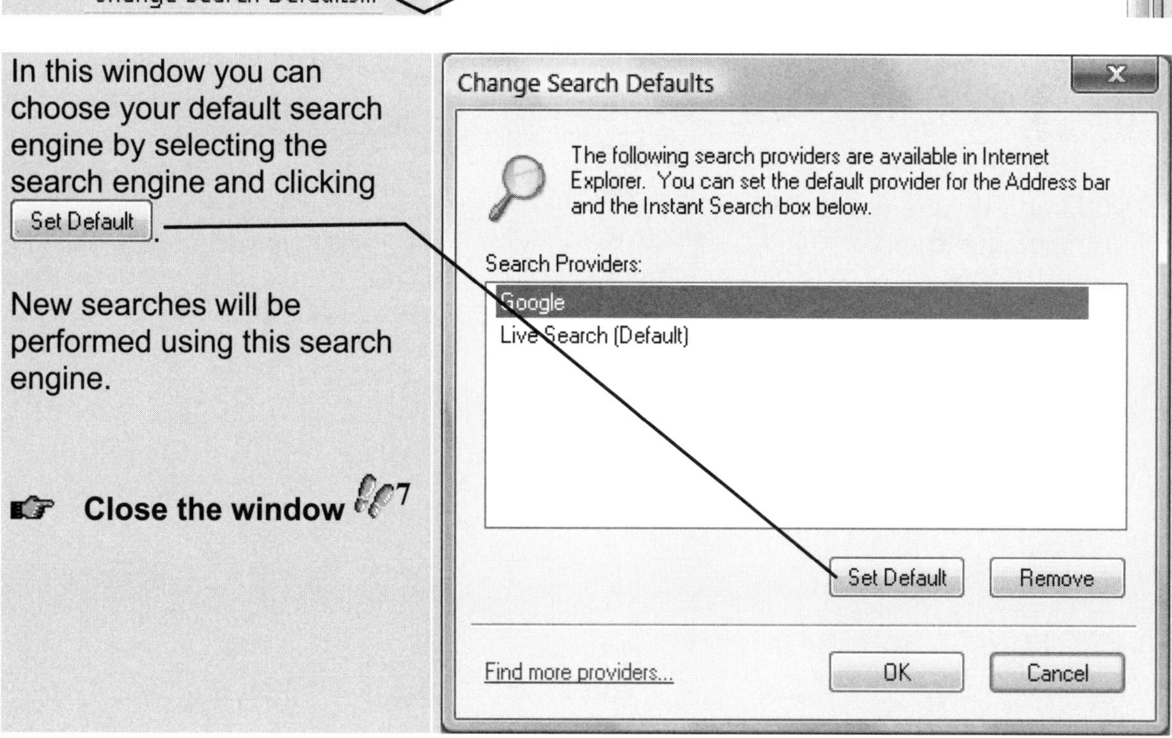

In this window you can choose your default search engine by selecting the search engine and clicking Set Default.

New searches will be performed using this search engine.

Close the window 7

7.4 RSS Feeds

News agencies like CNN, newspapers and other dynamic websites offer a service called *RSS feeds*. The acronym RSS stands for *Really Simple Syndication*, a format used to publish frequently updated digital contents, such as news headlines or sports scores.

Internet Explorer has a built-in feed reader that can display these feeds. When you subscribe to a news agency feed for example, the latest headlines are automatically sent to your computer when you connect to the Internet.

Internet Explorer looks for RSS feeds on every webpage you visit. When available feeds are found, the *RSS feed* button will change from gray to orange.

On the CNN website you can subscribe to a free RSS feed:

Surf to www.cnn.com

If necessary, close the window information bar

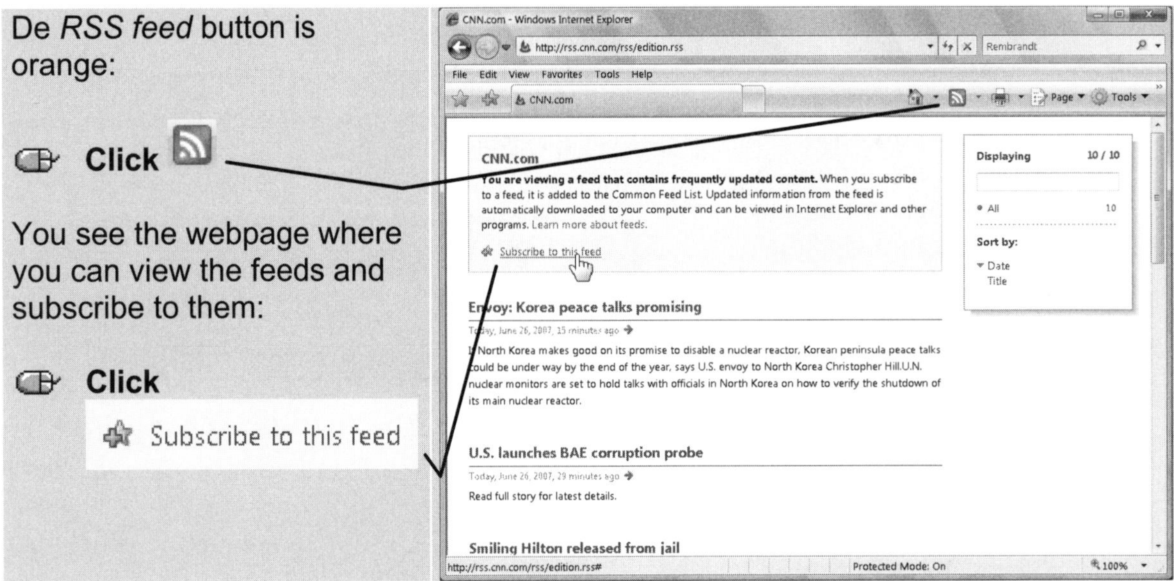

De *RSS feed* button is orange:

Click

You see the webpage where you can view the feeds and subscribe to them:

Click Subscribe to this feed

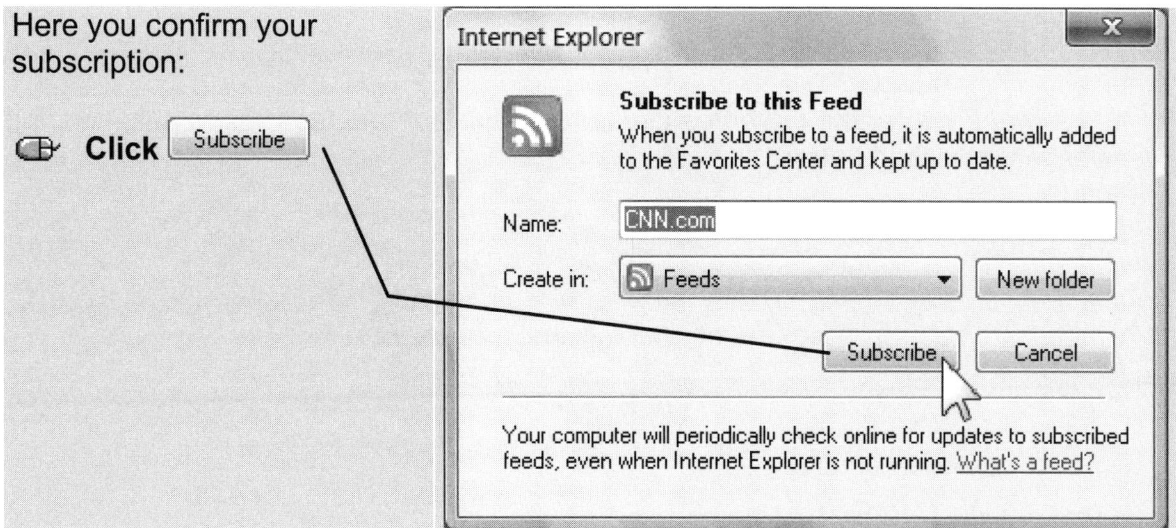

Now that you have subscribed to this feed, it has been added to the *Common Feed List* in the *Favorites Center.* You can verify this:

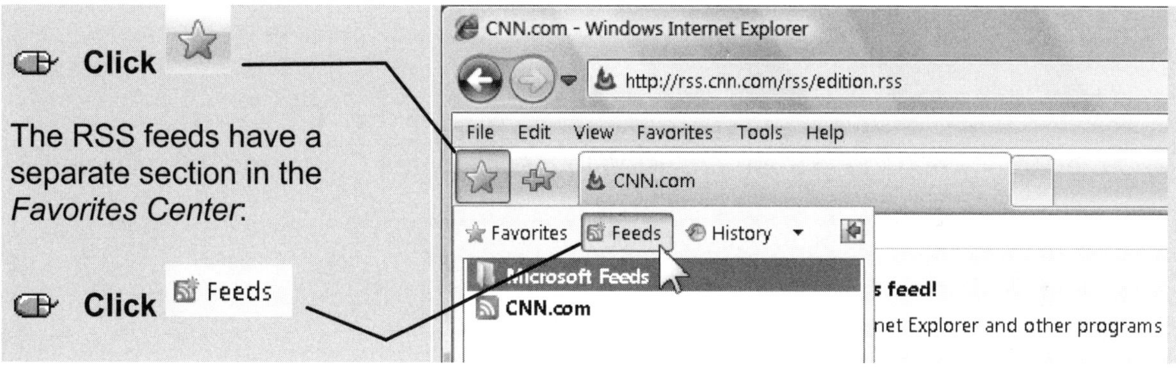

Here you can view the feeds you have subscribed to. In this example you only see the CNN feed.

7.5 The Favorites Center

In *Internet Explorer* the *Favorites Center* contains several features to help you find a website you visited before.

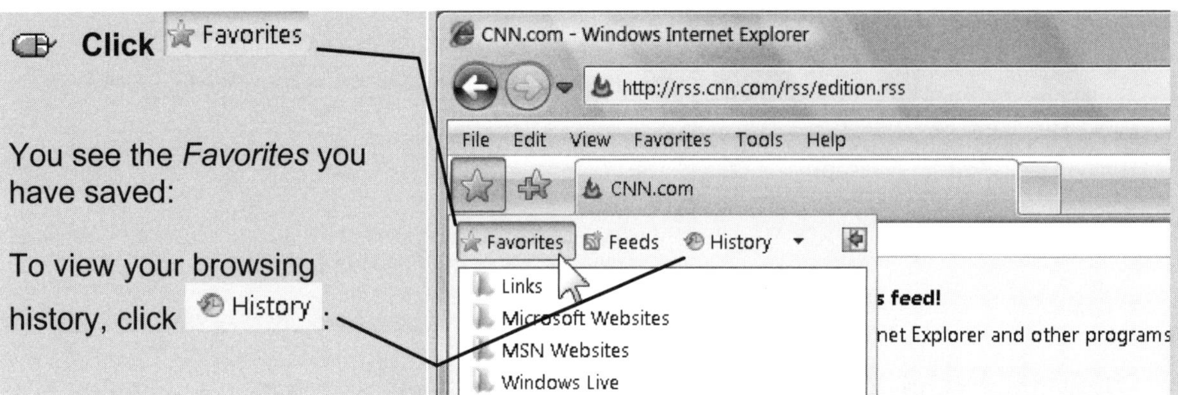

Click Favorites

You see the *Favorites* you have saved:

To view your browsing history, click History:

To close the *Favorites Center*:

Click

To add the webpage you are browsing to the *Favorites Center*, do the following:

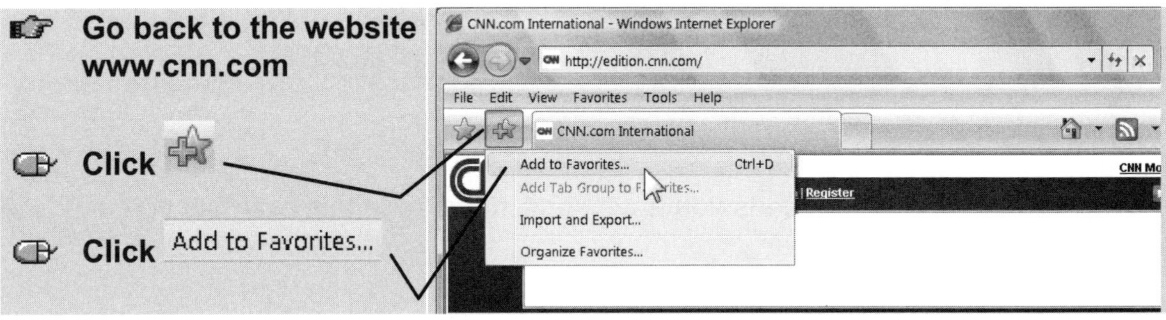

Go back to the website www.cnn.com

Click

Click Add to Favorites...

In this window you can enter a name for your *Favorite* and you can choose a folder. Then click Add.

If you do not want to add this webpage to your *Favorites*:

Click Cancel

Close the *Internet Explorer* window

7.6 Setting Up Windows Mail

Windows Mail is the successor to *Outlook Express.* Although many features remain unchanged, the program has received quite a facelift. This is how you start *Windows Mail*:

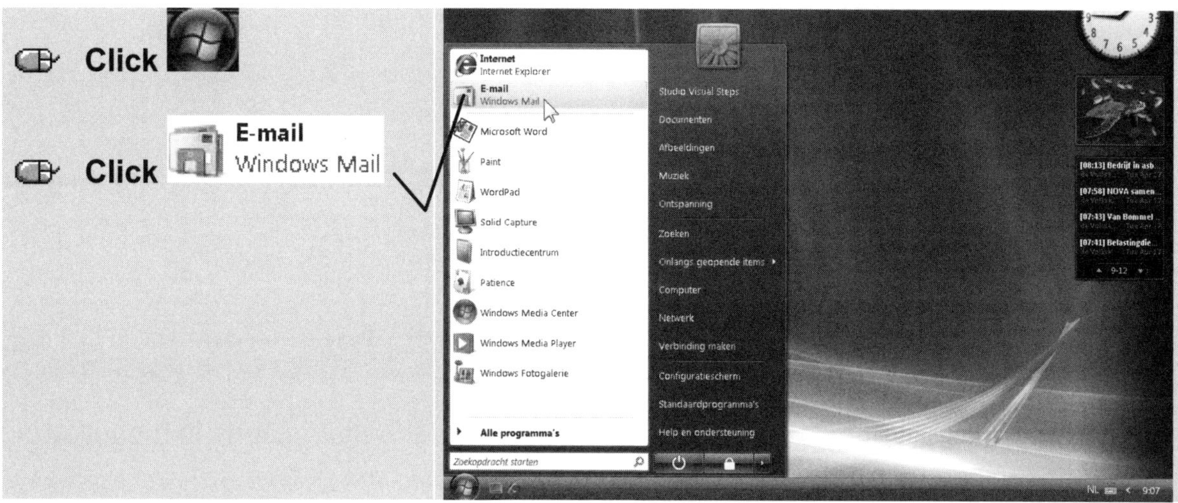

If you have a new computer and your e-mail accounts have not yet been transferred, you have to set these up first. You need the information provided by your *Internet Service Provider* to be able to do so.
When you open *Windows Mail* for the first time, you are asked to set up an e-mail account. Here is how to set up an account:

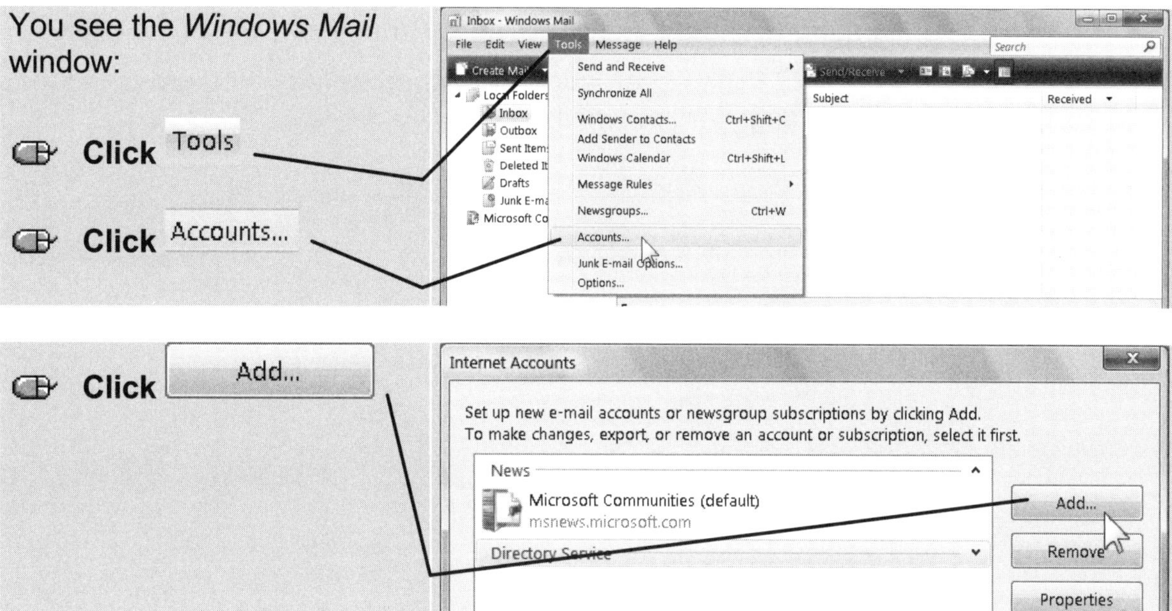

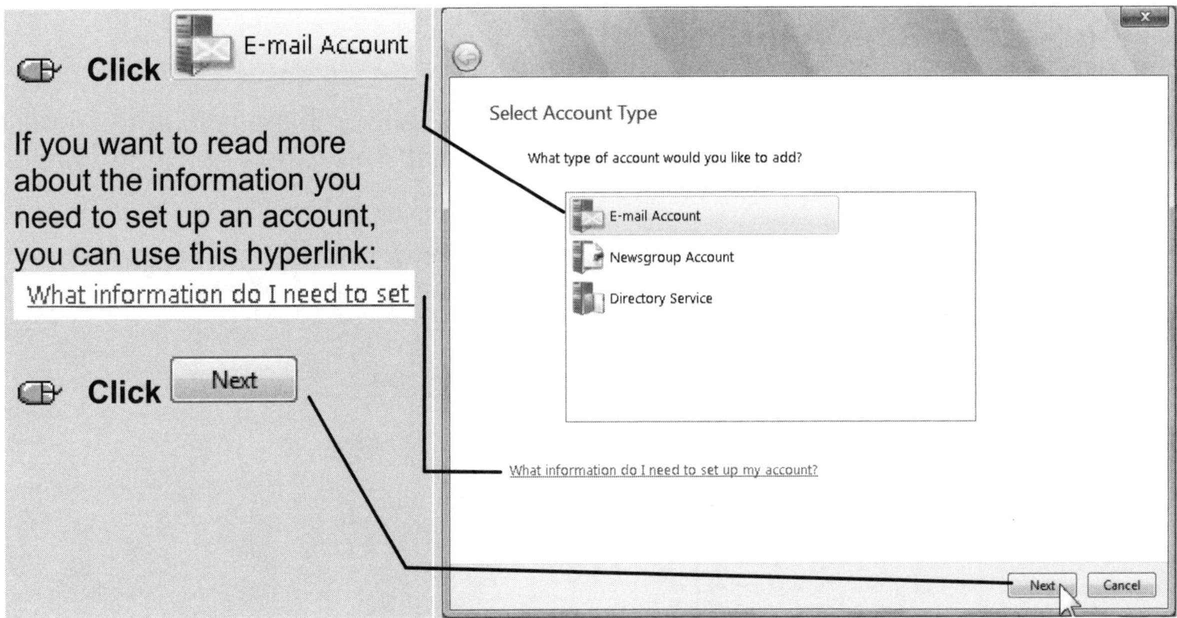

A wizard will take you through the procedure. Read the instructions in the following windows and enter the requested data.
After you have finished the setup process, your e-mail account is ready .

Close the window *Internet Accounts*

7.7 Junk Mail

To be able to separate unwanted e-mails like spam from your normal mail, the separate folder Junk E-mail has been added to *Windows Mail*. You are going to take a look at the general settings for junk mail:

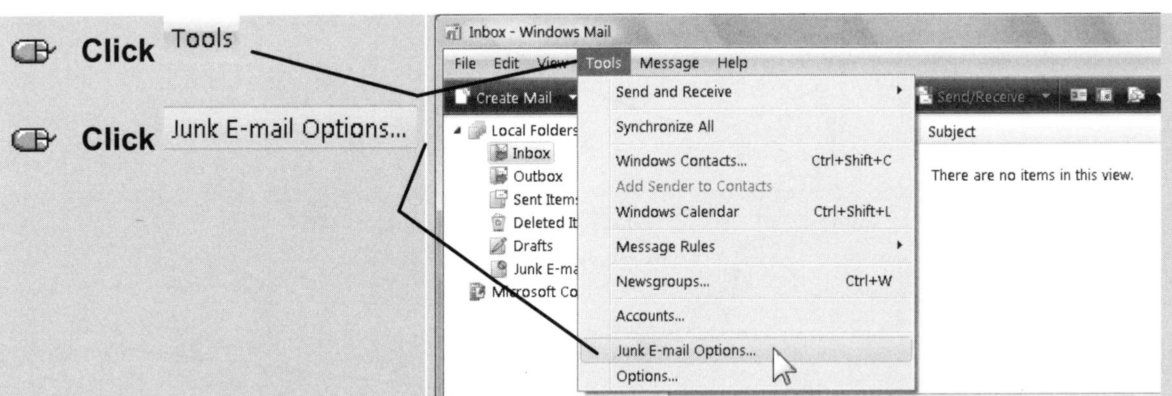

In this window you can adjust settings on multiple tabs:

For example, you can add senders to the *Safe Senders list* or to the *Blocked Senders list*. E-mail from senders on the *Blocked Senders list* will be moved to the *Junk E-mail* folder. Automatic protection against *phishing* has been added as well.

Look at the options on the tabs

Adjust the settings if necessary

To confirm the settings you can use the button Apply.

If you do not change anything:

Click Cancel

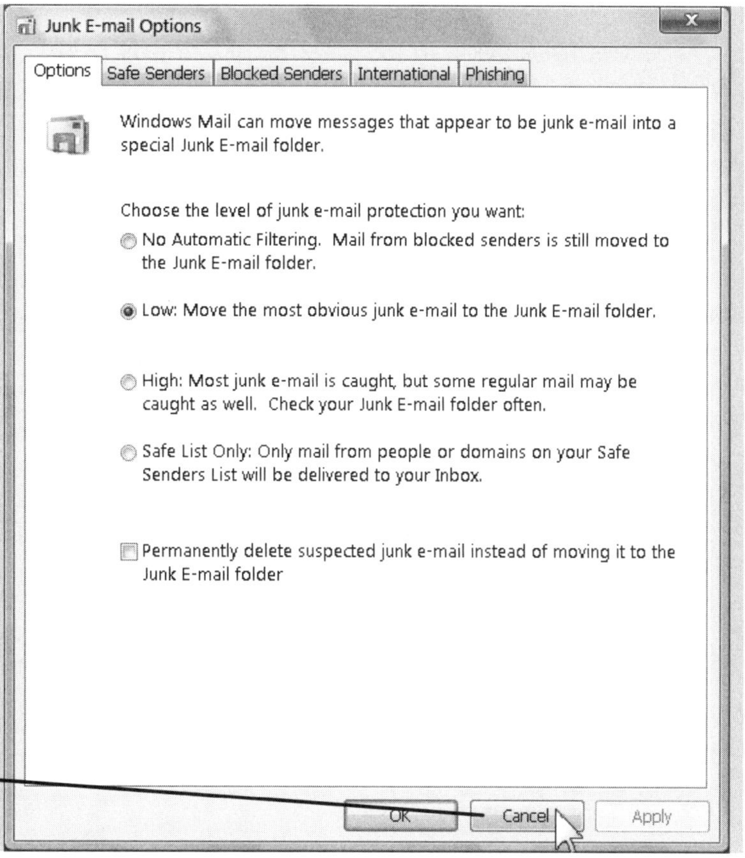

Tip

Check the folder Junk E-mail regularly to see if the e-mails that have been moved there are really junk e-mail. If the folder also contains regular e-mail, you can change your settings.

7.8 Windows Contacts

The address book in *Outlook Express* has been replaced by *Windows Contacts* in *Windows Mail.* You can add contacts or change the current contacts list like this:

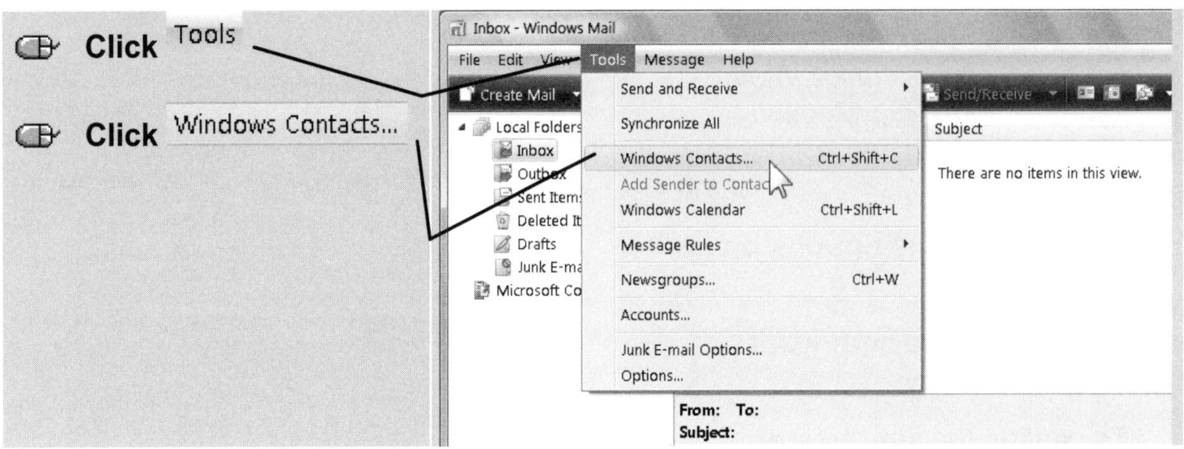

You see your *Contacts* folder with the names of contacts that have been saved:

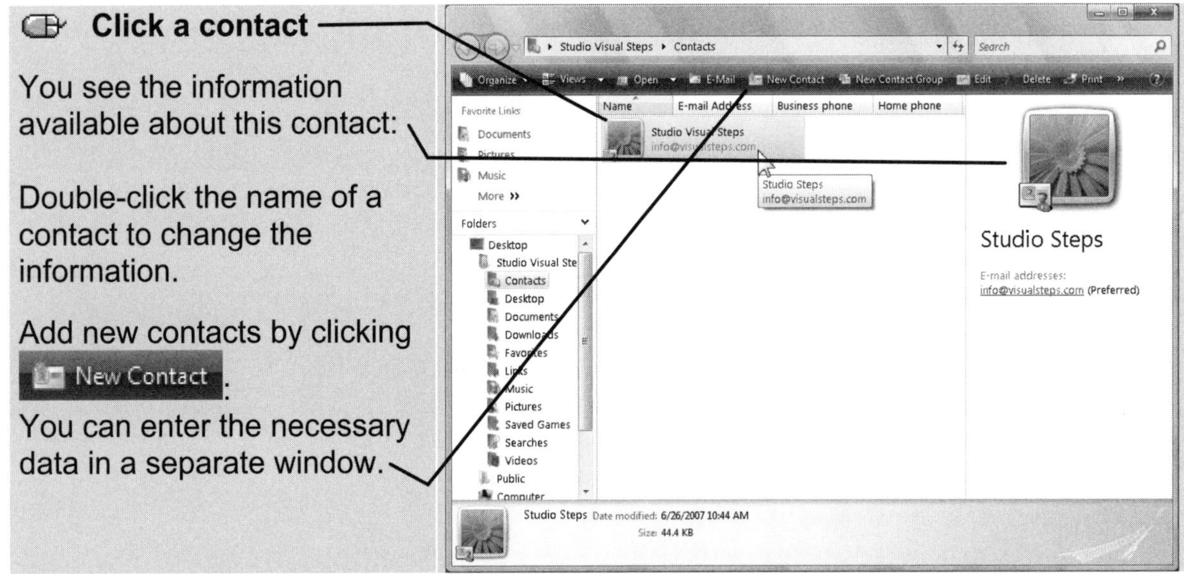

Close the window *Contacts* and the program *Windows Mail*

In this chapter you have been introduced to the most important changes and new features in *Internet Explorer* and *Windows Mail.*

7.9 Tips

Tip

Feed headlines in the Windows Sidebar
Now that you have subscribed to the CNN RSS feed, these headlines are also shown in the gadget named *Feed Headlines* in the *Windows Sidebar* on your desktop.
Usually all feeds you have subscribed to are displayed in random order. If you want this gadget just to display the CNN headlines, do the following:

- **Right-click the *Feed Headlines***
- **Click** Options
- **Click** ▾
- **Click** CNN.com
- **Click** OK

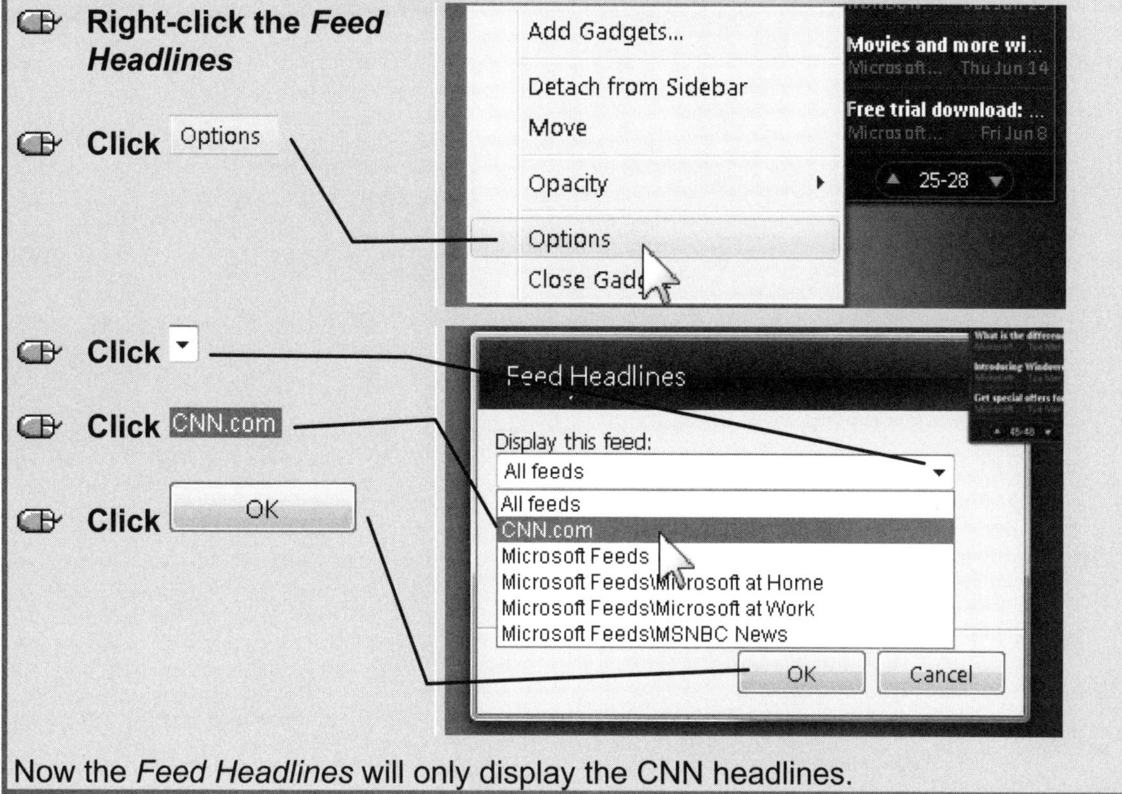

Now the *Feed Headlines* will only display the CNN headlines.

Tip

You can add senders to the *Blocked Senders list* in *Windows Mail* by right-clicking a message from this sender and choosing Junk E-mail, Add Sender to Blocked Senders List.

Tip

A message that has been placed in the *Junk E-mail* folder by mistake, can be moved to the *Inbox* by selecting the message and clicking Not Junk in the *Windows Mail Toolbar.*

Notes

Write your notes down here.

8. Security

Compared to *Windows XP*, the most important improvement in *Windows Vista* is the security. You probably already noticed that. You frequently see your screen go dark and you need to give your permission to perform a task. This is controlled by *User Account Control*. This will prevent changes being made to your computer by users who do not have permission to do so.

Windows Vista has more security options, for example to protect your computer from the dangers of the Internet. By default, *Windows Firewall* is used to manage the incoming and outgoing data traffic between your computer and the Internet and/or other networks. Depending on your settings, data traffic is blocked or allowed. *Windows Defender* actively protects your computer against the unwanted installation of spyware or other unwanted software. You can monitor the status of these two programs in the *Security Center*. Here you also find the item *Automatic updating.* This feature continuously checks for available *Windows Vista* updates. Installing these software updates keeps your operating system up to date.

Windows Vista does not contain an antivirus program. This means you have to purchase and install an antivirus program yourself. The presence and the status of your antivirus program will be monitored by the *Security Center*.

A new feature in *Windows Vista* is *Parental Controls*. You can use this feature to set limits on when other users, for example your (grand)children, are allowed to log on to your computer. You can also control the programs they can run and the websites they can visit.

In this chapter you will learn about:

- *Windows Security Center;*
- *Windows Firewall;*
- *Windows Defender;*
- *Windows Live OneCare;*
- *Windows Update;*
- *User Account Control;*
- *Parental Controls.*

8.1 Windows Security Center

The *Security Center* in *Windows Vista* monitors the security settings of your computer and lets you know when new *Vista* updates are available. You can open the *Windows Security Center* like this:

Open the *Control Panel* 3

Click

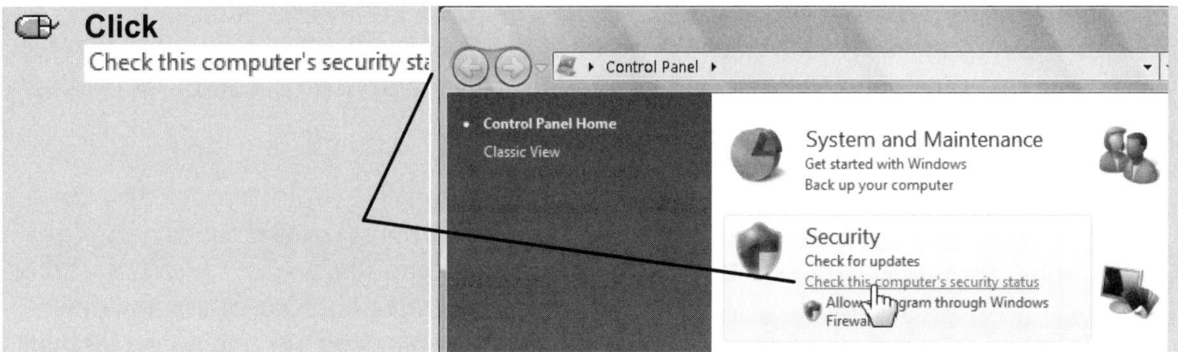

In this window you see the status of the four most important components of your computer's security:

- *Firewall*
- *Automatic updating*
- *Malware protection*
- *Other security settings*

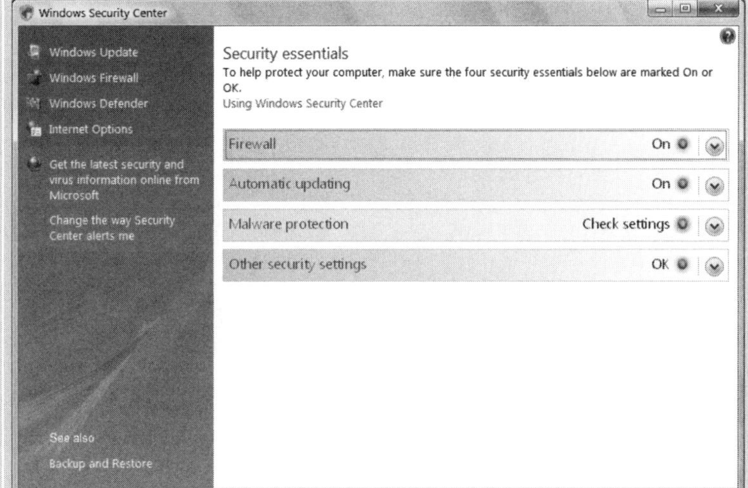

In this example three items have the status On or OK. These items do not need your attention.

The malware protection shows Check settings. It is possible that an antivirus program has not been installed, or that the installed program can not be recognized by *Vista*. If you switched off an item manually you see the status Off.

The settings of your computer may be different than what you see in this example.

8.2 Windows Firewall

A firewall is software or hardware that manages the incoming and outgoing data traffic between your computer and the Internet and/or other networks. Depending on your firewall settings, data traffic is either blocked or allowed to pass through to your computer.

The word firewall sounds safer than it actually is: a firewall **does not** protect your computer against viruses. If your e-mail program is allowed access to the Internet through your firewall, you can still receive an e-mail with an attachment that contains a virus. The firewall does not check the contents of the data traffic.

Click Windows Firewall

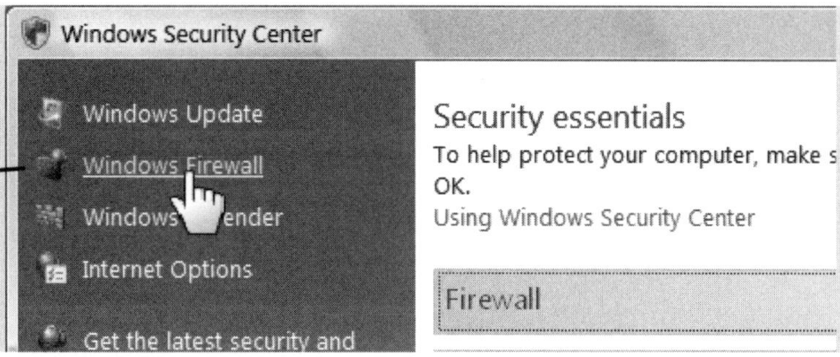

In this example *Windows Firewall* is used. It is possible that a different firewall has been installed on your computer. In that case *Windows Firewall* must be turned off using the link Turn Windows Firewall on or off:

Otherwise the two firewalls might interfere with one another.

Click Change settings

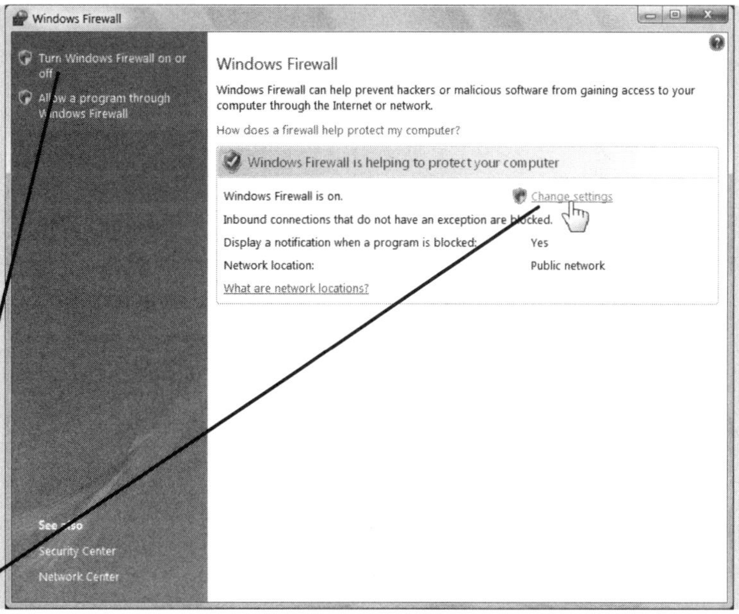

Your screen goes dark and you see a window where you need to give your permission to continue.

Now you see the window *Windows Firewall Settings*:

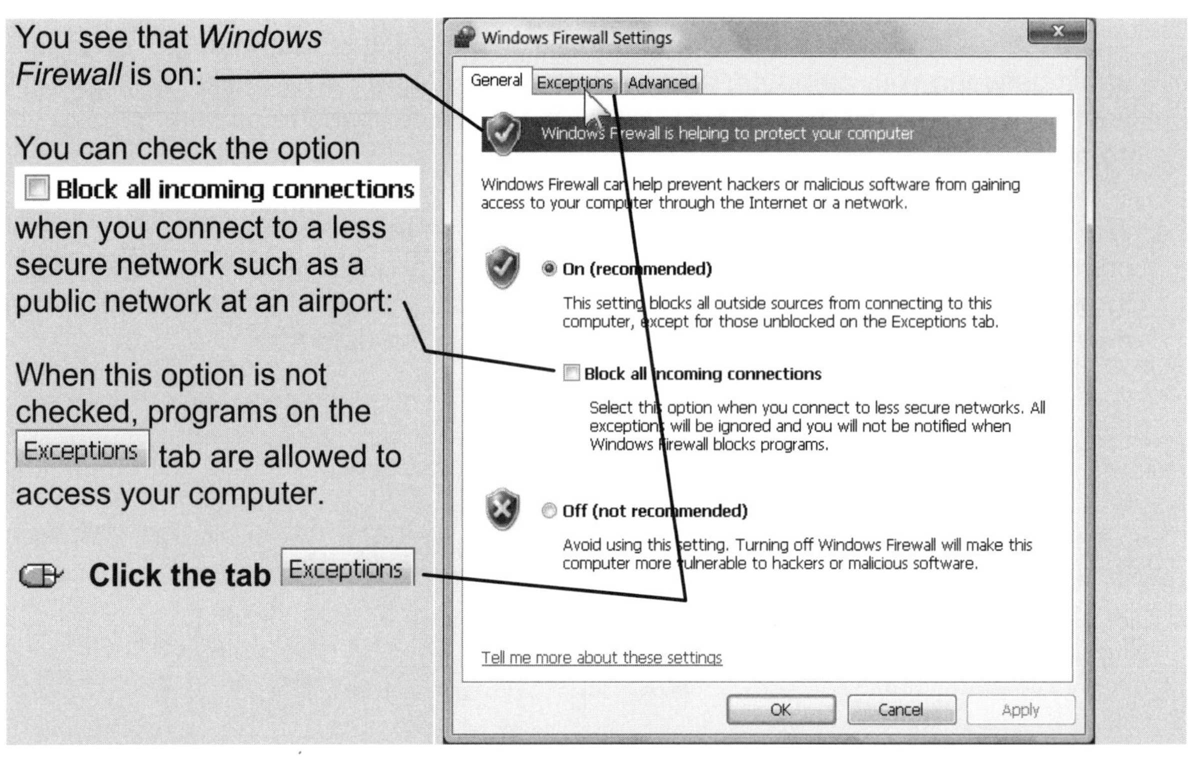

You see that *Windows Firewall* is on:

You can check the option **Block all incoming connections** when you connect to a less secure network such as a public network at an airport:

When this option is not checked, programs on the Exceptions tab are allowed to access your computer.

Click the tab Exceptions

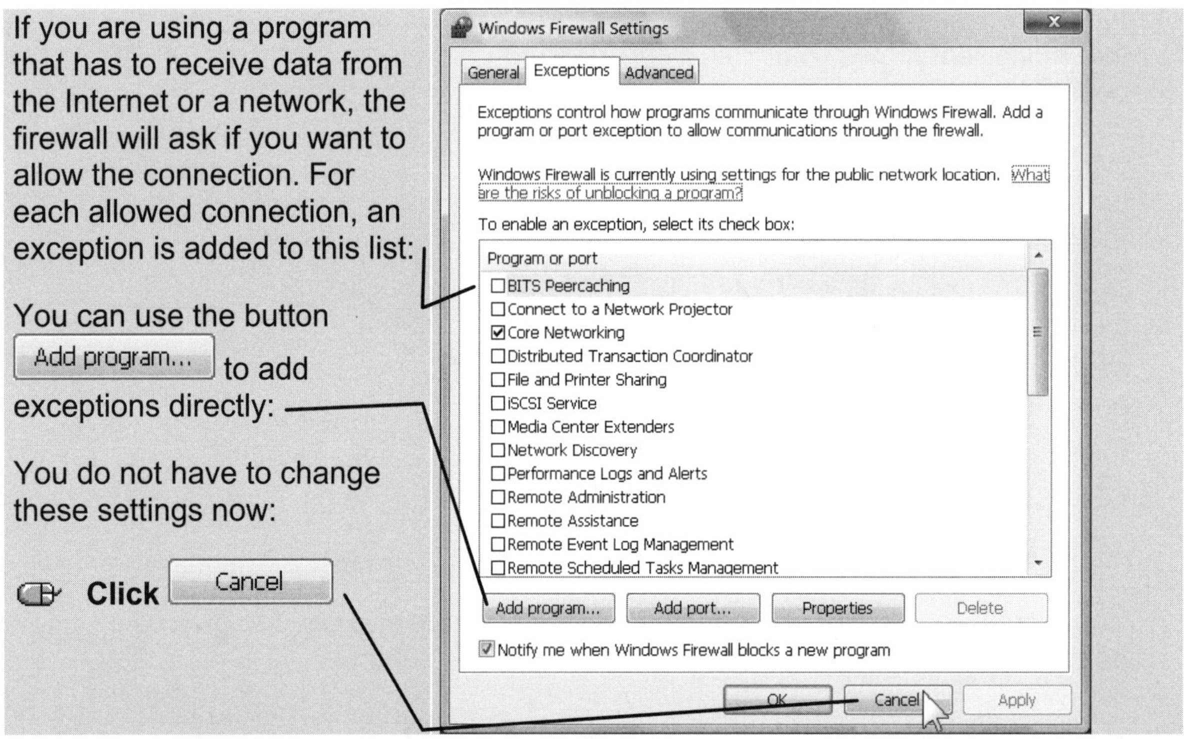

If you are using a program that has to receive data from the Internet or a network, the firewall will ask if you want to allow the connection. For each allowed connection, an exception is added to this list:

You can use the button Add program... to add exceptions directly:

You do not have to change these settings now:

Click Cancel

Close the *Windows Firewall* window

8.3 Windows Update

A very important part of the *Security Center* is *Windows Update.* This is a system that checks if you are using the most recent version of *Windows Vista*. *Windows Vista* is constantly being modified, expanded and made more secure. The additions and improvements are distributed by *Microsoft* in the form of *software updates*.

Please note:

Microsoft **never** sends software updates by e-mail. Anyone who receives an e-mail claiming to contain *Microsoft* software or a *Windows* update is strongly advised not to open the attachment and immediately delete the e-mail. Do not forget to delete it from the folder *Deleted items* as well. Mails like that are sent by criminals that try to install malicious software on your computer.

If you want to make sure your version of *Windows Vista* stays up to date, you should make sure *Automatic Updates* is turned on.

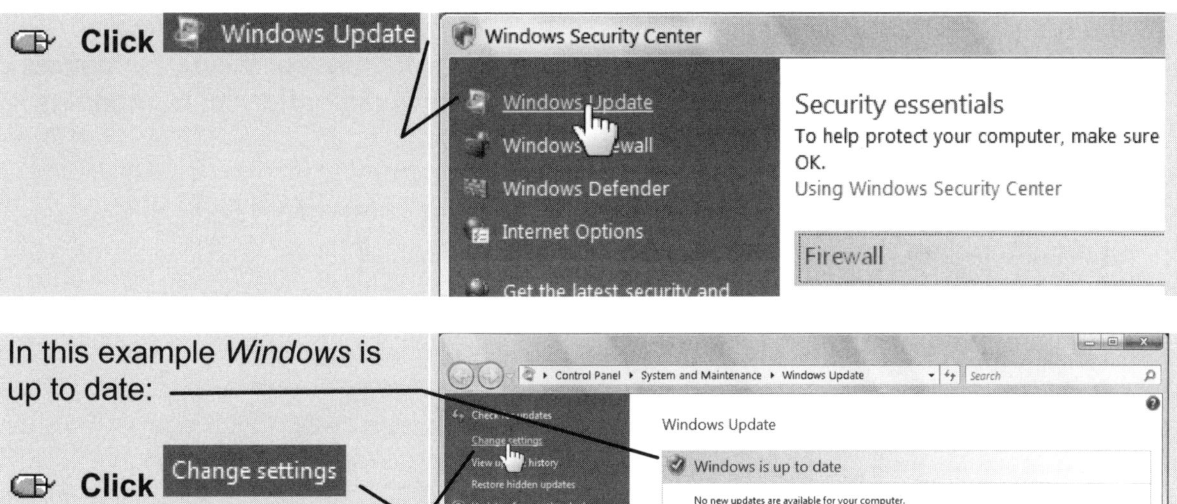

You see the current settings on your computer:

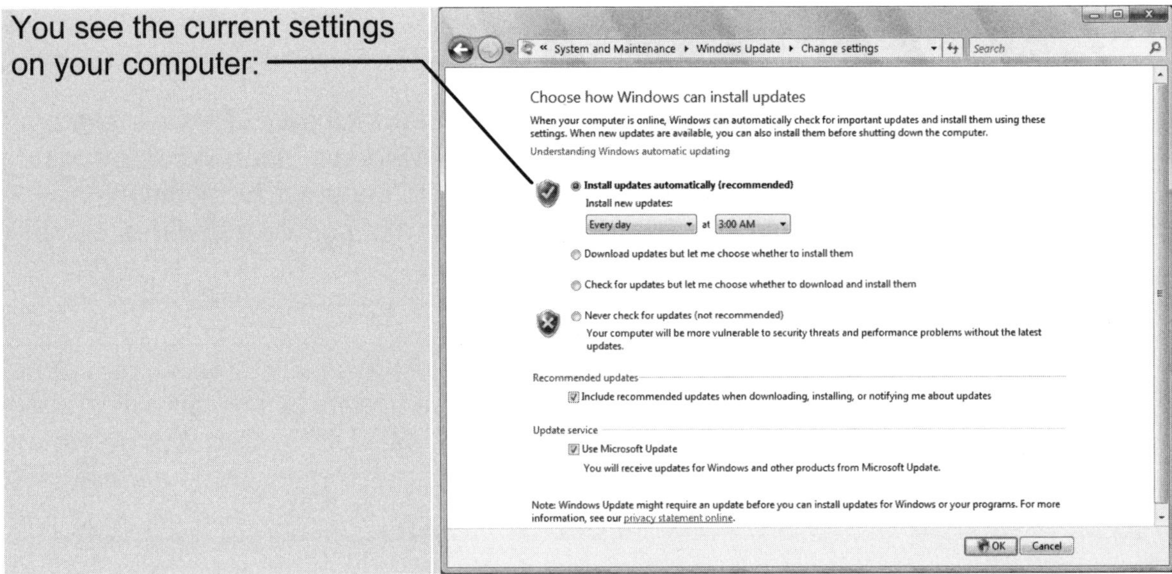

In this example, *Automatic Updates* is set to check for new updates and install these daily at 3:00 AM. If the computer was turned off at that time, the check will take place the next time the computer is turned on. The updates are then automatically downloaded and installed. *Windows* places a notification about this at the bottom of the screen, but in most cases you can just keep on working. For critical updates it may be necessary to restart your computer.

It is a good idea to select the **Install updates automatically (recommended)** setting. You can change the time to a moment that is most convenient for you.

Did you change a setting?

Click **OK**

Your screen goes dark, *Windows* needs your permission to continue. You can use the button **Continue** to give permission.

If you do not want to change anything:

Click **Cancel**

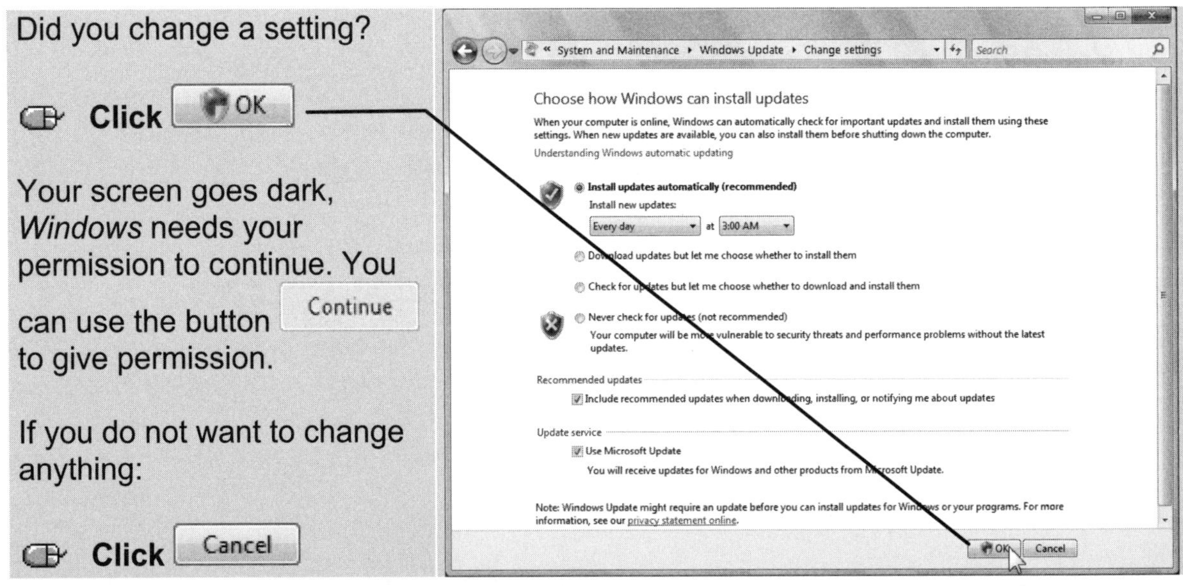

Close the *Windows Update* window

8.4 Malware protection

Malware is short for 'malicious software', software that is designed to deliberately harm your computer. Viruses, worms, spyware and Trojan horses are forms of malware. These types of software are an increasing threat to every computer connected to the Internet. The source of infection may be an attachment to an e-mail message or a file downloaded from the Internet. Your computer can also become infected by exchanging USB sticks, CDs or other storage media.

The *Malware protection* component of *Windows Security Center* checks to see if an up to date antivirus program is installed on your computer.

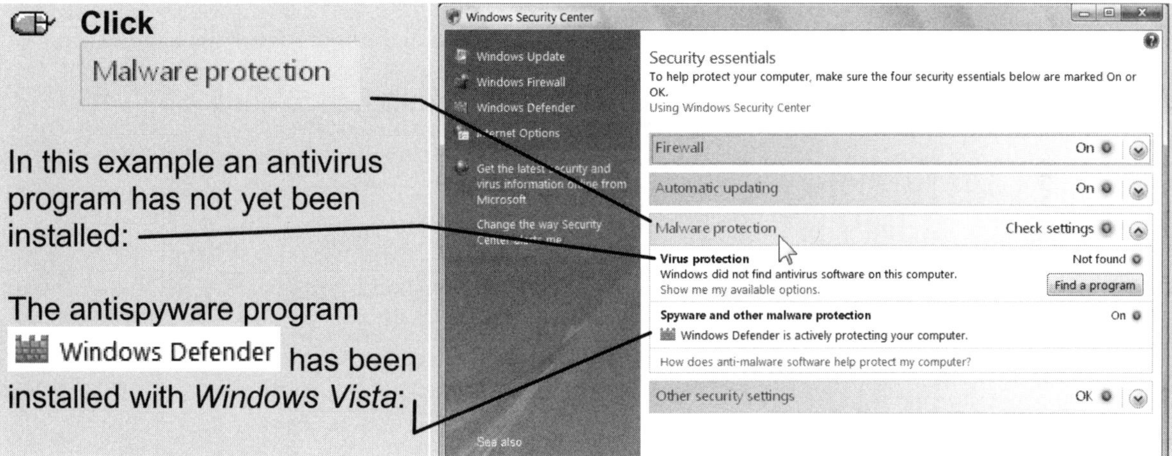

If you did not install an antivirus program, you will also see this message appear at the bottom of your screen from time to time:

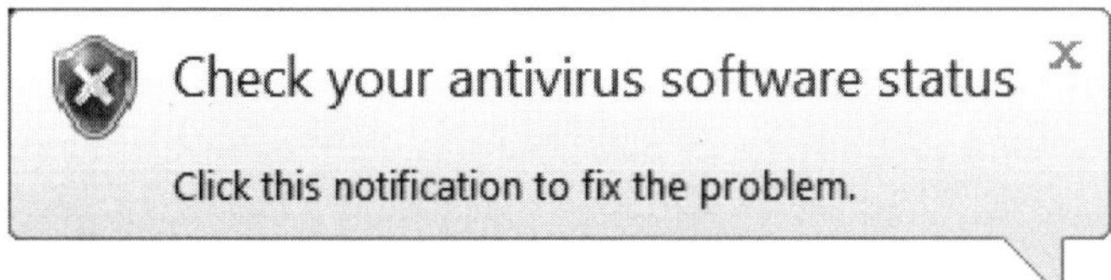

You will also see Check settings if you have installed an antivirus program that is not (yet) recognized by *Windows Vista*. There are excellent programs on the market where this is possible. In that case you can monitor your antivirus program yourself:

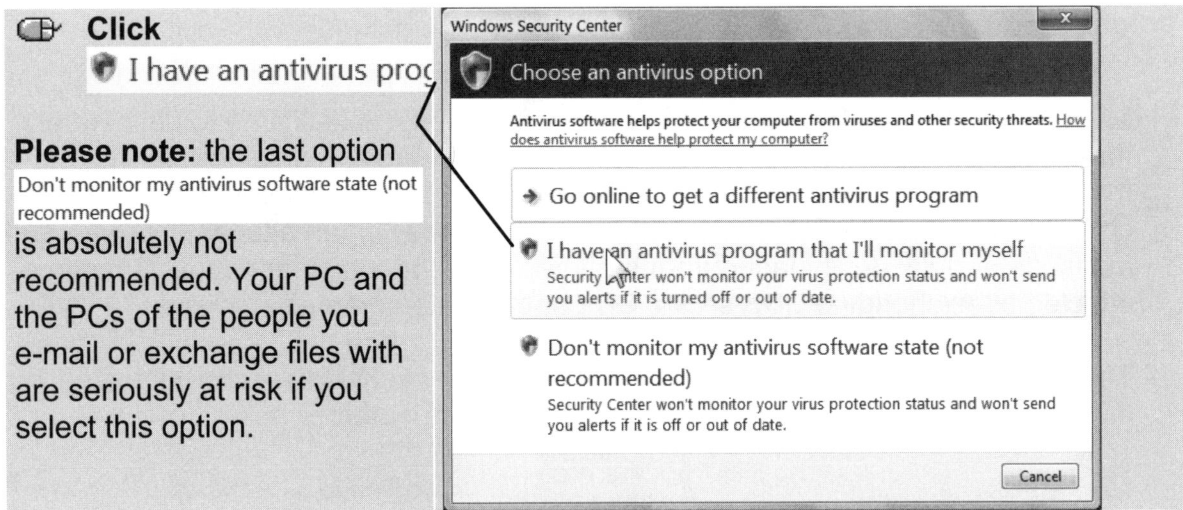

Your screen goes dark and *Windows* asks your permission to continue:

Click Continue

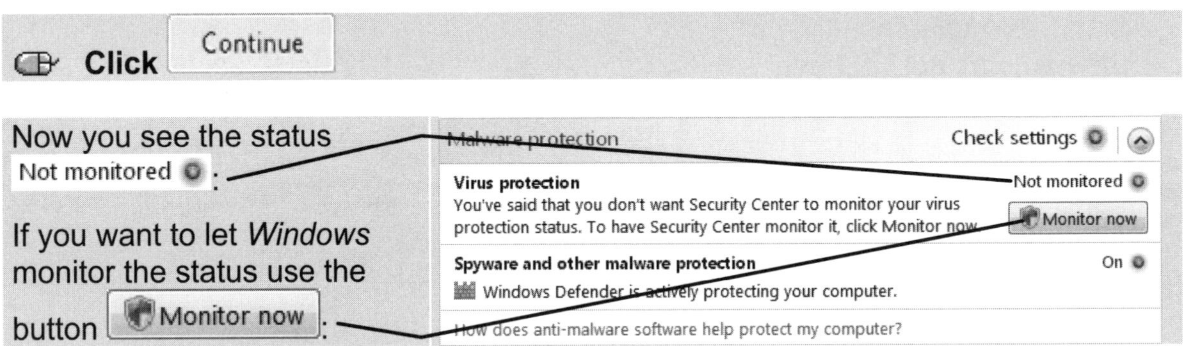

In the next section, you can read about the antispyware program *Windows Defender*. In the section after that, you can read about the 90-day free trial version of the *Microsoft* antivirus program *Windows Live OneCare.*

8.5 Windows Defender

Most Internet users will occasionally take advantage of one or more of the many free programs available. However, many people do not realize that some of these applications can contain components that gather information about users and send the information to the software's creators, for example about the websites you visit. It is even more annoying when settings on your computer are changed, like a different home page in your Internet browser or the insertion of an extra toolbar. Programs that do these kinds of things are called *spyware.*

Windows Defender is a program from *Microsoft* that is packaged with *Windows Vista*. You can use it to find and remove known spyware from your PC. Its continuous protection allows you to use the Internet safely.

Please note:

Windows Defender is not enough to protect your computer against viruses!
There is no antivirus program packaged with *Windows Vista*. This means you have to purchase and install one yourself. In the sections about *Windows Live OneCare* you will learn more about protecting your computer against viruses.

You can open *Windows Defender* from the *Security Center*:

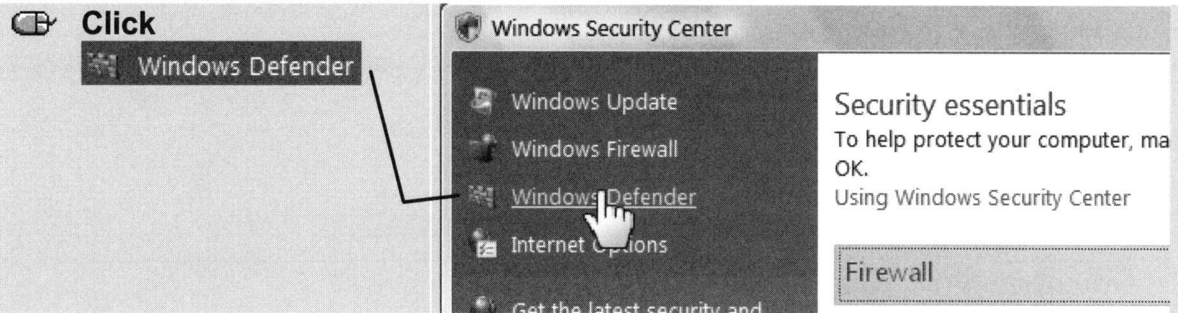

The *Windows Defender* opening screen appears.

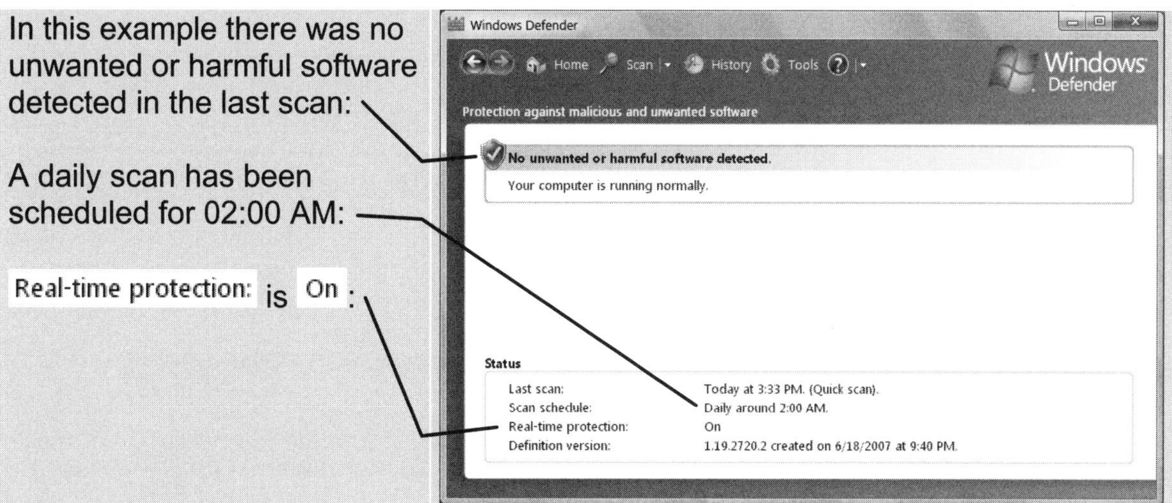

The real-time protection will alert you as soon as spyware attempts to install itself on your computer. *Windows Defender* works closely together with *Windows Update*: as soon as there are new spyware definitions available they are downloaded and installed. This way the program always uses the latest information. By default an extra check is made before a scan (automatic or manual) is performed.

You can take a look at the *Windows Defender* settings to verify this:

You see a large number of settings for *Windows Defender*. Take your time to read through these settings.

It is recommended to use the default settings.

When you have finished reading:

Click Cancel

Tip

Help and Support
In *Windows Help and Support* you will find more information about spyware and using *Windows Defender*.

If you use the button you will see the following information:

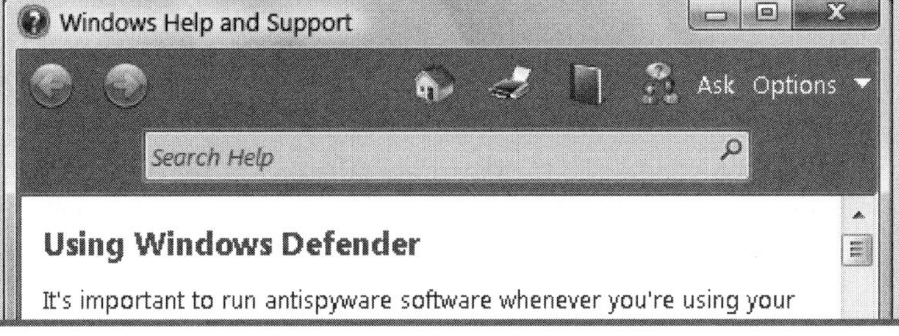

In *Windows Defender* you can choose between three scan types:

- Quick Scan : only scans locations where spyware is often found.
- Full Scan : scans all files and folders on your computer.
- Custom Scan... : only scans the folders you specify.

You can start a quick scan like this:

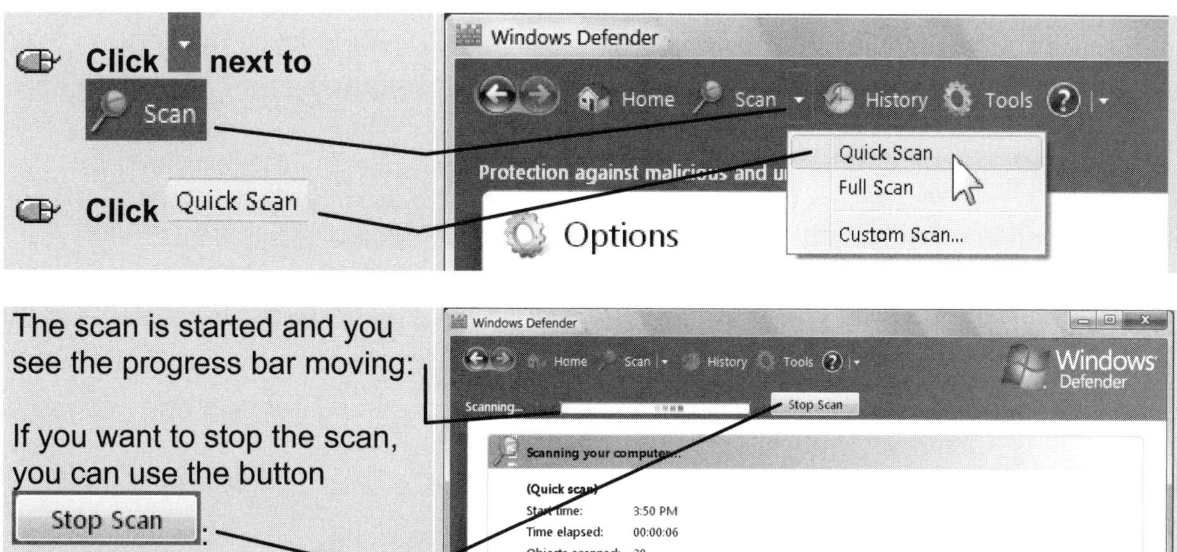

A full scan takes fifteen to thirty minutes, depending on the speed of your computer and the number of files. The quick scan takes a lot less time.

If nothing is found, you see this message:

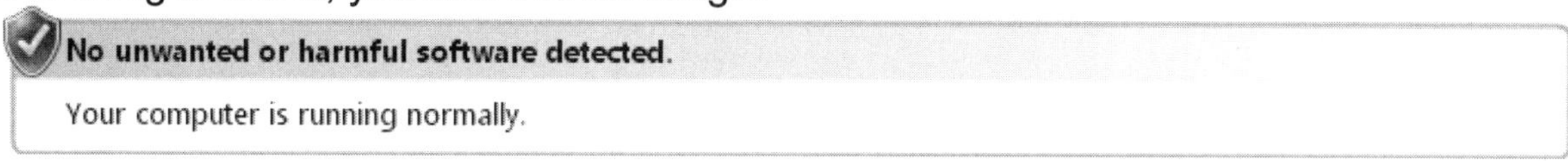

If something is found, you will see a message like the one in this example:

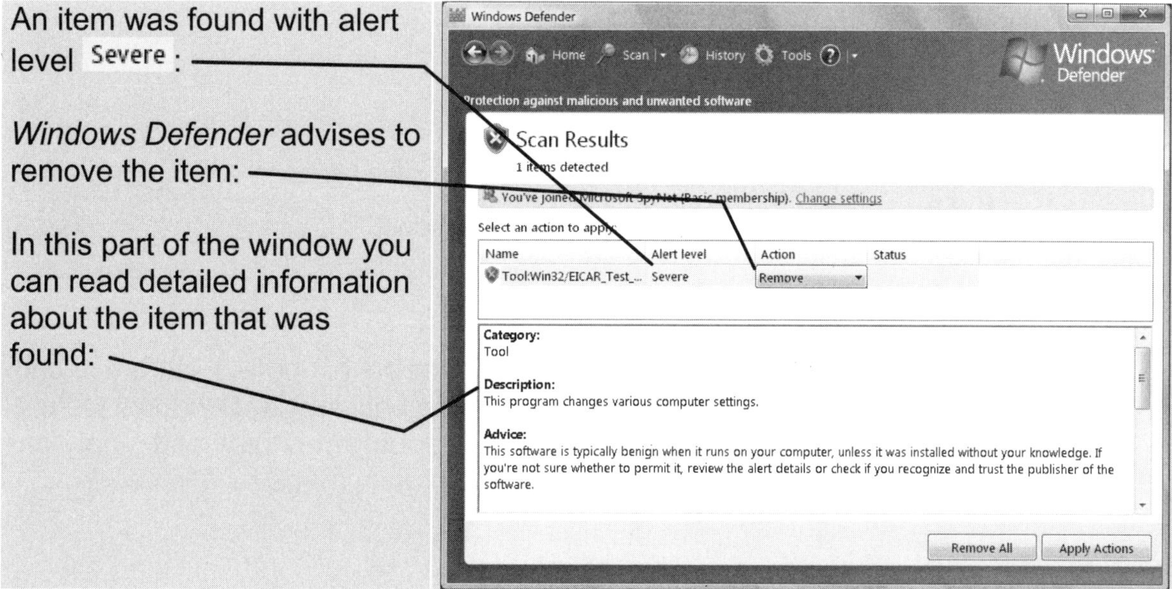

In addition to Remove, you have three other options:

- Ignore : select this option if you are certain you want to keep the item.
- Quarantine : select this option if you are not sure about an item. The item will be placed in a folder where it can do no harm. If it turns out to be something you need, you can put it back where it belongs.
- Always allow : select this option if you are familiar with the item and you are sure you want to keep it. The item will no longer be shown in future scans.

If more than one item was found on your computer, you can select a different action for each separate item. With the button Apply Actions you can carry out the selected actions at once. If you would rather just remove all items in one go, you can use the button Remove All.

When you have removed the item for example, you see this:

Name	Alert level	Action	Status
Tool:Win32/EICAR_Test_...	Severe	Remove	Succeeded

Close the *Windows Defender* window

8.6 Windows Live OneCare

If you do not yet have an antivirus program, you can visit a website where you can download an antivirus program from one of *Microsoft's* partners. You can reach this website through the *Security Center.*

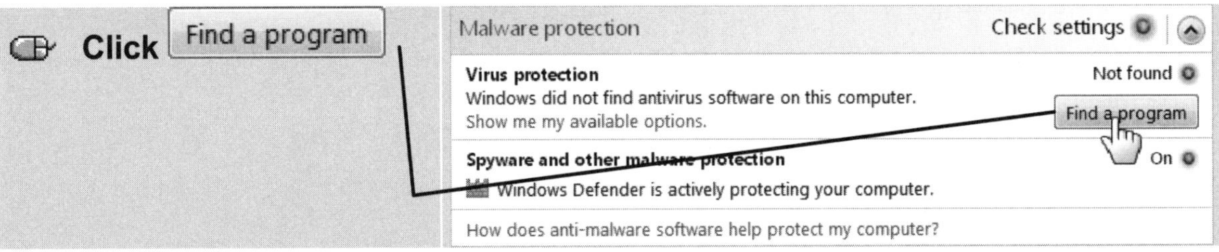

The website *Windows Vista Security Software Providers* is opened. Here you can download free trial versions of security software compatible with *Windows Vista.* The length of the free trial period varies per provider between thirty and ninety days. *Windows Live OneCare* is the complete security solution made by *Microsoft.*

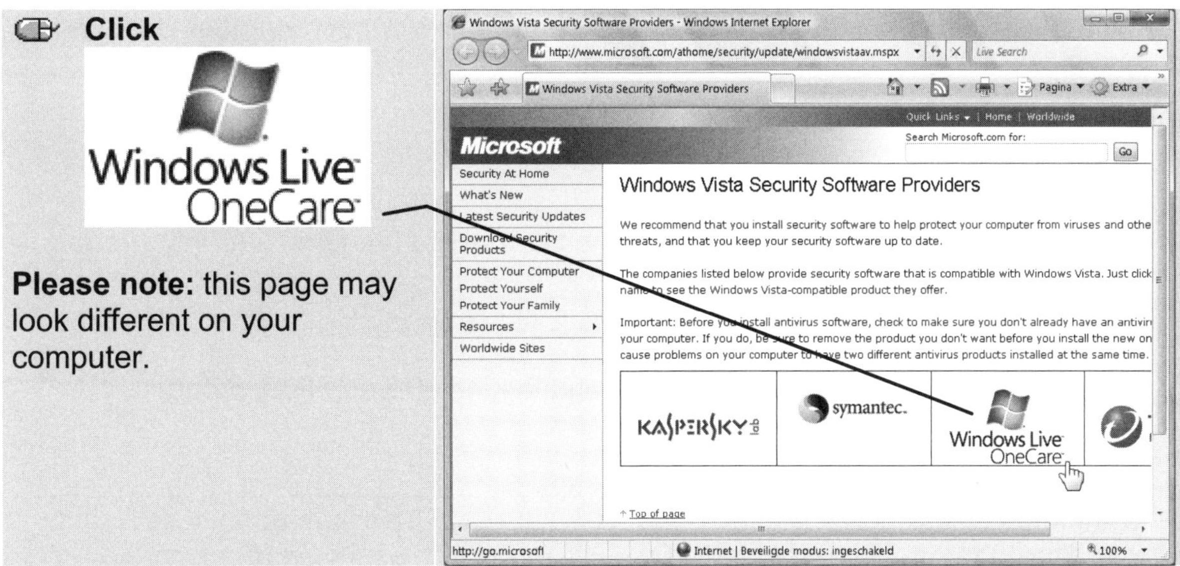

Click

Please note: this page may look different on your computer.

Please note:

You do not have to download and use *Windows Live OneCare*. You can also buy an antivirus program in a computer store. In the following section, downloading and installing *Windows Live OneCare* is used as an example of an antivirus program.

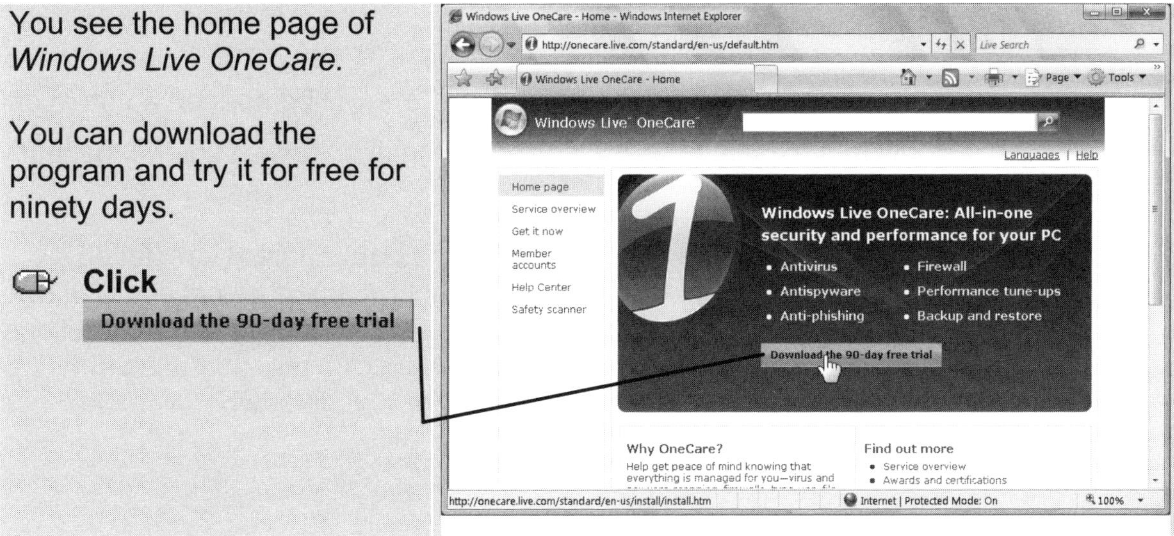

You see the home page of *Windows Live OneCare*.

You can download the program and try it for free for ninety days.

Click Download the 90-day free trial

It is very easy to download and install *Windows Live OneCare*:

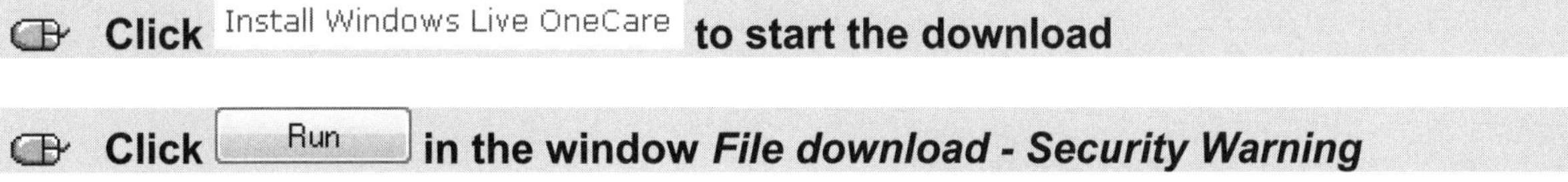

Click Install Windows Live OneCare **to start the download**

Click Run **in the window *File download - Security Warning***

The download is started and you see the progress. Your screen goes dark and *Windows* asks your permission to continue the installation:

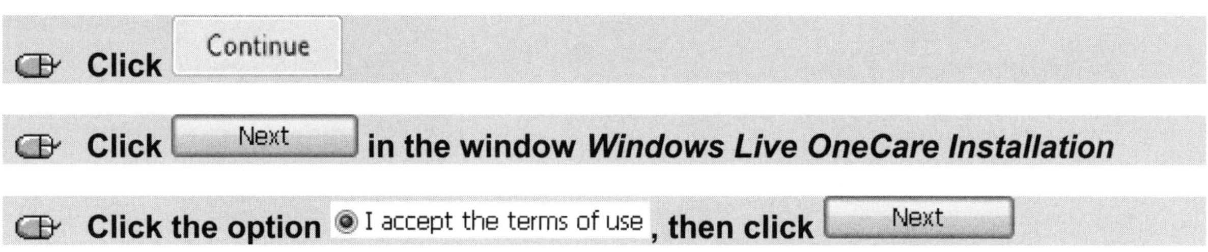

Click Continue

Click Next **in the window *Windows Live OneCare Installation***

Click the option I accept the terms of use**, then click** Next

You see the progress of the download and the installation of the program.

Please note:

When the installation is almost done, you will see a message about a security problem. This is due to *Windows Firewall* and *Windows Defender* being turned off during the installation. *Windows Live OneCare* uses its own firewall and antivirus program instead of these packaged *Vista* programs.

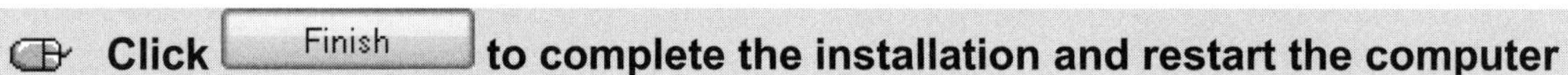

Click Finish **to complete the installation and restart the computer**

8.7 Using Windows Live OneCare

After restarting your computer, *Windows Live OneCare* will be opened automatically.

You see a window that explains the icon in the notification area of the taskbar. You can close this window.

Windows Live OneCare has a built-in firewall that has automatically replaced *Windows Firewall*. When a program wants to contact the Internet, access is allowed automatically when the program is recognized. You will frequently see text balloons appear in the bottom right corner of your screen that inform you about the status of the program or the actions that have been taken. For example, when you check your e-mail in *Windows Mail* you see this message:

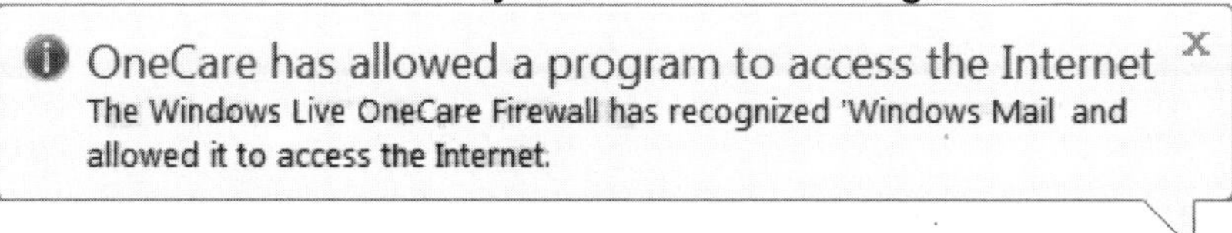

The antispyware component of the program has replaced *Windows Defender*. When you open the *Security Center*, you can see the current protection levels:

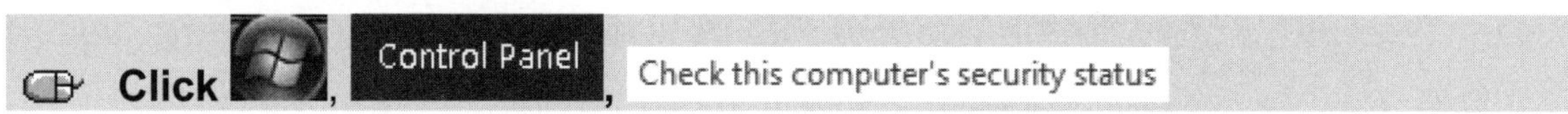

Click , Control Panel, Check this computer's security status

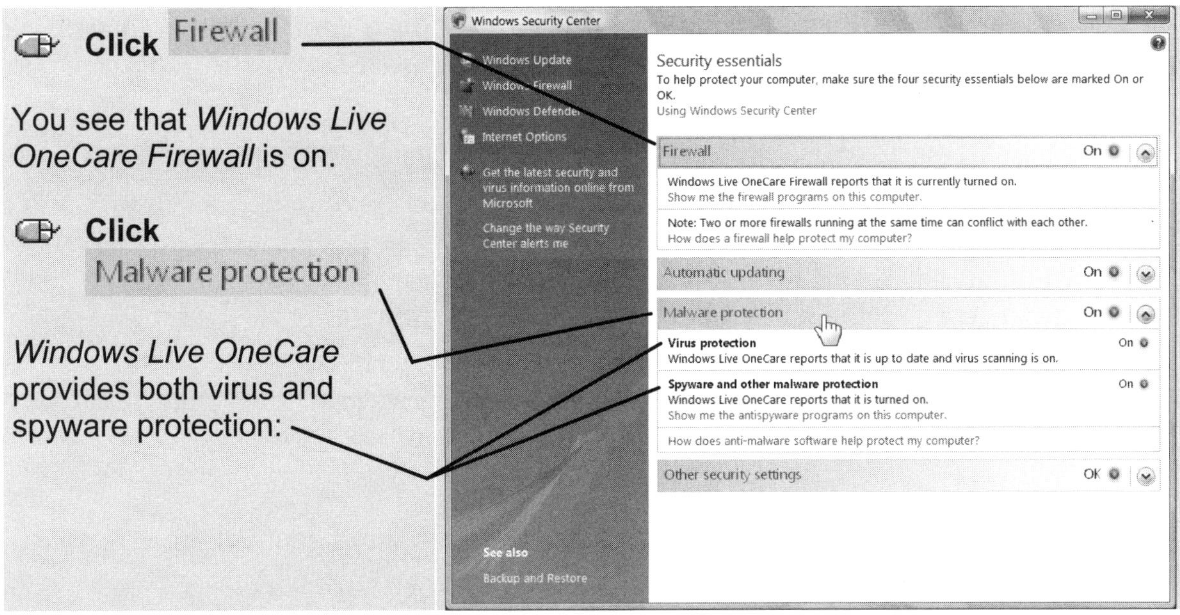

Click Firewall

You see that *Windows Live OneCare Firewall* is on.

Click Malware protection

Windows Live OneCare provides both virus and spyware protection:

Close the *Windows Security Center* window

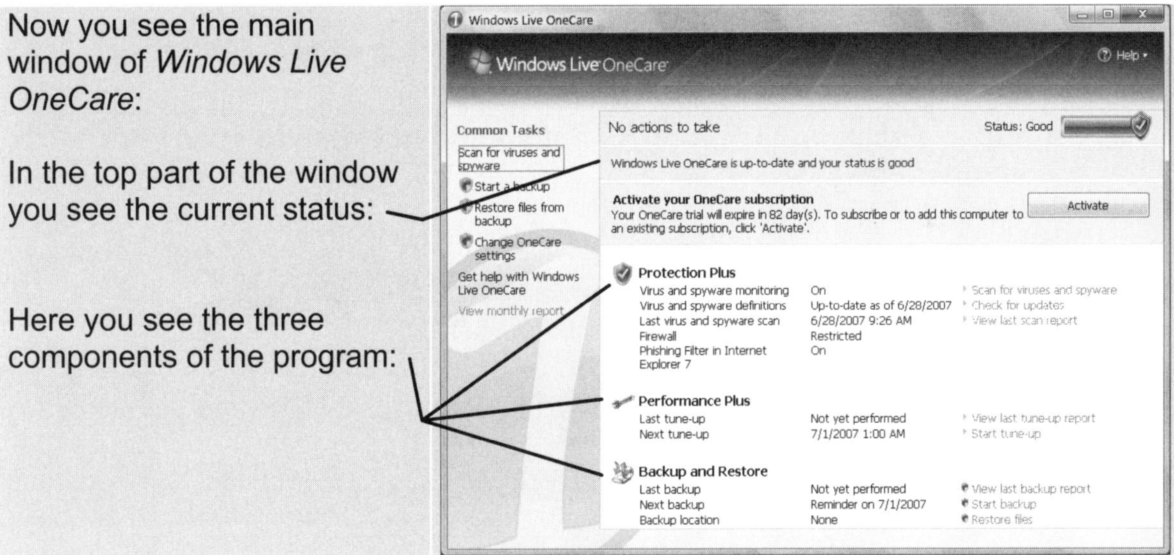

Now you see the main window of *Windows Live OneCare*:

In the top part of the window you see the current status:

Here you see the three components of the program:

These are the three components of *Windows Live OneCare*:

- Protection Plus: this component provides virus, spyware and phishing protection and manages a two-way firewall.
- Performance Plus: you can use this tool to perform maintenance tasks to keep your computer running smoothly.
- Backup and Restore: this component helps to protect your files in case of accidental deletion or hardware failure.

To make sure your computer has not been infected by a virus or other malware, you can let *Protection Plus* perform a scan of your computer:

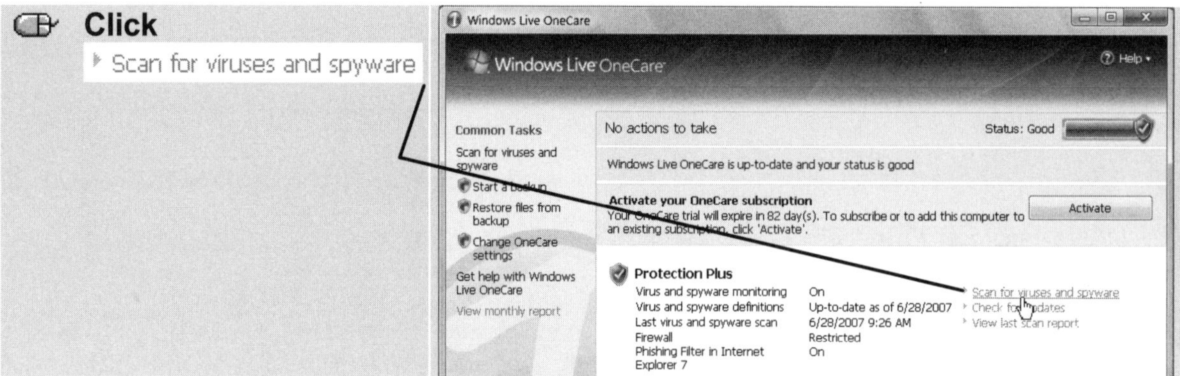

In the window that appears you can choose between three scan types:

- **Quick Scan**: only scans the locations where malware is often found.
- **Complete Scan**: scans all files and folders on your computer.
- **Custom Scan**: only scans the folders you specify.

Choose a scan or click Cancel if you do not want to scan your computer now

During the scan you see this window:

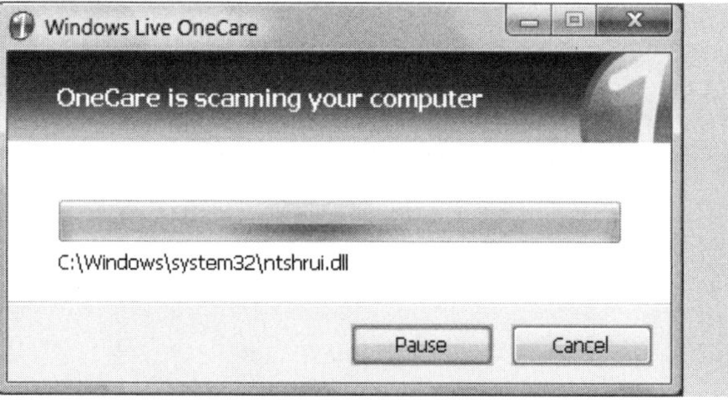

OneCare takes automatic action against potential harmful software rated high or severe. You will be notified about this in the scan report that is displayed when the scan is completed.
For low risk items you can choose between repairing the file, placing the file in quarantine or removing the file.

You can also let the scan start automatically.

The screen goes dark and *Windows* asks your permission to continue:

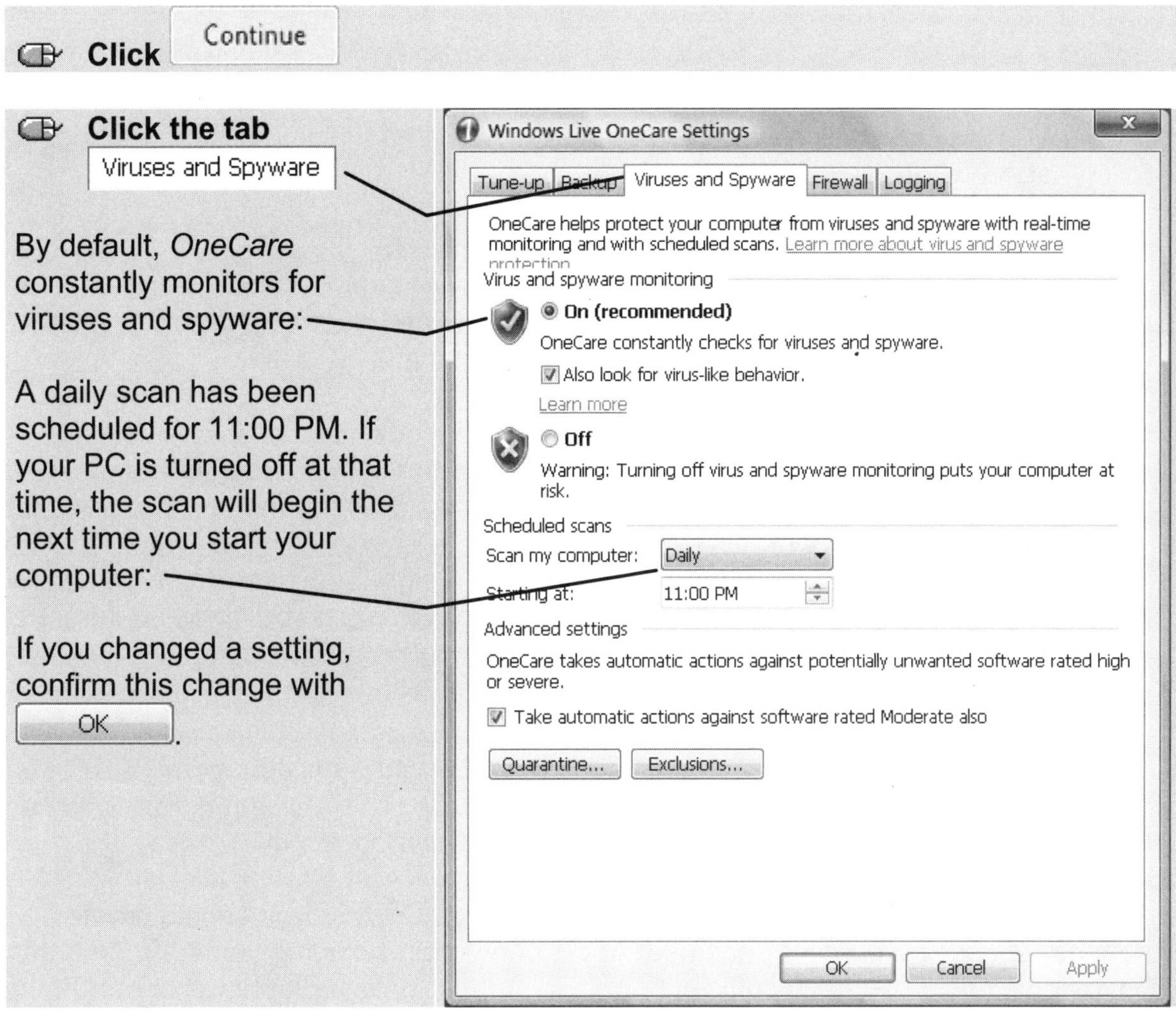

Click Continue

Click the tab Viruses and Spyware

By default, *OneCare* constantly monitors for viruses and spyware:

A daily scan has been scheduled for 11:00 PM. If your PC is turned off at that time, the scan will begin the next time you start your computer:

If you changed a setting, confirm this with OK.

Close the *Windows Live OneCare* window

8.8 User Account Control

You have probably already noticed the rigorous *User Account Control* in *Windows Vista*. Your screen darkens and a window appears, asking for your permission to continue. This action prevents changes being made to your computer by users who do not have permission to do so. When you see a message from *User Account Control*, read through it carefully. Make sure that the name that is displayed, corresponds to the task you want to perform or the program you want to open.

In a darkened screen you will see one of several different messages from *User Account Control*:

Windows needs your permission to continue
You see this message when you start a *Windows* function or program that can affect other users of this computer.

A program needs your permission to continue
This message is displayed when you open a program that is not part of *Windows*, but does have a valid digital signature (electronic security). This means you can assume this program is legitimate.

An unidentified program wants access to your computer
This message is displayed when you open an unknown program that does not have a valid digital signature from its publisher. This means that you are unable to check if the program is legitimate. It does not necessarily indicate danger, as many older, legitimate programs do not have signatures. However, you should take extra caution and only allow this program to run if you obtained it from a trusted source, such as the original CD or a publisher's website.

This program has been blocked
When your computer is connected to a network, the network administrator can block programs from running on your computer. To run this program, you can contact your administrator and ask to have the program unblocked.

If you want to use the full potential of *User Account Control*, you should create a *standard user account* for each user of the computer (including yourself). With this type of account you have sufficient rights to send e-mails, edit photos or surf the Internet.

You keep one *administrator account* that you protect with a password. You can add a password to your existing administrator account:

Open the *Control Panel* (if necessary) 3

Click Add or remove user accounts

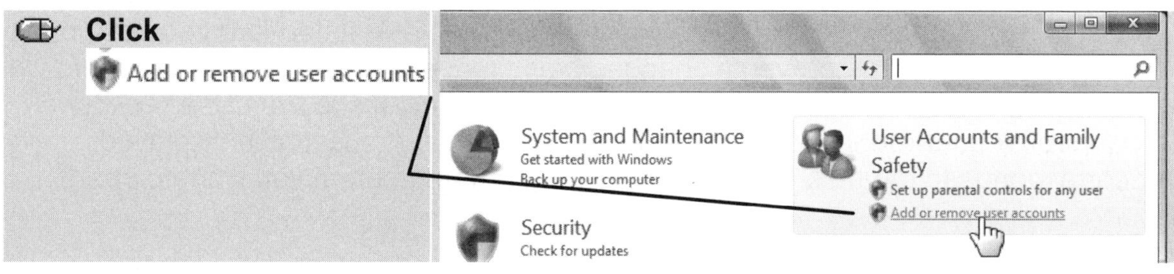

Your screen goes dark and *Windows* asks for permission to continue:

You see all user accounts on your computer.

Click the account you want to change

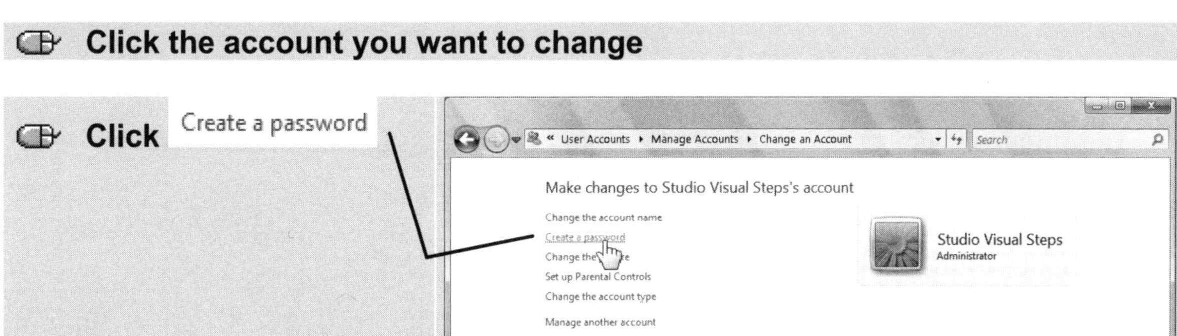

Now you can enter a password and a password hint.

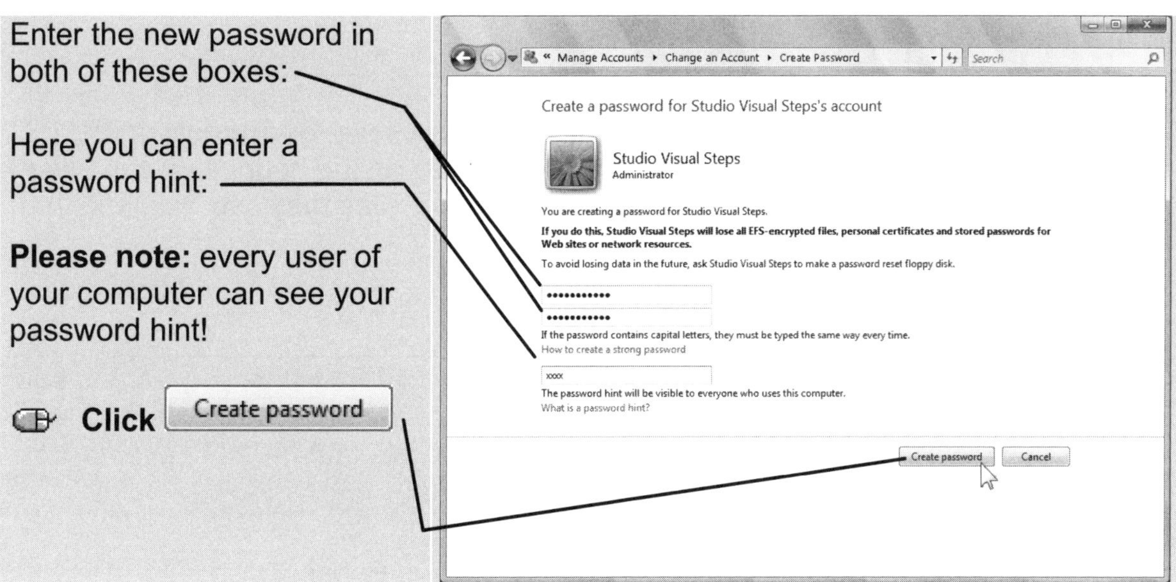

Your administrator account is now password protected. It is advisable to (have the other users) do the same for the standard user accounts.

Close all windows

When someone who has a standard user account tries to install software, the screen will go dark. *Windows* will ask for the password of the administrator account. This way, software can not be installed without your knowledge and permission.

The user with the standard user account has to enter the administrator password to be able to continue with this task:

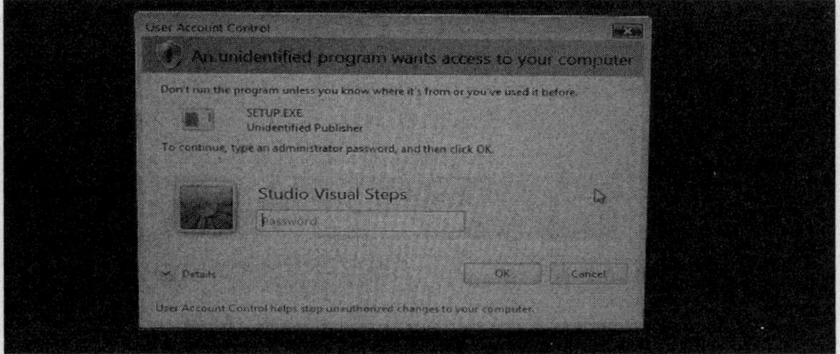

The administrator password must be entered each time before tasks can be performed that might:

- affect the settings of the computer or
- change the settings of other users.

For example, to set up *Parental Controls* you also need to enter the administrator password. In the next section you can read more about *Parental Controls*.

8.9 Parental Controls

You can use *Parental Controls* to control how other users, for example your (grand)children use the computer. You can set limits on the hours they can use the computer, the types of games they can play, the websites they can visit, and the programs they can run.

 **Please note:**

Before you get started, make sure that the (grand)child for which you want to set *Parental Controls* has a standard user account. Like the other accounts, this account must be password protected. If there are user accounts that are not password protected, the *Parental Controls* might be bypassed.

You can set up *Parental Controls* through the *Control Panel*:

Open the *Control Panel* 3

Click

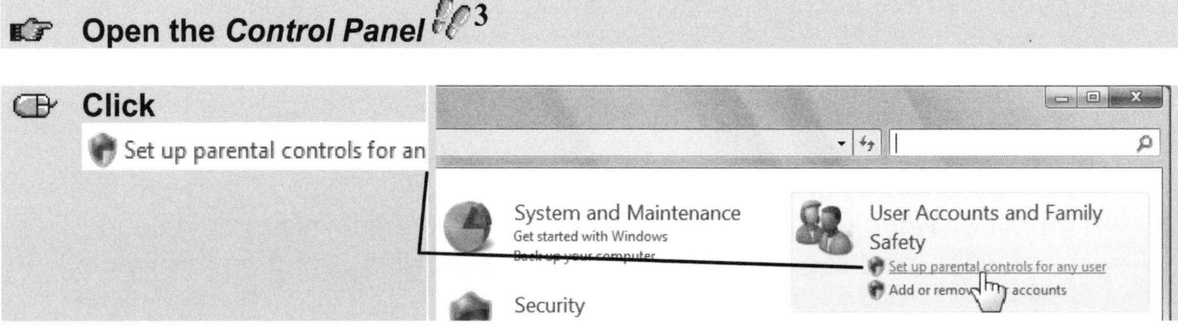

Your screen goes dark and you need to give permission to continue. If you are using a standard user account yourself, you must enter the administrator password.

Click Continue

You see all user accounts on your computer.

Click the account for which you want to set *Parental Controls*

Next turn on *Parental Controls*:

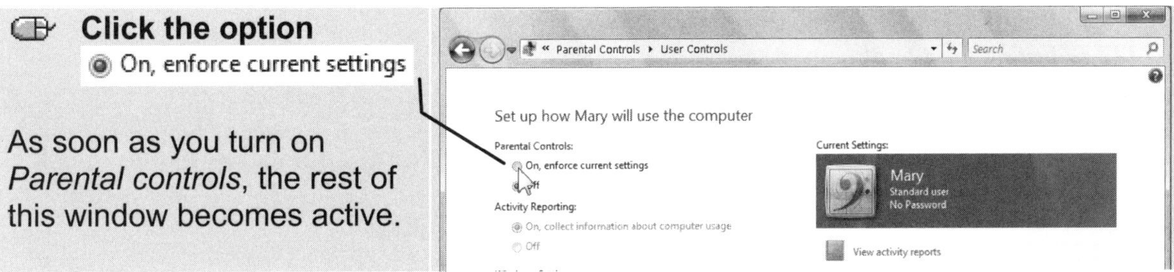

Click the option On, enforce current settings

As soon as you turn on *Parental controls*, the rest of this window becomes active.

Now you can adjust the separate settings for each component of *Parental Controls*.

With the option Windows Vista Web Filter you can set limits on the information your (grand)child can access on the Internet:

Click Windows Vista Web Filter

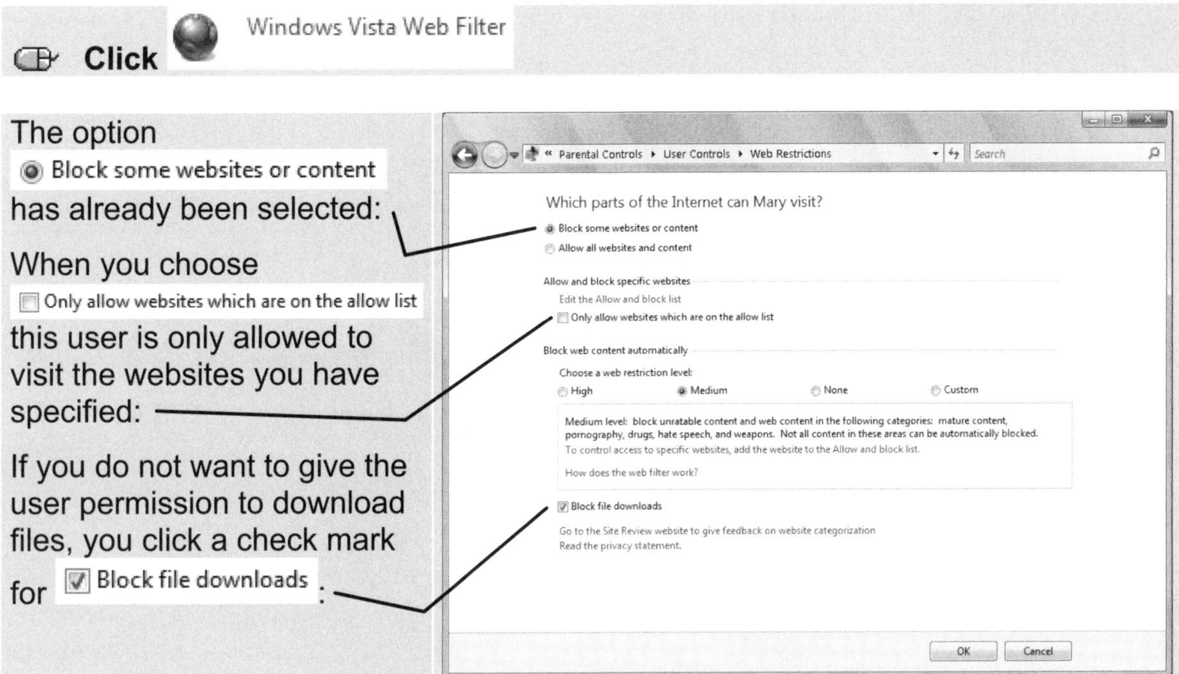

The option Block some websites or content has already been selected:

When you choose Only allow websites which are on the allow list this user is only allowed to visit the websites you have specified:

If you do not want to give the user permission to download files, you click a check mark for Block file downloads:

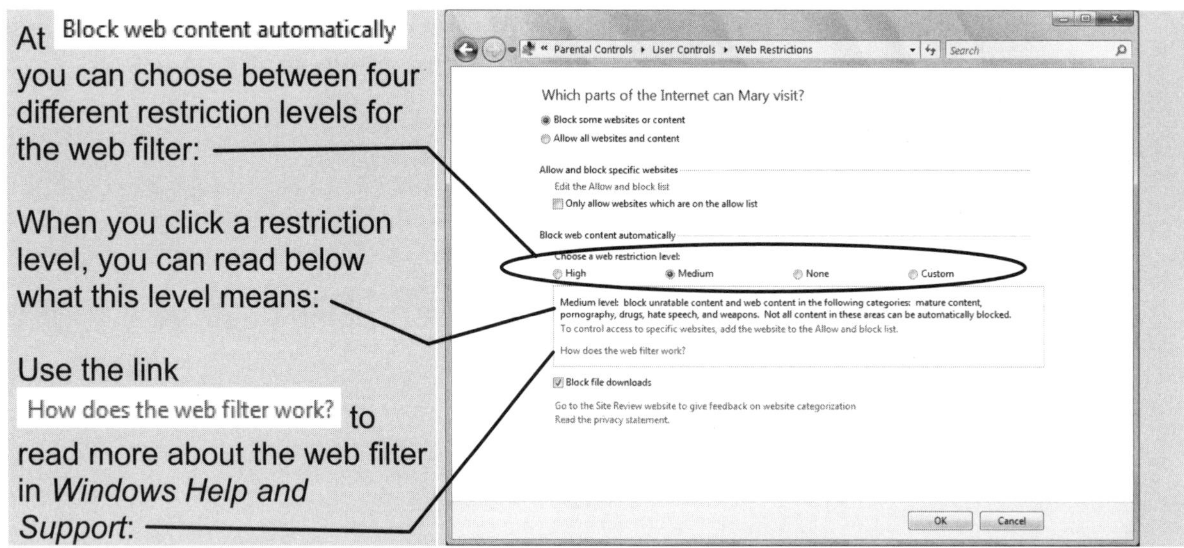

At Block web content automatically you can choose between four different restriction levels for the web filter:

When you click a restriction level, you can read below what this level means:

Use the link How does the web filter work? to read more about the web filter in *Windows Help and Support*:

You can combine the web filter with blocking or allowing specific websites. Click Edit the Allow and block list to do so.

When you have finished changing your settings:

Click OK to confirm your settings

Now you can set up the next component of *Parental Controls*.

The option Time limits allows you to set time limits to control when the user is allowed to log on to the computer:

Click Time limits

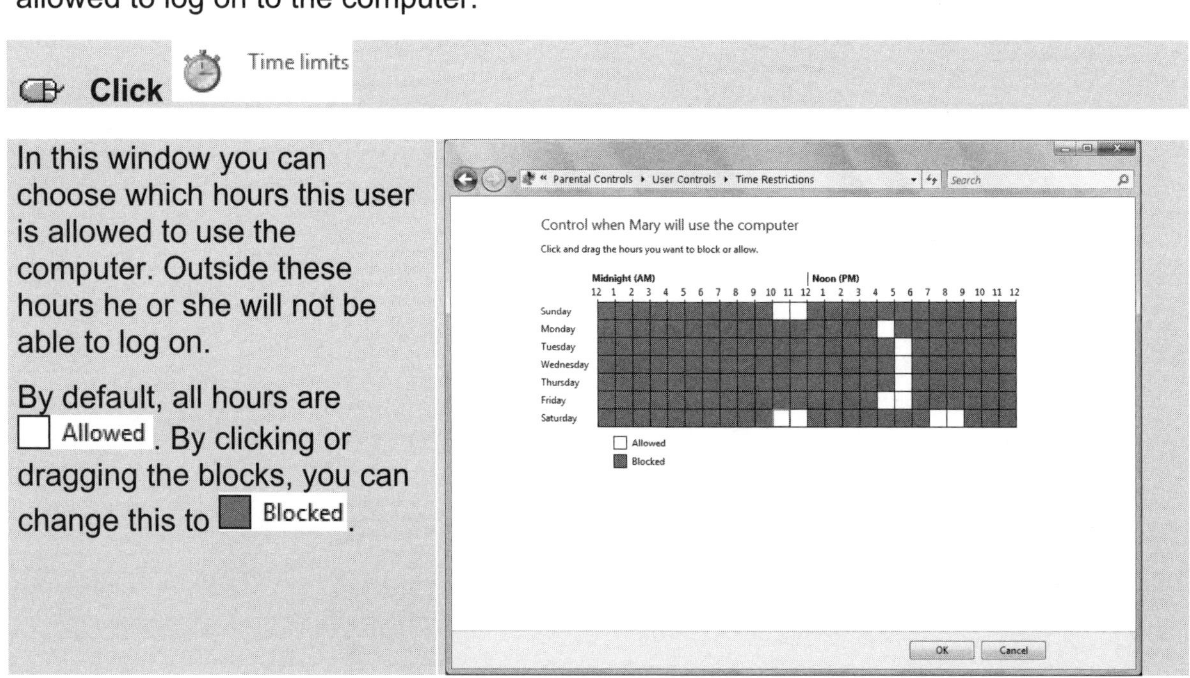

In this window you can choose which hours this user is allowed to use the computer. Outside these hours he or she will not be able to log on.

By default, all hours are Allowed. By clicking or dragging the blocks, you can change this to Blocked.

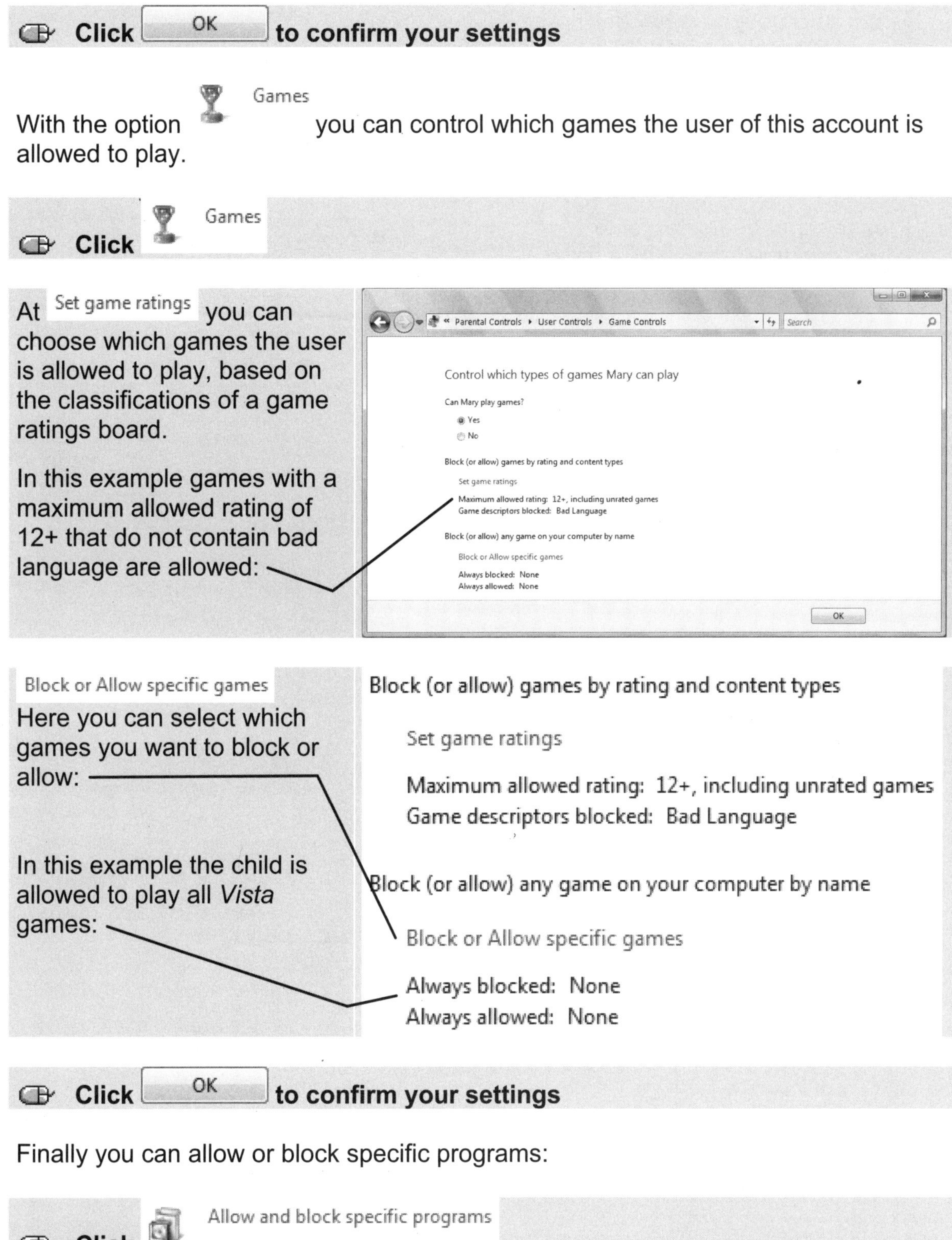

Click OK **to confirm your settings**

With the option Games you can control which games the user of this account is allowed to play.

Click Games

At Set game ratings you can choose which games the user is allowed to play, based on the classifications of a game ratings board.

In this example games with a maximum allowed rating of 12+ that do not contain bad language are allowed:

Block or Allow specific games
Here you can select which games you want to block or allow:

In this example the child is allowed to play all *Vista* games:

Click OK **to confirm your settings**

Finally you can allow or block specific programs:

Click Allow and block specific programs

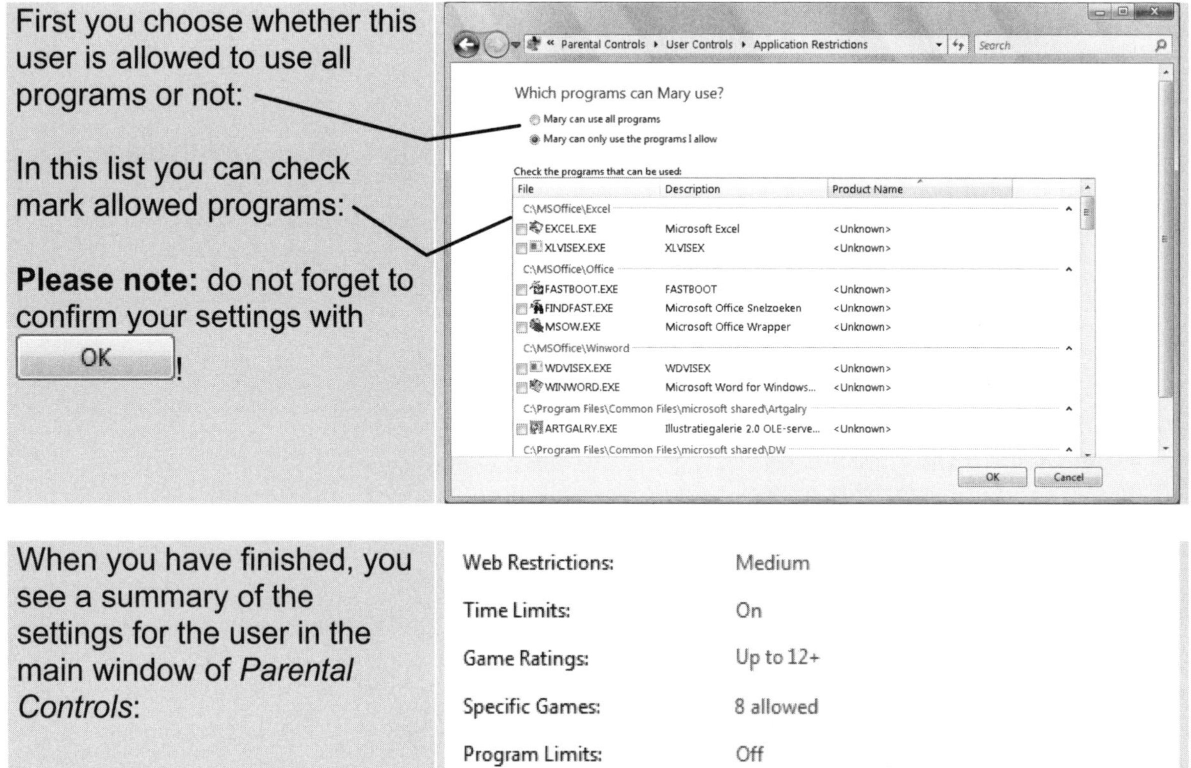

First you choose whether this user is allowed to use all programs or not:

In this list you can check mark allowed programs:

Please note: do not forget to confirm your settings with OK!

When you have finished, you see a summary of the settings for the user in the main window of *Parental Controls*:

Once you have set up *Parental Controls*, you can use *Activity Reporting* to keep a record of the computer activity of the user of this account.

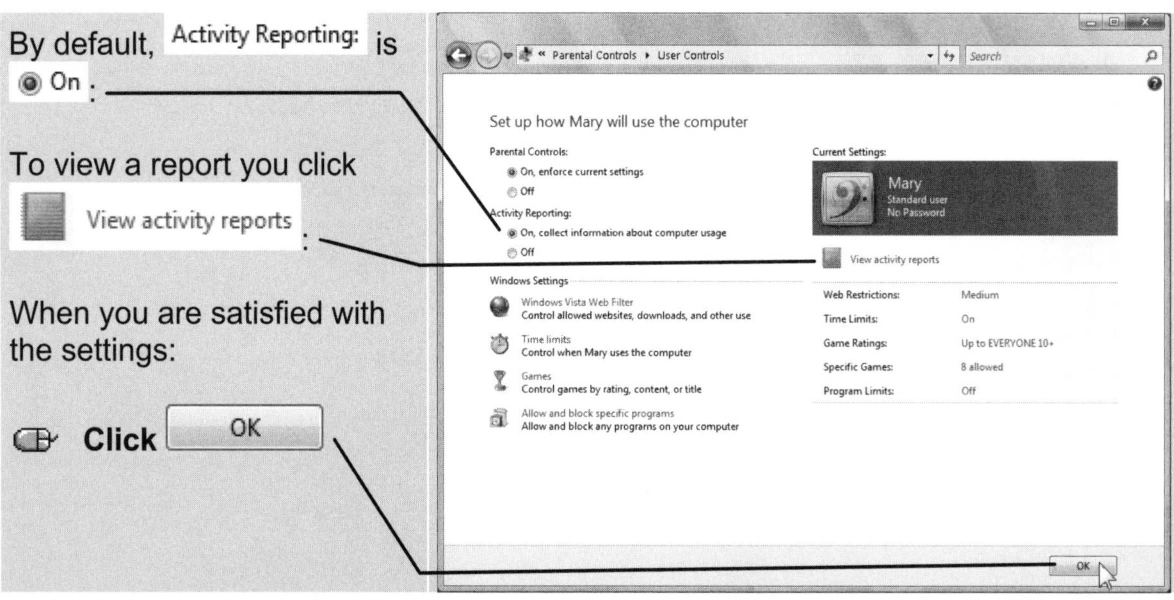

By default, Activity Reporting: is On:

To view a report you click View activity reports:

When you are satisfied with the settings:

Click OK

Close the open window using the button X

Here you see the layout of an *Activity report*:

From time to time a message will appear at the bottom of your screen, to remind you to read the *Activity report*. Clicking this message will open the report.

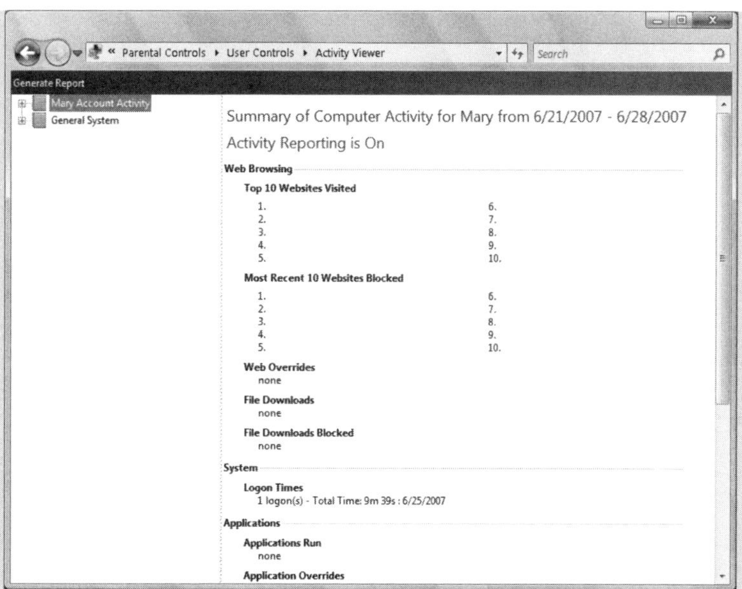

8.10 Windows Help and Support

Would you like to know more about the subjects of this chapter? Then you can read the articles in *Windows Help and Support.* There are different ways to get to these articles:

- In many windows you see the blue button with the question mark. When you click this button, the article that accompanies this window is opened in *Windows Help and Support.*
- Frequently you see questions in blue text like What is a user account? . When you click the question, the article with the answer to that question is opened.
- If you have a specific question, you can also search for a keyword in the *Windows Help and Support* window.

In this chapter you were presented with an overview of the different security features of *Windows Vista*.
In the next chapter you will be introduced to the new programs that are included in *Vista*.

8.11 Tips

Tip

Windows Vista demos

Windows Help and Support contains two narrated video demonstrations about the subjects of this chapter: Demo: Security basics and Demo: Understanding user accounts.

Open *Windows Help and Support* 4

In the *Search Box*:

Type: demo

Click

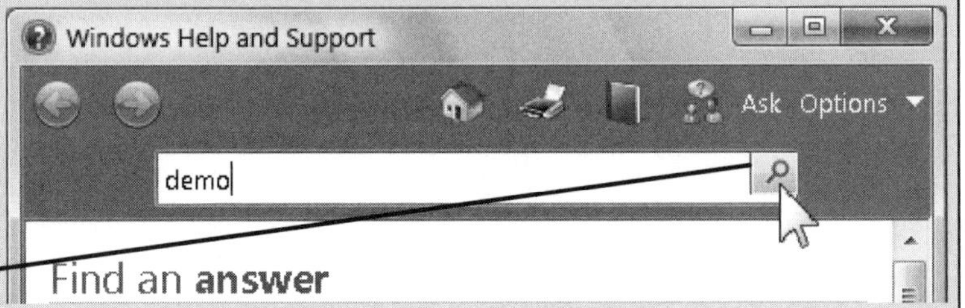

You see a list of demos.

For example, click Demo: Security basics

In the next window:

Click → Watch the demo

The program *Windows Media Player* opens and the demo starts playing:

Watch the demo

When this demo is finished, you can repeat the steps above to watch the demo about user accounts.

9. New Programs

So far, you have been introduced to some of the new and improved features of the latest version of the *Windows* operating system: *Vista*. You have also looked at some of the functional changes in programs that you were already familiar with from earlier versions of *Windows*.

In this chapter you can read about a new *Vista* program, *Windows Photo Gallery*. With *Windows Photo Gallery* you can manage all your digital photos and perform some basic photo editing tasks, such as fixing red eye, cropping photos and making color adjustments. This program contains a direct link to another new *Vista* program: *Windows DVD Maker.* In this program, you can put your digital photos in a slide show and then write it to DVD.

Other interesting new programs are *Windows Calendar* which you can use to schedule tasks and appointments and the *Snipping Tool* that can be used to capture screenshots (snips) quickly and easily.

In this chapter you will be introduced to:

- *Windows Photo Gallery*;
- *Windows DVD Maker*;
- *Windows Calendar*;
- the *Snipping Tool*.

Please note:

Windows DVD Maker is only available in the editions *Windows Vista Home Premium* and *Windows Vista Ultimate*.

9.1 Windows Photo Gallery

Windows Photo Gallery is a practical and easy-to-use program for managing, organizing and viewing your images and videos. You can find the program in the list *All programs* in the *Start menu*:

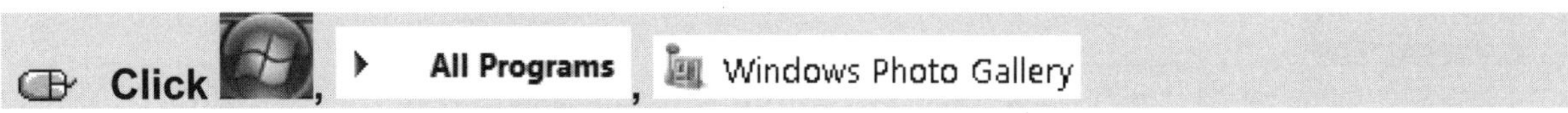

Windows Photo Gallery is opened.
In this example you see the sample pictures that are included in *Vista*:

On the left you see the *Navigation Pane* with the thumbnails of the images next to it:

In the *Information Pane* on the right the properties of a selected image will be shown:

If you do not see this part of the window:

Click Info on the toolbar

Click all arrows next to All Pictures and Videos, 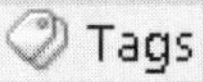 Tags and other options in the *Navigation Pane*

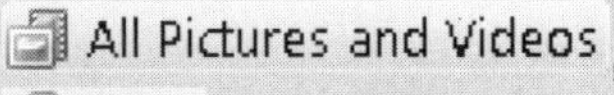

All options are now opened.

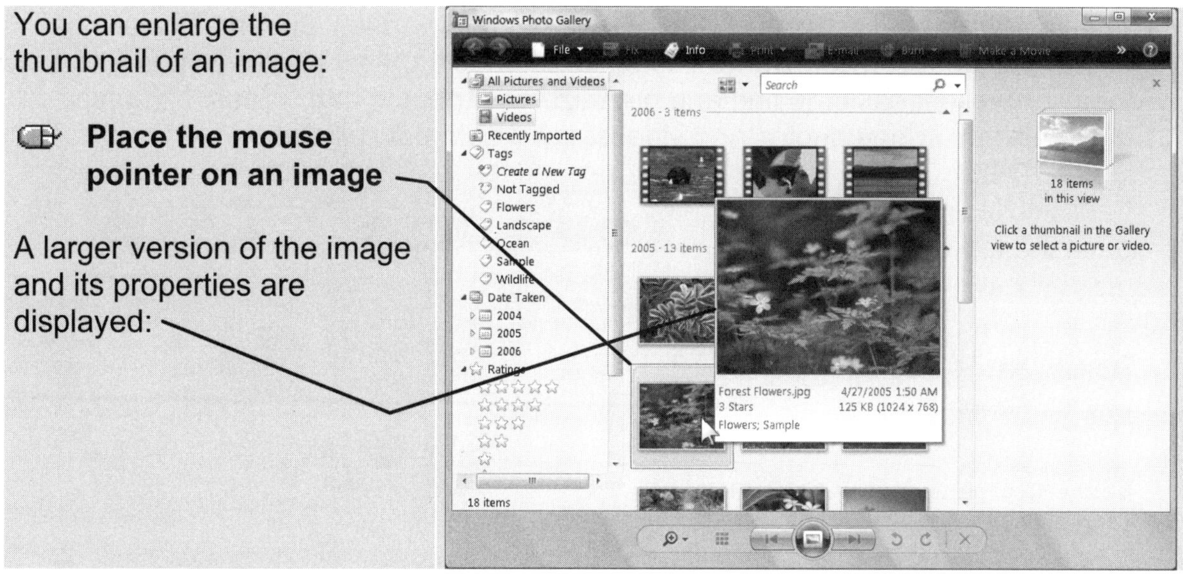

You can enlarge the thumbnail of an image:

Place the mouse pointer on an image

A larger version of the image and its properties are displayed:

9.2 Tags and Ratings

Finding a specific photo on your computer can be difficult when you have a large photo collection. *Windows Photo Gallery* offers useful tools to quickly find your photos:

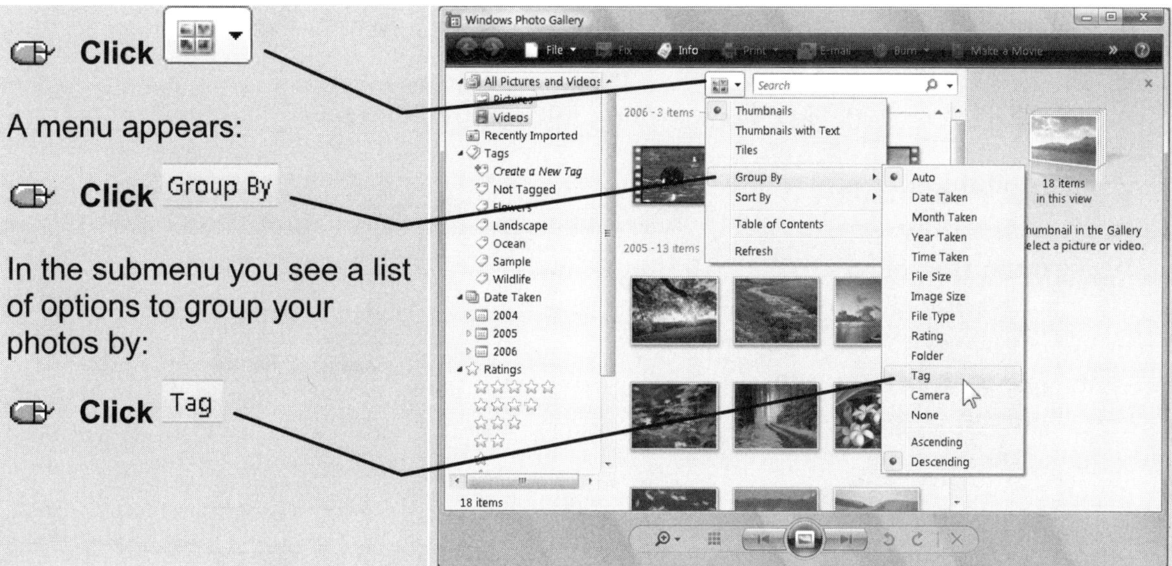

Click [button]

A menu appears:

Click Group By

In the submenu you see a list of options to group your photos by:

Click Tag

The images are now displayed grouped by their tags. Tags are small pieces of information that you can create yourself and attach to your photos and videos. These tags will make it easier to find and organize your photos and videos. If you specify a tag when you import photos and videos, it will automatically be added to each file.

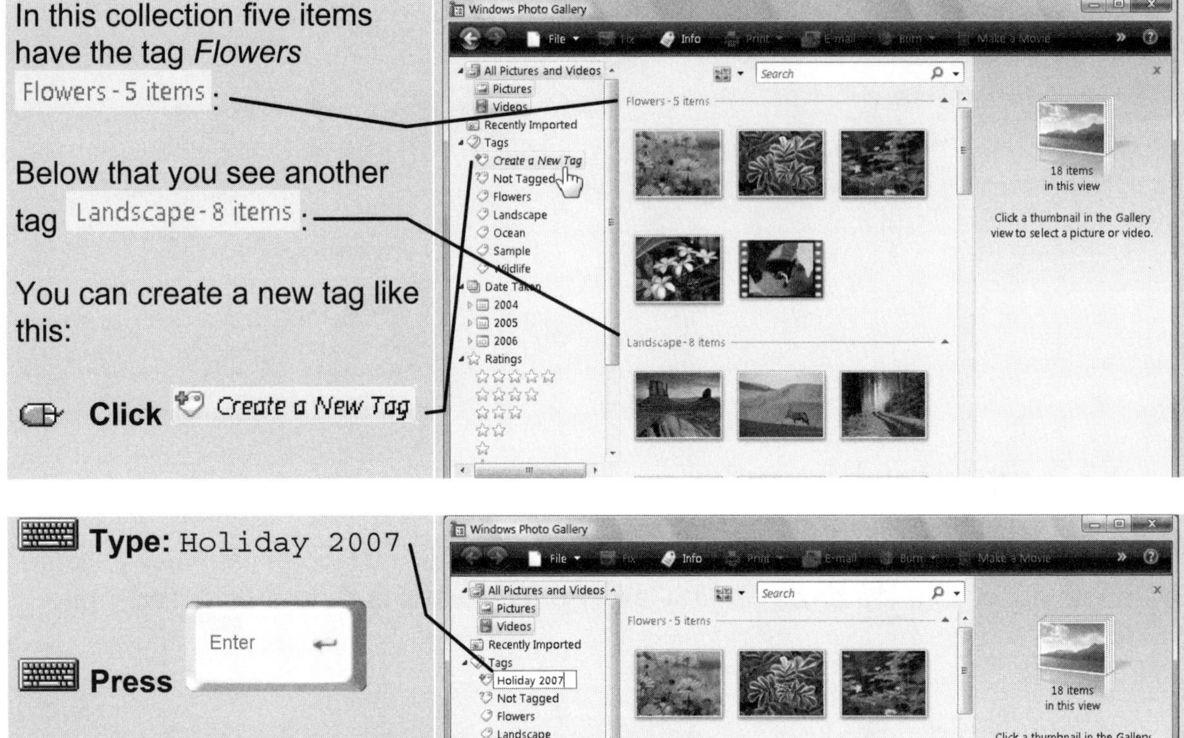

In this collection five items have the tag *Flowers* Flowers - 5 items.

Below that you see another tag Landscape - 8 items.

You can create a new tag like this:

Click Create a New Tag

Type: `Holiday 2007`

Press Enter

A new tag is created. Now you can add this tag to an image:

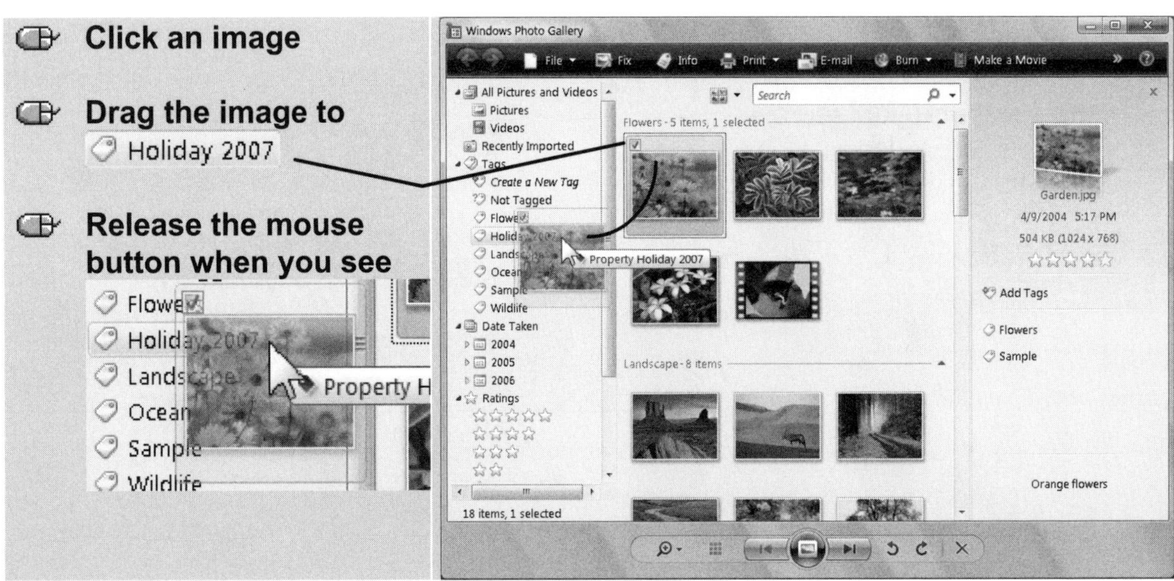

Click an image

Drag the image to Holiday 2007

Release the mouse button when you see

The tag is added to the image. You can do the same thing for a group of images: select the series of images and drag them all to Holiday 2007 in one go.

Tip

Nesting tags
To keep the number of tags manageable, you can 'nest' groups of related tags. This means that you add multiple lower level tags to a top level tag.
You can add a lower level tag by right-clicking an existing tag, and select Create Tag in the menu that appears. Here you see an example:

Holiday
2006
2007

You can also view images grouped by the date each photo was taken, or by its rating (the number of stars). You can add stars to your images in the *Information Pane* on the right side:

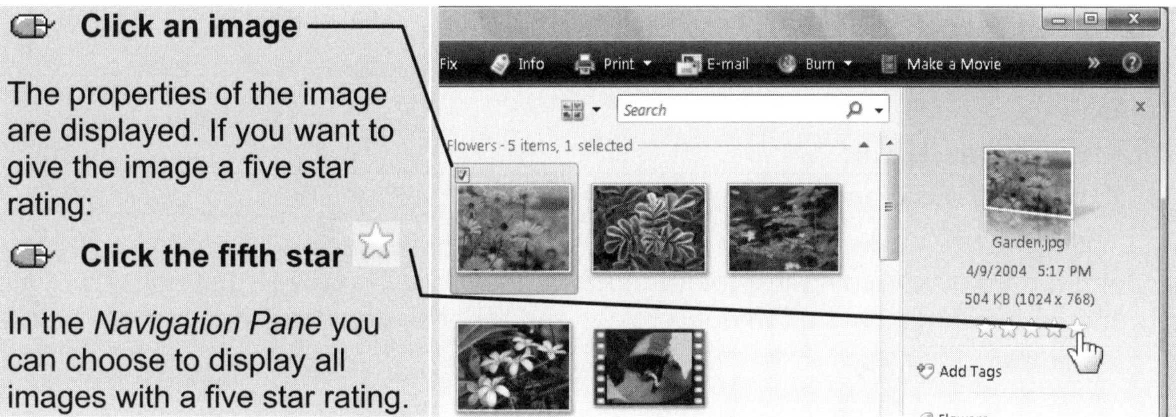

Click an image

The properties of the image are displayed. If you want to give the image a five star rating:

Click the fifth star

In the *Navigation Pane* you can choose to display all images with a five star rating.

9.3 Adding Folders to Windows Photo Gallery

By default, *Photo Gallery* shows all photos and videos in the *Pictures* folder, but you can add other folders to *Photo Gallery* as well. You can add folders one at the time, so you need to repeat the following steps for each folder you want to add.

Click File

Click Add Folder to Gallery...

In this window you can choose which folder you want to add:

By clicking the arrows ▷, you show the subfolders:

Click **Cancel**

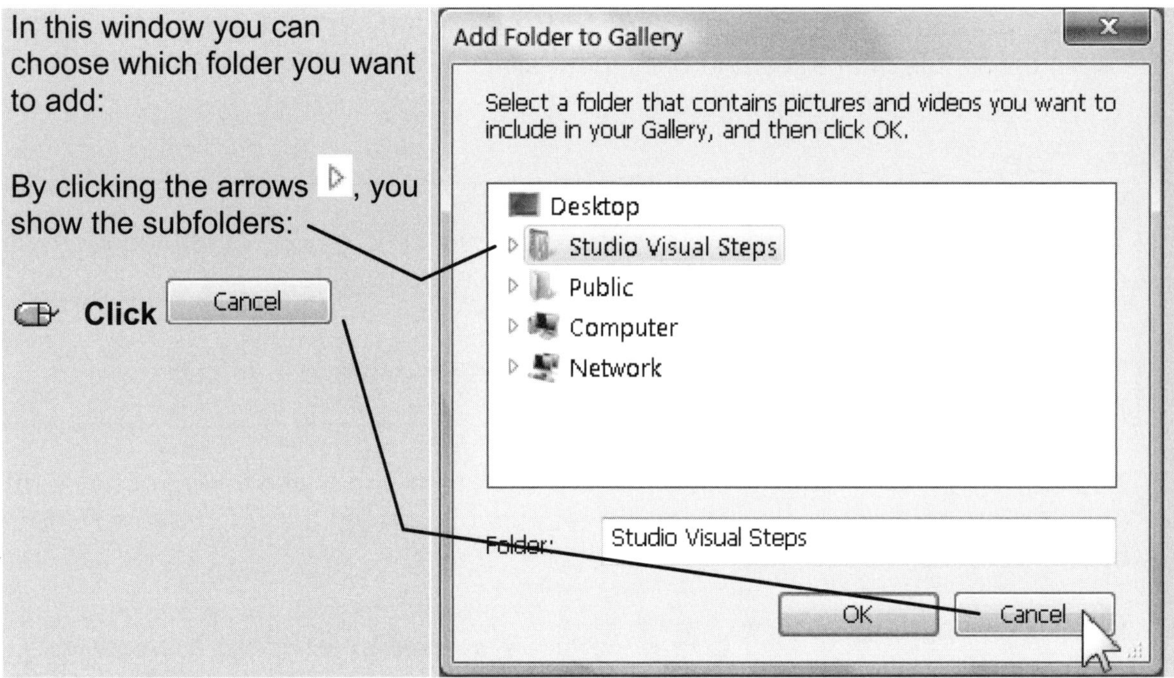

Please note:

You should avoid adding certain folders to *Photo Gallery*. The *Local Disk* folder ▷ Local Disk (C:), for example, is called the root folder because it represents your entire hard disk. Adding this folder to *Photo Gallery* will make it run very slowly. You should avoid adding the *Windows* folder and other system locations to *Photo Gallery* for similar reasons.

9.4 Photo Editing and Slide Show

You can perform a few basic photo editing tasks on your images in *Photo Gallery*. Take a look at the possibilities:

Click an image

Click Fix

You see several options on the right side of the window:

- **For example, click** Crop Picture

Below the button other options appear that you can try out for yourself:

If you are not satisfied with the result of your editing:

- **Click** Undo

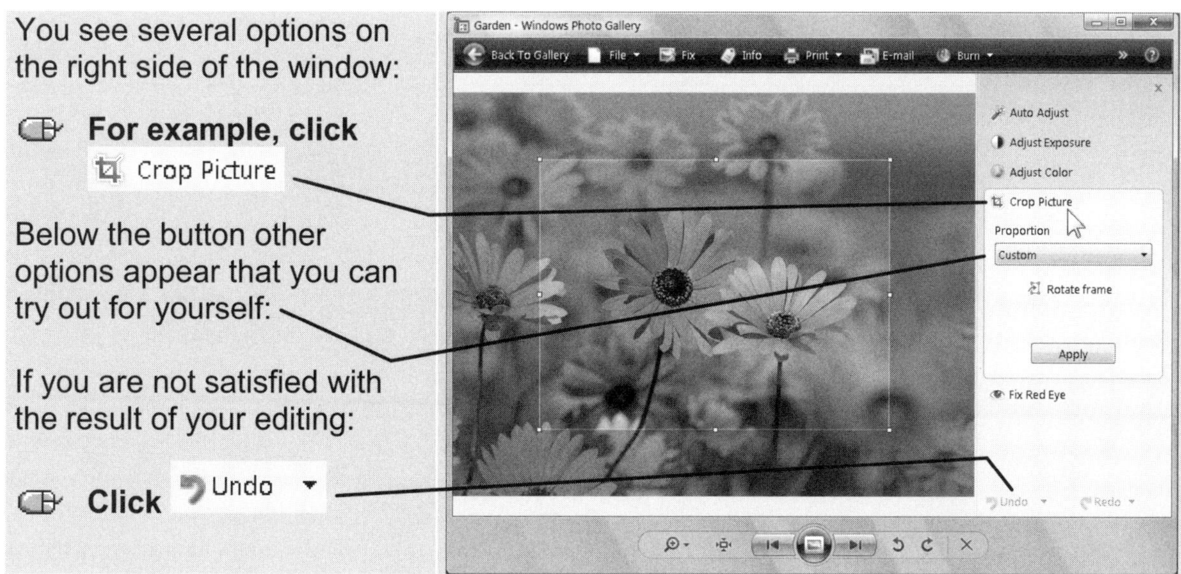

Please note:

If you delete an image using the button ✕ (at the bottom of the window), you will be asked for a confirmation before the image is moved to the *Recycle Bin*.

You can use the toolbar at the bottom of the window to start a slide show of your images in *Photo Gallery*:

- **Click**

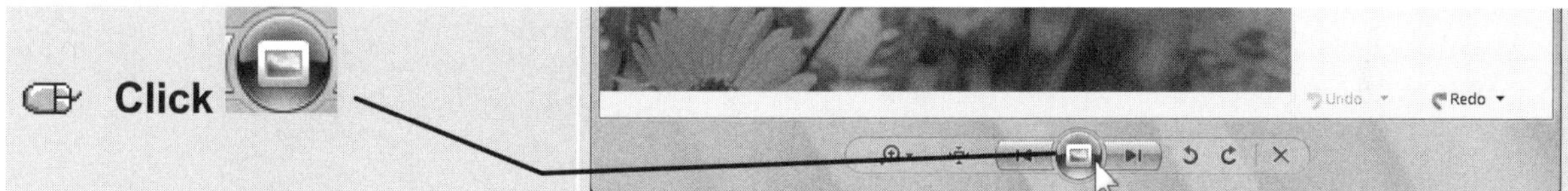

The screen goes black for a moment, then the slide show begins:

At the bottom of the screen you see various buttons that you can use to adjust the settings for the slide show.

- **Try the different buttons**

To stop the slide show:

- **Click** Exit

HELP! I do not see any buttons

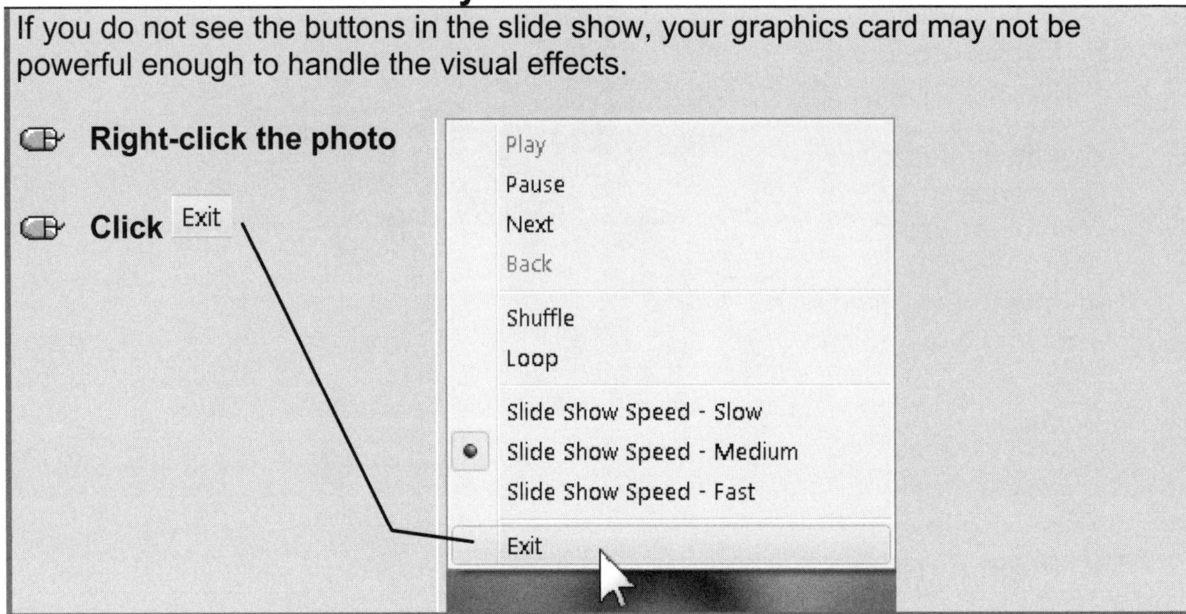

If you do not see the buttons in the slide show, your graphics card may not be powerful enough to handle the visual effects.

Right-click the photo

Click Exit

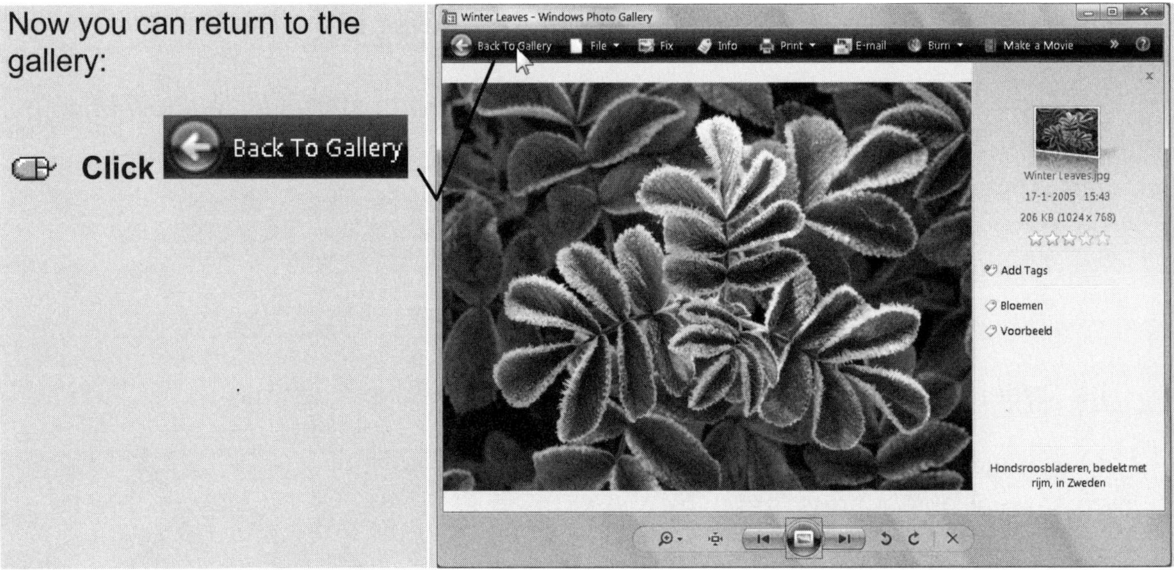

Now you can return to the gallery:

Click Back To Gallery

9.5 Printing and E-mailing Images

Just like *Windows XP*, *Vista* is equipped with a convenient printing wizard that makes it very easy to print your images in different sizes:

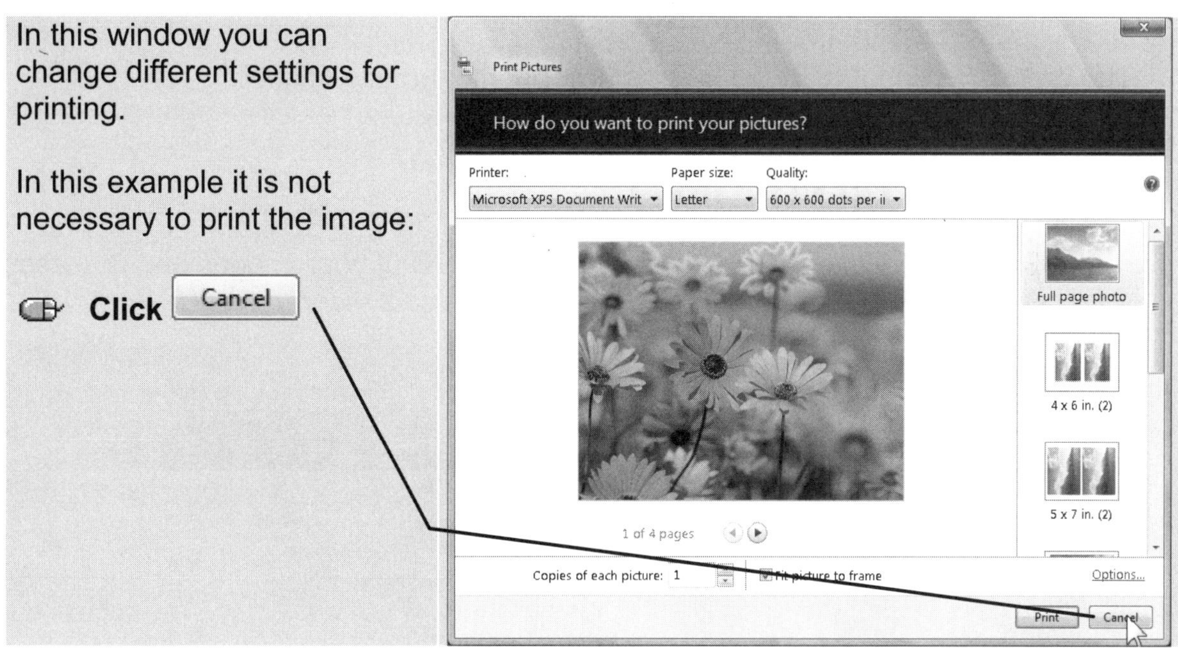

Another convenient option on the *Photo Gallery* toolbar is the button E-mail. Use this button to add one or more selected images directly as attachment(s) to an e-mail. First, you will be prompted to choose the size of the images. Then your default e-mail program is opened automatically and the images are added as attachments to a new message.

9.6 Writing Images to Disc or Video DVD

A new feature in *Vista* is the ability to write a video DVD containing your images. A video DVD can be played on your computer and in the DVD player connected to your TV.

- **Select a couple of images**
- **Click** Burn

If you click Data Disc... you will write a data disc of your images using the *Live File System*.

In this example, you will choose to write a video DVD:

- **Click** Video DVD...

The program *Windows DVD Maker* is now opened automatically.

9.7 Windows DVD Maker

In *Windows DVD Maker* you can create a video DVD of your images and/or videos in a few easy steps. The files you selected are added to a video *project*.

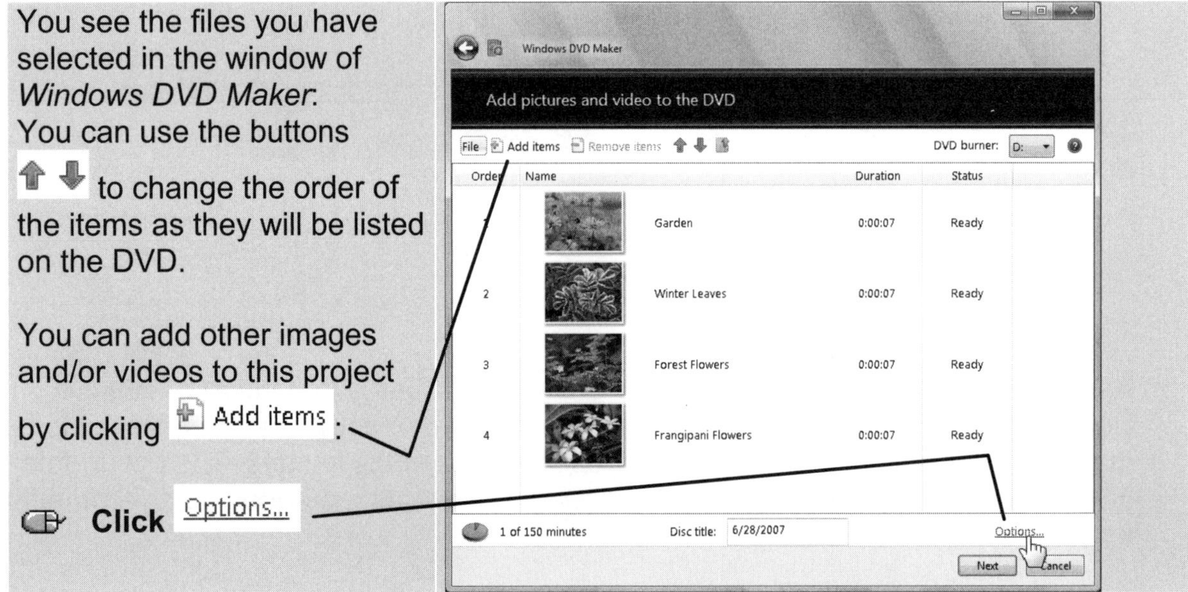

You see the files you have selected in the window of *Windows DVD Maker*.
You can use the buttons ⇧ ⇩ to change the order of the items as they will be listed on the DVD.

You can add other images and/or videos to this project by clicking Add items:

- **Click** Options...

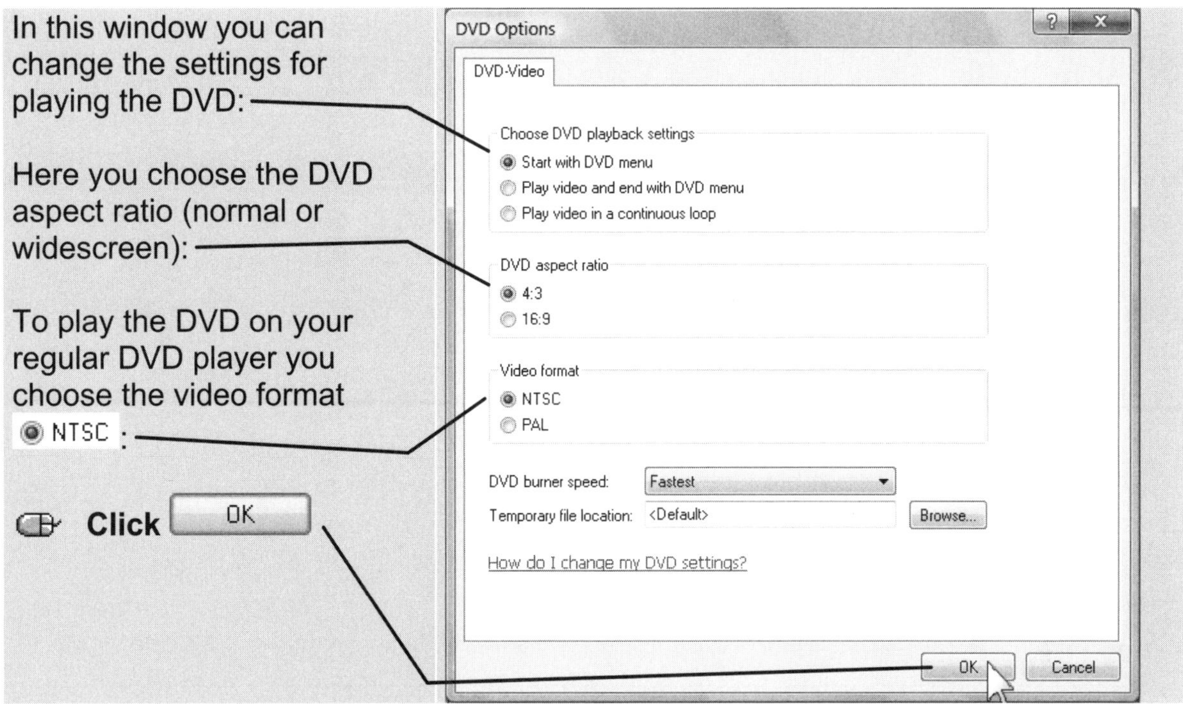

You see the previous window again. In this window:

You see the next window of the wizard. The content of each video DVD is displayed in a disc menu. This means you can use a remote control to play the DVD. The disc menu can be adjusted to your own preferences.

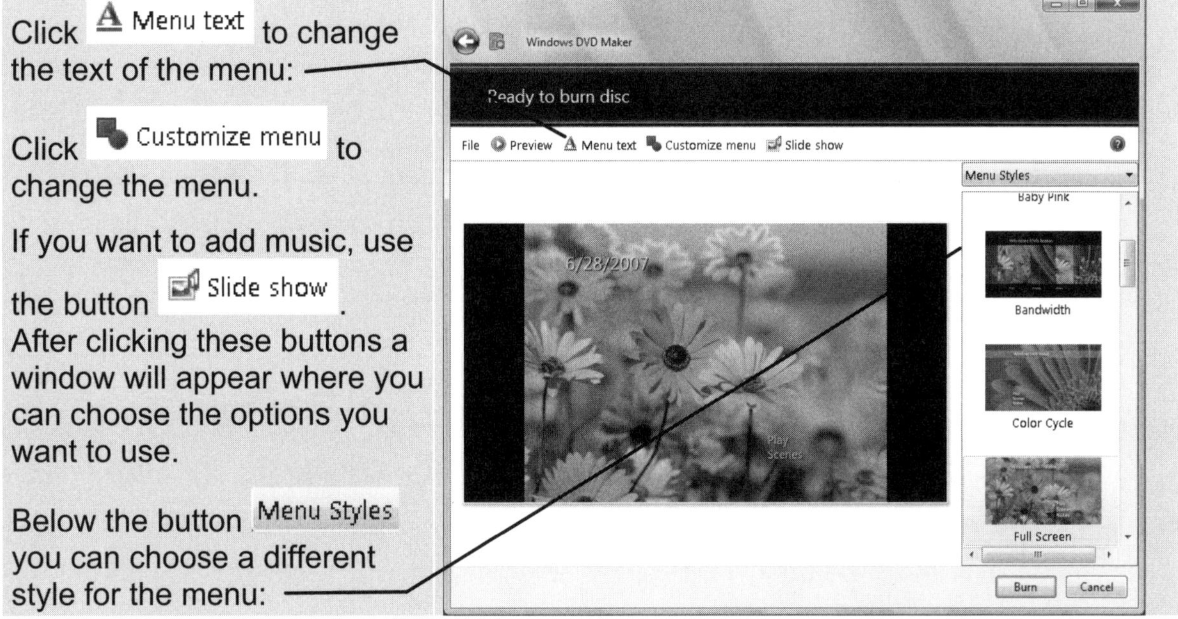

As soon as you have made your choices, you can preview the result using the button Preview. If you are satisfied, you can write the video DVD project to your DVD.

If you do not want to write a video DVD now:

Click Cancel and do not save the project

If you want to write the video DVD:

Insert a blank DVD in the DVD writer

Click 

The DVD will be written.

Tip

Saving a project
Do you want to save your project so you can continue working on it later?

Click File, Save.

The following window appears:

The folder *Videos* is selected:

Type a file name

Click Save

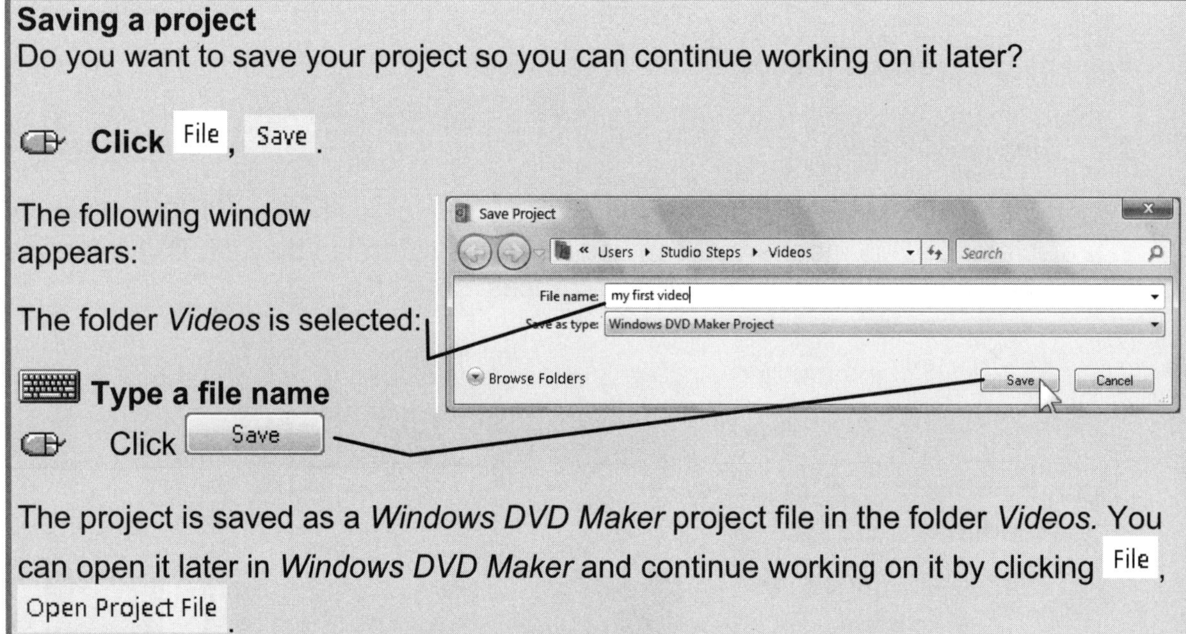

The project is saved as a *Windows DVD Maker* project file in the folder *Videos.* You can open it later in *Windows DVD Maker* and continue working on it by clicking File, Open Project File.

Tip

Opening Windows DVD Maker
You can open *Windows DVD Maker* from the *Windows Photo Gallery* window as well as from the list *All programs* in the *Start menu.*

Tip

Would you like to know more about Windows DVD Maker?
In *Windows Help and Support* you can find extensive information and tips about working with the program *Windows DVD Maker*. Type the name of the program in the *Search Box* and the corresponding articles will appear.

☞ **Close the *Windows DVD Maker* window (if necessary)**

☞ **Close the *Windows Photo Gallery* window**

9.8 Windows Calendar

Windows Calendar is a new program that comes packaged with *Windows Vista.* You can use this program to replace your paper calendar. You open *Windows Calendar* like this:

Click , **All Programs** , Windows Calendar

You see the *Windows Calendar* window:

The calendar shows the current day and time:

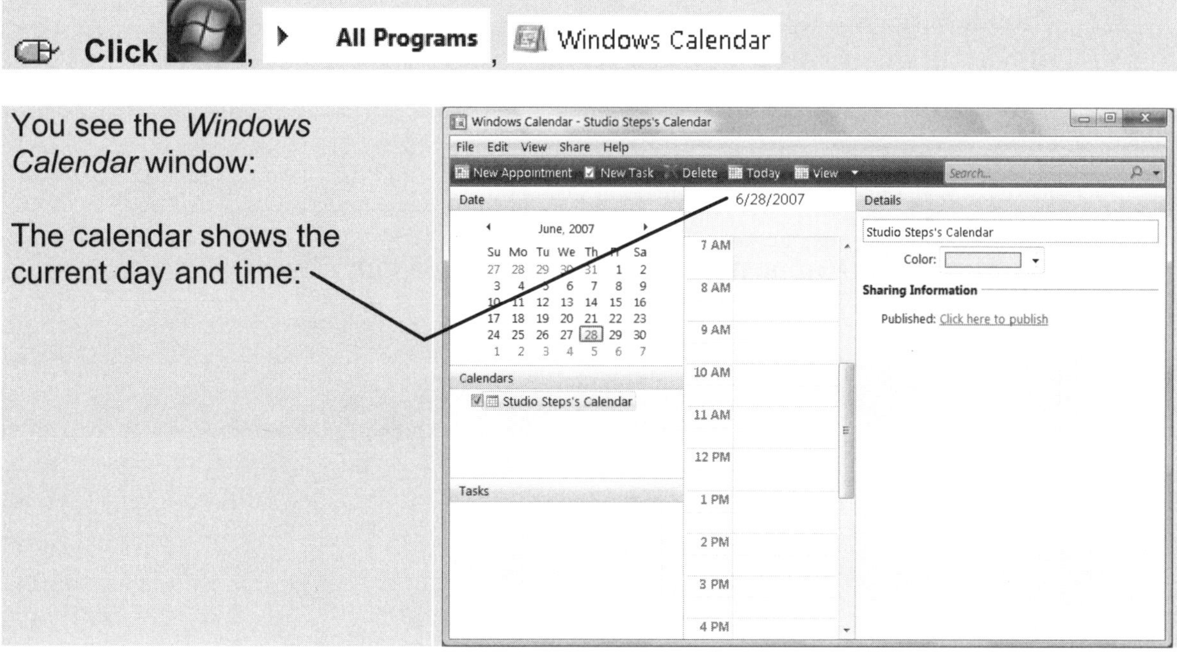

Tip

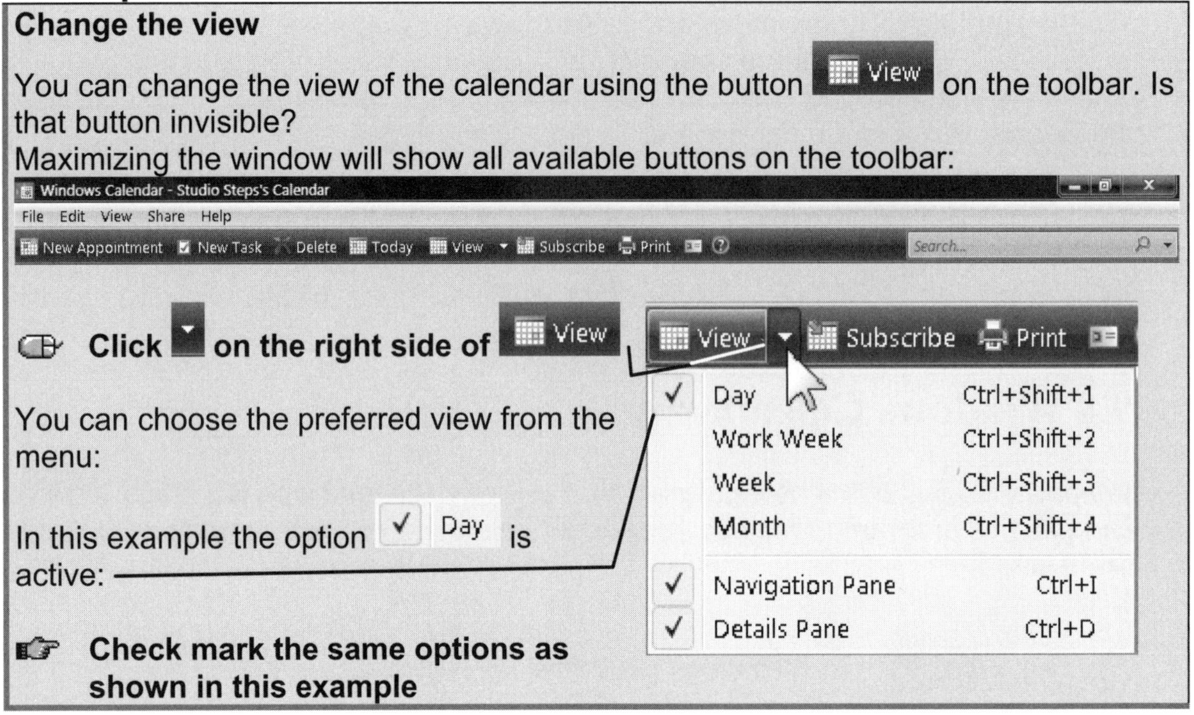

Change the view

You can change the view of the calendar using the button View on the toolbar. Is that button invisible?
Maximizing the window will show all available buttons on the toolbar:

Click ▾ on the right side of View

You can choose the preferred view from the menu:

In this example the option ✓ Day is active:

Check mark the same options as shown in this example

9.9 Adding a New Appointment

You can create a new appointment in *Windows Calendar*.

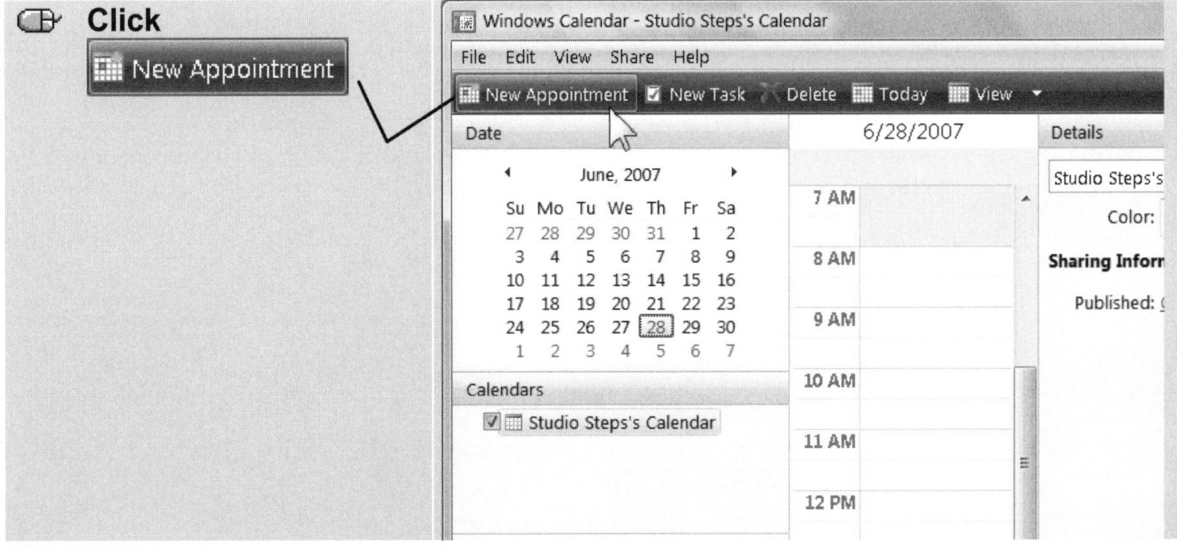

Click New Appointment

The new appointment appears on the current day and time:

You can enter the type of appointment:

Type: `Meeting`

Press Enter

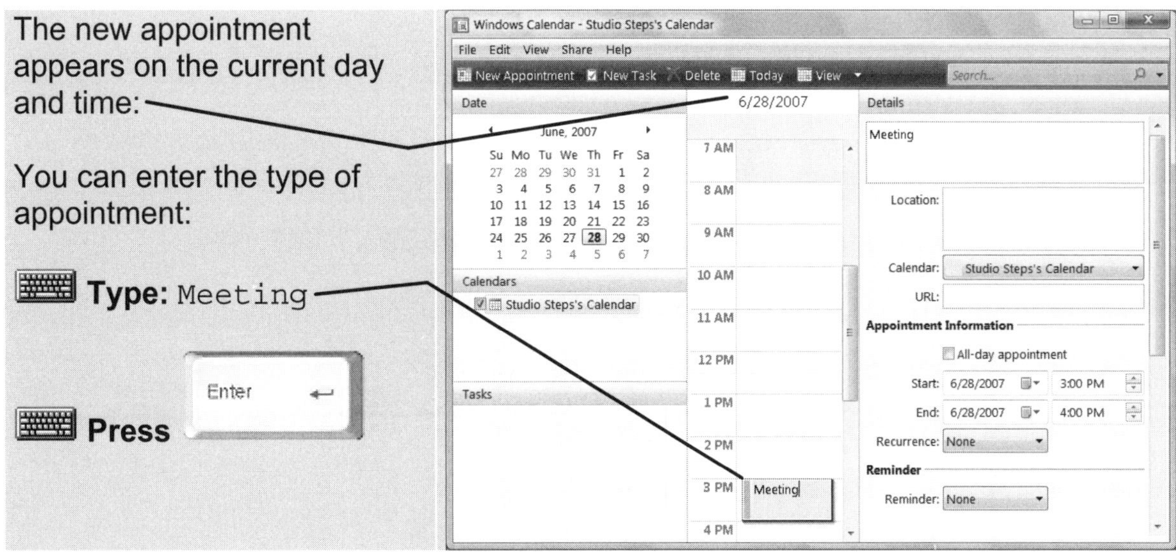

In the *Details Pane* on the right side you can enter additional information about this meeting:

Click the box next to Location:

Type: `Office`

You can enter more details for the meeting under **Appointment Information**.

For a recurring appointment you can choose the interval (weekly, monthly etcetera) at Recurrence:

Enter the details for this meeting

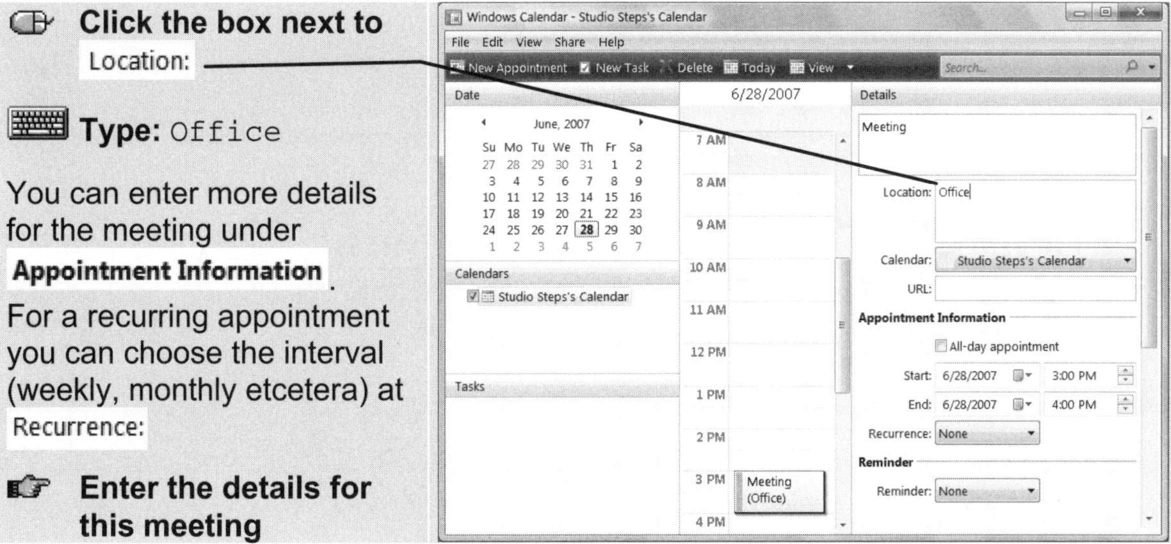

Tip

Quickly set a date and time

In *Windows Calendar* you can quickly set a date and time for an appointment:

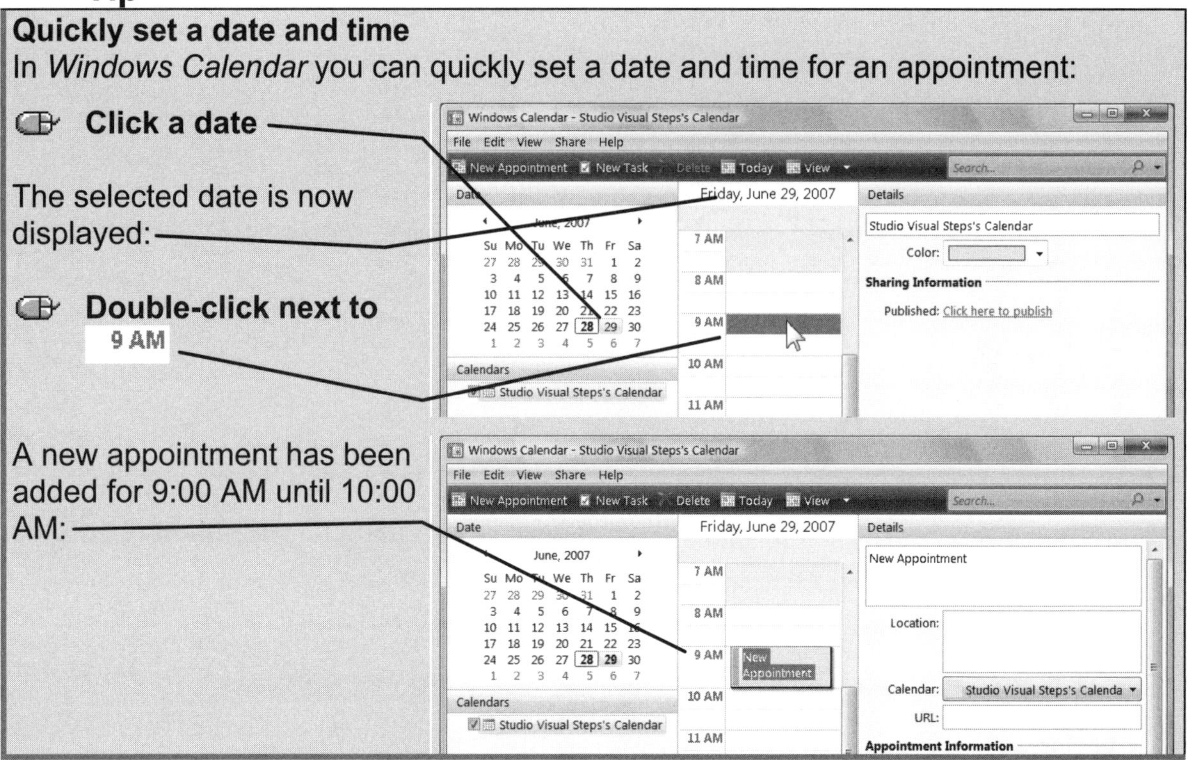

9.10 Inviting Others for an Appointment

Would you like to invite other people for an appointment? You can do that by e-mail.

Please note:

The people you invite for an appointment must use *Windows Calendar* or a comparable calendar feature, for example the one in *Microsoft Outlook*. Otherwise they can not read the invitation.

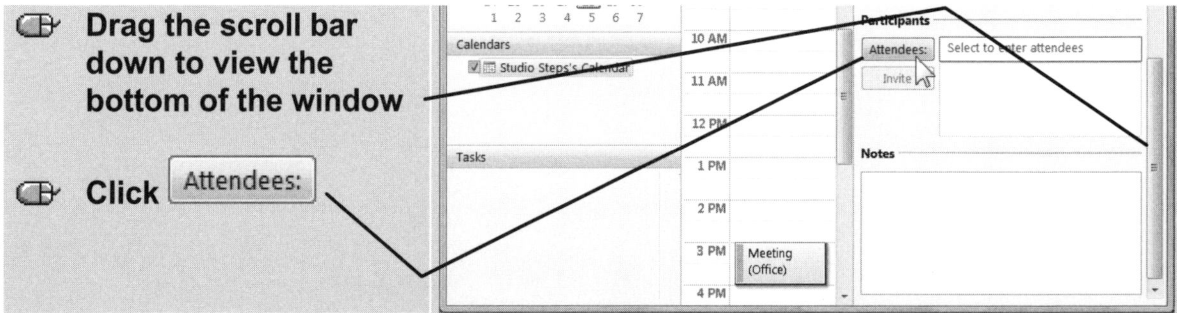

A new window appears where you can select a name. To be able to see what happens when you receive an invitation, you are going to add yourself as a contact:

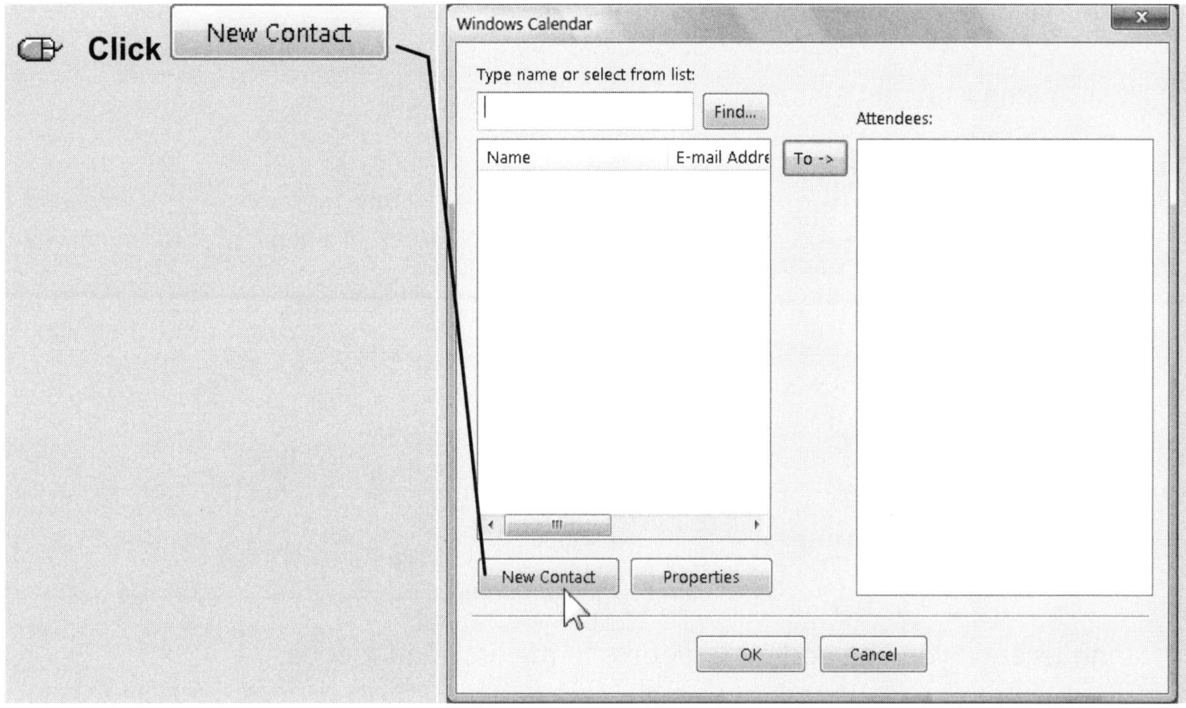

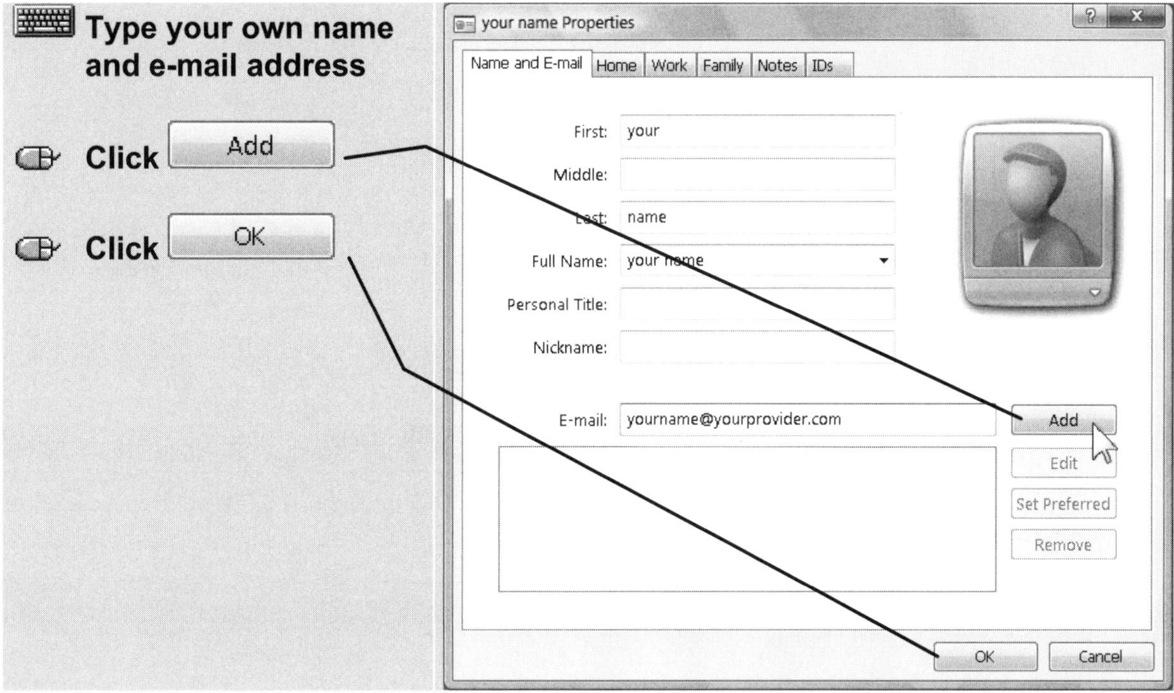

Your name is added to the *Contacts* folder.

Click your name

Click To ->

Your name is added to the list of attendees:

Click OK

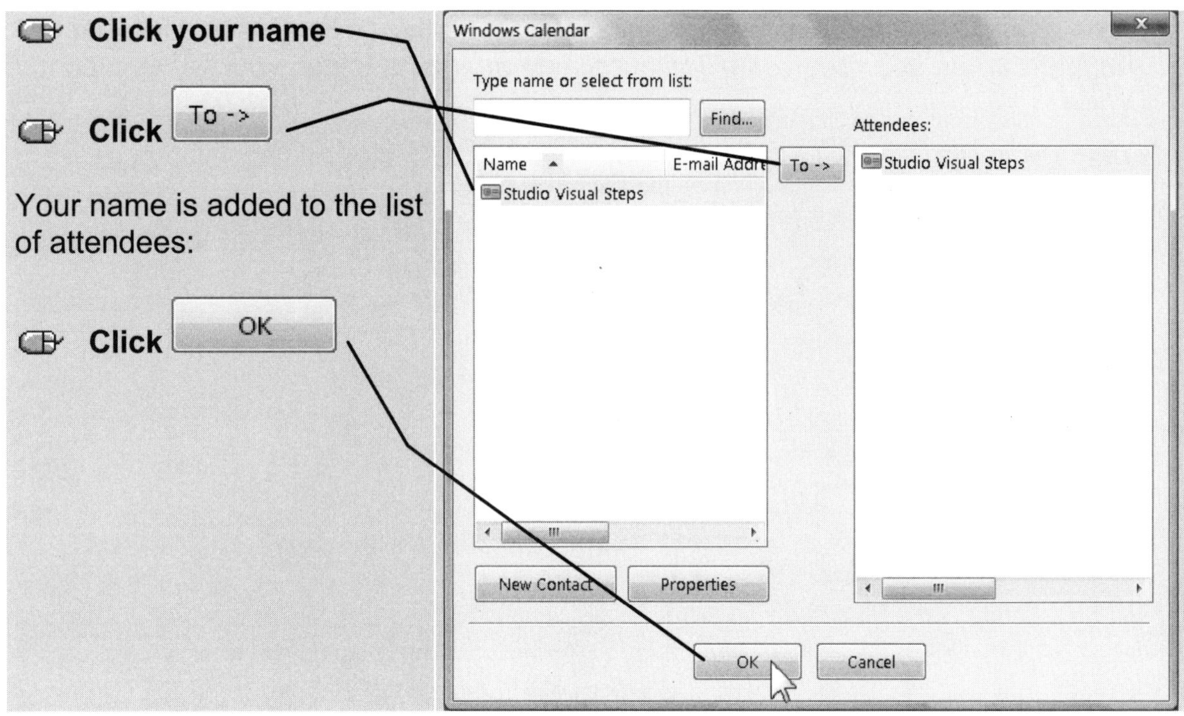

If necessary, you can add more people to the list of attendees.

You send the invitation as follows:

Click Invite

Your default e-mail program is opened automatically. A new message with the invitation appears:

Click Send

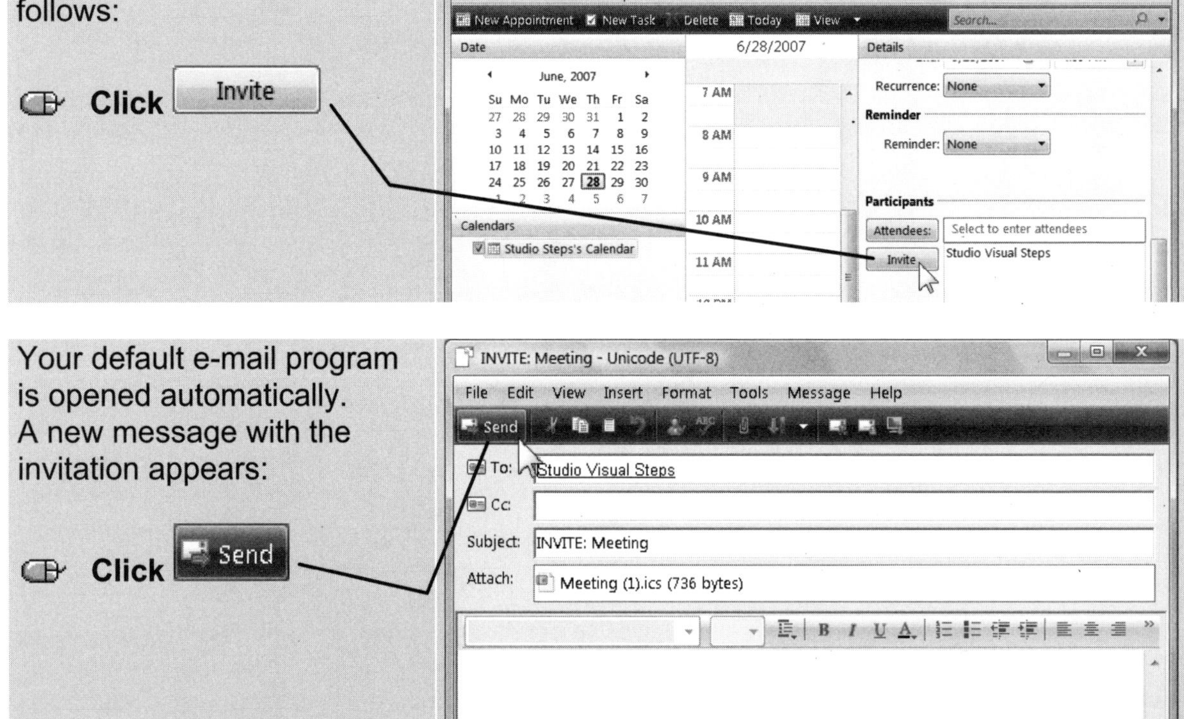

Open *Windows Mail*

Send and receive your e-mail

When you have received the invitation in your *Inbox*:

Double-click the message INVITE: Meeting

Double-click the attachment Meeting (1).ics (736 bytes)

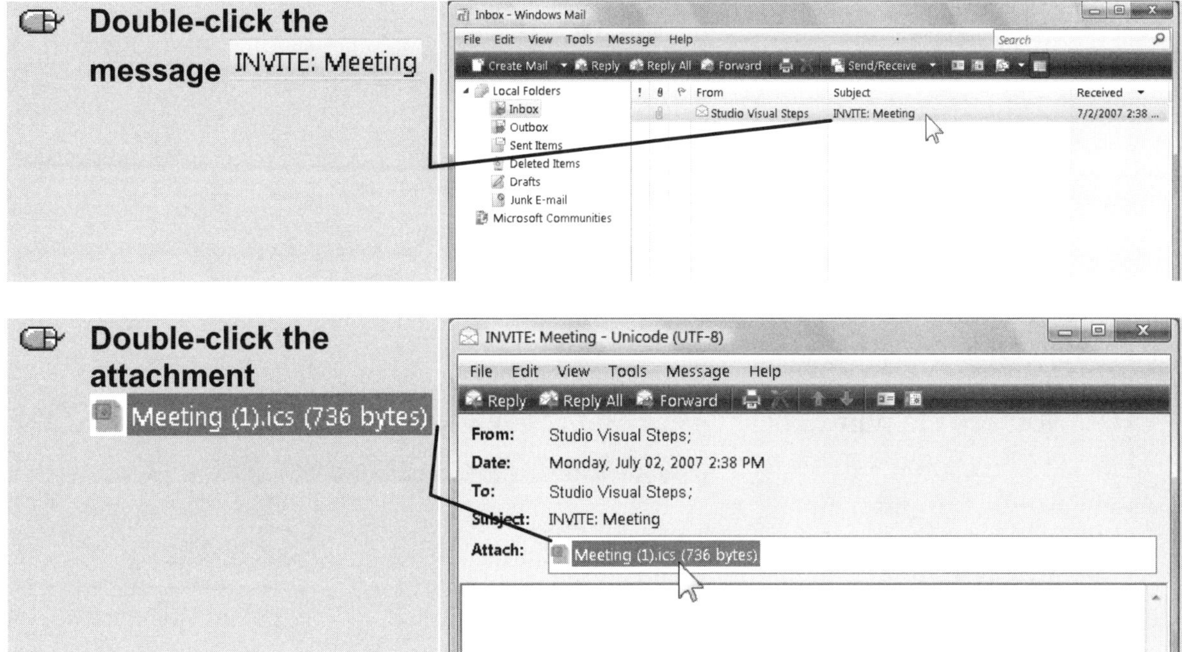

The attachment is an .ICS-file. ICS is the extension for *iCalendar*-files. *iCalendar* is the standard for exchanging calendar data. This means you can add appointments in this format to your own calendar.

Click Open

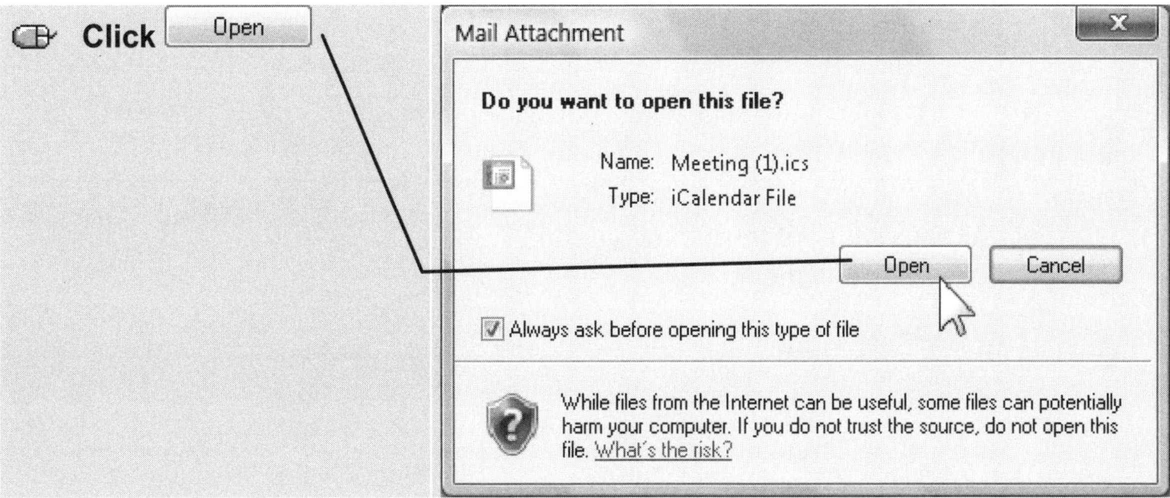

When you receive an invitation by e-mail, you can import it in *Windows Calendar*.

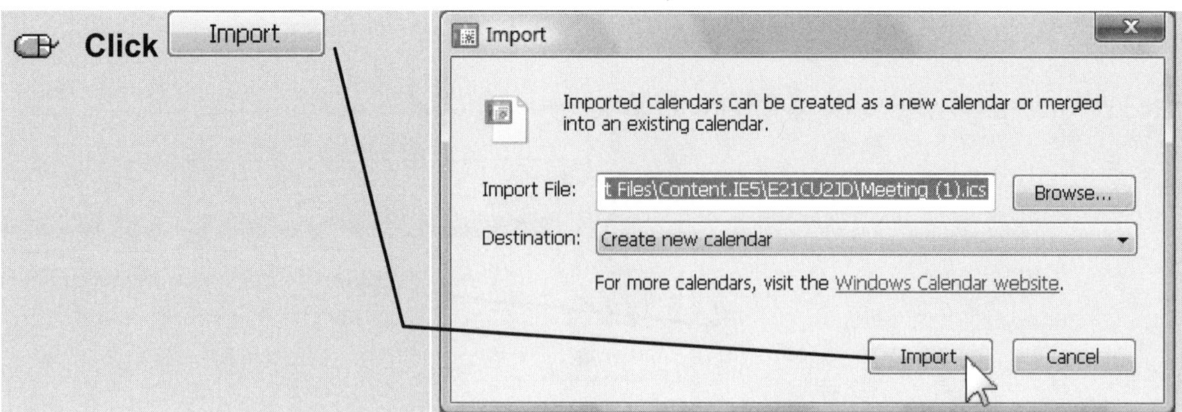

The appointment has been added to your *Windows Calendar*. A new calendar is created for imported appointments:

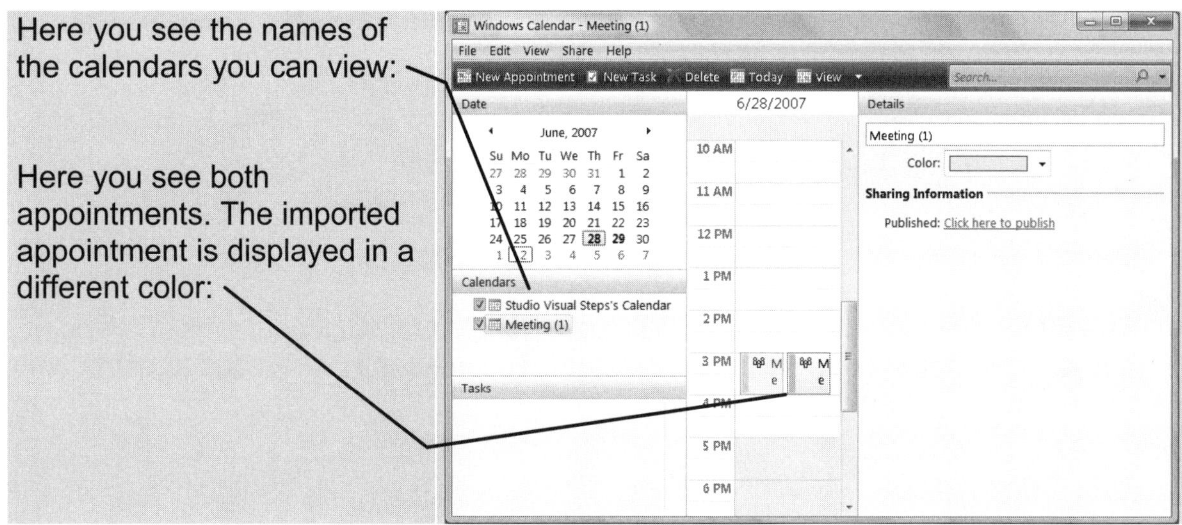

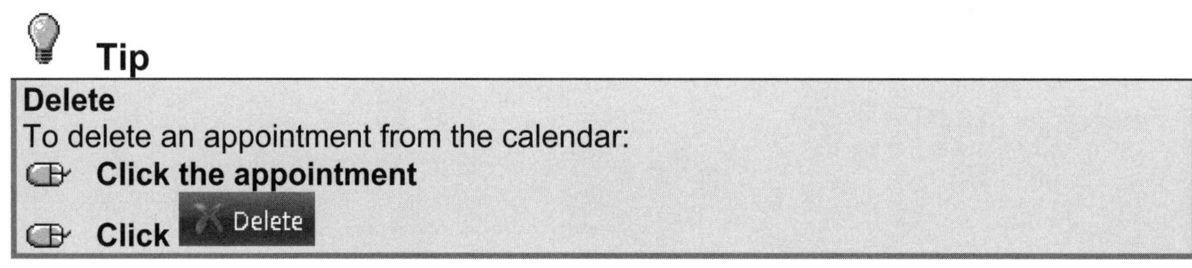

Tip

Delete

To delete an appointment from the calendar:

Click the appointment

Click Delete

9.11 Setting and Receiving a Reminder

When you enter an appointment in your calendar, you can also set a reminder. You will be alerted at the time you select before the meeting.

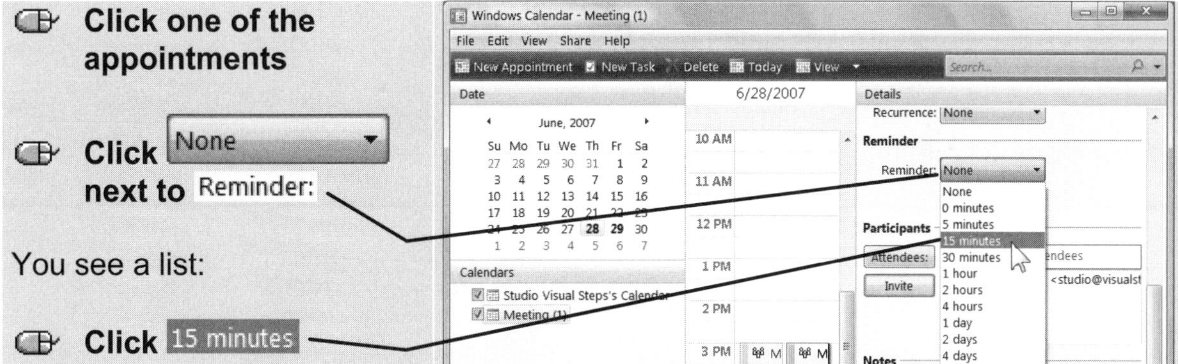

Fifteen minutes before the time of your scheduled appointment, this window will appear to remind you:

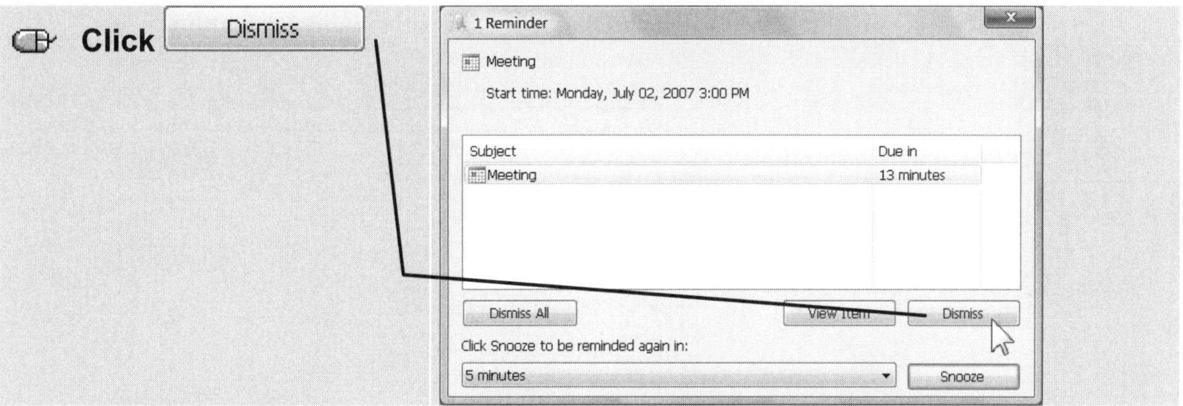

Close all windows

You have learned how to work with *Windows Calendar.* Would you like to know more about this application? In *Windows Help and Support* you can find more information about *Windows Calendar.*

9.12 The Snipping Tool

Windows Vista contains a useful program that you can use to capture a screenshot (snip) of any object on your screen. You open the *Snipping Tool* like this:

Click , All Programs , Accessories , Snipping Tool

When you start the program for the first time, this window appears:

Snipping Tool

Would you like to add the Snipping Tool to your QuickLaunch bar?

Yes No

Click No

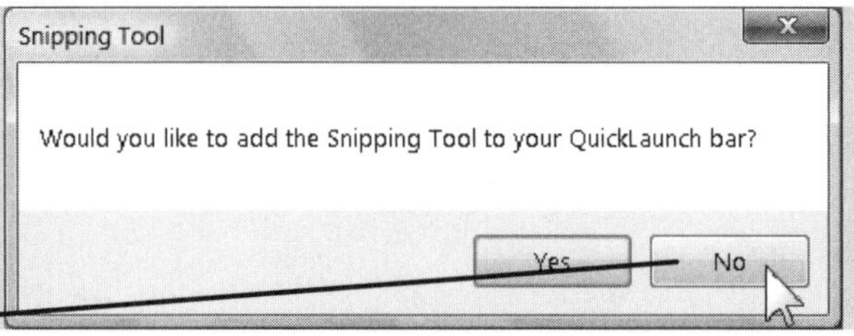

Click on the right **side of** New

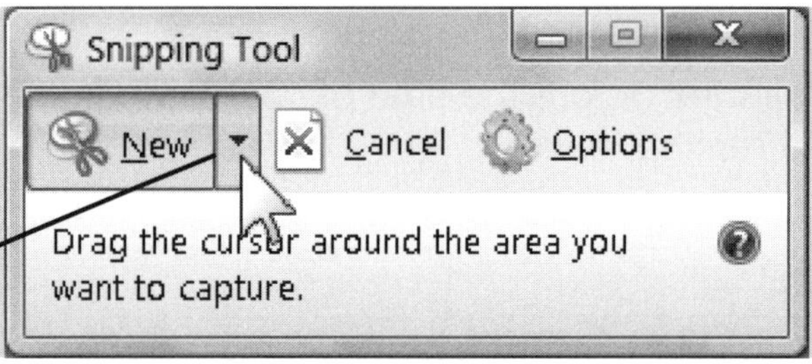

Snipping Tool

New Cancel Options

Drag the cursor around the area you want to capture.

You see several options in the menu:

Click Free-form Snip

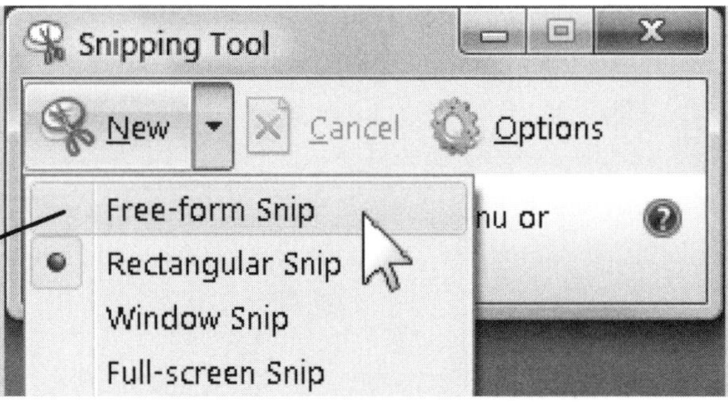

Free-form Snip
Rectangular Snip
Window Snip
Full-screen Snip

Now you can draw a free form around an object on your screen, for example a part of *Windows Sidebar*:

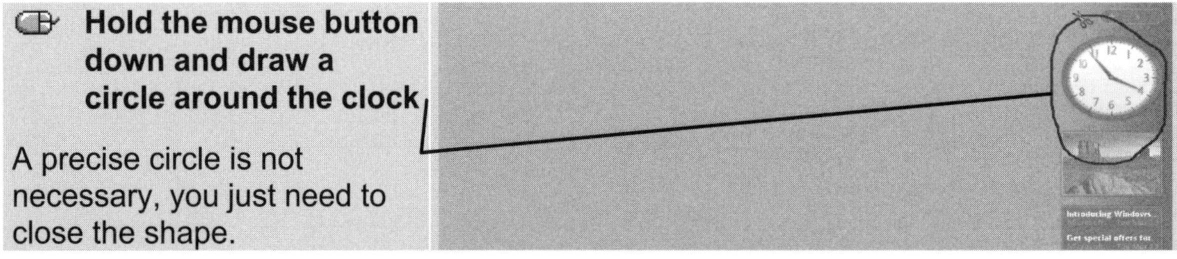

Hold the mouse button down and draw a circle around the clock

A precise circle is not necessary, you just need to close the shape.

After you capture a snip, it will be copied automatically to the mark-up window of the *Snipping Tool*.

Use the pen or highlighter to add something (writing or drawing) to this snip. With the eraser you can erase your addition.

Use the button to save the snip.

With you copy the snip. Then you can paste it in another program.

Use this button to send the snip by e-mail.

Would you like to know more about this handy program? In *Windows Help and Support* you can find more information.

Close the *Snipping Tool* window and do not save the changes

Tip

How to continue?

This book has given you a 'look under the hood' of *Windows Vista.* You have seen some of the new features in *Windows*, looked at what is different in some familiar programs and you have been introduced to some interesting new applications packaged with *Vista*. Now you can try experimenting on your own. Read about items you are not sure about in the extensive *Windows Help and Support* section. In this way you will continue to learn more about this new operating system. Gradually you will feel just as comfortable using *Vista* as you did using *XP*.

Would you like to gain more skills by using the easy step by step approach of the Visual Steps books?

Then another book in the *Vista* series will be an excellent choice, such as **More Windows Vista for SENIORS** (978 90 5905 055 6)

On the webpage **www.visualsteps.com** you will find a list of available *Vista* titles. For each book there is a complete table of contents and a chapter excerpt available online. In this way, you can determine which book best suits your needs and interests.

9.13 Background Information

Familiar and improved programs
In addition to the new programs you have been introduced to in this book, *Windows Vista* also contains programs that you are already familiar with from *Windows XP.*

The simple text editing program *WordPad* and the drawing program *Paint*, that you can also use to view images, remain largely unchanged. A feature that was added to *Paint* is that you can ´zoom out´ on a photo that is opened: click the magnifier on the *Tool Box*, then click the image with the right mouse button. This comes in handy when a photo is too large to fit in the active window.

Some of the familiar features or programs that you were used to in *XP* may seem difficult to locate in *Vista*. If this is the case, be sure to examine the list of files and folders in *All programs* or try searching *Windows Help and Support.* For example, the option *Run* that is found in the *Start menu* in *XP*, has been moved to the folder *Accessories* in *Vista. Windows Explorer* can also be found there. You can find the folder *Accessories* in the *All programs* list in the *Start menu.*

The games that are included in *Windows Vista* have also undergone improvements. You can find the folder *Games* in the *All programs* list in the *Start menu*.

Tip: The *Welcome Center* window that you see when you start your computer, contains a separate hyperlink What's new in Windows Vista. When you click this link you get extensive information about the new features and programs of *Vista.* You can also open the *Welcome Center* from the *Start menu.*

Appendices

A. How Do I Do That Again?

In this book some actions are marked with footsteps: 1
Find the corresponding number in the appendix below to see how to do something.

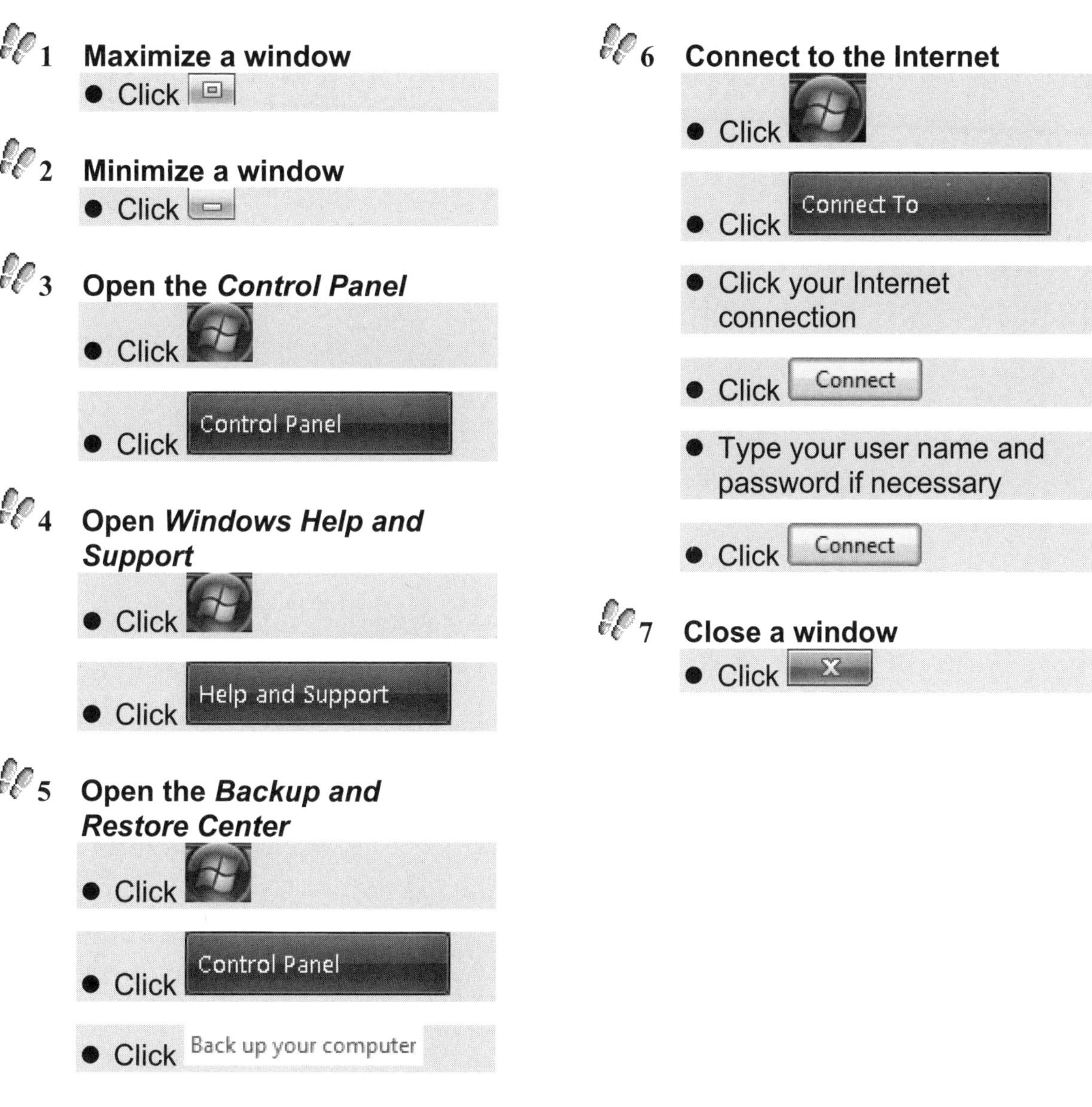

1 **Maximize a window**

- Click

2 **Minimize a window**

- Click

3 **Open the *Control Panel***

- Click
- Click Control Panel

4 **Open *Windows Help and Support***

- Click
- Click Help and Support

5 **Open the *Backup and Restore Center***

- Click
- Click Control Panel
- Click Back up your computer

6 **Connect to the Internet**

- Click
- Click Connect To
- Click your Internet connection
- Click Connect
- Type your user name and password if necessary
- Click Connect

7 **Close a window**

- Click

B. Index

A

B

C

D

E

F

Notes

Write down your notes here.

Notes

Write down your notes here.